International Law and the Global South

Perspectives from the Rest of the World

This book series aims to promote a complex vision of contemporary legal developments from the perspective of emerging or developing countries and/or authors integrating these elements into their approach. While focusing on today's law and international economic law in particular, it brings together contributions from, or influenced by, other social sciences disciplines. Written in both technical and non-technical language and addressing topics of contemporary importance to a general audience, the series will be of interest to legal researchers as well as non-lawyers.
In referring to the "rest of the world", the book series puts forward new and alternative visions of today's law not only from emerging and developing countries, but also from authors who deliberately integrate this perspective into their thinking. The series approach is not only comparative, post-colonial or critical, but also truly universal in the sense that it places a plurality of well-informed visions at its center.

The Series

- Provides a truly global coverage of the world in reflecting cutting-edge developments and thinking in law and international law
- Focuses on the transformations of international and comparative law with an emphasis on international economic law (investment, trade and development)
- Welcomes contributions on comparative and/or domestic legal evolutions

More information about this series at http://www.springer.com/series/13447

Muhammad Azeem

Law, State and Inequality in Pakistan

Explaining the Rise of the Judiciary

Springer

Muhammad Azeem
Shaikh Ahmad Hassan School of Law
Lahore University of Management Sciences
Lahore
Pakistan

ISSN 2510-1420 ISSN 2510-1439 (electronic)
International Law and the Global South
Perspectives from the Rest of the World
ISBN 978-981-10-3844-0 ISBN 978-981-10-3845-7 (eBook)
DOI 10.1007/978-981-10-3845-7

Library of Congress Control Number: 2017938145

Printed on acid-free paper

This Springer imprint is published by Springer Nature
The registered company is Springer Nature Singapore Pte Ltd.
The registered company address is: 152 Beach Road, #21-01/04 Gateway East, Singapore 189721, Singapore

To my family, Sara and Sumana

Acknowledgements

This book is, in a way, an outcome of my long legal and political practice with workers, peasants, students and marginalized sections of Pakistan. The list of friends is long, ranging from the 1950s peasant leaders Ghulam Nabi Kallu to present day Allah Buksh Baloch in southern Punjab and includes especially, former student activists, Sabir Ali Haider and Mushtaq Chaudry, as well as lawyer Abid Hasan Minto. The Progressive Writers' Association and its poets Abid Hussain Abid, Afzal Saahir, Maqsood Khaliq, IftikharBaig and many others were apart of struggles against privatizations, peasant ejectments by land mafia and the firings from these processes. During these struggles, I learnt from the experiences of the working class and where I could, I carried them to courts as a part of the overall struggle. Khawaja Imran Advocate always tolerated and helped me in the courts.

Based on my experiences, my quest in Ph.D. was to theoretically understand the limits of liberal legal project and the role of the judiciary for the emancipation of the marginalized. During my years of graduate study, I frequently visited Pakistan, and critically engaged with my prior perceptions. The critical environment of Osgoode Hall School, and York University in the Toronto area was very conducive to my quests. I thank my supervisor Ruth Buchanan and supervisory committee Liora Salter and especially the kind support and encouragement of Dr. Tariq Amin-Khan. They let the project originally grow and kindly nourished it with their insights and also trimmed its excesses. I thank Dr. Kamran Asdar Ali for being the external reader and for debating my views vigorously with me.

I would like to thank my political friends and family who stood with me in the disappointments and joys of producing this piece of literature. I would specially like to thank my loving daughter Sumana Abraham and wife Sara Abraham who supported me throughout these past years as I was doing my research. In Sara, I was greatly fortunate to have an activist and a critical observer look over and contribute to my writings. My sister Farida patiently waited for me to return to Pakistan.

Other critical scholars in Toronto are Profs. Raju Das, Obiora Okafor, Peer Zumbensen, Greg Albo, Sam Gindin, Aparna Sundar, Malavika Kasturi, Alok Johri, Kajri Jain, Dhruv Jain, Horace Campbell and Shubhra Gururani, and I thank them for their intellectual engagement with my project. While studying law my political engagement with peoples' rights in Toronto was possible through a wonderful galaxy of graduate students and friends. Here I thank Steve de Silva running a community newspaper promoting peoples' journalism, Basics. I thank Noaman, Arsalan and Urooj for running a campaign against drones in Pakistan, Mike and Kabir for organizing black neighbourhood against the police, as well as Laura working with indigenous people. Sukhdev, Navkiran and Punjabi struggles in Brampton offered lessons at a very different level.

After week-long hectic intellectual engagements, my creative writers and poets offered cheerful compounds with soothing effect. Amir Jaffery and Seemi, Khalid Sohail, Rafiq Sultan, Malik Khan, Rasheed Nadeem, Askariand Zehra with their poetry, fiction and songs kept my soul alive and steady for the time I was researching, during those eight years. I was fortunate to have a few graduate students as my friends and want to thank Qamar, Humayun, Tahir Amin, Paula, as well as Aqeel, Nadeem, Halida and Ahamad.

After completing my research, I was fortunate to move back to Pakistan, Lahore for a job at LUMS University. These past two years I have worked on changing my thesis into this book. I found new empirical evidence to fill some gaps. During this time, my colleagues Dr. Zubair Abbasi, Sadaf Aziz, Dr. Ali Qazilbash, Sikandar Shah, Uzair Kayani, Khyzer, Dean Martin Lau and Vice Chancellor Dr. Sohail Naqvi were very supportive and I want to thank them. Rizwanna, Sadaf Shahjehan, Yumna Arshad and Asad Ullah Khan really worked hard on editing and other support.

Dr. Itty Abraham deserves a special thanks, for he guided me in a very special way at every stage of my work.

Finally, the staff of Sheikh Ahmed School of Law (SAHSOL) Shah Nawaz, Imran, Khalid and Iftikhar have kept things working smoothly around teaching and dealing with students. I thank them for making such a peaceful environment.

Contents

About the Author

Muhammad Azeem is Assistant Professor at Shaikh Ahmad Hassan School of Law, Lahore University of Management Sciences (LUMS), Lahore, Pakistan, where he teaches 'Labour Law,' 'Critical Legal Theory,' as well as 'International Law from the South: A Critical Perspective to Decolonize.' He has published multiple books on political economy in Urdu and was a political activist in subaltern sectors, particularly bonded labour, before becoming more theoretically engaged and writing about judicial activism in his Master of Laws (LLM) and Ph.D. at the Osgoode Hall Law School, York University, Toronto.

Abbreviations

AJP	Access to Justice Program
ANP	Awami National Party
APSEUA	All-Pakistan Small Enterprises Unions Association
BD	Basic Democracy
BLLF	Bonded Labour Liberation Front
CDF	Comprehensive Development Framework
CJ	Chief Justice
CJBHC	Chief Justice Baluchistan High Court
CJLHC	Chief Justice Lahore High Court
CJSHC	Chief Justice Sindh High Court
CMLA	Chief Martial Law Administrator
COAS	Chief of the Army Staff
HDI	Human Development Index
ICS	Indian Civil Service
IFIs	International Financial Institutions
IMF	International Monitory Fund
JJs	Justices
LFO	Legal Framework Order
LHC	Lahore High Court
MLD	Monthly Law Digest
MNAs	Member of the National Assembly
MPAs	Member of the Provincial Assembly
MRD	Movement for the Restoration of Democracy
NAB	National Accountability Bureau
NAP	National Awami Party
NGOs	Non-Governmental Organizations
NRO	National Reconciliation Ordinance
NSC	National Security Council
NWFP	North-West Frontier Province
PCO	Provisional Constitutional Order

PCS	Pakistan Civil Service
PHC	Peshawar High Court
PIA	Pakistan International Airlines
PIL	Public Interest Litigation
PLC	Pakistan Labour Cases
PLD	Pakistan Legal Decisions
PLJ	Pakistan Law Journal
PM	Prime Minister
PML	Pakistan Muslim League
PML-N	Pakistan Muslim League—Nawaz
PML-Q	Pakistan Muslim League-Quide-i-Azam
PNA	Pakistan National Alliance
PTV	Pakistan Television
PWA	Progressive Writers' Association
RCO	Restoration of the Constitution Order
SAP	Structural Adjustment Policy
SCMR	Supreme Court Monthly Review
SHC	Sindh High Court
WAPDA	Water and Power Development Authority
WB	World Bank

Part I
Law Under Modernization: Foundational Discourse (1947–1990)

Chapter 1
The Law and Judiciary in Pakistan: Beyond a Liberal Understanding

1.1 The Liberal Legal Project in Pakistan

In 2007, the world saw a gigantic and powerful lawyers' and judge's movement led by the Pakistani Chief Justice against the military ruler, General Pervaz Musharraf. It lasted for two years and seemed to shake the foundations of the society. Harvard Law School was quick to award the Medal of Freedom to Supreme Court Chief Justice Iftikhar Chaudhry and the Canadian Bar Association President participated in a march of Ontario lawyers in solidarity with the Pakistani lawyers. The Quebec Bar and Law Society of Upper Canada also responded strongly and favourably to this movement. No doubt the lawyers' movement was historic, its aims laudable, and the image of Pakistan presented to the world through the media refreshingly different. The aim of this book, however, is to demonstrate that such praise for the legal profession and judiciary from global elite legal sectors arise from a highly limited grasp of the complexity of state and society in Pakistan. Identifying a 'rise of the judiciary' is a flawed basis for optimism for a country's development. The source of this limited understanding is the extant abundant law and political science 'liberal' literature about postcolonial Pakistan. The dominant legal and social science literature takes 'liberal' democracy, 'rule of law', 'separation of powers', 'independence of judiciary', and 'human rights' as inherently good institutions and 'values'. Governmental regimes are measured as greater or lesser deviations from these ideals. A dictatorial regime is a large deviation from an 'ideal' type of democracy. The horizon for political scientists, therefore, is limited to the perceived attack on the judiciary by the military or civilian authoritarian governments. The judiciary in this analysis is always under attack, though at times compelled to support dictators.[1] The judiciary is seen as deserving support and its independence

[1]M Hussain & A Hussain, *Pakistan: Problems of Governance* (Vanguard, Lahore, 1993) 54-58; see also JM Dawood, *The Role of Superior Judiciary in the Politics of Pakistan* (Royal Book Company, Karachi, 1994) 2.

M. Azeem, *Law, State and Inequality in Pakistan*, International Law and the Global South, DOI 10.1007/978-981-10-3845-7_1

is to be guarded. Pakistan is itself seen as a 'constitutional state' only when it absorbs political and economic changes through the judiciary.[2]

The place of the judiciary is thereby inherently vaulted and its decisions or even inclinations are viewed as portentous for the country's history. This is particularly true for Pakistan with its fragile and continuously threatened foray into democracy over the past 60 years. For example, it is popularly said within Pakistan that if the Pakistani judiciary under Chief Justice Munir in the 1950s could have been pro-legislature, the entire postcolonial history of Pakistan could have unfolded differently.[3] Or, there is much regret that the judiciary did not step forward to 'save democracy' at various junctures.[4] The judiciary, hence, has seemingly played a central role in the dynamics of regime change, with both political actors seeking favours from it or seeking to limit its legitimizing potential.

My argument is that the liberal narrative, which identifies a dichotomy between dictatorship and democracy[5] or between modernity and Islam (which we will get to later in the text), only tells one part of the story. It fails to understand the class nature of the state, and grasp more fundamental contradictions in the state and society. It also fails to identify the limited role of law and the judiciary in the state structure of Pakistan. In explaining why the judiciary in fact cannot defend democracy, this book explores the nexus between elite institutions, their composition, and their interests. It shows that laws and decisions were blunted at the legislative level or at the implementation stage, leaving no further remedy. It also shows that the judiciary was only seriously engaged with struggles around accountability of politicians and constitutional engineering. Where the legislature made legislation after successful class struggle and reproduced the political power of the common man (like during a brief period of nationalization and land reforms), the judiciary strongly resisted these.[6] Whereas the judiciary struck down many

[2]M Waseem, *Politics and the State in Pakistan* (NIHCR, Islamabad, 2007) 2.

[3]H Khan, In the Memory of Justice (ret) AR Cornelius: A Great Judge, *PLJ* (1992) Magazine Section 70.

[4]PR Newberg, *Judging the State: Courts and Constitutional Politics in Pakistan* (Cambridge University Press, New Delhi, 1995).

[5]As argued in HA Rizvi, *Military, State and Society in Pakistan* (Palgrave: Macmillan, UK, 2000) xiv-xix; Waseem's opinion is that this dichotomy does not tell what is on the ground because the military regimes keep the constitutional set up intact, see M Waseem, The Causes of Democratic Downslide, in, SA Zaidi (ed) *Continuity and Change: Socio-Political and Institutional Dynamics in Pakistan* (City Press, Karachi, 2003) 59, 65.

[6]The Federal Shariat Court declared land reforms as un-Islamic. In an appeal against this decision, in the *Qazalbash Wakf* case, the Supreme Court also declared land reforms un-Islamic, *see* *QazalBash Waqf v Chief Land Commissioner, Punjab, Lahore and others,* PLD 1981 FSC 23; see also PLD 1990 SC 99; Similarly, in the celebrated Steel Mill case, Chief Justice Iftikhar Chaudhry cancelled the privatization of a public sector steel mill on the basis of corruption and procedure, but did not challenge the privatization as a policy, see *Watten Party through its President v Federation of Pakistan*, decided on 23 June 2006 in Constitution Petition No 9 of 2006 & Civil Petition Nos 345 & 394 of 2006, online: <http://www.supremecourt.gov.pk/web/user_files/File/CJD_Pakistan_Steel_Mills_Case.pdf>.

laws, calling inter-elite struggles as unconstitutional, it never declared any labour law unconstitutional despite considerable evidence to the contrary.[7] To simply find the judiciary as worthy of defense then is to play on a wicket far removed from daily struggles and popular democracy.

Academic legal literature analysing law and state in Pakistan can be divided into two eras: that which was produced before the mid-1990s, which saw the judiciary as being under pressure, and the other as post-mid-1990s, where the judiciary is supposed to foster good governance. Tayyab Mahmud's writings fall in the former category and offer a common sense liberal 'constitutionalist' explanation of the times.[8] Paula Newberg's study of state and judiciary of Pakistan offers the most nuanced attempt yet to understand the state of postcolonial Pakistan, though it too is confined within liberal tradition in legal literature. It identifies a mismatch of people's ideals in a constitution with the politics in an executive dominated state of postcolonial Pakistan and the judges' interpretation of it according to their ideals. Her work has a strong view of judicial capacity and clearly argues that the courts have influenced the development of the constitution and the state structure of postcolonial Pakistan.[9]

After the judiciary's rise as an institution in the 1990s and its decisions around the separation of power, appointment of judges, and public interest litigation (PIL) confronting elected governments of Benazir Bhutto and Nawaz Sharif as well as military ruler Musharraf, launched a second type of literature. Anil Kalhan found Pakistan's lying in a 'grey zone' between authoritarianism and democracy, with an 'institutional imbalance' or 'a persistent institutional disequilibrium'.[10] He urges for a balance between judicial autonomy and constraint. His work borrows heavily from proponents of common sense liberal projects in Pakistan. Its theoretical framework explains the causes of disequilibrium as flowing uni-directionally from 'military and deep state interests' to judiciary and from judiciary to representative interests.[11] Osama Siddique's work analyses the different interpretations of dissolutions of assemblies' cases by different judges. He explains how the contradictory and inconsistent interpretations led to an adverse impact on judicial neutrality and

[7]F Mohammed, Protecting Pakistani Labourers Post-Eighteenth Amendment: Recognizing Rights After the Devolution of Power, 9 *Loy U Chi Int'l L Rev* (2012) 265, 285.

[8]T Mahmud, Praetorianism and Common Law in Post-Colonial Settings: Judicial Responses to Constitutional Breakdowns in Pakistan, *Utah L Rev* (1993) 1225; T Mahmud, Jurisprudence of Successful Treason: Coup d'Etat & Common Law, 27 *Cornell Int'l L J* (1994) 49; also MM Stavsky, The Doctrine of State Necessity in Pakistan 16 *Cornell Int'l L J* (1983) 341.

[9]Newberg, *supra* note 4, 5.

[10]A Kalhan, "Gray Zone" Constitutionalism and the Dilemma of Judicial Independence in Pakistan, 1 *VJTL* (2013) 1, 12, 10.

[11]*Ibid* 1, 10, 12; Fig. 3 at 37.

its public perceptions.[12] Articles on the lawyer's movement have stayed within the dichotomy of democracy and dictatorship (detail in Chap 5).[13]

Another parallel trend is a critique of Islamization of Pakistani laws, launched most strongly in the 1980s by the women's movement and subsequent feminist analyses. This approach gained hugely in 'market value' after 9/11 and the entrapment of Pakistan as a state that produces global terrorists. Charles H. Kennedy, an eminent scholar on Pakistani state and politics, commenting Islamization of laws since Zia's time, argues that support for Islamic law, though loud and strong, was not enough for the adherents in public policy and implementation.[14] According to him, being discouraged at the legislative level, Islamists started using the superior judiciary with an activist approach to scrutinize laws repugnant to the injunctions of Islam.[15] Martin Lau's research concurs with this and usefully shows how the Islamization of laws in Pakistan has been primarily a judge-led process. Judges use the vocabulary of Islam consciously as a way of enhancing judicial power and independence.[16] These writings correctly pointed out the rise of judiciary and its use of Islam but as a deviation from liberal arrangement. Counter to the liberal framework, Shaheen Sardar Ali, Rubiya Mehdi, Ralph Briabanti, and Clark B. Lombardi relate Islam with the liberal legal project in Pakistan justifying it with reference to Islam's compassion, pluralism, and cultural and traditional roots.[17] Shaheen Sardar Ali's argument is that women's human

---

[12]O Siddique, The Jurisprudence of Dissolutions: Presidential Power to Dissolve Assemblies under the Pakistan's Constitution and its Discontents, 23:3 *Ariz J Int'l & Comp L* (2005–06) 713.

[13]TA Qureshi, State of Emergency: General Pervez Musharraf's Executive Assault on Judicial Independence in Pakistan 35: XXXV *N C J Int'l L & Com Reg* (2009–2010) 485; also JA Mintz, Introductory Note: A Perspective on Pakistan's Chief Justice, Judicial Independence, and the Rule of Law 15:1 *ILSA J Int'l & Comp L* (2008-09) 1. Related to this is T Hasan, The Need of Judicial Activism and CJSC Iftikhar Chaudhry as a "judicial activist" on the basis of PIL, 15:1 *ILSA J Int'l & Comp L* (2008-09) (2008-09) 9-14; see also N Ahmad, The Rule of Law- A Substratum of Justice (2012) *8:2 J Commonwealth L & Legal Educ* 11; also SA Ghias, Miscarriage of Chief Justice: Judicial Power and the Legal Complex in Pakistan under Musharraf 35:4 *Law & Social Inquiry* (2010) 985.

[14]CH Kennedy, Islamization and Legal Reforms in Pakistan: 1979-1989, 63:1 *Pacific Affairs* (1990) 62.

[15]CH Kennedy, Repugnancy to Islam- Who Decides? Islam and Legal Reforms in Pakistan 41:4 *ICLQ* (1992) 769; CH Kennedy, Pakistan's Superior Courts and the Prohibition of Riba, in, RM Hathaway & W Lee *Islamization and the Pakistani Economy* (eds) (Woodrow Wilson International Center for Scholars, Washington DC, 2004) 101.

[16]M Lau, *The Role of Islam in the Legal System of Pakistan* (Martinus Nijhoff Publishers, London/Boston, 2006).

[17]SS Ali, *Gender and Human Rights in Islam and International Law: Equal Before Allah, Unequal Before Man?* (Kluwer Law International, Hague, 2000); R Mehdi, *The Islamization of Law in Pakistan* (Curzon Press, UK, 1994); CB Lombardi, Can Islamizing a Legal System Even Help Promote Liberal Democracy?: A View from Pakistan, 7:3 *University of Saint Thomas Law Journal* (2010) 649; R Braibanti, *Chief Justice Cornelius of Pakistan: An Analysis with Letters and Speeches* (Oxford University Press, Karachi, 1999).

rights in Islam are not irreconcilable with UN mandated fundamental rights. What is needed is 'progressive' as opposed to 'literalist' interpretation of the sources of Islamic law.[18] Shoaib, using an 'institutionalist' approach, argues that Sharia's courts are 'the least dangerous branch' because political regimes kept them under their control.[19] In the same vein, Werner Menski's tries to 'indigenize' the liberal tradition of human rights public interest litigation in Pakistan.[20] To sum up, this stream of critical literature in the name of 'tradition' does not escape the theoretical confines of Islam versus liberalism. It seeks to institutionally modernize Islam, and more pertinently, as it understands secularism and Islam as linked respectively to democracy and dictatorship respectively.

The quest for an alternate theoretical approach in this book emanates from three interlocked questions: first, if the judiciary in Pakistan has indeed risen, why have the lives of people not been changed by an activist judiciary? Second, does the class nature of this judicial activism, meaning, who are the judges matter? What is the significance that they are mostly from certain families and chambers only? Third, what is the significance of the same sitting judges during both dictatorial and democratic regimes, and no shift in political balance despite a few 'bold' and celebrated decisions?[21] Two small examples point to how the law is itself caught up in a machinery far larger than its making. After the passage of the *Bonded Labour Liberation Act 1991*, as bonded labourers were freed from brick kilns, soon after they were caught up in another debt bondage situation. Despite laws with clauses in their favour, like the *Industrial Relations Act, 2012; The Payment of Wages Act, 1936; The Workmen's Compensation Act, 1923*, the working class on the whole has not received favourable results.[22] Rather it has been extremely vulnerable under

---

[18]*Ibid* Ali, 3.

[19]SA Ghias, *Defining Shari'a: The Politics of Islamic Judicial Review*, A PhD dissertation (University of California, Berkeley, 2015) 44.

[20]W Menski, Public Interest Litigation: A strategy for the future, The Fourth Cornelius Memorial Lecture, in W Menski, AR Alam & MK Raza (eds) *Public Interest Litigation in Pakistan* (Platinum publishing limited & Pakistan Law House, London & Karachi, 2000) 106.

[21]*Asma Jilani v Government of the Punjab*, 1972 PLD SC 139, the court declared that Yahya Khan was a usurper of power; Another example is the restoration of Nawaz Sharif's government by Chief Justice Nasim Hassan Shah in 1993, *Muhammad Nawaz Sharif v President of Pakistan*, 1993 PLD SC 473.

[22]The laws are mostly inclined towards the interest of the employer. For example, *Workmen's Compensation Act, 1923* is a strict liability and utilitarian logic colonial law which is still applicable in Pakistan, creating a ceiling on compensation. This law along with the *Factories Act, 1934* and *Mines Act, 1923* are bureaucratic Commissioner and Inspector based laws in a society ripe with corruption. Similarly, *Employees Old-Age Benefit Act, 1976* makes government contribution optional, have no effective deterrent for non-payment of dues, and covers a limited range of industries, excluding a huge increasing informal sector. For a situation on minimum wage inspite of *Minimum Wages Act*, see SA Rasheed, Minimum Wages, *Dawn*, Karachi, (10 March 2015) last visited August 21, 2015 <http://www.dawn.com/news/1166560>; See *Workmen's Compensation Act, 1923* (Act No. VIII of 1923), Ch 34; *Old Age Benefits Act, 1976* (Act No. XIV of 1976) Ch 21; *Minimum Wages Ordinance, 1961* (Ordinance No. XXXIX of 1961), Ch 30; *Payment of Wages Act, 1936* (Act No. IV of 1936), Ch 31, in M. Shafi & P Shafi, *Labour Code of Pakistan*,

local bureaucratic control, despite ILO and IFIs pressure.[23] This book is an attempt to get at how underlying political-economic structures shape the terrain of legal struggles, cause the rearrangement of legal institutions, which lead in turn to the daily complaints about bad judges, poor laws and the need for 'governance'. In terms of practice, this means primacy of political struggles over legal struggles and this is particularly the only way for the most marginalized sections of society.[24]

I also hope to challenge the belief of my law colleagues in the 'rule of law' which gives law 'a life of its own' in 'in terms of its own logic'.[25] These issues are unexplored in Pakistan. There is little critique of modernity from within. 'India' as a foil for Pakistani sensibility has added its own gloss to this—as Pakistan did not experience a sustained liberal democracy and a period of secularism (as compared to India) such institutional arrangements have only gained in status. The liberal understanding in political science and law is presented as the virtue of its own, and blame for the lack of progress is placed on dictators or religious figures or mullahs alone.

Theoretical framework in this book draws on Gramsci's idea of hegemony as a political practice of state formation, which is different from the commonsense descriptive approach to political events in prevalent legal analyses. When analysing law and judiciary, this analysis connects them to ideological, political and economic instances of the social whole in a detailed, expository fashion and through complex mediations. Later it links *judges*' legal ideologies and ideals of political development as gleaned from their judicial biographies, speeches and writings to their legal decisions. *Decisions*, in turn, are related to *events*, and *events* to the *political* hegemonic project. Finally, the analysis is linked with the deep structures within which these institutions were enabled or restrained, such as the unequal distribution of land and wealth, and Pakistan's imperialist hegemonic centre–periphery dependency relations over the decades from modernization to current global 'good governance'.

(Footnote 22 continued)

Vol 2 (Bureau of Labour Publications, Karachi, 2014); See also *Factories Act, 1934* (Act XXV of 1934) Vol I of Shafis.

[23]Even the laws amended after a long time pressure of ILO like *Industrial Relations Act, 2012* went against the working class. In this Act 2012, the major change is ousting labour courts by the National Industrial Relations Commission (NIRC). Section 57(5) of this Act gave final say to NIRC on Registrar, Labour Courts, and Labour Appellate Tribunal. See for discussion *ibid* Shafi, Ch 16, 13 about the *Industrial Relations Act, 2012* (Act No. X of 2012); see also K Ahmed, Impact of 18th Constitutional Amendment on Labour Issues, in *Labour Movement in Pakistan: Past and Present* (Institute of Workers Education and Labour Studies, Lahore, 2009)136.

[24]Anjum Altaf, based on his study conducted in Shaikhupura concluded that "activism is needed to advance labour's cause." See A Altaf, Helping Labour, *Dawn* (23 January 2015) last visited 21 August 2015 <http://www.dawn.com/news/1158751>.

[25]EP Thompson, *Whigs and Hunters: The Origins of the Black Act* (Penguin Books, London, 1975) 260.

1.2 Theoretical Grasp of the Liberal Legal Project in Pakistan

1.2.1 Institutionalism and Functionalism of Liberal Understanding

"The liberal theory of the state is 90% a legal theory of the state". Pashukanis thus emphasizes the confusion created by bourgeois sciences around the essence of law.[26] The primacy of law advocates for a modern state to mean legal and constitutional arrangements with three organs, legislature, executive and judiciary, having a stark separation of power. Politics and analyses in postcolonial countries start from this 'ideal' are to reach this 'idea' in a Hegelian sense.[27] From John Locke to Hobbes, a modern capitalist state has wanted a man 'free' from coercive feudalism for commodity exchange and to enter 'freely' in a social contract.[28] This social contract is for the protection of property and enforcement of contract by free individuals. Liberalism refuses to develop a useful analysis of the state, which is divorced from property rights, as seen in a study of the work of Douglas C. North, the main proponent of new institutionalism. This is the theory behind the current phase of interventions in developing countries by international financial institutions.[29] But, with the next stroke, the liberal state snatches this freedom in liberalism and asks the individual to submit to a neutral, autonomous state, separate from civil society and above the classes (separation of the political from the economic).[30] Max Weber thought of capitalism and its legal system (order) as mutually causative, and believed that the laws in Europe before the full development of an industrial capitalist system were partially responsible for the rise of capitalism. He then interlinks the legal system with the political system—with the focus on a

---

[26]P Beirne & R Sharletedt, *Pashukanis: Selected Writings on Marxism and Law* (Academic Press, London, 1980) 281.

[27]In Hegel, the structure of thought or the shapes of consciousness take the shape of human social life. The sequence of this progress is subjective spirit, objective spirit, and the absolute spirit. See Hegel's Logic, Being Part One of the *Encyclopedia of the Philosophical Sciences (1830)* by G.W.F. Hegel, translated by Wiliam Wallace with Foreward by Andu Blunden and published by the Marxist Internet Archives, 2009.

[28]J Locke, *Two Treatises of Government* (The New American Library, New York, 1965).

[29]DC North, *Structure and Change in Economic History* (WW Norton & Company, New York, 1981) 21.

[30]See Hobbes for this anxiety. Though Hobbes believed in social contract, yet he was pessimistic about human nature which for him is selfish. Therefore, Hobbes wants a strong state which was monarch with unlimited powers in his times of chaotic civil war (1642-1649). John Locke was also in favour of monarch but with his power limited by the collective subjects, see Locke, *supra* note 28; and also J Locke, Essays concerning human understanding <http://www.earlymoderntexts.com/assets/pdfs/locke1690book1.pdf>.

centralized bureaucratic state constructed through rational decisions which had gained people's loyalties.[31]

The liberal legalist paradigm accommodates these concerns. In this paradigm, individuals have consented to the state's domination, which in turn needs to further the individuals' welfare. The state uses law to control individuals, and itself is also constrained by the law. To achieve social purposes, rules are consciously designed. This law making is to be fair, that is, not driven by race and wealth. Furthermore, pluralist processes are adopted to formulate laws. Once the rules are made, these are applied equally for all according to their purpose. Courts have the responsibility of defining and interpreting these laws. This process of adjudication should be autonomous and based on knowledge and learning. The process of tutelage of the citizenry is top down, so vividly observed in any courtroom, and social actors have to learn to conform to these rules in their behaviours.[32]

I am troubled by the institutionalist and functionalist aspects of liberal legal paradigm as it is being imported into the postcolonial world, and being grafted onto a postcolonial state which itself has been constructed out of the colonial state and its law and order machinery. By the 1990s, institutions in the form of the judiciary, laws and constitutions are considered to be essential for a country to politically and economically develop. I am borrowing the theoretical critique of institutionalism and functionalism of liberal legal project from Poulantzas as a theoretical prerequisite, yet my critique of law and judiciary of Pakistan is in its particularity and in turn will add to borrowed theoretical understanding. For functionalism, according to Poulantzas, 'collective consciousness', 'motivations', 'desires', and 'values' are important for the 'functioning' of a society.[33] This simply means what are the driving forces, 'values', 'consciousness', etc., at the individual level in institutionalism is considered as the central point of analysis at a collective/society level in functionalism. When social 'values,' 'social ends,' 'consciousness,' or 'hegemony' becomes a dominant factor in organization of the social whole, this reflects a Weberian type of functionalism. For Weber, 'values' or 'social ends' are taken as subject of history. From these 'values', the formation of the political, 'the spirit of capitalism' and the analysis of the bureaucracy is undertaken.[34] Any approach having these aspects being the basis of liberal legal paradigm is Hegelian–Weberian

---

[31]DM Trubek, Towards a Social Theory of Law: An Essay on the Study of Law and Development 82:1 *The Yale LJ* (1972) 12-14. Weber is far more complex than this but I am taking his methodology of analysis as a particular way of understanding law and legal institutions. See other commentaries about Weber in above mentioned articles of Trubek about Weber's sociology of law.

[32]Based on a summary of Trubek and Galanter see R Buchanan, A Crisis and its Afterlife: Some Reflections on 'Scholars in Self-Estrangement,' in deBúrca, Kilpatrick & Scott (eds) *Critical Legal Perspectives on Global Governance* (forthcoming Hart, 2014).

[33]E Durkheim, *The Division of Labour in Society* (The Free Press, New York, 1983); also E Durkheim, *The Rules of Sociological Method* (Free Press, New York, 1985).

[34]Poulantzas (1966), "Marxist political theory in Great Britain" in James Martin (ed) *The Poulantzas Reader: Marxism, Law and the State* (Verso, London & New York, 2008) 120, 124-125. First translation published in New Left Rev 43 (May/June 1967) at 57-74.

institutionalist-functionalist understanding. How has this travelled to postcolonial societies?

1.2.2 *Institutionalism and Functionalism in Postcolonies*

After independence, postcolonial leaders wished to build a modern nation-state and 'believed' in modernity.[35] Yet, as has been widely noted and theorized, modernization meant the reinsertion of these countries into the rapidly globalizing capitalist economic order, and the new political leadership was forced into alliance with its indigenous elite. Ambitions of nation-building around modernity took a further leap in liberal legal project under modernization in structural functionalism of Talcott Parsons.[36] Parsons moved away from rationality of classical economic theory and Pareto and brought non-rational factors in human action like Max Weber. He also relied heavily on Durkheim for social order leaving aside totalitarian monarchy in Hobbes. Poulantzas called Talcott Parsons the leader of 'functionalist' school in contemporary sociology under the influence of Max Weber.[37] New constitutions, laws and institutions were developed for the service of a developmental state in postcolonies. Law became the reflection of the developmental state in newly independent countries devoted to nation-building. David Trubek called this the first phase of law and development. After the failure of the developmental state in postcolonial countries, "law was understood as the foundation for market relations and as a limit on the state" in 1980s.[38] This gives centrality to law and liberal legal project under new institutionalism in 1990s. From the 1990s through 2000s, we have been living in the era of new institutionalism which has given a centrality to law for political and economic development.[39] Instead of a developmental state

---

[35]In India, even before independence, the "Bombay Plan" was approved in 1944 and in 1945 signed by five of the leading industrialists about future development and industrialization of India. See V Chibber, *Locked in Place: State-building and late industrialization in India* (Princeton University Press, Princeton, 2003) 85. In Pakistan, analysis in book will show the evidence from the speeches of one of the founding fathers Liaqat Ali Khan.

[36]T Parsons (1937), *The Structure of Social Action* (Free Press, New York, 1968); T Parsons (1951) *The Social System* (Routledge, London, 1991); see also Talcott Parsons and Edward A. Shills (1957) *Towards a General Theory of Action* (Harvard University Press, Harvard, 2013).

[37]N Poulantzas, *Political Power and Social Classes* (NLB, London, 1975) 40.

[38]DM Trubek and A Santos, Introduction: The Third Movement in Law and Development Theory and the Emergence of a New Critical Practice, in, DM Trubek & A Santos (eds) *The New Law and Economic Development: A Critical Appraisal* (Cambridge University Press, Cambridge, 2006) 2.

[39]This is evident from three Nobel Prizes in this area for Ronald Coase 1991, Douglas North 1993, and Oliver Williamson 2009 in last few decades. New Institutionalism is based on classical economics like rational choice theory, self interested individual, methodological individualism, utility maximization and equilibrium. A black box is common to all varieties of institutionalists, by which I mean the link between political demands and ultimate outcomes. Williamson placed emphasis on transaction costs adopted from Coase's theory of the firm. He saw transaction costs

leading development, the market was assigned the task of development because it would better allocate resources. IFIs and foreign investors only need laws for the market economy and an independent and strong judiciary for the protection of foreign investment (property) and contract enforcement. This means laws should be present *before* development occurs (in Weberian sense) and legal institutions for a particular function of market-oriented development in functionalist terms. The deductive school of thought in new institutional economics came back to the usefulness of institutions as the 'Ideal Type' in the vein of Max Weber.[40] Hence, Hegelian–Weberian institutionalist-functionalist understanding is the core in the current phase of liberal legal project under neoliberalism in the era of 'good-governance'.

Particular to this 'institutionalist' thrust are legal institutions. The emphasis of lender agencies has shifted from hard infrastructures (roads, dams, hospitals and schools) to soft infrastructure (judges, custom officials, legal aid and human rights organizations).[41] When the market failures happened at the end of the 1990s, the judiciary's role came to the centre of the liberal legal project in the postcolonial countries. Law and judicial reforms led by a strong judiciary are at the core of the good governance paradigm. For example, indicators like 'Regulatory Quality' (sometimes referred to as 'regulatory burden'), which is an assessment of all laws and policies by how they measure up against an ideal market economy. Through this, a whole body of enactments, amendments, legislations and repeals of laws in developing countries, including Pakistan, are measured for governance of the market economy.

Yet, people should also be made to respect these 'laws', in a Hobbesian sense, and here we find the sub-paradigm of 'Rule of Law'. This comprises several indicators, which measure the extent to which foreign investors and 'agents' have confidence in and abide by 'the rules of society'. The predictability of judicial decisions and contract enforceability are key here. I will call this entire complex the Project of the Judiciary.[42] The judge, according to Trubek, is the leader of this

(Footnote 39 continued)

being negotiated within a 'governance structure. See OE Williamson, The Institutions of Governance 88:2 *The American Econ Rev* (1998) 75.

[40]As claimed by Kristen Ford (2011). See K Ford (2011), The Veblenian Roots of Institutional Political Economy (Department of Economics Working Paper Series, University of Uttah Working Paper No. 2011-07) 12.

[41]V Taylor, The Law Reform Olympics: measuring the Effects of Law Reform in Transition Economie, in, Tim Lindsey (ed) *Law Reform in Developing and Transitional States* (Routledge, London New York, 2007) 87.

[42]D Kaufmann, A Kraay & Zoido-Lobaton, Governance Matters [7-8], last visited 6 December 2013 <http://elibrary.worldbank.org/action/doSearch?AllField=daniel+kaufmann&startPage>; see also D Kaufmann, A Kraay & Zoido-Lobaton, Governance Matters: From Measurement to Action, 37:2 *Finance & Development: a quarterly magazine of the IMF* (1999) 10-13.

phase of law and development.[43] That was the height of the liberal legal project in postcolonial societies.

Why did strong judiciaries arise in Pakistan, India, Bangladesh, Egypt, and elsewhere?[44] Apart from explanations of judges' bravery and lawyers' commitment for the rule of law or IFIs push for legal reforms, the new place of the judiciary should be analysed as a part of current level of complex hegemonic project in its historical trajectory from the colonial period to modernization under neoliberalism. The continuous failure of the liberal legal project in postcolonial countries is not because of bad judges, military intervention, corrupt politicians or implementation issues (governance) *only*.[45] All the liberal analyses in Pakistan never challenge the assumptions within the institutionalist-functionalist understanding of law, state, society and development.

1.2.3 Critique of Institutionalist-Functionalist Paradigm: The Issue of Change in Postcolonies

In postcolonial societies particularly, highly unequal property relations are a fundamental cause of conflict and a hindrance on the path of political and economic development. As opposed to this, institutionalist analyses, take property relations and relating laws as the empirical base upon which successful development occurs.[46] Liberal legal project does not look at above contradiction rather, it reduces all the problems of the liberal state formation to differences, paradoxes, opposition, strain, tension, disequilibrium, dislocation or imbalances and, if open strife, as conflicts.[47] But these contradictions in laws and constitutional arrangements are the

---

[43] "The hero figure of third globalization is unmistakably the judge, who brings either policy analysis or neo formalism to bear, as best s/he can, on disputes formulated by governmental and nongovernmental organizations claiming to represent civil society," see D Kennedy, Three Globalizations of Law and Legal Thought, in, DM Trubek & A Santos (eds) *The New Law and Economic Development: A Critical Appraisal* (Cambridge University Press, Cambridge, 2006) 65.

[44] See for example R Hoque, *Judicial Activism in Bangladesh: A Golden Mean Approach* (Cambridge Scholars Publishing, 2011).

[45] 'Governance' is defined as, 'how the decisions are made and implemented. In 1999, Daniel Kaufmann et al. adapted the definition of governance as put forward by the IMF, IDEA, and the Institute of Governance, and came up with "the traditions and institutions by which authority in a country is exercised, see D Kaufmann, A Kraay & Zoido-Lobaton, Governance Matters II: Updated Indicators for 2000-01 (Policy Research Working Paper No. 2772/1999) 4.

[46] For North, Athens based their structure of property rights on law, and the Romans elaborated a complete system of civil law undergirding the contractual relationships of the highly developed exchange economy. This developed throughout the Mediterranean world in the first two centuries AD, and the heritage of which has survived into modern times in Continental Europe. See North, *supra* note 29, 107.

[47] Bert Ollman, *Dance of the Dialectics: Steps in Marx's Method* (University of Illinois Press, Urbana/Chicago, 2003) 18.

contradictions of the political and the social in postcolonial societies. In postcolonies, the volatile nature of legal arrangements seems a clear indication of instability at the political and social level, arising out of the exclusion of large masses of the people at a structural level (property).

Contradictions are greater in class-divided postcolonial societies than in the class societies of the West. The latter have inequalities, but the former have a far more highly unequal distribution of resources. The more these contradictions are at the structural level, the more is the complexity of the hegemonic project of the ruling elite, that is, hegemony along with coercion.[48] Instead of answering the question of the extreme nature of contradictions, the exclusion and marginalization of huge sectors of the population, it is glossed over in the liberal legal project by reducing the issues to 'managerial' level of 'governance'. For example, institutional explanations show that the working class is represented in the assembly whereas they are not. Even turning out for elections for many times, there is not a single working-class person in the assemblies of Pakistan. Quite contrary to this, no constitutional and legal explanation can reveal the presence of U.S. imperialism (a very structural issue of Pakistan's dependency relation). Whereas, the U.S. was part of all the overthrows of democratic regimes and backing of the dictatorial regimes, from modernization to the current era of neoliberal governance. So the institutional and constitutional analyses hide what is present but not visible (structure) but shows or expects what is not present, that is, equality before law and representation.

My intention is to unearth that layer or instance of social reality where this exclusion is naked, that is, structure. As well as, the analysis in this book wants to counter individualistic and voluntarist view, which means that social processes are reproducible to apparently unconstrained actions of individuals. It also wants to conclude that overemphasis on the need of institutions or the overextended institutional analysis of our times is problematic in developing countries like Pakistan. Similarly, legalism in legal practice or a toll for politics, as an overextension of institutionalism, is fundamentally antithetical to a broader and deeper democracy. This is a matter of change in these postcolonial societies and the law has very limited emancipatory value. Anyone concerned with change in postcolonial societies, should be clear that laws, regulations and rules of the game (institutions) in New Institutionalism behind good governance are for organizational stability, not change.[49] Rather, revolution and illegal struggles are considered as disorder.[50]

---

[48]Hegemony is the active consent of the dominated classes to the dominant classes. Apart from coercion in social formation, the active consent of the dominant is obtained through an entire complex of political and theoretical activity. This 'political hegemony' does not depend on material force and power but is an ideological appropriation. See Q Hoare & GN Smith, (eds and trans) *Selections from the prison notebooks of Antonio Gransci* (International Publishers, New York, 2012) 57.

[49]K Thelen & S Steinmo, *Structuring Politics: Historical Institutionalism in Comparative Analysis*, (Cambridge University Press, New York, 1992).

[50]DC North, *Understanding the Process of Economic Change* (Princeton University Press, Princeton & Oxford, 2005) ch 8, 103.

Therefore, to properly grasp the change in postcolonial societies, analysis should bring into consideration the space around and beyond law while analysing law. This space is where the marginalization of the marginalized actually happened, that is, the economic instant of social formation. Furthermore, there is a need to know the role of law in the reproduction of system. That is, to include in legal analyses a certain 'consciousness' of the 'legal subject' and law as a part of 'hegemonic' project by the elite. Below is such an attempt to broaden the analysis of law and judiciary beyond the confines of institutionalism and functionalism.

1.3 Legal Analysis in Relation to State and Society: Theoretical Departure from Liberal Legal Analysis

The decade of 2000s in Pakistan was full of discourse of rule of law, good governance, rights, constitutionalism and a powerful judiciary using it to challenge democratic and dictatorial regimes alike in Pakistan. Connected to this were hectic legal activism and persistent exploitation, marginalization and exclusion of the subalterns. How can one study this development of the legal enterprise as it evolved through time? Below is an attempt to develop such a theoretical framework used in this book.

First step for this is to explore the surface appearances, which present themselves as including the historical development of the object, that is, judiciary in this case. Based on this, a prior conception is to build, that can lead to the selection of empirical material. Next step is, with the concrete material before us, 'to ascend from the concrete to the abstract'. This means pulling out the actual constituent elements from the concrete and look at them connected and in motion in the abstract. For example, from the empirical material about judiciary, I tried to see how the judiciary and political development are in the concrete in constant motion, developing in a particular direction due to contradictory and mutually affecting determinations. As a next step, abstraction helped me in pulling out the most decisive of these contradictions to build the reproduction of the concrete-in-thought through the criteria of social practice. This stage of abstraction also helped to determine the general mutual connections of the decisive, abstract elements in moving the social phenomenon. After this I was able to reconstruct the concrete going through the empirical material. This was not a one-time process, it was a repeated process of conceptualization that led to new ways of appropriating and abstracting empirical material.

There is a need to elaborate more on this particular stage of abstraction due to its difficulty and accusations levelled against it. Abstraction here is not in terms of its common sense use meaning 'vague' or 'removed from reality'.[51] Objects and their relations are not transparent. Actually 'abstraction' (or theoretical matters) is familiar, for instance, people know that things have been the same for the last

---

[51]A Sayer, *Method in Social Science: A Realist Approach*, 2nd edn (Routledge, London & New York, 1992) 87.

66 years in Pakistan in terms of lack of betterment in their lives. Everyday life includes concepts that are abstract and theoretical like 'we are mortal'. And concreteness cannot necessarily be familiar or be lay knowledge, as we mostly deal with, is apparent and superficial knowledge.[52] But remember, that from Perry Anderson, Andrew Sayer, to Poulantzas, everyone warned that abstraction will not offer *concrete* descriptions (Sayer 1992: 98). [Emphasis added by Sayer][53]

I picked the constituent elements of political development (hegemony as a political practice in Gramscian sense) in relation to the approach and actions of the judiciary. One constituent element, in case of Pakistan, was centre–periphery relations, with the U.S. as the hegemonic class (a class analysis of Pakistani state to follow in the next half of this chapter). This hegemonic class brought the reigning classes (feudal, capitalists) under its political project using civil-military bureaucracy as a seat of power. This was complex. A second constituent element is inter-elite struggles around and with civil-military bureaucracy. This is the *political instance* of social formation in Pakistan. In this instance, the inclusion and exclusion (or pretentious inclusion) of the dominated classes in the hegemonic project happened. This inclusion and exclusion of the dominated is third and the most important constituent element. I look at how this exclusion was made possible in both democratic and dictatorial regimes. So we are to see the development of the above three constituent elements at the structural level, that is, economic instance of social formation. How the centre–periphery economic dependency relations joined hands with local elite in economic arrangements excluding dominated classes travelling in a particular direction. This is called articulation of the mode of production but changing ones, and the key for change is class struggle, which we will discuss later.

But our object of study is law and judiciary, that is, to look at the relation of above-mentioned political and economic instance's development with law and judiciary (legal instance). That is, those constituent parts of the legal enterprise (law and judiciary) which form part of the hegemonic project. *This is the legal instance that gives the most legitimacy to political and economic instances in the post-colonial Pakistan.* This is where most of the hegemonic project is concentrated. Pakistan shows an active judiciary and legal field as an arena of political struggle. This is not only politicization of judiciary but is also judicialization of politics, that is, most of political battles are fought in the courts. The legal instant gives legitimacy to political and economic conflicts which are contradictions. This suggests that most of the work of reproduction of the 'system' happened in the legal and ideological (Islam) instances in Pakistan. Since hegemony is a political practice, this is the reason of politicization of judiciary and judicialization of politics in Pakistan. *The objective of this book is to elaborate how a particular rule of law, separation of power, human rights, judicial review and a rhetoric of independent*

[52]*Ibid* [145, 146].

[53]*Ibid* 98.

judiciary, collectively as a legal instant, carry three constituent elements; namely, centre–periphery dependency relations, inclusion of reigning classes, and the exclusion of the dominated classes, in relation to political and economic development/change (instant) in a particular direction in a constant motion in an empirical concrete.

In this elucidation, incoherence and inconsistency of the judicial decisions will be apparent. The attempt is made to trace back this inconsistency to the contradictions in the political and the economic. This book studies the judicial discourses around judicial review, fundamental rights, separation of power, PIL, appointment of judges and even the politics of the bar in an interconnected manner to understand its role in the political development. Rather than getting to the bottom line quickly, sufficient time in this book is given to the complex mediations over space and time to discover the relation of political governance and judiciary.

Legal and judicial activism happens within a complete system. To be effective, it needs to take into account social, political, economic, cultural and ideological aspects. This invokes serious questions of methodology and theory. To make this introductory chapter simple, I try to confine myself to the method I use to analyse the legal developments in Pakistan in relation to changes in broader society. This may seem like laying down the contours of a theoretical framework but not settling all theoretical questions. Based on this method, once the historical and empirical account is narrated, then in concluding chapter, I will reflect on how this theoretical framework has implications for critical legal tradition in academia like 'social' and 'cultural turn,' law and development, Third World Approaches to International Law (TWAIL), and Critical Legal Studies (CLS). That is, how it adds to this critical tradition.

Proper grasp of the relation of legal enterprise with other instances of the social whole also needs a nuanced understanding of politics, relation of law and politics with economy. It needs to avoid mechanical and reductionist attempts to divide social whole into ontological discrete spheres such as culture, economy, politics or consciousness. Orthodox Marxism reduced law and other superstructural phenomena to economy. Reacting to this current reductionist trend of social theory and culture in academia seems allergic to any nuanced understanding of political and economic in legal analyses. Theoretical framework in this book originally builds upon Gramsci's idea of hegemony as political practice and Althusser's dynamic relation of economic instance of social whole with law and ideology. While doing this, E.P. Thompson's contribution to emphasize importance of cultural aspect of law can be accommodated to avoid economic reductionism. This means to bring back nuanced understanding of 'critical political economy' in legal analyses which dominantly are under the influence 'social' and 'cultural turn'. This is to bring a broader social theory in legal analyses.

Concept of hegemony by Gramsci is to understand that ruling class does not rule through coercion only but it gets active consent of the dominated by persuading them. For Gramsci, this ideological appropriation of the dominated classes by the ruling class is hegemony.[54] This is not only a false consciousness but dominated classes accept the universal promises of freedom and equality. In that sense hegemony is not the hegemony of one class but a political practice in which consent is sought and ideas are contested in one cultural and social space. That is why hegemony may be complex and indeed it is in postcolonies where the hegemonic class negotiates with other dominant and dominated classes to construct a hegemonic order and form a 'historic bloc'. To do that, legal and ideological constructs and discourses are developed by the dominant classes. In case of Pakistan, this book shows a real effort on behalf of judges and jurists to address the requirements of the hegemonic bloc to construct legal (liberal) and ideological (Islam) instant of the social whole. In that effort while the contradictions in the hegemonic bloc make it volatile, the tremendous pressure came on legal and ideological instances of the social whole to give legitimacy to these regimes and state formations.

But in postcolonial class-divided societies there is no separation of political from the economic and hence economic is a very important part of the social and is related to hegemony, that is, political practice and consequent state formations for 'developmental state' of modernization and 'state for the market' of current neoliberal globalization. Whereas Gramsci rightly emphasized the importance of politics reacting to economic reductionism of orthodox Marxism, Althusser re-articulate the importance of the economic instant of the social whole. This is particularly important in postcolonies where the hegemony is all about exploitation and exclusion of the subaltern at the structural level.

Althusser in his writings from *For Marx*, *Reading Capital*, to his famous essay *Ideology and Ideological State Apparatuses* insisted that 'social whole' consists of 'levels' 'instances' (economic, political, legal and ideological) which distinguishes Marxism from Hegelian 'totality'.[55] Economic level (base or infrastructure) consists of the productive forces and the relations of production. Superstructure consists of two levels or instances: the political-legal (including law and state) and the ideological level/instance (religious, moral, legal, political and so on).[56] In Althusser's formation legal, political, ideological instances of social formation (superstructure) are *relative autonomous* but are *determined* by the *effectivity* of the economic. Superstructure reacts back to the base but economic is determinant *in the last instant*[57] but through complex mediations. For example, literature and culture react

---

[54]This concept and its relation to overall aspects of social whole is elaborated by Gramsci in his prison notes. To make it simple, I am using Kalyan Sanyal's summary. See K Sanyal, *Rethinking Capitalist Development: Primitive Accumulation, Governmentality and Post-colonial Capitalism* (Routledge, London, 2007) 27; see Gramsci in Q Hoare & GN Smith, (eds and trans) *Selections from the prison notebooks of Antonio Gransci* (International Publishers, New York, 2012).

[55]See for the detailed articulation of these concepts, L Althusser, *For Marx* (trans Ben Brewster) (Verso, London, 2010); L Althusser & E Balibar, *Reading Capital* (trans Ben Brewster) (Verso, London, 2009).

[56]L Althusser, *On the Reproduction of Capitalism: Ideology and Ideological State Apparatuses* (Verso, London, 2014) 53.

[57]*Ibid* 54.

back to other instances of social whole like philosophy and politics as well as to the economic base. This simply means that superstructure is relative autonomous having specific effectivity, that is, have its own history. We can trace it to economy through complex mediations. According to Althusser, Marx had given us two ends of the chain, one is determination in the last instant by the economic (mode of production) and on the other end is relative autonomy and specific effectivity of the superstructure. We are to find between them a complex set of mediations.[58] This proposition of Althusser made any social phenomenon, from political parties to literary texts as *over-determined*, that is, caused in varying degree by events and actions in all levels of the base and superstructure by which it is constituted.[59] So it is clear that economy is not the sole determinant factor of a historical event. 'Dominance in the last instance' does not mean 'dominant role'.[60] Though the economy is determinant in the last instant. In reality, 'the last instance' never comes.[61]

Viewing it this way, Althusser's theory of social formation is open, dynamic, and takes into account different levels of social formation even with unevenness in their own development and in their mutual relationship. What one needs is to avoid a degree of functionalism and structuralism in Althusser. He did not identify oppositional ideologies within the state structure, so it pulled his analysis strongly towards functionalism.[62]

Althusser is accused of being a structuralist by E.P. Thompson. For Stuart Hall this impression is right, but the real advances in Althusser's theory are more important than this,[63] which we have mentioned above. Althusser did not align himself with structuralism of Sassure, Levi and Lucan. He was not interested in a complete system. He distanced himself from what he called 'structuralist ideology'.[64] Edith Kurzweil's position is that though Althusser denounced being a structuralist, he shared preoccupations about unconscious structures with Levi-Straus, Foucault and Lacan.[65] That said, I want to make clear that to take into account structure in my analysis of relation between legal institutions and political development, the above-mentioned understanding of social formation can be the only theoretical base to start with. This theoretical prerequisite of understanding of social whole will not automatically generate analysis but only show 'how things are

---

[58]Althusser, For Marx, *supra* note 55, 111.

[59]See for a summary of these concepts L Ferretter, *Louis Althusser* (Routledge, London & NY, 2006) 40.

[60]Poulantzas, Towards a Marxist theory, (trans Gregory Elliot), *supra* note 34, 139, 159.

[61]Althusser, For Marx, *supra* note 55, 113.

[62]Comments of James Martin on this article of Poulantzas, *supra* note 60, 10.

[63]S Hall, Signification, Representation, Ideology: Althuser and the Post-structuralist Debates, 2 *Crit Stud in Mass Comm* (1985) 91, 96.

[64]T Benton, *The Rise and Fall of Structural Marxism* (Macmillan Publishers, London, 1984) 14.

[65]E Kurzweil, *The Age of Structuralism: From Levi-Straus to Foucault* (Transaction Publishers, New Brunswick/London, 1996, first published in 1980) 39.

in a social whole'. The burden on the research is to show 'this is how the things are' in a particular social formation.

This invokes the question of structure, history, culture and human agency. This also brings theory and empirical research in an antithetical position in these debates. Known Marxist historian E.P. Thompson around history of Black Acts gave tremendous detail of events of that time, like class interests, crimes committed against property, forest bureaucracy's rationality, their conflicts with forest formers, wealth of South Sea Company and its bribes.[66] But throughout his study, Thompson connects historical evidence randomly. Perry Anderson called this a catalogue of system without causal hypothesis, that is, 'a listing is not explanation'.[67] This means history is equal to past—a record of everything that has happened.[68] A historian is not free of the duty of conceptualizing. To capture the process of change in history, one is to formulate and specify historical concepts with care. This duty becomes more where there is diversity and historical flux.[69] Perry went to the extent that Marxist history should be different from historiography in general. Former needs a formal construction of theoretical concepts but Perry at the same time warned that these concepts can only produce real knowledge if return to and derive from a controllable research.[70]

As opposed to this, E.P. Thompson deliberately demolished the above-mentioned theoretical understanding of a social whole proposed by Althusser at the end of his study of Black Acts.[71] Thompson was reacting to an impression in Althusser's work, which Poulantzas correctly pointed out. That is, Althusser tried to find 'theoretical' solutions to 'theoretical problems'.[72] To avoid this, Thompson went to the other extreme of empiricism. Althusser was not putting theoretical practice before history but before historical investigation. This means conceptualizing. Perry Anderson is right that in order to understand change in history, one needs to conceptualize. Economic itself was a social phenomenon for Thomson and he tries to set free culture, consciousness and human agency from the economic. Later it was difficult to conceptualize the causal relations of the legal struggles with that of the social of the economic. It lost the historicity of the legal practice. Any legal analysis needs tracing the legal struggles on historical premise going through complex mediations to see how do they develop. But to have their contemporary material-ideological analysis, one needs a structural premise. Therefore, legal analysis should be integrally on both premises. History and structure are two distinct concepts. One cannot be reduced to another. What connects structure and history is investigation of the political practice which is hegemony. It needs

[66]Thompson, *supra* note 25, 83, 95 99, 130 and 176.

[67]P Anderson, *Arguments Within English Marxism* (Verso, London, 1980) 81.

[68]*Ibid* 13.

[69]*Ibid* 10.

[70]*Ibid* 66.

[71]Thompson, *supra* note 25; Last Chapter.

[72]Poulantzas, *supra* note 60, 139, 157.

concrete study of class struggle, where agents are not free-floating empirical facts of historiography nor doped slaves of structures.

After distancing from structuralism and functionalism,[73] the related issue of neglect of human agency also needs some clarification, For Giddens, this is common to all structural writers. In Derrida, writers' intentions are separate from the writing. Similarly, in Sassure, Levi and Barthes, social practices are separate from our intentions.[74] For me, agency in relation to class struggle means independence of human agency to wage class struggle against structures as opposed to pretentious liberty and freedom of human agency under liberalism. By continuously keeping an eye on classes and class struggle in my analysis, I bring the main strength of the Marxist analysis. Marxist analysis of structures hinges on class, that is why, the mention of structures for class analysis in this book has nothing to do with structuralism. Based on this, my only claim is that, in this age of institutional analyses, ignoring structures is just ignoring class struggle (the actual potency of human agency), be it done by liberals or by poststructuralists. For both of them, 'values', 'hegemony', 'consciousness', 'discourse', is the start as well as the end objective of analysis.

Then what is the place of ideology, discourse and consciousness of the legal subject in legal analyses? 'Consciousness' is mostly used as awareness and opposite to 'ideology' considering it 'false consciousness'. But in contemporary research, just like power/resistance and structure/agency are not opposite, ideology and consciousness are considered as internal components of a larger process of social construction.[75] In that sense, consciousness of the legal subject is neither false consciousness nor is neutral as some contemporary social theorists think.[76] This context of discussion of ideology is at the expense of social experience of the ideology by people. If actual experience of the people is exclusion and marginalization through deception of ideology, as is the case of Pakistan, why not to accept this role of ideology in its particularity? Rather, through discourse, ideology is institutionalized to become a material reality. Social organization gains legitimacy through legal consciousness.[77] In terms of dealing with ideology, there can be two types of missions for those who want change in society. One is to use legal ideology as a contesting field and give a new content. Speculative content of ideology is not enough either. Furthermore, ideologies are not empty sack that can be filled with new content. Another way is to delegitimize ideology and change consciousness for

---

[73]For Giddens, 'functionalism' and 'structuralism' share similar origins and have many important factors in common, see A Giddens, *Central Problem in Social Theory: Action, Structure and Contradiction in Social Analysis* (University of California Press, Berkeley, 1979) 9.

[74]*Ibid* 41.

[75]P Ewick, Consciousness and Ideology, in, A Saratedt (ed) *The Blackwell Companion to Law and Society* (Blackwell Publishing, US, 2004) 80, 80.

[76]SE Merry, Concepts of Law and Justice among Working-Class Americans: Ideology as Culture, 9 *Legal Studies Forum* (1990) 59.

[77]Ewick, *supra* note 75, 86.

a counter-hegemony.[78] Gramsci's idea of hegemony explains that ideas play a role in politics to get the consent of the governed. But why people submit to ideology? Gramsci could not answer. Althusser's seminal work explains how ideology is a medium in which one 'lives out' ones relation to society. It binds social structure.[79]

Based on above understanding of the social whole what should be the methodology for legal analysis?

1.3.1 Few Comments About Methodology

I connect *judges*' legal ideologies and ideal of political development as gleaned from their judicial biographies, speeches and writings to their legal decisions. I relate *decisions* to *events*, and *events* to the *political* hegemonic project. Finally, I link this analysis with the deep structures within which these institutions were enabled or restrained, such as the unequal distribution of land and wealth, and Pakistan's imperialist hegemonic centre–periphery dependency relations over the decades from modernization to current global 'good governance'.

While reading available literature on Pakistani judiciary and its decisions on different component of legal enterprise like judicial review, rights, etc., I noticed two problems. One, as already stated, that the decisions were discussed at the level of deviation from some 'ideal' legal and political arrangement and hence labelling judges as good or bad. Second, there were development of one legal component from piece meal case law and legal struggles disconnected from other components of the legal enterprise. Finally, the development of legal concepts was either doctrinal or with very superficial understanding of politics and society.

First, I gave a new reading to most of the cases in dominant legal literature in relation to political development in Pakistan. At this stage I use elements of discourse analysis, deconstruction, and immanent critique. Apart from judges' decision in favour of democracy or human right, I tried to understand judges' ideas about democracy and rights from their speeches, writings and autobiographies. All Pakistan Law Decisions (PLD) has a journal section which covers writings and all important speeches of judges and jurists. In these writings and speeches judges comment about their cases and politics also. Almost all the important judges and jurists also publish their autobiographies. Here again judges talk about their cases and political opinions. What I did is to construct a model of political, social and cultural development of judges from these sources and connect it, on one hand, with their cases and on the hand with overall political hegemonic project as a political and state practice. To do the former, I again use critical approach to go beyond

[78]CLS adopted this mission see DM Trubek, Where the Action is: Critical Legal Studies and Empiricism, 36 *Stan L Rev* (1984) 575; Example of such a work is Duncan Kennedy, The Structure of Blackstone Commentaries, 28 *Buff L Rev* (1979) 209.

[79]DS Brosnan, Serious but not Critical, 60 *S Cal L Rev* (1987) 259.

descriptive liberal understanding about Pakistani state, politics, culture and economics. The different analysis of law and judiciary was not possible without a new critical understanding of the postcolonial state and politics of Pakistan. Most of the social science literature reduces the understanding of Pakistan to an omnipotent military bureaucracy. Related to this is the analysis of Islamization of Pakistan by the military in these writings. The judiciary in these analyses seems under attack, helpless, compromising and hence, deserving of sympathy. Legal analyses superficially borrow understandings of state and politics from these already descriptive liberal analyses. This book adds a few new insights to the state theory of postcolonial Pakistan by demonstrating a close nexus of the civil-military bureaucracy with the judiciary during modernization. That is, it was not a civil-military bureaucracy but a juridico-bureaucratic structure that defined state formation in legal and constitutional terms.

The research project in this book emerges from my prior life in hectic legal struggles for the labour, bonded labour and peasantry. I interviewed lawyers to fill the gaps in my research. To add Bar politics in my analysis, I interviewed those who were involved because their writings were not commonly available. I interviewed labour leaders and their views were crucial as being marginalized in this struggle for 'democracy' and 'rights'. Most of all I hope that my experience as a legal practitioner with marginalized communities and my quest for relevant legal theory merge in this book in such a way that it allows for readers to conceptualized a theoretically informed legal activism, with a theory which can broaden the political horizon in theory as well as practice.

Finally, before critically engaging with judges' and jurists' writings and decision in empirical chapters, one thing should be clear that this book is not meant to defame Pakistani judiciary or judges. The role of judges and judiciaries in other class-divided societies is the same to varying degrees. This is true even with class societies of the west. It is just a matter of theoretical framework and methodology that can bring it to light. That is why, concluding chapter pointed out the problems of insufficiency of critical legal to expose the liberal legal project in the west.

1.4 A New Theoretical Understanding of State and Politics of Postcolonial Pakistan

1.4.1 'Liberal' Understanding of Law and State in Postcolonial Pakistan

The liberal approach to the state in Pakistan holds that political governance moves between dictatorship and democracy, and that the judiciary decides which it is to be. For this approach, the military is a main player of governance in Pakistan. In general, the military uses the civil bureaucratic structure and the judiciary, through constitutional engineering and legal manoeuvering, to keep the legislature under its control.[80] For instance, Charles H. Kennedy's explanations are an example of common sense liberal understanding of the Pakistani state. He correlates Musharraf's first 5-year regime with other three dictatorial regimes and devises a 'A User Guide to Guided Democracy'. These steps include avoiding legal chaos (continuity of the government), making things legal in the short term (judiciary's stamp), eliminating political opponents, arranging to become a president, reinventing local government, intimidate the civil bureaucracy and superior judiciary, rewriting the constitution and orchestrating elections. This description assumes the passivity of politicians and sees the military as the only active agent. The 'reluctant conclusion' of the writer is that the fault lies in both military and politicians for not developing a stable constitutional system.

This is true at a descriptive level that all the military regimes in Pakistan (Ayub Khan, 1958–1968; Zia ul-Haq, 1977–1988; Pervez Musharraf, 1999–2009) came to power through bloodless coups, suggesting that there was widespread agreement among power holders that the prior political democratic regimes were not functioning properly. The military regimes also maintained the continuity of the constitution through a malleable judiciary, which gave their rule constitutional approval. This judiciary helped them at times to eliminate their political opponents.

In order to consolidate themselves as being elected and design their version of governance, the three military heads took a particular path to constitutional engineering. They invented and reinvented local governance to create a new electoral college so as to create a new party in order to bargain with the existing feudal and business elite. This way, the dictator could be elected as a president, and later the assembly could approve the constitutional arrangements for the designed governance mechanism. During such transitions, an intimidated civil bureaucracy had to control the masses.

All the quasi-democratic regimes[81] led by mass parties, on the other hand, have attempted to loosen the grip of the executive/president over the governance structure. The base of these parties has been the rural elite, the majority of whom have been recruited through political defection (horse-trading, buying and/or terrifying the opposition and rewarding the new ruling party Members of National Assembly). They readjust the judiciary to implement certain legal and constitutional arrangements, which usually ends in confrontation with the judiciary.[82] They also use the judiciary to focus on the opposition's corruption and to bring attention away from their own corruption cases. The regimes try to control the civil and military

[80]See CH Kennedy, A User's Guide to Guided Democracy: Musharraf and the Pakistani Military Governance Paradigm, in CH Kennedy & CA Botteron (eds) *Pakistan: 2005* (OUP, Karachi, 2005) 120, 150.

[81]Heeger (1977) thinks that even when the military is not in power it has control over resource allocation and decision-making. See GA Heeger, Politics in the Post-Military State: Some Reflections on the Pakistani Experience, 29 *World Politics* (1977) 242; See also M Aziz, *Military Control in Pakistan: The Parallel State* (Routledge, New York, 2008).

[82]The second term of Benazir Bhutto (1993-1996) and Nawaz Sharif (1997-1999) are marked with this confrontation.

bureaucracy and to appoint their own 'sincere' Chief of Army Staff. Every time they attempt this, however, the assembly is dissolved and cannot complete its tenure. The judiciary has always been there to put its stamp on this dissolution of assembly as 'constitutional deviation'.

According to analysis in this book, this much-touted dichotomy of dictatorship versus democracy removes class and class relations from an understanding of the political dynamics of the state and, as a result, the law. The dichotomy emphasizes that the state is completely autonomous from society and social relations. This autonomy is in the sense of the state's own will devoid of classes for its own interests and not neutral above classes in the sense of western state. By implying that the legislature is weak because of a strong military, the liberal paradigm stresses that the military is the primary problem in Pakistan's politics. In these 'democracy-centric' analyses, as opposed to non-democracy or lack of democracy (dominance of military), once democracy is universalized, no one can ask about representation in it. This means the death of other forms of representation.

In order to understand the totality of Pakistan's politics and how this structures the law, there is a need to go beyond this liberal approach.

1.4.2 From a 'Legal State' to a 'Class State'

Instead of reducing Pakistan's political development as a deviation from an ideal type of democracy (due to military) and a *legal state*, this book will argue Pakistani state as a *class state*. That is, how metropolitan bourgeoisie as a hegemonic class, under the leadership of U.S. imperialism, used military and civil bureaucracy as its *seat of power* to secure a complex hegemony for the inclusion of the reigning classes (feudal and capitalist elite) and the exclusion of the dominated classes. For this analysis, social formations including political and cultural are the actual sites of the reproduction as well as its existence. This means that these sites are the sites of class struggle and hence the history of political struggles can elaborate the theory of a postcolonial state.[83] This understanding suggests a simple formula that the state formation which came into being, should be linked to the class formation. Borrowing from Poulantzas, state formation as a class formation, would permit an assessment whereby class is dominant in state formation. Below is the step-by-step elaboration of this understanding.

[83] I am borrowing this idea from Poulantzas. His theory is about capitalist state. N Poulantzas (1978), *State, Power, Socialism* (Verso, London & New York, 2000) 25.

1.4.3 Postcolonial Pakistani State: Factual or Theoretical Departure?

The Pakistani state has not developed through the European path of state formation[84] and requires theorization that can account for its particular characteristics. But this particular different does not mean that there is some fault line separating east and the west and rejecting everything that is western.[85] The link of the east and the west is at the factual economic, political, cultural and ideological level in terms of imperialist presence from colonization to neo-colonization. The new understanding of the non-western states raised many genuine concerns,[86] very particular to postcolonial state but this does not need complete theoretical departure from the West as is claimed by these theories. Rather, the different contextual differences of east and west should be enriching theoretical understanding in both.

For example, there is no separation of state and civil society in postcolonial Pakistan. Separation of the state and civil society is the theoretical basis of the liberal understanding of western capitalist state and society. The concept of civil society, borrowed from Hegel and eighteenth century political theory, connects 'concrete man' for world needs into a national political unity through universal suffrage. The 'equality' and 'liberty' of individual citizens is in their relation to the abstract laws form a 'legal state' separated from civil society or above the citizens. The problem with this preposition, even in western capitalist society, let alone postcolonial one, is that it prevents us from understanding the relation of the state to the class struggle. Similarly, individuals are told so equal that it is not possible to constitute social classes from this. In this way, state comes at the origin of the economic individual agents and one cannot start from classes to understand the

---

[84]As explained by Tariq Amin-Khan (2012) in his engagement with the stream of western scholarship for which the natural social and, political form of the modern world is anchored in the nation-state. See T Amin-Khan, *The Post-Colonial State in The Era of Capitalist Globalization: Historical, Political, and Theoretical Approaches to State Formation* (Routledge, New York, 2012) 48. See also A Wimmer and NG Schiller, Methodological Nationalism and Beyond: Nation-State Building, Migration and Social Sciences, 2:4 *Global Networks* (2002) 301. Other theorists of nationalism and nations are Ernest Gellner, Eric Hobsbawm, ElieKouderie, and Benedict Anderson. They link the industrial revolution with the beginning of nationalism and nation state. See B Anderson, *Imagined Communities: Reflection on the Origin and the Spread of Nationalism* (Verso, London, 1991).

[85]For rebuttle of postcolonial theory's this claim, see Vivek Chibber's powerful arguments taking subaltern studies as an example of postcolonial theory. V Chibber, *Postcolonial Theory and the Specter of Capital* (Verso, London, 2013) 284.

[86]Similarly Tariq Amin Khan gives a critique of ethnographic studies of state like G Joseph & D Nugent, *Everyday Forms of State Formation: Revolution and the negotiation of rule in modern Mexico* (Duke University Press, Durham, 1994); A Gupta & A Sharma, Globalization and postcolonial States, 47:2 *Current Anthropology* (2006) 277, 278; SA Radcliffe, Imagining the State as a Space: Territoriality and the Formation of the State in Ecuador, in, TB Hansen & F Stepputat, (eds) *State of Imagination: Ethnographic Explorations of the post-Colonial State* (Duke University Press, Durham, 2001) 125. See T Amin-Khan, *supra* note 64, 48; *ibid* Chibber.

state.[87] The separation of state and civil society based on Hegel stayed in Marx but later he evolved the concept of a 'class state', with 'objective structures' giving birth to a 'specifically political' concept of the state. Consequently, Marx and Gramsci conceived of politics as a practice of power.[88] When I say that in postcolonial Pakistan, there is no separation of state and civil society, this means it is not a state above classes or outside classes (relative autonomous *only*). This is a *class state*. It serves the interests of the dominant classes (instrumental aspect of the state) and disperses the dominated classes keeping law and order (functional aspects). But in my analysis, these relative autonomous and functional aspects of the state are not *aclass* as in Weber and Parsons as discussed above. Similarly, these aspects are not because dominant classes control the state (on *behest* of the capitalist class, as is in Miliband). Rather, I refer the nature of each aspect (instrumental, functionalist and relative autonomous) to particular conjecture of class struggle in a particular society in a particular period of time. This should be the basis of looking at the state formations going from democracy to dictatorship in postcolonial Pakistan rather than democracy and dictatorship as deviations from an ideal type.

Similarly, in postcolonial Pakistan, there is no separation of political from the economic. In western capitalist society, the state is assumed to be above the economic interests of all the classes and individuals, and protects the property and ensures contract enforcement. There is an assumed consensus in regards to the economic base or infrastructure, or the organizing principles of the society. The state's involvement in the economy is assumed to be on behalf of all classes. So there is complete separation of political from the economic.

My take on the issue is that there is no actual separation of the political from the economic in postcolonial societies. In postcolonial Pakistan, the presence of an industrialist class, along with capitalist agriculture, under the hegemony of the metropolitan bourgeoisie was crucial for determining political development and not the civil and bureaucracy *only*. Of course, this represents the contradictory unity of the dominant classes but the state and its legal arrangements for these classes. This is true from structural adjustment policies (SAP) and privatization under neoliberalism. Based on this, one can define the functionalist aspects of the postcolonial state. It is true that the state is not merely an object or 'authorized author' or representing the will of the dominant class. But it can be used 'instrumentally' as a repressive force with 'internal unity' of the state to that will.[89] Yet, in a postcolonial society, the 'political practice' of the dominant classes overtly or covertly makes intensive use of the state apparatus and hence the state has an instrumental aspect. However, this instrumentality should be found in the political practice (class struggle) and not in the 'will' of the dominant classes. It is this very political practice that, at once, also gives 'relative autonomy' to the state. When the

---

[87]Poulantzas, *supra* note 37, 123.

[88]Martin (ed), *supra* note 34, 8.

[89]Vyshinsky's formula which Poulantzas rejected, see Poulantzas, Preliminaries to the study of hegemony in the state, *supra* note 34, 74, 76.

dominated classes are organized, the state accommodated their demands as after 1968 in Pakistan.[90] Given that there is no separation of political from the economic in postcolonial Pakistan, we should reconsider the instrumental and functionalist aspects of the state and examine the direct involvement of the state in protecting the structures of society. Invoking this buried concept has implications for considering different forms the postcolonial state can take.

Based on the above discussion, few very basic factual and theoretical departures from the prevalent liberal and Marxist liberal understanding about postcolonial Pakistan are very clear. First, in postcolonial Pakistan, the state is not relative autonomous *only* above classes as is in western liberal understanding. Nor the postcolonial state is relative autonomous in Alavian's understanding that the military is running the affaires of the country.[91] In Alavi's formation, postcolonial state of Pakistan has relative autonomy with respect to three contending fundamental classes (the indigenous bourgeoisie, the metropolitan bourgeoisie and the landed class). Since no class can dominate in the formation mentioned above, this gives relative autonomy to the military-bureaucratic structure that Alavi conceptualized as an 'overdeveloped state'. This is clearly another form of liberal *aclass* autonomous state with bad rationality as opposed to 'good' rationality of western Weberian state. In my theoretical understanding, the state of postcolonial Pakistan has instrumental and functional aspects *also* along with its relative autonomy. The natures of all the three above aspects vary and the change depends upon the changing nature of class formations due to class struggle. What is the nature of class formation in Pakistan?

1.4.4 Hegemonic Class?: Redefining the Place of Centre–Periphery Relations in State Formation

Alavi argues that there is a 'plurality of fundamental classes' in postcolonial societies like Pakistan, namely the indigenous bourgeoisie, the metropolitan bourgeoisie and the landed class. There is accordingly no one 'ruling class'. This is in contrast to the fundamental classes in the West, namely the bourgeoisie and the proletariat, where the bourgeoisie rules.[92] In Alavi's class formation about Pakistan, the working, or dominated, class is missing. Furthermore, the metropolitan bourgeoisie is mentioned in the bloc of the dominant classes, but is not explained in the 'overdeveloped' state formation. That is, how does it affect democracy and dictatorship?

[90]Working class upsurge as a part of popular uprising against Ayub in 1968 made his successors Yahya and Bhutto to bring structural changes (See chapter about 1970's of this book).

[91]H Alavi, The State in Post-Colonial Societies: Pakistan and Bangladesh 74 *New Left Rev* (1972) 59.

[92]*Ibid*, 71.

To bring to light the presence of metropolitan bourgeoisie and the exclusion of the dominated classes in state formations (in so-called democracy versus dictatorship debates) are the most crucial points of my understanding. As far as the working class is concerned, it always deserves a footnote in liberal analyses. The U.S. "role is considered in liberal analyses regarding inter-elite struggles" literature of Pakistan but is very superficially theorized. The neglect of imperialist design is a phenomenon of the 1990's under rising 'institutionalist' analyses linked with the decline of the Left. Till the 1980s, this 'neutral' imperialist presence was not neutral. It was argued, "Pakistan hardly enjoys any degree of freedom in its external relations".[93] Now Pakistan's political elite is fully convinced that the road to Islamabad lies through Washington,[94] and its liberal elements argue that the U.S. should intervene for democracy in Pakistan. Responding to why the U.S. has supported every authoritarian regime in Pakistan, Siddiqa thought that the U.S. support of dictatorships is just an excuse that dictatorial regimes used. She wants U.S. support for internal movements of democracy to reduce the role of military just like U.S. did in Latin America.[95] Siddiqa is an example of a more contemporary theorist who has lost the old plotline, that imperial interests work within and through the Pakistani state, and that they have always done this through the military.

In my understanding, the lack of liberal democracy in postcolonial Pakistan can only be explained due to the presence of metropolitan bourgeoisie in the state formation as a relational condensate during cold war as well as post-cold war period in Pakistan. In contrast, in India's case, the presence of a strong bourgeoisie vis-à-vis the relatively lesser presence of a metropolitan bourgeoisie (along with other social relations and class struggle) explains the 'level' and 'nature' of liberal democracy. In other words, the weakness of the bourgeoisie vis-à-vis a strong state is not the key to explain a dictatorial state formation, as is Liberals and Alavi's position. Rather, weakness of the political elite vis-à-vis the metropolitan bourgeoisie in class formation is a reason for the lack of democracy. This presence is not institutional but structural. It is important to remove 'neutral' (with respect to imperialist design) explanations of judicial, legal and constitutional issues as part of political development.

How is imperialism, particularly U.S. imperialism, *in* the state and society of postcolonial Pakistan? Imperialism under the leadership of the U.S. is not only connected in the circulation of capital sphere but in the production sphere in the form of aid under modernization to the dictates of IFIs under SAP to current 'good

---

[93]WP Zingel, S Zingel & A Lallemant (eds) *Pakistan in the 80's: Law & Constitution* (Vanguard, Lahore, 1985) 3; This is the compilation of papers read at the international conference 'Pakistan in its Fourth Decade: Test Ahead for the Islamic State', held on 27-30 May 1980 in Hamburg. All the participants were of the above opinion.

[94]Hussain *supra* note 1, 41.

[95]A Siddiqa, *Military Inc.: Inside Pakistan's Military Economy*, (OUP, New York, 2007) 24.

governance'.[96] Foreign investment is not only present dominantly but imperialist countries quotas, licenses and statuses determine the direction and the nature of development of the production sphere. In this mode of production, feudal (currently agricultural capital) exist with the capitalist development with increasing informal economy. The point I want to make is that direct sort of imperialist presence in Pakistan as a front line state compromised with the pre-capitalist formations or local capitalist formations and produced uneven development within the domain of capitalist development. This uneven development is the relative unevenness of the different instances, that is, legal more developed than the political and political more developed than the economic, etc.

A continuous reproduction of the above system is assured in the political, cultural and the ideological instances, all connected for a complex hegemony (political instant). But the complexity of this hegemony is the irresolvable contradictions of the structure and not the problems of its own *only*. Below are some more details of the nature of this complex hegemony in postcolonial Pakistan.

1.4.5 Myth of Miserable Politicians vis-a-vis Military: Nature of Hegemony

Liberal theses are generally of the opinion that politicians are not allowed to rule by a strong military and civil bureaucracy. As opposed to this, one can see that landed and capitalist elite in Pakistan succeeded in protecting their interests throughout the history after independence in Pakistan, and acted as the reigning class under the hegemony of metropolitan capital. To acquire that hegemony, the U.S. imperialism used military and civil bureaucracy as its seat of power and consequent removal and restoration of democratic regimes.

It is commonly argued that the state (military-civil bureaucratic structure) has never focused on protecting the economic interests of the landed class. Rather, the state's policies have an urban bias.[97] Land reforms and labour policies went against this class's interests. Alavi has shown that the landed elite opposed land reforms and agriculture tax but could not change the long-term bias against agriculture.[98]

---

[96]For dependency structuralists like Frank, developing countries are engaged in unequal exchange relations with capitalist countries and hence are underdeveloped. This analysis is at the level of circulation of capital. This neglected the production sphere of capital in developing countries. Whereas in my analysis they are connected. See A G Frank, *Latin America: Underdevelopment or Revolution (Essays on the underdevelopment of development and immediate enemy)* (Monthly Review Press, London & New York, 1969).

[97]MH Khan, Changes in the Agrarian Structure of Pakistan, in SM Naseem & K Nadvi (eds) *The Post-Colonial State and Social Transformation in India and Pakistan* (Oxford University Press, Karachi, 2003).

[98]H Alavi, Class and State in Pakistan, in H Gardezi & J Rashid (eds) *Pakistan: The Unstable State* (Vanguard Books, Lahore, 1983) 40, 59.

Indeed, many studies have shown that there had been no necessary connection between holding or controlling land and having an effect on power in social formation.[99] Land control is not the guarantee of prominence in government decision-making.[100] Ayesha Jalal found that the interests of the landed class as well as the state can be the same but not necessarily all the time, calling the convergence a 'politics of compromise'.[101] Aasim S. Akhtar concludes that the landed elite have become less committed to the autonomy and corporate interests of their class. According to this position, both the major propertied classes are fragmented and are guided by a cynical logic of gaining access to the state to distribute (or access) patronage and both are incapable of following the specific *class* interests of the party leadership.[102] All of the above shows one side, that is, the relative weakness of the landed elite as a coherent class to assert itself against the state while balancing the interests of other contending classes.

The other side of the story is of how the landed elite posed a restraint on the autonomy of the state vis-à-vis subordinate classes, particularly by having blunted the efforts of land reforms. Burki suggested the names of prominent landed elites as those who made history, as opposed to the typical 'who's who' of Liaquat Ali Khan, Ayub Khan, Bhutto, Benazir Bhutto, etc.[103] Rather he gave a list of Khizar Hayat Khan as opposed to Jinnah, Mushtaq Ahmad Gurmani not Liaqat, Amir Muhamad Khan (Nawab of Kalbagh) not Ayub. He selected them because they were highly effective in impeding change.[104] Similarly, Naim Ullah highlights how the suppression of a series of reports on land reforms and tenancy rights was in fact a forceful defense of the landed elite against land reforms. Zia declared on 16 Oct 1979 that 'Inshaallah' (God willing) there will be no land reforms. In 2003, Prime Minister Jamali announced that there will be no more land reforms as far as our government is concerned.[105] That is to say, the fundamental interest of the landed elite, their ownership of land, has in fact been protected.

Similarly, we cannot say that state ever went against the capitalist class, except during a short period during Bhutto's reign. For Ishrat, the market was rigged and distorted for the benefit of the elite, whereas the instruments of the state did not

---

[99]R Sobhan, State and governance as factors in development in SM Naseem & K Nadvi (eds) *The Post-Colonial State and Social Transformation in India and Pakistan* (Oxford University Press, Karachi, 2003) 8-9.

[100]R Laporte, Jr, *Power and Privilege: Influence and Decision-making in Pakistan* (University of California Press, Berkeley, 1975) 92.

[101]A Jalal, The State and Political Privilege in Pakistan, in A Banuazizi & M Weiner (eds) *The Politics of Social Transformation in Afghanistan, Iran and Pakistan* (Syracuse University Press, Syracuse, 1994) 157.

[102]AS Akhtar, *Overdeveloping State: The Politics of Common Sense in Pakistan, 1971-2007*, SOAS - University of London, PhD Thesis (2008) 111.

[103]SJ Burki, *A Revisionist History of Pakistan* (Vanguard, Lahore, 1998).

[104]*Ibid.*

[105]See the detail in M Naim Ullah, Pakistan in the Stranglehold of Feudalism [*Pakistan Jagirdari Zamindari Nizam Ke Shikaney Men*], (Jumhoori Publications, Lahore).

correct these inequalities but benefitted the same small group of people.[106] Recently, the role of the capitalist class in local politics has been increasing.[107] The new business class of the 2000s is more closely linked to the popular classes than the business class of the 1960s. Prime Minister Nawaz Sharif integrated the business class with the intermediate classes in Punjab.[108] Weiss, after studying the steel rolling, pharmaceutical, and sporting goods industries in Punjab found industrialists to be well connected with the local formation and local politics.[109] Now they fund, back and even participate in political parties.[110]

Furthermore, the bourgeoisie, through their personal relations with the state personnel, have been directly involved in the formation and implementation of the state policies.[111] They also affect the legislature in democratic regimes, advising governments sitting on the committees, commissions and regulatory boards. They do not make many decisions, or present or write actual bills for legislative consideration, but no policies go against their overall interests within the capitalist system as explained below.

The point I want to make is that the landed elite has largely succeeded in protecting its interests throughout the history after independence in Pakistan, and has acted as the reigning class. Despite lacking coherence in terms of following economic interest, propertied classes have persuaded the state to protect their property and let them increase their property holdings. Every major policy (like the 'Green Revolution' of 1960s and privatization of 1990s), though adopted under the pressure of the International Monetary Fund and World Bank, has been in favour of the capitalist class as well as the landed class.[112] Capitalist development, as a part of the liberal project of state building, has always been central for state building in Pakistan. From the available literature, we can only find a positive relation between the three fundamental classes, though at times contradictory: the relation is non-antagonistic, whether under democratic or military-bureaucratic governance. The few episodes of failed and half-hearted land reforms and non-antagonistic

[106]I Husain, *Pakistan: The Economy of an Elitist State* (Oxford University Press, Karachi, 1999) 348.

[107]The number of MNAs from 1985 onward has increased. This was 54 in 1985 elections but decreased subsequently. See S Shafqat, Democracy and Political Participation in Pakistan, in, S Mumtaz, Jean-Luc Racine & I Ali (eds) *Pakistan: The Contours of State and Society* (Oxford University Press, Karachi, 2003) 225.

[108]AR Wilder, *The Pakistani Voter: Electoral Politics and Voting Behaviour in Punjab* (Oxford University Press, Karachi, 1999) 143.

[109]A Weiss, *Culture, class and development in Pakistan: the emergence of an industrial bourgeoisie in Punjab* (Westview Press, Boulder, 1991) 11.

[110]Best illustrations are Shahid–ur-Rahman (1997) *Who owns Pakistan*, online, last visited 21 November 2013, <http://www.scribd.com/doc/125960792/Who-Owns-Pakistan>; see also I Husain, *Pakistan: The Economy of an Elitist State* (Oxford University Press, Karachi, 1999).

[111]In Chapter 3, we will see how the capitalist class moved along with the state building project in Pakistan.

[112]Shahid–ur-Rahman, *supra* note 110.

'governance disputes' around corruption, democracy and dictatorship have done little, if anything, to affect the material interests of these fundamental classes.

Now let me lay down the specific features of hegemony in postcolonial Pakistan. This hegemony is complex and in this hegemony, the U.S. imperialism is the hegemonic class. But in postcolonial countries under neo-colonialism, the imperialism cannot rule directly[113] Nor the hegemonic imperialism can rule through the military directly for a long time. Even during the dictatorial regimes, a quasi-democratic regime had to come very soon. In postcolonial Pakistan, the hegemonic class brought the weak and feeble feudal and the capitalist class under its hegemony. But imperialism did not use the reigning class (legislature) as a seat of power because it was weak vis-à-vis popular challenges unleashed by anti-colonial struggles. To control this, hegemonic imperialism used civil and military bureaucracy as a seat of power. The weakness of this reigning class in the hegemonic bloc vis-a-vis imperialism (to build a counter narrative of hegemony) and vis-a-vis working-class and centrifugal nationalist challenges (bearing a counter narrative of hegemony) is the key to understand the instability, volatility, and slippery nature of political instant in postcolonial Pakistan. Connected to this is the relative effectiveness of the legal (court as the centre of politics for legitimacy) and use of ideological (Islam) instances in the case of postcolonial Pakistan.

Poulantzas insisted on looking into objective coordinates of political domination within this ideological formation. For him, this is particularly useful when we are examining several politically dominant classes or class fractions, of which only one takes the hegemonic role, a situation typified by capitalist Britain.[114] Fair enough. Based on this, to analyse the particular changing ideological formation of legal and ideological instances of postcolonial Pakistan, we are to first distance ourselves from the dominant liberal dichotomy of secularism versus Islam with its conceptions the Pakistan's actual problem after military is Islam and Objectives Resolution.[115] Related to this is common connection between military and Islam, particularly the ISI, wanting Islam. Theoretically, this means that the state is creating ideology which is dominantly military. This is true at descriptive level but again this is poor theorizing with Islam in its particular form in Pakistan an *aclass* concept. First of all, the ideology of Pakistan in its particularity is liberal as well as Islamic. Rather than the state giving birth to ideology, Islam should be looked at in the perspective of the Cold War as a defense against communism and its application as a defense against land reforms by Jamaat Ahmedia and then Moudoodi of the Jamaat-e-Islami. Furthermore, this is not something fixed, we should look at the nature of this ideology (Islam as a changing part of it) with changing class formation. U.S. as a hegemonic class used Islam for Jihad during cold war and its

[113]This is even true about the western societies as pointed out by Poulantzas. During transition from feudalism to capitalism, the commerce class was the hegemonic class but the landed class was the reigning class, see Poulantzas, On Social Classes, *supra* note 34, 186, 208.

[114]Poulantzas *supra* note 34, 132.

[115]Article 2-A of 1973 Constitution of Pakistan.

height was 1980s. So this is not a coincident that this was the height of support for Islam by the postcolonial state. Later, the same state was conducting war against fundamentalist Islam. We are to understand the importance/place of Islam in its materiality. This means knowing which classes are dominant in Pakistan's state formation.

This book will demonstrate that the Pakistani state has used Islam for its legitimacy (as during the Zia regime) but also resisted it to some extent (as during the Ayub and Musharraf regimes) through state apparatuses but on the demand of the hegemonic class. What common throughout was the deepening influence of international capital, and the growing hegemony of the ruling elite as actual problem and not Islam as the main focus of analysis. Where religion was used by the state formation for legitimizing oligarchic rule, it also came in conflict with the above liberal project of the state.

The use of Islam by the hegemonic class and the feudal class is clear so far. But why the local capitalist class and the merchant class did not resist conservative pre-capitalist modes of production and thinking? Rather, the merchant class was a big supporter of religious parties.[116] First of all, the very nature of Pakistan's dependency capital is merchant because of quota- and licenses-based industrialization. Metropolitan bourgeoisie and this merchant nature of local industrialist class are not interested in the labour process and organization of capital. This simply means changing the pre-capitalist modes, irrelevant to their agenda and status quo and compromises with conservatives is common. The very merchant nature of capital needs the uninterrupted flow of goods only. Therefore, to co-opt the pre-capitalist modes of production like feudalism and tribalism were not the compulsion of political instance *alone* but were reflective of the very nature of the mixed mode of production *also*.

To sum up, overemphasis on Islam is not because of the 'rationality' of the state apparatus be it civil bureaucracy or military establishment. State apparatuses do not create ideologies. In my understanding, law and constitution in Pakistan is neither liberal nor Islamic. It should not be analysed as a deviation from one of them. The grafting of Islamic law onto liberal legal institutions, I suggest, was to protect liberal institutions, including legal institutions, against theocracy. The function or purpose or intent or effect of all the regimes was to promote the liberal project, with the help of legal engineering, which in Gramscian terms was a key element of the formation of the historic bloc.

Apart from the role of Islam in the lives of Pakistan, why do all the classes in class formation overemphasize Islam as ideology? As is already pointed out, Pakistan's political instant was highly volatile and unstable and hence the burden of legitimacy heavily fell on legal and ideological instances.

Based on this, to correctly understand the crisis of democracy in Pakistan, a final crucial departure from liberal understanding is needed. That is, rather than looking

[116]Aasim in his thesis tried to understand through the lens of state's patronage. See Akhtar, *supra* note 102.

at the crisis of the state in disequilibrium of the institutional arrangements among state apparatuses (military overstepping legislature), what one needs to analyse is the crisis in the hegemony as changing class formation due to challenges from below.

1.4.6 Crisis of the Hegemony as the Crisis of the State

Common sense understanding of the postcolonial state of Pakistan is that military is doing everything even to the extent of spreading Islamic fundamentalism, etc.[117] This simply means that the state has its own rationality, though bad in case of postcolonial Pakistan. So, the Pakistani state is a *subject*. This is a liberal concept except that rationality in case of the Pakistani state is a bad rationality.[118] It is also extensively argued that the U.S. supported/used the military for its geopolitical ends.[119] This means that the postcolonial state of Pakistan is an *object*. A third problematic and widely accepted so-called Marxist liberal understanding, rejecting instrumental and functionalist aspects of a state, is that the civil and military bureaucracy is relatively autonomous of its own in Pakistan and hence 'overdeveloped'.[120]

No doubt, the Pakistan military's role has increased, over and apart from its constitutional role under Article 245 to defend the country against external aggression and to support the civilian government during disasters. There is plenty of literature available pointing out the manipulative role of the military in political life,[121] whether in terms of 'Military Inc.,'[122] Garrison state,[123] or literature

---

[117]M Aziz, *Military Control in Pakistan: The Parallel State* (Routledge, London & New York, 2008).

[118]The Weberian state has its own internal unity, rationality, and relative autonomy from civil society as a whole (there is a separation of state and civil society). Here political theory is the state's 'rationality' (the 'universal' character of the state.

[119]H Abbas, *Pakistan's Drift into Extremism: Allah, the Army, and America's War on Terror* (ME Sharpe, Armonk, 2005).

[120]A Hamza, The State in Post-Colonial Societies: Pakistan and Bangladesh, 74 *New Left Rev* (1972) 59.

[121]S Shafqat, *Civil-military relations in Pakistan: from Zulfikar Ali Bhutto to Benazir Bhutto* (Westview Press, Boulder & Colorado, 1997) 21; H Haqqani, *Pakistan Between Mosque and Military* (Carnegie Endowment for International Peace, Washington DC, 2005).

[122]In a recent study, Ayesha Siddiqa (2007) pointed out the role of military through the concept of "Milbus" or military capital different from defense budget, and being the military's internal economy and responsible for direct/indirect control of governance of the country. The military's predatoriness is cause and effect of the feudal authoritarian and nondemocratic political system; see Siddiqa *supra* note 95.

[123]I Ahmed, *Pakistan: The Garrison State (origins, evolution, consequences 1947-2011)* (Oxford University Press, Karachi, 2013).

articulating how the military bears a *qualitatively* greater role than that of a mediator.[124] Instead of a 'rational' state, the concept of a 'class state' with 'objective structure' can give a 'specifically political' concept of state. 'Political practice' and 'objective structures' give birth to specific forms of state (democracy or dictatorship) through hegemony. Hegemony explains *political power* of the dominant class with respect to dominated classes through a combination of consent and coercion which the state crystallizes.[125] This means that not only the dominant, but the dominated classes are also included in the hegemonic project. Connected to this is the dominant class and its fractions which are structured into an ensemble through the mediation of the state. The structure of the ensemble *is* the state. At the postcolonial level, the 'specific' interests of dominant classes are concentrated to form a 'power bloc'—a contradictory unity of dominant classes, themselves 'under the dominance' of the hegemonic class or fractions.[126] So, particular changes in the state forms of postcolonial Pakistan should be analysed with its specific internal unity and the position of objective system of branches. But each particular changing form of the state should be referred back to important modifications of the relations of production as well as to the important stages of class struggle. I have already explained the hegemonic and the reigning classes in postcolonial Pakistan. Now throughout my dissertation, I will show how the particular state forms while moving from democracy to dictatorship to quasi-democratic and quasi-dictatorial regimes were the changing specific determinations of the dominant classes responding to class struggle. Here the bad rationality or self-interest of the military will not be explaining the nature of postcolonial state of Pakistan as is in abundant liberal literature about Pakistan. Different changing class formations due to class struggle will also explain the changing rationality and the nature and extent of the relative autonomy as well as instrumental and functional aspects of the state. But still the questions about strong military and crisis of the state need answers.

Based on the above explanation, I am going to present an understanding about the strong military and the crisis of state in postcolonial Pakistan, which is very different than liberal understanding. In most of the abundant liberal literature available on Pakistan, the crisis of democracy is reduced to the crisis of the state, that is, because of the 'overdeveloped' military and civil bureaucracy. The political crisis in the state apparatuses sometimes is reflected in the conflict of personalities, as seen with the Chief of Army Staff conflicting with the parliamentary leader, or Chief Justice differing with the elected Prime Minister or the crisis of a wrong decision in a writ petition. These conflicts of personalities must be traced back to

---

[124]Since the landed class and the indigenous bourgeoisie wants access to the state so the military enjoys implicit consent of both in the form of no resistance. See AS Akhtar, *Overdeveloping State: The Politics of Common Sense in Pakistan, 1971-2007*, SOAS - University of London, PhD Thesis (2008).

[125]James Martin explains Gramsci and his influence on Poulantzas, see Martin (ed), *supra* note 34, 7-8.

[126]Borrowing from Poulantzas, Preliminaries to the study of hegemony in the state, *supra* note 34, 74,103.

political crises and the crisis in the class formation. When political crises led to the problem of state's own unity, the dominant class (the metropolitan bourgeoisie) created networks to oversee different branches of the state. An example is that of the National Accountability Bureau (NAB), which was created to control corruption, and other governance mechanisms initiated by the World Bank. As another example, the U.S. Gulf states brokered an agreement between Musharraf and Benazir and Nawaz. This was the National Reconciliation Ordinance.[127]

This is very particular to 'institutionalist-functionalist' and 'system' analyses of bourgeois sociology and political science. Here, the crisis is a dysfunctional moment in an otherwise harmonious functioning of the 'system' and will pass after the equilibrium is re-established because the state is assumed to be an integrated pluralist society of 'powers' and 'counter-powers' resulting in 'the institutionalization of social conflicts'. In addition, conflicts are taken to the level of conflicts of 'ideas', 'opinions', 'values' or crisis of 'legitimation'.[128] The above illustration shows the dislocation within branches of the state where the compromises of the allied classes are being crystallized, as well as the dislocations in ideological and political forms that are trying to unify allied classes. But where are the origins of this dislocation of state apparatus as crisis? The actual contradictions between dominant and dominated classes in the postcolonial society can be explained when the state is understood as a class formation engaged in politics defined as class struggle. So it is not a crisis of institutions, but rather a structural crisis that has resulted in the crisis of hegemony.[129] This means there is a challenge posed by class struggle of the dominated classes and within the 'power bloc' of dominant.

Based on all of these points of critique, I argue we should depart from liberal's and liberal Marxists Alavi's explanation of the state's actions as being motivated by its self-interest. Oppressive regimes are not only due to the self-interest of dictators. It is necessary to locate class struggle against which repression is unleashed.[130] Bringing back class struggle simply means to understand the power of the state as a class power. The military in Pakistan and other newly developed countries operated for the benefit of the fundamental classes, particularly metropolitan capital, and

[127]This ordinance was a result of the deal between Musharraf and Benazir Bhutto and was issued on 5 October 2007, see the ordinance. <http://www.pakistani.org/pakistan/legislation/2007/NationalReconciliationOrdinance.html>. Supreme Court of Pakistan declared the ordinance "null and void" on 16 December, 2009, see the order of the SC in *Dawn, Karachi (17*, December 2009), online: <http://www.dawn.com/news/688541/timeline-from-nro-to-memogate>.

[128]Poulantzas, The Political Crisis and the Crisis of the State, *supra* note 34, 294, 297, 299.

[129]*Ibid* 299.

[130]Leys questioned the formulations on postcolonial state and its bureaucracy developed by Hamza Alavi, Rogers Murray and John Saul. He challenged the 'over-developed' notion and proposed that peripheral capitalist countries produce fewer surpluses as compared to advanced capitalist societies, so they had to appropriate a large share directly, which is the reason for class struggle, see C Leys, The Overdeveloped Postcolonial State: A Re-evaluation, *Review of African Political Economy* (1976) 39; see also Rogers Murray, Second Thoughts on Ghana 42 *New Left Rev* (1967 March/April); see also John Saul, The State in Post-Colonial Societies - Tanzania *The Socialist Register* (1974) 349.

against the subordinate classes. This was an institutional arrangement to keep the structure intact. What Liberals and liberal Marxist Alavi tried to debunk was the idea that the working-class struggles in these countries mattered.

Bringing back class struggle of the dominated classes is the main contribution of this book.

1.4.7 Bringing Class Struggle Back in State Formation

Working class does not deserve a footnote in liberal analyses. Even the Marxist liberal Alavi dropped the subordinate and intermediate classes from his analysis as either weak or irrelevant. Alavi found economic competition as the main reason preventing poor peasants from revolt. For Alavi, the helplessness of the poor peasant is not subjective but an objective fixed reality.[131] The same neglect of class struggle is carried by all liberal writings. Yet in 1968, the working classes did get organized, and did gain victories in Pakistan. The state did not stay impartial. The concessions were greater when the working classes were better organized and lesser when they were disorganized. Poulantzas was clear that the working class has specific ideological elements even without a revolutionary party, which Lenin called a 'class instinct', as an autonomous discourse. They behave differently even under bourgeois ideology. He gave an example of the U.S. working class without a revolutionary party. The absence of a politics of resistance in postcolonial societies can be traced to the absence of class struggles that focus on the fundamental structures in order to change those structures. Poulantzas stated that it is class struggle that determines how the apparatuses are modified.[132] In the complex relation between class struggle and state apparatuses, it is class struggle that has the principal role.[133] Not taking working class struggle as a constituent element of the state formation left Alavi discussing the state as removed from class relations. I will show how the class struggle (through leftist class politics) and even the class in different class formation, such as the translation of the working-class movement in the ethno-nationalist idiom of the National Awami Party-NAP, has serious consequences for class formations and hence state formations in Pakistan.

---

[131]Alavi tried to prove that not the poor peasants but the middle peasants led the revolution in Russia and China. This is also true regarding peasants struggles in India, see H Alavi, Peasants and Revolution, in, R Miliband & J. Saville (eds) *The Socialist Register* (1965) 241, 274.

[132]Poulantzas, On Social Classes, *supra* note 34, 186, 212.

[133]*Ibid.*

References

A Giddens, *Central Problem in Social Theory: Action, Structure and Contradiction in Social Analysis* (University of California Press, Berkeley, 1979).

A Kalhan, "Gray Zone" Constitutionalism and the Dilemma of Judicial Independence in Pakistan, 1 *VJTL* (2013).

A Saratedt (ed), *The Blackwell Companion to Law and Society* (Blackwell Publishing, US, 2004).

A Sayer, *Method in Social Science: A Realist Approach*, 2nd edn (Routledge, London, 1992).

A Siddiqa, *Military Inc.: Inside Pakistan's Military Economy* (OUP, New York, 2007).

A Weiss, *Class, Culture and Development in Pakistan: The Emergence of an Industrial Bourgeoisie in Punjab* (Westview Press, Boulder, 1991).

AR Wilder, *The Pakistani Voter: Electoral Politics and Voting Behaviour in Punjab* (Oxford University Press, Karachi, 1999).

B Brewster (trans), L Althusser & E Balibar's *Reading Capital* (Verso, London, 2009).

B Brewster (trans), L Althusser's *For Marx* (Verso, London, 2010).

B Ollman, *Dance of the Dialectics: Steps in Marx's Method* (University of Illinois Press, Chicago, 2003).

CB Lombardi, Can Islamizing a Legal System Even Help Promote Liberal Democracy?: A View from Pakistan, 7:3 *University of Saint Thomas Law Journal* (2010).

CH Kennedy & CA Botteron (eds), *Pakistan: 2005* (OUP, Karachi, 2005).

CH Kennedy, Islamization and Legal Reforms in Pakistan: 1979-1989, 63:1 *Pacific Affairs* (1990).

CH Kennedy, Repugnancy to Islam - Who Decides? Islam and Legal Reforms in Pakistan, 41:4 *ICLQ* (1992).

D Kennedy, The Structure of Blackstone Commentaries, 28 *Buff L Rev* (1979).

DC North, *Structure and Change in Economic History* (W. W. Norton & Company, New York, 1981).

DC North, *Understanding the Process of Economic Change* (Princeton University Press, Princeton, 2005).

DM Trubek & A Santos (eds), *The New Law and Economic Development: A Critical Appraisal* (Cambridge University Press, Cambridge, 2006).

DS Brosnan, Serious But Not Critical, 60 *S Cal L Rev.* (1987).

E Durkheim, *The Division of Labour in Society* (The Free Press, New York, 1983).

E Kurzweil, *The Age of Structuralism: From Levi-Straus to Foucault* (Transaction Publishers, London, 1996).

EP Thompson, *Whigs and Hunters: The Origins of the Black Act* (Penguin Books, London, 1975).

F Mohammed, Protecting Pakistani Labourers Post-Eighteenth Amendment: Recognizing Rights After the Devolution of Power, 9 *Loy U Chi Int'l L Rev.* (2012).

GA Heeger, Politics in the Post-Military State: Some Reflections on the Pakistani Experience, 29 *World Politics* (1977).

H Abbas, *Pakistan's Drift into Extremism: Allah, the Army, and America's War on Terror* (M. E. Sharpe, Armonk, 2005).

H Alavi, The State in Post-Colonial Societies: Pakistan and Bangladesh, 74 *New Left Rev.* (1972).

H Gardezi & J Rashid (eds) *Pakistan: The Unstable State* (Vanguard Books, Lahore, 1983).

H Haqqani, *Pakistan Between Mosque and Military* (Carnegie Endowment for International Peace, Washington DC, 2005).

HA Rizvi, *Military, State and Society in Pakistan* (Palgrave: Macmillan, UK, 2000).

I Husain, *Pakistan: The Economy of an Elitist State* (Oxford University Press, Karachi, 1999).

J Locke, *Two Treatises of Government* (The New American Library, New York, 1965).

J M Dawood, *The Role of Superior Judiciary in the Politics of Pakistan* (Royal Book Company, Karachi, 1994).

J Martin (ed), *The Poulantzas Reader: Marxism, Law and the State* (Verso, London, 2008).

JA Mintz, Introductory Note: A Perspective on Pakistan's Chief Justice, Judicial Independence, and the Rule of Law, 15:1 *ILSA J Int'l & Comp L* (2008-09).

K Ahmed, *Labour Movement in Pakistan: Past and Present* (Institute of Workers Education and Labour Studies, Lahore, 2009).
K Thelen & S Steinmo, *Structuring Politics: Historical Institutionalism in Comparative Analysis*, (Cambridge University Press, New York, 1992).
L Althusser, *On the Reproduction of Capitalism: Ideology and Ideological State Apparatuses* (Verso, London, 2014).
L Ferretter, *Louis Althusser* (Routledge, London/New York, 2006).
M Aziz, *Military Control in Pakistan: The Parallel State* (Routledge, New York, 2008).
M Hussain & A Hussain, *Pakistan: Problems of Governance* (Vanguard, Lahore, 1993).
M Lau, *The Role of Islam in the Legal System of Pakistan* (Martinus Nijhoff Publishers, London/Boston, 2006).
M N Ullah, *Pakistan in the Stranglehold of* Feudalism (*Pakistan Jagirdari Zamindari Nizam Ke Shikaney Men*) (Jumhoori Publications, Lahore, 2003).
M. Shafi & P Shafi, *Labour Code of Pakistan*, vol 2 (Bureau of Labour Publications, Karachi, 2014).
MM Stavsky, The Doctrine of State Necessity in Pakistan, 16 *Cornell Int'l L J* (1983).
M Waseem, *Politics and the State in Pakistan* (NIHCR, Islamabad, 2007).
N Ahmad, The Rule of Law- A Substratum of Justice, 8:2 *J Commonwealth L & Legal Educ.* (2012).
N Poulantzas (1978), *State, Power, Socialism* (Verso, London/New York, 2000).
N Poulantzas, *Political Power and Social Classes*, 2nd edn (NLB, London, 1975).
O Siddique, The Jurisprudence of Dissolutions: Presidential Power to Dissolve Assemblies under the Pakistan's Constitution and its Discontents, 23:3 *Ariz J Int'l & Comp L.* (2005-06).
P Anderson, *Arguments Within English Marxism* (Verso, London, 1980).
P Beirne & R Sharletedt, *Pashukanis: Selected Writings on Marxism and Law* (Academic Press, London, 1980).
PR Newberg, *Judging the State: Courts and Constitutional Politics in Pakistan* (Cambridge University Press, New Delhi, 1995).
Q Hoare & GN Smith (eds & trans) *Selections from the Prison Notebooks of Antonio Gramsci* (International Publishers, New York, 2012).
R Braibanti, *Chief Justice Cornelius of Pakistan: An Analysis with Letters and Speeches* (Oxford University Press, Karachi, 1999).
R Hoque, *Judicial Activism in Bangladesh: A Golden Mean Approach* (Cambridge Scholars Publishing, 2011).
R Mehdi, *The Islamization of Law in Pakistan* (Curzon Press, London, 1994).
RM Hathaway & W Lee (eds) *Islamization and the Pakistani Economy* (Woodrow Wilson International Center for Scholars, Washington DC, 2004).
S Hall, Signification, Representation, Ideology: Althusser and the Post-structuralist Debates, 2 *Crit. Stud. M Comm.* (1985).
S Mumtaz, Jean-Luc Racine & I Ali (eds), *Pakistan: The Contours of State and Society* (Oxford University Press, Karachi, 2003).
S Shafqat, *Civil-military Relations in Pakistan: From Zulfikar Ali Bhutto to Benazir Bhutto* (Westview Press, Boulder/Colorado, 1997).
SA Ghias, Miscarriage of Chief Justice: Judicial Power and the Legal Complex in Pakistan under Musharraf, 35:4 *Law & Social Inquiry* (2010).
SA Zaidi (ed), *Continuity and Change: Socio-Political and Institutional Dynamics in Pakistan* (City Press, Karachi, 2003).
SE Merry, Concepts of Law and Justice among Americans: Ideology as Culture, 9 *Leg. Stud. Forum* (1990).
SM Naseem & K Nadvi (eds), *The Post-Colonial State and Social Transformation in India and Pakistan* (Oxford University Press, Karachi, 2003).
SS Ali, *Gender and Human Rights in Islam and International Law: Equal Before Allah, Unequal Before Man?* (Kluwer Law International, Hague, 2000).
T Benton, *The Rise and Fall of Structural Marxism* (Macmillan Publishers, London, 1984).

T Hasan, The Need of Judicial Activism and CJSC Iftikhar Chaudhry as a "Judicial Activist" on the basis of PIL, 15:1 *ILSA J Int'l & Comp L* (2008-09).

T Lindsey (ed), *Law Reform in Developing and Transitional States* (Routledge, London/New York, 2007).

T Mahmud, Jurisprudence of Successful Treason: *Coup d'Etat* & Common Law, 27 *Cornell Int'l L J* (1994).

T Mahmud, Praetorianism and Common Law in Post-Colonial Settings: Judicial Responses to Constitutional Breakdowns in Pakistan, *Utah L Rev* (1993).

T Parsons (1937), *The Structure of Social Action* (Free Press, New York, 1968).

T Parsons (1951), *The Social System* (Routledge, London, 1991).

T Parsons and EA Shills (1957), *Towards a General Theory of Action* (Harvard University Press, Harvard, 2013).

TA Khan, *The Post-Colonial State in The Era of Capitalist Globalization: Historical, Political, and Theoretical Approaches to State Formation* (Routledge, New York, 2012).

TA Qureshi, State of Emergency: General Pervez Musharraf's Executive Assault on Judicial Independence in Pakistan, 35 *N C J Int'l L & Com Reg* (2009-10).

V Chibber, *Locked in Place: State-building and late industrialization in India* (Princeton University Press, Princeton, 2003).

V Chibber, *Postcolonial Theory and the Specter of Capital* (Verso, London, 2013).

W Menski, AR Alam & MK Raza (eds), *Public Interest Litigation in Pakistan* (Platinum Publishing Ltd./ Pakistan Law House, London/Karachi, 2000).

WP Zingel, S Zingel & A Lallemant (eds), *Pakistan in the 80's: Law & Constitution* (Vanguard, Lahore, 1985).

Chapter 2
Law in the Era of Capitalist Modernization (1947–1960s)

From the 1940s to 1960s, Pakistan moved from being under British colonial rule to coming under the influence of the United States (U.S.). Jinnah, the 'founder' of Pakistan was a Lincoln's Inn graduate, as was his successor and the first Prime Minister, Liaqat Ali Khan. The major jurists in Pakistan were either British lawyers hired by the government or local barristers who trained at Lincoln's Inn and cited Privy Council decisions. The colonial state legacy continued to affect the civil servants who served in the judiciary, the number of these rising to 65 members in 1964. Pakistan at this point experienced the imposition of modernization under the guidance of experts from Harvard and Massachusetts Institute of Technology (MIT). The transition was seamless and the existing judiciary facilitated the assimilation of 'modern' U.S. legal norms in Pakistan. After the writing of the 1956 constitution, judicial decisions in Pakistan started leaning towards U.S. Supreme Court precedents on the issue of the arbitrary use of administrative and legislative powers against fundamental rights, claiming it was because of the written constitution. Politically, Pakistan adopted a presidential system in the 1962 constitution.

This chapter will argue that during this period of transition, the juridico-bureaucratic structure came to undermine the legislature, not because "it did not like politicians" as is commonly stated,[1] but rather because it surmised that the legislature could not be trusted to control the population. The general thrust of legal discourse in the 1950s was in support of a move from Privy Council decisions to 'modern' U.S. legal norms as a way of accommodating political and economic change. The main legal issue raised before the courts in this period was not regarding the supremacy of the legislature or bureaucratic dictatorship (as goes the common explanation), but rather, which arrangement could best keep the structure of the government intact against popular struggle. Navigating through the confusion of the 1950s, legal discourse and constitutional arrangements in Pakistan ended

[1]The particular instance referred to is Ayub's action against politicians by creating a parallel system of Basic Democracies (BD System). See *Elective Bodies (Disqualification) Order* 1959, President's Order No 13 of 1959, PLD (1959) Central Statutes 101.

M. Azeem, *Law, State and Inequality in Pakistan*, International Law and the Global South, DOI 10.1007/978-981-10-3845-7_2

with a set of institutions not dissimilar to that of the U.S. presidential system, with indirect elections, controlled democracy, and rights as a substitute for this democratic deficit. The idiom of Islam was deployed both as a cohesive force for the nation-building project and as a substitute for 'morality' in U.S. legal discourse. But in its 'particular' materiality, it was to achieve the same end along with the U.S. type of legal system, that is to stop deeper and broader democracy unleashed by anti-colonial struggle and socialist ideas. The judiciary, drawn from the civil bureaucracy and leading the process of modernization, was an indispensable part of the project.

Before moving on, let us briefly unpack the use of the terms 'capitalist modernity', 'socialist modernity', and 'modernization theory'. At the end of the first quarter of the twentieth century, world politics saw two competing models of political modernity, namely socialist and capitalist models. Most anti-colonial struggles came to be inspired by the experience of socialist modernity in the middle of the twentieth century. These national mobilizations hoped for real democracy, economic and political, in the newly independent countries. To counter these hopes, the capitalist bloc, under the hegemony of the U.S., theorized its own experiences of 'colonization' into what it pushed as 'modernization theory', or the material benefits of the capitalist path to modernity.

Both models were linked to different laws and development theories, as theorized by David Trubek.[2] For the socialist model, law was an instrument of a vanguard party and legitimacy came from faith in the vanguard and/or from popular participation, rather than constitutional fidelity. Both models assumed a dissolution and transformation of pre-capitalist society and social structures.[3] Hamza Alavi, the best-known Pakistani theorist, was clear that theories of "modernization" are implicitly or explicitly theories of capitalist development because they were based on the premises of capitalist societies, such as private property and mass consumption. He wished for Pakistan to see a 'revolutionary change', to break with its internal feudal structures as well as from the encompassing global capitalism. He wished, in other words, for a version of a socialist modernization model.

2.1 Law and State During Colonial Rule

Legal literature by academic historians about the process, nature and affect of British legal codification of Indian law during the colonial era, differs from the understanding of legal commissions and jurists in postcolonial Pakistan. The latter outrightly admired the legal system they inherited, the detail to follow in a while.

[2] DM Trubek, The Owl and the Pussy-cat: Is there a future of Law and Development, 25 *Wis Int'LJ* (2007) 235, 237.

[3] H Alavi, State and Class Under Peripheral Capitalism, in, H Alavi & T Shanin (eds) *Introduction to the Sociology of "Developing Societies"* (Monthly Review Press, New York and London, 1982) 289.

The former category of historians on colonial India had divergent views about the codification of laws in British India accommodating traditional laws.

The 'expropriation'[4] of law in India, but as a decisive step towards a modern system went through three stages, according to Marc Galanter. The first was Warren Hasting's re-organization of the state in 1772 in Bengal, which was a general expansion of the government in isolation from courts and legislation; the second, after 1860, with extensive codification of laws and rationalization of the court system, where legislation provided the laws; and third, the post-independence stage.[5] Apart from continuity and discontinuity from the traditional Mughal era laws, the colonial system came to be based on the extraction of taxes with the state's penetration in society working through the land revenue system. Existing social structures at all district and sub-district levels were given meaning through legal protection of landed property and its lawful usage exercised by the formal state structure. In West Bengal, the British East India Company (EIC) introduced the Law of Permanent Settlement and created a rural elite to extract surplus from the peasantry.[6] Addressing the issue of accommodating traditional law, for David Washbrook, that 'pseudo-traditionalism' was a reintroduction of more hierarchical and feudal structures.[7] Later, the state protected this class from moneylenders who had been strengthened due to increases in usury in the agrarian economy. Landowners were converted into landlords and preserved through legislation.[8] According to Waseem, society was connected with the new state through the revenue bureaucracy mediated by the rule of law.[9] It was the law that tied India to the British Empire, both politically and economically.[10]

Current Foucauldian translated these colonial indulgences in legal formations as 'discourse formations' by the 'power-knowledge' paradigm[11] and the building of 'pan opticon' prisons[12] and 'rationalization' of administrative bureaucracy as

---

[4]Weber used this term and according to him, through 'expropriation' the monopoly of the Govt declared, and applied the law, see M Weber (1958), Politics as a Vocation, in, HH Gerth & CW Mills (eds) *From Max Weber: essays in sociology* (Routledge & K Paul, London, 1970) as cited by M Galanter, The Displacement of Traditional Law in Modern India, in, Rajeev Dhavan (ed) *Marc Galanter: Law and Society in Modern India* (Oxford University Press, Delhi, 1989) 17.

[5]*Ibid* 17, reprinted from 24 *J Soc Issues* 65.

[6]M Waseem, *Politics and the State in Pakistan*, 3rd edn (NIHCR, Islamabad, 2007) 29.

[7]DA Washbrook, Economic Depression and Making of Traditional Society in Colonial India 1820-1855 in 3 *Trans Royal Hist Soc*, (1993) 237, 239.

[8]Like, *the Punjab Alienation of Land Act* 1901 and *Sindh Encumbered Estates Act* 1878, see I Habib, *Essays in Indian History*: *Towards a Marxist Perception* (Tulika, New Delhi, 1995).

[9]Waseem, *supra* note 6, 45.

[10]Waseem, *supra* note 6, 21.

[11]BS Cohen, *Colonialism and its Forms of Knowledge*: *The British in India* (Princeton University Press, Princeton, 1996).

[12]M Kaplan, Panopticon in Poona: An Essay on Foucault and Colonialism, 10:1, *Cult. Anthropol* (1995) 85.

'techniques of disciplining power'.[13] Where were the excluded, dispossessed and the marginalized in these legal formations? The motives behind laws, i.e. to protect British trade and industry, were equally behind the crafting of trade union and workers' legislation. After the Ghadr (revolt) of 1857, the wage-related disputes in public sector came within the ambit of jurisdiction of magistrates under The Employers and Workmen Dispute Act of 1860. The Act criminalized breach of contract by an employee but not employer.[14]

Exclusion by the East India Company was racial, placing British civilian bureaucracy on the top administratively. 'Difference' and 'separation' sharpened identities and added fears in the minds of the marginalized and excluded, dividing them further.[15] Chief Justice Munir of Pakistan (29 June 1954 to 2 May 1960) noted that legal codifications in British India sharpened divisions. For example, the Government of India Act, 1919 presumed communal electorates and diarchy, and the classification of subjects into 'reserved' and 'transferred'.[16]

The relationship of the local polity with law-making, meanwhile, went through two phases. Before the extensive *Ghadar* (revolt) of 1857, military struggle and occupation were followed by colonial laws, such as the Permanent Settlement laws. In the second phase, after 1857, the relation of the polity to laws changed and protests *followed* law-making. For example, *The Government of India Act*, 1858 came just after the revolt (Ghadar) of 1857 and was a constitutional document for colonial India, which transferred the administration territory under East India Company to the Crown.[17] The *Indian Council Act* of 1861 further deepened the local administration in colonial India.[18] Still, the local population was not included in the administration. Later, the formation of the Indian National Congress created a cadre of native politicians to include in the administration in 1892.[19] It expanded the Council of the Governor-General. Muslim minority consciousness was triggered, resulting in demand of separate electorate and formation of the Muslim League (ML) in 1906, leading to the Minto-Morley Reforms 1909.[20] Afterwards, the politics of Congress and Muslim League followed the indigenization of Indian politics through *The Government of India Act*, 1919[21] and finally *The Government*

---

[13]P Chatterjee, *The Nations and its Fragments: Colonial and Postcolonial Histories* (Princeton University Press, 1993).

[14]F Mohammed, Protecting Pakistani Labourers Post-Eighteenth Amendment: Recognizing Rights after the Devolution of Power, 9:2 *Loy U Chicago LJ (*2012*)* 265, 269.

[15]F Robinson, *Separatism among Indian Muslims: The Politics of the United Provinces Muslims*, 1860-1923 (Oxford University Press, Delhi, 1993); see also, A Jalal, *Self and Sovereignty: Individual and Community in South Asian Islam since* 1850 (Routledge, New York, 2000).

[16]M Munir CJSC (Ret as he then was), *From Jinnah to Zia* (Vanguard, Lahore, 1979) 6.

[17]*The Government of India Act* 1858, in, Constitutional Documents (Pakistan), Vol I, (Law Div, Ministry of Laws & Parliamentary Affairs, Karachi, 1964) 332.

[18]*The Indian Council Act* 1861, in, *supra* note 17, 399.

[19]*The Indian Councils Act* 1892, in, *supra* note 17, 408.

[20]*The Indian Councils Act* 1909, in, *supra* note 17, 413.

[21]*The Government of India Act* 1919, in, *supra* note 17, 513.

of India Act, 1935.[22] Eventually, we see the 'constitutional' or 'legal birth'[23] of two independent states in subcontinent in 1947.[24] Pakistan was arguably created through an Act of the British Parliament and not through a prior existence of a 'revolutionary' movement as in other colonized countries.[25]

2.2 Did Pakistan Inherit a Good Judicial System?

As already explained, after the defeat of Ghadar, the local polity followed the legal and constitutional changes introduced by the British authorities. These new ideas of 'constitutionality' and 'legality' became the dominant mode for legal policy at the national level (both Congress and Muslim League-ML), with exception of the Ghadar Party (1913), Bhagat Singh's movement (1930) and finally Subhash Chandra Bose (1940s).[26] The rule of law became so pervasive that by the 1950s, the dominant opinion was that Pakistan had inherited a good judicial system.[27] The Law Reforms Commission (1967–1970) found that the essential principles of the Mughal system of administration of justice were sound and efficient and that the British had only changed the system in those areas which were previously unregulated. According to the commission, British influences on India were assimilated and were no longer foreign.[28] Even the critique of this view of the 'inherited good

[22]*The Government of India Act* 1935, in, *supra* note 17.

[23]H Khan, *Constitutional and Political History of Pakistan*, 2nd ed. (Oxford University Press, Karachi, 2009) 41.

[24]Pakistan was arguably created through an Act of the British Parliament, and not through a prior existence of a 'revolutionary' movement as in other colonial countries, See *The Independence Act* 1947, in, *supra* note 17.

[25]*The Independence Act* 1947, *supra* note 17.

[26]The Ghadar party was formed by the Punjabi Indians in 1913 in U.S. and Canada to liberate India. Bhagat Singh (1907-1931) was a socialist in United British India struggling for independence. He was accused of murdering British police officer Saunders by throwing a bomb in the Punjab Legislative Assembly. A trial by Special Tribunal and appeal at Privy Council in England found him guilty. He was hanged on March 23, 1931. Subhash Chandra Bose was an Indian nationalist who formed the Indian National Army (INA) to liberate India out of the British Indian Army in the battle of Singapore during the Second World War. Bose was assisted by Germany. The British Raj charged 300 INA soldiers for treason. Bose escaped but died in a plane crash in Taiwan.

[27]S Anwar-ul-Haq CJSC (Ret, as he then was), Administration of Justice.
PLJ (1983) Journal Section 42; See SA Haque, Laws Delays - A Study: Diagnosis and Cure, XXVIII *PLD* (1976) Journal Sections 64, 65.

[28]S Anwar-ul-Haq has summarized the report, see Anwar-ul-Haq, *ibid* 50. He is also of the view that Civil Services should not be discarded as "ruling elite" which is a relic of the colonial past and he resented Yahya's Civil services reforms in 1970-71, see S Anwar-ul-Haq, *Revolutionary Legality in Pakistan* (Pakistan Writers' Co-operative Society, Lahore, 1993) 303; This opinion was shared by Justice (Ret) Saiduzzaman Siddiqui in a speech delivered at National Defense College, Islamabad to the Senior Cadre Officers of the Armed Forces of Pakistan and Friendly Countries in

judiciary' only extended to the issue of appointment of British only judges.[29] The profound social and political changes that had accompanied the transplantation of British law went unremarked upon, and little was changed by the successive governments in two decades after independence.[30]

The only exceptional voice in this regard was that of Chief Justice Cornelius. He discussed the diversity of the courts and laws before the British arrival. According to Cornelius, during the period of Hindu rulers, there was also a gradation of courts. Landowners or *Zamindars* had jurisdiction over the population in the courts of the territories. Gradually, in his view, British rule displaced the prior forms of justice and discriminated against the locals, as they could not sue any British person. All of the judges were European, with the East India Company having jurisdiction all over the subcontinent. Few locals served as judges in these courts, those who did were called 'Black Judges'. The Indian Civil Services, after the Parliamentary Act of 1761, were exclusively British.[31] Cornelius also pointed out that it was the beneficiaries of the system, like certain judges and lawyers, who believed in the British system.[32]

And yet, Cornelius did not extend his critique to more fundamental questions such as the purpose and function of the British legal system in India in terms of exploitation or oppression. While he did not indulge with the hierarchies and exploitation within the legal system in British or pre-British India, he never asked if independence would mean delinking from the colonizers, or how the state and legal structure might have to change. This reflected a lack of a critique of neo-colonialism and it was no accident he became one of the main architects of U.S. modernization project in Pakistan under Ayub. Cornelius also did not mention the nature of indignity and the extent of exploitation in the informality which for him was 'Islam'.

To sum up, Pakistan not only inherited a colonial state apparatus and the personals on the key posts in judiciary, military and civil services, but also a consciousness accepting modernity and enlightenment as a part of colonial conquest.

(Footnote 28 continued)

Asia, Africa, Europe and North America, see Justice (Ret) S Siddiqui, Judiciary in Pakistan: An Overview *PLD* (2000) Journal Section 52, 53.

[29]A Ahmad, Judicial Review of Administrative Actions and Independence of Judiciary in Pakistan, XXII *PLD* (1970) Journal Section 135, 139.

[30]S Ahmed, Administration of Justice- A Hoax, (1971) *XXIII PLD* 123.

[31]AR Cornelius, Restoration of Judicial Responsibility to People; Repairing Damage Done to National Character During Period of Subjugation XV *PLD* (1963) Journal Section 7, address delivered at a gathering of Military officials at G. H. Q., Rawalpindi on 11 July 1962.

[32]*Ibid* 3.

2.3 Modernizers Even Before Modernization

As a rapidly constructed state, Pakistan did not inherit a centralized state machinery.[33] It could have experimented with new forms of governance, but did not. What are the explanations for this? One may be that the founding father had internalized the ideas of the colonizers.[34] The founding father of Pakistan, Jinnah, was a Lincoln Inn's graduate, and under the influence of liberal British parliamentarians.[35] The first Prime Minister of Pakistan, Liaquat Ali Khan, was also a student of Exeter College, Oxford. He completed his studies in law and was called to the bar of the Inner Temple in 1922. Jinnah was a lawyer of outstanding eminence.[36] Munir CJ's claim is that Jinnah was secular and against theocracy.[37] Most of these claims of Jinnah are based on his speech addressing the constituent assembly on the 11th of August 1947.[38] Sharifuddin Pirzada, one of the most prominent jurists of Pakistan, rejected this view that Jinnah wanted a secular state[39] but a modern state which was neither a Western type or nor a theocratic state.[40] For Nasim Hassan Shah CJ, Jinnah's vision of Pakistan was as a liberal democratic Islamic welfare state.[41] Since socialist ideas were also prominent at the time, Jinnah also offered a haphazard condemnation of landlords and capitalists.[42] He stated that major key industries and public utility services would be socialized.[43] Jinnah wanted socialist

[33]As opposed to India, Pakistan started with a completely new state, See SJ Burki, *A Revisionist History of Pakistan*, (Vanguard, Lahore, 1998).

[34]F Fanon. *The Wretched of the Earth* (Grove Press, New York, 2004); See, Also, F Fanon. *Black skin, white masks* (Grove Press, New York, 1968) as cited by A Khan (2012) 33, 45. See TA Khan, *The Post-Colonial State in The Era of Capitalist Globalization: Historical, Political, and Theoretical Approaches to State Formation* (Routledge, New York, 2012).

[35]As a student in England, Jinnah used to visit Hyde Park Corner to listen to Soap Box orators and he was a regular visitor of the House of Commons to listen to the speeches of Gladstone, Lord Morley, Joseph Chamberlain, Balfour, etc. See S. Anwar-ul-Haq "Quaid-i-Azam as a Constitutionalist" (1976), a paper read at the Third Jurist Conference held on 9 December, 1976 at Karachi, in Anwar-ul-Haq, *supra* note 28, 251.

[36]For a detailed account of Jinnah's legal cases and achievements, See SS Pirzada, *Quaid-i-Azam Muhammad Ali Jinnah: As a Lawyer* (Nazaria-i-Pakistan Trust, Lahore, 2000).

[37]Munir, *supra* note 16, ix.

[38]Jinnah's speech on 11 August on his election as first president of the Constituent Assembly of Pakistan, See *Quaid-i-Azam Mohammad Ali Jinnah, Speeches and Statements as Governor General of Pakistan 1947-48* (Government of Pakistan, Ministry of Information and Broadcasting, Directorate of Films & Publications Islamabad, Islamabad, 1989) 42.

[39]SS Pirzada, Pirzada's interview with MH Faruqi, Jinnah's Pakistan: Islamic or Secular? in *supra* note 36, 22.

[40]*Ibid.*

[41]Shah, *infra* note 103, 140.

[42]Jinnah addressing Muslim League on 24 April 1943.

[43]Jinnah talking to the Associated Press of America on 8 November, 1945.

modernization but Munir CJ made it clear 'immediately' that he wanted to combine the moral principles of Islam and socialism and did not mean a practicing theory of socialism.[44]

Apart from Jinnah's position on Islam and Pakistan, one thing is certain, after 1857 Ghadr, Muslims of the subcontinent had a fear of exclusion at a political level. Materiality of the idiom of Islam or Muslim identity was only to that extent and should be traced in those class formations. Munir is right that Jinnah was not a communalist.[45] Then what about two-nation theory he espoused, that Muslims are a separate 'nation' from Hindus? This was a later development in its 'particular'. To understand the later developments of the grafting of Islam on the modernist constitutionalist version of Jinnah's state, there is a need to explore the class formations under Liaqat Ali Khan after Jinnah's sudden death in September 1948.

2.4 Class Formation Behind 'Overdeveloped' State

After independence, state formation and legal/constitutional formation did not change under Jinnah. Indian Act of 1935,[46] with a few modifications, became the constitution of the newly independent Pakistan. Jinnah became Governor-General with 3 out of 4 provincial governors as British technocrats. All British chiefs of armed forces stayed in their offices and the important ministries of finance and foreign affairs were given to Ghulam Muhammad and Muhammad Zufrullah Khan, who were technocrats of international reputation and had 'connections'. Whereas the delinking of the colonial hegemony was not substantial, rather non-existent leading to deep centre–periphery relations of Pakistan, the reigning class in post-colonial Pakistan was in transition. A number of key political and economic figures of the time concurred, including Iskandar Mirza, Akhtar Hussian, Amjad Ali, Yousaf Haroon and Chaudhri Salahuddin. Amjad Ali and Haroon (Karachi) were from influential business families, and Salahuddin was the General Secretary of the Muslim League. Habib Bank gave Rs. 80 million as a loan equal to half of the revenue.[47] The statement of Industrial Policy came in 1948. This was the beginning of a capitalist class. In the 1950s, 99% of the growth was through Import

[44]M Munir, Stateless and Classless Society, in NH Chaudhry, *Chief Justice Muhammad Munir: his life, writings and judgments* (Research Society of Pakistan, Lahore, 1973) 170, 176, first published in Pakistan Times, 23-24 March, 1972, 170, 176.

[45]Munir, *supra* note 16, 20.

[46]*The Government of India Act* 1935, in, *supra* note 17.

[47]Shahid-ur-Rehman, *Who owns Pakistan*? (Mr Books, Islamabad, 1998) 9.

Substitution Industrialization (ISI).[48] We can see, therefore, how "the alliance between big business and the bureaucratic-military axis was already well-established in the 1950s".[49]Unlike India's congress, the Muslim League had thin roots in the territory which became Pakistan. Internally, the Muslim League was facing pressure for land reforms from Doltana and left-wing Mian Iftikhar-ud-din. In 1947, the Government Hari Committee was formed, which declared landlords as friends of the peasants, whereas a dissenting opinion of an ICS Muhammad Masud portrayed the real miseries of the peasantry in Sindh and recommended urgent land reforms. The report was stopped and not published till 1949. The Muslim League had to make an agrarian Reforms Committee under Mumtaz Daultana in February 1949. The East Bengal Land Acquisition and Tenancy Act, 1950 abolished large land holdings by fixing a ceiling of 33 acres self-cultivated land.[50] Landlords started ejecting tenants, so the situation began to deteriorate and took on 'semi-revolutionary' proportions.[51] Hence, the agrarian question continued to be volatile. According to Toor, the ruling classes were concerned with an increasingly unruly populace and were determined to expel socialism/communism from the realm of legislative politics. The left was seeking to articulate an alternate narrative of nationalism and the nation-state project on the basis of 'vision' of progressive society as opposed to liberal anti-communists. She has discussed this conflict between the liberal capitalist vision and socialist progressive vision in 1950–1960s in detail.

After Jinnah's death, under the leadership of Liaqat Ali Khan, the Muslim League was not united and lost popular support.[52] This led to a process of creating parties internally from within state which Waseem called as 'official' parties. These were to counter an emerging anti-colonial popular alliance of ethno-nationalist (Bengali, Pashtoon and Baluchi) and socialists.[53] To make it possible, Liaqat Ali Khan took two steps; first, he decided to rely on West Pakistan's landed elite as his natural constituency as a big landlord; second, he brought the Objectives Resolution

[48]AR Kemal, Patterns and growth of Pakistan's Industrial Sector, in, SR Khan (ed) *50 Years of Pakistan's Economy: Traditional Topics and Contemporary Concerns* (Oxford University Press, Karachi, 1999) 152.

[49]A Jalal, *The State of Martial Rule: The Origins of Pakistan's Political Economy of Defense* (Vanguard & Cambridge University Press/UK, Lahore, 1991) 176 fn 122.

[50]Hari Enquiry Committee, Govt of Sindh, *Minutes of Dissent* by M. Masud (Karachi), See, Also *Report of the Agrarian Committee appointed by the Working Committee of the Pakistan Muslim League* (S. Shams-ul-Hasan, 1949).

[51]The report of AR, Preston, American Consul General, as cited by Ayesha Jalal, see Jalal, *supra* note 49, 105.

[52]M Munir CJSC (Ret, as he then was), *Highways and Bye-ways of Life* (Law Publishing Company, Lahore, 1978) 74.

[53]For example, National Awami Party-NAP, which was formed after 1956 and started representing communists, nationalists, and masses outside the state formation which Waseem called as an external party, see Waseem, *supra* note 6, 118.

to please Mullahs, who had already opposed land reforms declaring them as un-Islamic.[54]

The vulnerability of the feeble reigning class of Pakistan made it dependent on neo-colonial powers also. Liaqat's 1950 visit to the U.S., ostensibly in response to President Truman's Point IV Program to let the developing world benefit from the technical advances of the U.S., was a starting point for this. It was the acceptance of the new hegemonic project of the U.S. by the reigning class. Liaqat's request for private investment from the U.S.[55] in 1950 was for Pakistan to catch up and make up for lost centuries within the shortest possible time.[56] One can note that this rhetoric of 'catch up' fits with the rhetoric of Truman's speech and with the dominant modernization approach to development. He was convinced that the modernization of Pakistan could not be accomplished without the help of advanced countries like the United States.[57] Thus, he took a clear stand in the Cold War, siding with the U.S. He predicted that 'liberal civilization' and its institutions were under attack by 'dark forces' and identified the U.S. as the torchbearer of 'civilization'.[58] He emphasized the common values of individual enterprise, civil liberties and private ownership as opposed to distribution.[59] In his formation of modernization for Pakistan, he replaced U.S. morality with Islam as "the best security of law and the surest pledge of freedom" for Pakistan. According to Ali Khan, Islam was a necessary supplement due to the "mental confusion of the colonial world or their struggle".[60]

Soon after this came the support of Pakistan in Korean War and joining of the Southeast Asia Treaty Organization (SEATO) and later CENTO (the Baghdad Pact). In the wake of these moves, Pakistan lost the sympathy of the Soviet Union.[61] So far, the imperialist bloc wanted to use the legislature as a seat of power under the leadership of Liaqat Ali Khan and not military. Therefore, the *Pindi conspiracy* case was to clear communists from the military. Later, Nixon found the military under the leadership of Ayub to meet the daunting needs of cold war and

---

[54]Jammaat-e-Ahmadia's second caliph Mirza Bashiruddin Mahmud Ahmad wrote a book titled "*Islam and Masala Malkiat-e- Zamin*" in 1950. He rejected the recommendations of land reforms by Doltana Report. Muslim League formed this committee in response to the volatile question of land in the country. Similarly, Maulana Moudodi of Jammaat-e-Islami also wrote a book in 1950 titled "*Masala Malkiat-e-Zameen.*" He strongly opposed land reforms, see M Naim-Ullah, *Pakistan in the Stranglehold of Feudalism* [*Pakistan Jagirdari Zamindari Nizam Ke Shikaney Men*] (Jumhoori Publications, Lahore) 186.

[55]LA Khan, *Pakistan: The Heart of Asia*: *speeches by Liaqat Ali Khan* (Royal Book Company, Karachi 1989) 62, speeches delivered in 1950 but first issued in Pakistan in 1989.

[56]*Ibid* 30.

[57]*Ibid* 30.

[58]*Ibid* 22.

[59]He assured Americans that "we as Muslims believe in private ownership as opposed to Hindus whose laws were designed to promote the distribution of wealth and discourage vast unearned accumulation", see *Ibid* 56, 62.

[60]*Ibid* 45.

[61]MA Khan, *Friends not Masters*: *A Political Autobiography* (Oxford: London, 1967) 16.

Pakistan as a front line state. Nixon, after meeting with General Ayub in 1953 in Pakistan, described him in his memoirs as, "one Pakistani leader who was more anti-communist than anti-Indian".[62] Ayub credited himself as promoting U.S.–Pakistan relations. Jalal is of the opinion that the entry of Pakistan into Middle East defense pacts re-established the dwindling influence of the government.

To sum up, the state formation in Pakistan, from the outset, was a class formation, which included an alliance between three fundamental classes (metropolitan bourgeoisie, landed elite and an emerging merchant and industrial class). But the reigning class was unable to control the masses and fulfill the emerging needs of the cold war. Long before joining SEATO and CENTO, the reigning class under the leadership of Liaqat went through the test of the *Pindi Conspiracy* case and later, the consequent banning of the Communist Party and Progressive Association (PWA) and the take over of Progressive Papers Ltd.[63] Toor also connects this struggle with the McCarthy era, liberal anti-communist consensus.[64]

2.5 Pindi Conspiracy Case

All liberals take the defeat of democracy by dictatorship in the *Tamizzuddin* case of 1955 as the starting point of constitutional history of Pakistan. However, as the book will argue, the *Pindi Conspiracy* case can explain how the legal and constitutional institutions in Pakistan respond to class formations, irrespective of whether the country is governed by democracy or dictatorship. Askar Ali Shah of the Criminal Investigation Department (CID) of North Western Frontier Province of Pakistan—NWFP[65] disclosed a conspiracy in the military on 19 Feb 1951. Between 4 and 7 March, Major-General Akbar Khan and Latif Khan were dismissed and arrested under Bengal Regulation III of 1818. The charge against all of the accused was a conspiracy to wage war *against the King* [emphasis is mine].[66] The trial was held *in camera* in Hyderabad Jail. The accused were found guilty and convicted. The judgment, authored by Justice Abdur Rehman, pronouncing guilt, comprised of 852 pages along with 41 appendices.

---

[62]As quoted by M Hussain & A Hussain, *Pakistan: Problems of Governance* (Vanguard, Lahore, 1993) 30.

[63]S Toor, *The State of Islam: Culture and Cold War Politics in Pakistan* (Pluto Press, London 2011) 52; Kamran Asdar Ali also gave an account of communist perspective as a contesting voice on the intellectual and cultural scene in the early days of Pakistan, see KA Ali, Communists in a Muslim Land: Cultural Debates in Pakistan's Early Years 45:3 *Mod Asian Stud* (2011) 501.

[64]*Ibid* 79.

[65]Currently province of Khyber Pukhtunkhwa.

[66]H Zaheer, *The Times and Trial of the Pindi Conspiracy Case* 1951: *The First Coup Attempt in Pakistan* (Oxford University Press, Karachi, 1998) 248.

What was the context for this case, and what was its direct impact? General Gracy, while transferring to Ayub his position as Commander-in-Chief of the Army on 17 January 1951, informed him about a 'Young Turk' Party in the army. General Ayub himself had always been suspicious of Major-General Akbar Khan, his ambitions and his 'political leaning'[67] and hence the conspiracy was about class politics.[68] Zaheer (1998) insisted that the Communist Party was involved in the conspiracy.[69] General Akbar had been under the observation of U.K. intelligence agencies during his training there. He was seen with Andrew Roth, a leading American Communist intellectual.[70] Before his arrest under the conspiracy charges, Akbar Khan met with the Russian Progressive Writers' delegation between 19 and 20 November 1950. He was introduced to the delegation as the next Commander-in-Chief of Pakistan.[71] Based on the reports of intelligence agencies, the Communist party lost many of its cadre during partition, but in three years "a powerful party machine had emerged". The budget of the party was second to that of the ruling Muslim League and had more paid workers than any other party. It had many front organizations in powerful sections of the society, including those for journalists and students. It had an upward mobility with leaders such as Mian Iftikhar-ud-din, who moved into the upper layers of Pakistani society. The Party was remarkable in a feudal and tribal society.[72] This was also the early period of the Cold War.

The following legal account will explain how an elected government under one of the founding fathers of Pakistan, Liaqat Ali Khan, not necessarily a dictatorship, responded to the class struggle. Prime Minister Liaqat informed the constituent assembly that the conspiracy plan within the military was spearheaded by the support of Communists and revolutionary forces. He argued that the plan involved implementing a communist dictatorship. A bill was put forth in the national assembly on 13 April 1951 and was passed the same day after an intense debate.[73]

[67]He did not state it clearly here, but obviously these were communists, see Khan, supra note 61, 35.

[68]For Zaheer, the Left intellectuals propagated that there was actually no conspiracy, and that it was a conspiracy engineered by intelligence agencies of the Anglo-Saxon American bloc, see Zaheer, *supra* note 66, x-xi. He also disagrees with the position of Ayesha Jalal throwing blame on 'complex influence' like asserting the government to form a policy independent of Anglo-Saxon bloc, see Jalal *surpra* note 49, 121, 3.

[69]He insisted this based on 'A long interview with Major Ishaq,' 6 May 1972, 'What was the Rawalpindi Conspiracy Case? A Staff Study', 11 November 1972; 'Was the Rawalpindi Conspiracy a Myth?' Air Commodore M. K. Janjua (Ret) 13 January 1973, *The Outlook*, Karachi. Based on interview with Eric Cyprian, Islamabad 18 January 1995, the writer claimed that he criticized the adventurous steps of Sajjad. Hasan Zaheer himself threw the blame on the few rich feudal families of Lahore espousing the Russian model of economic and social progress, "without of course, missing out on the good things of life". See Zaheer, *supra* note 66, x, xi.

[70]*Ibid* 224, 25.

[71]*Ibid* 169.

[72]*Ibid* 207, 08.

[73]*The Rawalpindi Conspiracy (Special Tribunal) Bill* 1951.

Provisions of the Act were at variance with prevailing laws. The rights of the accused were abrogated explicitly by relaxing the standard of the prosecution's evidence and procedural requirements, and ignoring principles of administration of criminal justice. This law set an example of 'bad governance' and 'disregard of fundamental rights'.[74] Under the Act, statements made before the police were admissible and conclusive without cross-examination.

Four main areas violated the norms of natural justice, namely, the right of inquiry was waived, no appeal was allowed, a person's statement was admissible as evidence without cross-examination and even the statement before an investigating officer was admissible under Section 5(2) of the Act. The tribunal could convict any person, even if they were not charged on the basis of evidence produced before it. No appeal was allowed under Section 10 of the Act. This removal of the right to appeal was unprecedented in the history of British India.[75]

Section 2 of the *Rawalpindi Conspiracy (Special Tribunal) Act*, 1951, empowered the central government to set up a Tribunal in which to try the accused. Section 4 of the Act gave the Special Tribunal all the powers of a High Court in relation to a criminal trial. But, the Tribunal could not take the bail of any accused person. Under Section 5, the Tribunal could also try offences falling under the Army Act. The Tribunal consisted of Justice Amir-ud-din of the Dhaka High Court, Justice Sharif of the Lahore High Court and Justice Abdur Rahman of the Federal Court (as Chairman) of the Tribunal. Mr. A.K. Brohi, Advocate General, conducted the prosecution.

Through the *Pindi conspiracy* case, the Communist Party's underground apparatus was completely devastated due to large-scale arrests of all leadership and sympathizers and the seizing of documents, including records and bills, etc. All mass fronts of the party were also destroyed and the communist influence among the Trade Unions, Progressive Writers' Association P.W.A. and students decreased sharply. The Communist Party of Pakistan itself was banned in 1954.[76]

The long-term outcome of the case is even more interesting than the direct impact of the case, and this proves this case to be a decisive turning point in the 'constitutional' history of Pakistan. General Ayub strongly disliked defence counsel Suhrawardy's cross-examination of the army officers, but found himself helpless against a 'passive court' at the time. When Suhrawardy was going to be appointed as Prime Minister after the 1954 dismissal of the legislature, President Iskandar Mirza appointed Ayub as a defense minister. Ayub told Suhrawardy that he did great damage to military at the trial. Mirza advised Suhrawardy to negotiate, but never to interfere in the matters of the Army.[77] From *Pindi Conspiracy case* to the movement against him, Ayub's major anxiety was the rise of socialism.

---

[74]Zaheer, *supra* note 66, 18.

[75]*Ibid* 20.

[76]I Leghari, The socialist movement in Pakistan: an historical survey - 1940-1974, PhD Dissertation, Université Laval, Québec City 1979, 69.

[77]Khan, *supra* note 61, 37.

Even after the *Pindi conspiracy* case, the ban of the Communist Party and its fronts, PWA and DSF in 1954, reigning class under the banner of Muslim League could not stop its down fall and needed a reshuffling. This led to the dissolution of non-representative legislature and hence the *Tamizuddin* case.

2.6 Moulvi Tamizuddin Khan Case

On 24 October 1954, the first Constitutional Assembly was dissolved by Governor-General Ghulam Muhammad.[78] The grounds for dissolution were that the constitutional machinery of the country had broken down and the Assembly had lost the confidence of the people. According to Jan Mohammed Dawood (1994), the Assembly did not have a representative character. Most of the members did not have a constituency of their own in Pakistan. The fact was proved in the elections of 1954, when only 14 were re-elected. From West Pakistan, 28 out of 40 were landlords, whereas in East Pakistan, 20 out of 40 were lawyers.[79] This assembly had been making a constitution for the newly independent country since 1947 and meanwhile, the country was being run under an interim constitution which was an adaption of the Government of India Act, 1935. The president of the Constitutional Assembly, Moulvi Tamizuddin Khan, challenged this dissolution before the Sindh Chief Court (which later became Sindh High Court) as unconstitutional, illegal, *ultra vires*, without jurisdiction, inoperative and void. Moulvi requested that the court restrain the government from interfering under a writ of *mandamus,* and to determine the validity of certain appointments of the Governor-General's Council of Ministers under a writ of *quo warranto.* The lawyer for Moulvi Tamizuddin, Mr. I.I. Chundrigar, stated before the court that "the constituent assembly is a sovereign and sacred body, it can only be extinguished by a revolution or a *coup d' etat*".[80] The Sindh High Court decided unanimously in favour of Moulvi Tamizuddin Khan.[81] The court accepted the sovereign and supreme power of the Constitutional Assembly regarding the constitution and law-making and found no powers were vested in the Governor-General to dissolve the Constitutional Assembly in the *Indian Independence Act*, 1947. The decision was challenged in an appeal by the government in Federal Court. On 21 March 1955, the Federal Court, under the leadership of Chief Justice Munir, decided the case in favour of the government and against Moulvi by a majority of four to one. The court reversed the judgment of the Sindh High Court on technical grounds without addressing the question of whether

[78]Order No F 81/Pres./58, text of the proclamation is produced in J Ahmad (ed) *Constitution-Making in Pakistan* (National Assembly of Pakistan, Islamabad, 1973) as Annexure V 41; Order of the dissolution is partly produced in *infra* note 81.

[79]JM Dawood, *The Role of Superior Judiciary in the Politics of Pakistan* (Royal Book Company, Karachi, 1994) 17, 211.

[80]Shah, *infra* note 103, 57.

[81]*Moulvi Tamizuddin Khan v Federation of Pakistan*, PLD 1955 Sindh 96.

the assembly was rightly dissolved or not.[82] The dissenting judge in this case was Justice A.R. Cornelius. He placed the Constitutional Assembly above the Governor-General and found it to be a sovereign body.

As a result of the above judgment, 46 of the Acts on the statute's books became invalid. The Governor-General promulgated the Emergency Powers Ordinance IX of 1955 to frame the constitution, validate the laws already made by the Constituent Assembly and make central budgets.[83] This ordinance was challenged in the Federal Court. Chief Justice Munir, heading a full Federal Court bench in *Usif Patel case*, declared on 13 April 1955, that powers to make provisions to the constitution of the country could not be exercised by the Governor-General through an Ordinance.[84] After this declaration, the government requested that the Federal Court detail the constitutional steps to come out of this constitutional crisis in a Reference.[85] The courts had to fall back on the doctrine of state necessity to address the constitutional impasse by the Emergency Powers Ordinance, 1955.

The prompt statement from leading jurists against the original Federal Court judgment was that it paved the path of future "arbitrary, malicious and capricious acts of the executive on hyper technical grounds or self-serving theories or concepts".[86] Hamid Khan (2001) declared Chief Justice Munir, on this decision, as a "supporter of the feudal-bureaucratic establishment of West Pakistan which was headed by his old friend Ghulam Muhammad".[87] For Waseem, the decision 'over-expanded' the judiciary's institutional resources and established the tenacity of the rule of law for the time to come.[88] For Mir Khuda Bakhsh Marri CJBHC, Munir CJ could have stood like Abu Hanifa and Thomas More, which means uprightness and truth.[89]

Cornelius is portrayed as a savior of 'democracy' and protector of fundamental rights in the later touted liberal dichotomy of dictatorship versus democracy. There is a need to discuss the ideas of political change/development in the minds of Munir and Cornelius CJs in a coherent way connecting their legal decisions and writings after the *Dosso case* which adjudicated upon the 1958 coup. This is important right now to explore how *Tamizuddin case* tried to address the ongoing crisis in the political formations of postcolonial Pakistan.

Because the Constituent Assembly did not make a new constitution in seven years, the statutes available to the judges of Sindh Chief Court were old colonial

---

[82]*Supra* note 81.

[83]*Emergency Powers Ordinance of 1955* (Ordinance IX of 1955) PLD 1955 Central Acts and Notifications.

[84]*Usif Patel v Crown*, PLD 1955 FC 387.

[85]*Reference by His Excellency The Governor General*, 1955 PLD Federal Courts 435.

[86]Khan, *supra* note 23, 84.

[87]*Ibid* 235.

[88]Waseem, *supra* note 6, 129.

[89]MKB Marri CJBHC (Ret, as he then was),, *A Judge May Speak* (Ferozsons (Pvt) Ltd, Lahore, 1990) 17, 18.

Acts or Independence Act of 1947 to address that ongoing transition from colonial to independence. Constantine CJ and Justice Villani of Sindh Chief Court thought that the prerogative of dissolution of assembly by His Majesty were in Governor-General, because he represented him. On the other hand, Justice Muhammad Bakhsh's comments were a full assertion of independence for the people of India "to do what they liked with their own Constituent Assembly". In an appeal in the Federal Court of Pakistan (which later became Supreme Court of Pakistan), Munir CJ, and Justices A.S.M. Akram, Muhammad Sharif and S.A. Rahman found the Crown as a constituent part of the parliament in U.K. and all Dominion Legislature and his assent a necessity. Judges considered any possibility of the Constituent Assembly as a sovereign body 'a mistake' and that it was supposed to function within the confines of the Indian Independence Act, 1947. The word 'independence' was meaningless in this Act.

On the other hand, Cornelius J tried to interpret the "degree of independence' in 'independent Dominion' of Pakistan more than which was given in the Statute of Westminster, 1931 to other 'Dominions'. For Cornelius J, the Governor-General was only 'faithful' to Her Majesty and no one else. Similarly, the Constituent Assembly' was not the creation of British Parliament but a body which was representative of the "will of the people in relation to their future mode of Government". Cornelius was trying to break the colonial chains 'constitutionally', whereas political and economic formations in postcolonial Pakistan had taken neo-colonial turns under the cold war as explained above. For Paula Newberg, Cornelius's views about 'the will of the people' were an attempt to establish a link of legislative power with popular sovereignty.[90] I disagree. There is no such thing as 'popular sovereignty' in Cornelius's views. He was strongly against 'popular democracy' and details to follow in the coming section. In the absence of a new constitution, Munir CJ was compelled to rely on colonial statutes and available in Common Law to address this situation was the doctrine of necessity, though 'technically' for him.[91] Justice Cornelius did not challenge the doctrine of necessity but tried to limit the discretion derived from it. He pointed out that this principle should be the maxim, '*salus populi supre molex*' (the welfare of the people shall be the supreme law). Apart from the books (constitution) and the courts (institutions), Munir's mind was in the reason outside the courts. Enforcement of law in this case was against the sovereign and such cases are political or military for him. Therefore, the court should not decide in favour of one and against another, which may cause bloodshed.[92] He was clear about the 'disastrous' consequence of the judgment in the *Tamizuddin case* and he repeated the same in the *Reference* also. For him,

[90]For Newberg, "Justice A.R. Cornelius offered the equally forceful alternative notions of *popular sovereignty* and constitutional government" [emphasize is mine], See PR Newberg, *Judging the State: Courts and Constitutional Politics in Pakistan* (Cambridge University Press, New Delhi, 1995) 45.

[91]Munir, *supra* note 52, 251, 271.

[92]Munir's comments while addressing High Court Bar Association, see Chaudhry, *supra* note 44, 22.

responsibility rested on the legislature because it thoughtlessly proceeded with its business and assumed itself in the position of an irremovable Legislature. The Muslim League had lost in provincial elections of 1953 to the United Front[93] and won in Punjab with the help of landed aristocracy. Suhrawardy did not have the support to make the Muslim League a popular party.[94] Furthermore, Anti-Ahamdi disturbances and religious riots in 1953 had an impact on Munir as he headed the Commission made to resolve that issue.[95] He was very clear that law and order should be separate from politics because a district magistrate was enough to control the Anti-Ahamdi disturbances.[96] On the face of rising socialism, this disturbance could be fatal.

One thing is very certain, that Ayub was behind this dissolution.[97] Ayub's opinion was that the Constituent Assembly had lost its prestige and the demand for its dissolution was gaining support. Moreover, he believed that 'unfettered democracy' would be dangerous on the face of rising communism. Munir CJ warned that communism from within and without is quick to make use of this weakness of political governance.[98] Communism and sectarianism (Bengali) was connected in this dangerous political formation in the mind of Munir,[99] which emerged as National Awami Party—NAP in the years to come.

The fears of Munir and Cornelius, as well as other jurists were real and more detail about them is to come. Right now, it is suffice to argue that the *Tamizuddin case* can be connected with the *Pindi Conspiracy case* in structural terms. Whereas the weak and feeble reigning class comprising Constituent Assembly was unable to delink from the colonial relation, and they were equally fearful to go to people and re-elected. In that scenario, the hegemonic neo-colonial elite decided to use the civil and military bureaucracy as a seat of power to keep the exclusion of the masses. Landed and merchant elite happily accepted their reigning positions under this hegemony. This class formation gave birth to different state formations in Pakistan, which were the subject of legal and constitutional explanation. While liberal explanations give considerable attention to the dissenting judgment of Cornelius in this case, my own view is that there was no hero in this judicial battle. Rather, the judiciary in this case revealed itself to be part of the juridico-bureaucratic structure of the state. I will develop this explanation in the following section.

Before we conclude this case, it is not irrelevant to have a cursory look on the views of Maulvi Tamizuddin Khan, the petitioner who came 'to rescue' democracy. Maulvi Tamizuddin argued that he was against the presidential system based on

---

[93]Munir, *supra* note 52, 77.

[94]Munir, *supra* note 52, 85.

[95]For detail of the relation of religion, law and order and state in this report, see Chaudhry, *supra* note 44, 183, 190.

[96]Chaudhry, *supra* note 44, 200.

[97]Munir, *supra* note 52, 92.

[98]Khan, *supra* note 61, 188.

[99]Chaudhry, *supra* note 44, 20.

fear, due to the history of a one-man rule in Muslim states. Ayub's logic was that a presidential system like that of the U.S. was not a monarchical system and with so many political parties, a parliamentary system was not feasible. Tamizuddin responded by asking for a decree of law allowing only two parties. The response from Ayub was that "you cannot control people's conscience by legal contrivances".[100] We can see how each of these accounts do not represents a democracy which considered peoples representation as the basis. Munir CJ decision was not a deviation from an ideal type of 'independent' and 'neutral' judiciary, nor it was a 'historical' accident that the judiciary stood with the civil-military bureaucracy. Rather, in the first two decisive decades of the newly independent Pakistan, the judiciary was the part-state structure leading political development more than any other developing country in that age of decolonization.

2.7 The Judiciary as a Part of Juridico-Bureaucratic State Structure

Just like the civil-military bureaucracy, judiciary in Pakistan not only had a colonial legacy but also participated in the neo-colonial formations and political developments after independence. After partition, there were English judges and the foremost jurists in the leading cases in the 1950s were either British lawyers hired by the Pakistani government or local barristers trained at Lincoln's Inn.[101] Both judges and jurists continued to cite Privy Council decisions as "the expositions of the law by one of the highest judicial tribunals in the world composed of distinguished men".[102] As a result, most cases cited were from the United Kingdom or the United States, English continued to be the language of courts and judgments, and as in the English tradition, the judges would refer to one another as "my brother" and counsel would refer to the judges 'my Lord'. The "English concept of

---

[100]Khan, *supra* note 61, 205, 206.

[101]As in the first leading constitutional case of *Maulvi Tamizuddin*, the judges of the Sindh High Court deciding in favour were Chief Justice Constantine, Justice Bachal and Justice Vellani, who were all English judges. Sir Ivor Jennings and Sir Kenneth Diplock, Queen's Counsel, were engaged by the government of Pakistan in this case. British judges of the 1950s were Sir Edward Snelson, KBE, Joint Secretary of Law from 1947 to 1958. He served as Federal Law Secretary till 1961. He resigned after the conviction in the Snelson case, detail of the case to follow. There were nine appointments of judges or registrar in 1947 and were reduced to two in 1961. Sir George B. Constantine, KBE, and J. Ortchenson, CBE, from Lahore High Court retired in 1962 and 1965 respectively. From the ICS (Indian Civil Service) and IPS (Indian Police Service) a total of 158 officers opted for Pakistan, out of which 36 in the ICS and 17 in IPS were British. Even in 1951, out of 202 officers, 23 were British. Five Britishers were in the judiciary. See Braibanti, *infra* note 104.

[102]Comments of CJ Munir in *Noor-ul -Hassan and others v The Federation of Pakistan,* PLD 1956 SC 331.

justice remained the dominant factors in Pakistan's higher judiciary, and indeed these are the part of the Pakistani culture".[103] It took 50 years for Pakistan to abandon the wigs of English justices and the phrase 'your Lordship'. Indeed, barristers are still required to say 'my Lord' when addressing the court.[104] The traditions were so powerful that all the related political activities were also understood as "mere motions in a foreign mode,"[105] as we will see.

The judiciary itself arrived in two streams—from the Indian Civil Services (ICS, officially known as Imperial Civil Services),[106] and the Lincoln Inn Barristers.[107] The close entanglement of the judiciary and bureaucracy in Pakistan's early years was greater than in any other developing country.[108] Civil Servants could, and frequently did, opt for judicial service. In 1961, eight officers of the Civil Service of Pakistan (CSP) were justices of the courts, namely M. Shahbuddin, Sir George Constantine, A.R. Cornelius, S.A. Rehman J. Ortcheson, M.B. Ahmad, A.R. Khan, M.R. Kayani, Sheikh Anwar-ul-Haq. In 1964, there were 65 such members. Three hundred and sixty-six officers of the Civil Services were presided over by Chief Justices Kayani of Lahore High Court, followed by Supreme Court Chief Justices S.A. Rahaman and M. Shahabuddin. The judiciary also headed all administrative reform commissions.[109]

By 1958, the year of coup, the hegemonic shift in Pakistan's politics from the U.K. to the U.S. was happening. At the same time new deepening relation of judiciary with the establishment and the U.S. were developing. This culminated in a

---

[103]NH Shah, *Memoirs and Reflections* (Alhamra Printing, Islamabad, 2002) 138.

[104]R Braibanti, *Chief Justice Cornelius of Pakistan: An Analysis with Letters and Speeches* (Oxford University Press, Karachi, 1999) xxiii.

[105]Cornelius, *supra* note 31, 11, address delivered at a gathering of Military officials at G H Q, Rawalpindi on 11 July 1962.

[106]Chief Justices Muhammad Shahabuddin (3 May 1960 to 12 May 1960), AR Cornelius (13 May 1960 to 29 Feb 1968) and SA Rahman (01 March 1968 to 03 June 1968) were from this category. The point to remember is that they all served in the 1960s, the era of modernization in Pakistan.

[107]Chief Justices Sir Abdur Rashid (07 June 1949 to 29 June 1954) and Muhammad Munir (29 June 1954 to 02 May 1960) came before the start of modernization. Fazal-e-Akbar (04 June 1968 to 17 Nov 1968) and Hamood-ur-Rahman (18 Nov 1968 to 31 Oct 1975) also served in the post-capitalist modernization period and even in socialist modernization period of 1970s.

[108]Braibanti, *supra* note 104, 109, see the detail of this relationship in R Braibanti, Public Bureaucracy and Judiciary, in, Pakistan in Palombra, *infra* note 122, 360, see, also, R Braibanti, The Socio-Judicial Context of the Cornelius Era – 1950-70 in Braibanti, *supra* note 104. This essay was first published in Braibanti, *Research on the Bureaucracy of Pakistan* (NC Duke University Press, Durham, 1966).

[109]Justice Munir JSC headed the First Pay and Service Commission of 1949-50. Justice Cornelius headed the second Pay and Service Commission from August 1959 to 28 May 1962 and completed a 300-page report in 1962. See Government of Pakistan, Report of the Pay and Service Commission (Manager of Publications, Karachi, 1969). An important point to note here is that SM Haider reviewed this report in 1970, see SM Haider, *A Review of the Cornelius Report* (National Institute of Public Administration, Lahore, 1970).

close relation of Ralph Braibant and Cornelius CJ.[110] Braibanti became the Chief Advisor and Professor of the Civil Services Academy in 1960, Lahore. At the time he was on leave from Duke University and was on contract with United States Agency for International Development. I consider him the main architect of the liberal legal and administrative project to this date. By the 1960s, the judiciary became influenced by the U.S. legal tradition.

2.8 The Significance of the Shift in Hegemonic Influence from U.K. to U.S.

According to Jalal, the "Polite British and American rivalry in South Asia" began in the early 1950s and was accompanied by the declining prestige of the U.K. in the Middle East and South Asia with the increasing influence of the Soviet Union.[111] According to Bhutto, initially Pakistan gave considerable importance to the Commonwealth, without considering the waning British influence in the world. Upon realizing the change in the global power structure, it began to lean towards U.S. influence.[112] It was clear to Ayub that the situation had changed and the United Kingdom could no longer give military and economic cover to the members of the Commonwealth.[113] Soon, the military was replacing Sand hurst-trained generals with American-trained ones. This continued throughout the 1950s and 1960s under the auspices of the American Military Assistance Program (MAP).[114]

---

[110]Cornelius passed the Indian Civil Service examination, did two years of study in Selwyn College, Cambridge UK, and joined the ICS in 1926. He opted for judicial services in 1930. He was Justice in Lahore HC in 1946 to 1950, Secretary of law 1951, elevated to Federal/Supreme court, and became the CJSC in 1960-1968. After retirement, he was the Law minister of Yahya Khan from 1969 till Bangladesh independence. He joined a law firm, Lane and Mufti. For writings on Cornelius, see SM Haider (ed) *A.R. Cornelius, Law and Judiciary in Pakistan* (Lahore Law Times Publications, Lahore, 1981); See, H Khan, In Memory of Justice (Retd) A R Cornelius- A Great Judge, Magazine Section, *PLJ* (1992) 70; See also, NH Shah, A Salute to the SC (A Tribute to the Cornelius Court) *PLD*, Journal Section (1992) 17; also Braibanti, *supra* note 104.

[111]Jalal, *supra* note 49, 126, 137, 171.

[112]ZA Bhutto, *Political Situation in Pakistan* (1968), in, H Jalal and K Hasan (eds) *The Politics of the People- Awakening the People, Vol. Two, 1966-69* (Classic, Lahore, 1969) 89, 98. This speech was first published as a pamphlet. Bhutto served as a Foreign Minister in the 1960s under General Ayub.

[113]A letter on the Future of the Commonwealth to the PMs of UK, Australia, and New Zealand, in, Baxter, *infra* note 138, 93.

[114]The number of these trained officers was very high. For example, in 1967-69 alone, 60 officers were trained under this program, see SP Cohen, *The Pakistan Army*, (University of California Press, Berkley, Los Angles & London, 1984); See also, W Miles D, *Military Aid and Counterrevolution in the Third World* (Lexington Books, Lexington & Massachusetts, 1972).

Similarly, a substantial U.S. intellectual and financial investment was allocated to train the bureaucracy.[115]

The transition from the U.K. to the U.S. tutelage was tricky and the tension could be seen in the connection of the upper brass of the civil and military bureaucracy. The first Commander-in-Chief of Pakistan was British General Gracy. When he was leaving, Liaqat Ali Khan decided to appoint a Pakistani General as Commander-in-Chief, but not the senior most one. General Iftikhar was backed by the British,[116] however, it was General Ayub Khan who was appointed the first Pakistani Commander-in-Chief on 16 January 1951. Ayesha Jalal notes the detail of this "subtle but significant British-American rivalry". By early 1951, it was decided by American policy makers to bypass the British and directly contact the Pakistani establishment, for the defense of the Gulf.[117]

The transition away from under the influence of the U.K. was also tricky in terms of legal and constitutional arrangements. Dr. S.M. Haider (1988) has elaborated on the process of assimilation of 'modern' U.S. legal norms in Pakistan. In the beginning, the judges relied on British court decisions, but they also relied upon U.S. precedents. After the 1956 constitution, the court decisions began to reflect the U.S. Supreme Court, regarding arbitrary use of administrative powers against fundamental rights. Another factor, which made this task easy, was the already present legal institutional arrangement of the British.[118] Braibanti found a shift from the U.K. to U.S. precedents due to the change to the presidential system and federalism,[119] as well as the written constitution and a chapter on Fundamental Rights. English courts do not have a written constitution and their fundamental rights were assured through Common Law and legislators. The quickly growing appreciation of U.S. tradition, with the help of academics, can be explained as part of an active modernization project and an understanding of the role of law in this project.[120] Thus, judicial approaches started tilting more toward the U.S. judicial

---

[115]In 1960, under US guidance and assistance, the Administrative Staff College was established in Lahore. In 1961, three National Institutes for Public Administration were established in Karachi, Lahore and Dhaka.

[116]Khan, *supra* note 61, 34.

[117]A Jalal, *Democracy and Authoritarianism in South Asia* (Sang-e-Meel Publications, Lahore, 1995) 37.

[118]SM Haider, American Constitution and Assimilation of Modern Legal Norms in Pakistan, XL *PLD* 1988 Journal Section, 121, 126.

[119]Braibanti, *supra* note 108; See also R Braibanti, The Higher Bureaucracy of Pakistan, in, Braibanti et al. (ed) *Asian Bureaucratic Systems Emerging from the British Imperial Tradition* (N. C.: Duke University Press, Durham, 1966).

[120]SM Haider was Braibanti's student and on his advice wrote a dissertation on the writ jurisdiction in Pakistan. He worked for Law Reform Commission till his death. Braibanti, *supra* note 104, xxii.

system.[121] The judiciary at that point was led by Indian Civil Services judges, who were not only aware of the ongoing modernization project led by the civil bureaucracy, but were bringing interpretation to help the project and at the same time to reduce its excesses. The judiciary was the point of permeation of American norms of administrative techniques but also of its review and future reforms.[122] So until the end of the Cold War, the impact of American law was pronounced on the Pakistani legal system.[123] Ayesha Jalal explained, it as a presidential form of government based on the American pattern, the framers of the constitution had ingeniously superimposed it on a distorted version of the British's parliamentary system. She explained how it veered but could not deviate from a U.K. or U.S. model.[124] In my view, Jalal correctly pointed out the *form,* but does not adequately account for the *content* of this move from the U.K. to the U.S. legal system. It is the objective of my analysis in this dissertation to demonstrate how it was that the law took on a central role in this transition, from modernization to the failing of the modernization project and a rising participatory popular democracy. I will briefly elaborate on the U.S. modernization school alluded to above. The political dimensions of the modernization project, according to Michael Adas, were felt in China, the Philippines, Caribbean and Latin America even before World War I. The focus was to create a middle class committed to both democracy and supportive of continuing ties with the United States.[125] There was a consensus on some version of social democracy as the only way to organize society[126] and a basic political liberalism. Democracy was to follow, 'the elite theory of democracy' led by a rational, coherent, self-confident elite, as stated by political scientists David Easton and Robert Dahl.[127] Morris Janowitz appreciated the role of third world militaries in

[121]Ralph Braibanti, an American political scientist and Duke Prof Emeritus at Duke University, studied the judiciary in Pakistan in the 1950s until 2005. From his writings, AR Cornelius, Dr. SM Haider, and Justice Kayani are found as close to the US judicial system. This was at its height when the Cornelius was chief justice in 1960s. Ralph Braibanti's book on AR Cornelius reflects implicitly on the relation of the modernization project under way in Pakistan and the changing approach of the judiciary, see Braibanti, *supra* note 104.

[122]R Braibanti, Public Bureaucracy and Judiciary in Pakistan, in, Joseph La Palombra (ed) *Bureaucracy and Political Development* (Princeton University Press, Princeton NJ, 1967) 360-440

[123]SM Haider, American Constitution and Assimilation of Modern Legal Norms in Pakistan, XL *PLD* (1988) 121, 125.

[124]Jalal, *supra* note 49, 215.

[125]M Adas, Modernization Theory and the American Revival of the Scientific and Technological Standards of Social Achievements and Human Worth, in, DC Engerman, N Gilman, MH Haefele & ME Latham (eds) *Staging Growth: Modernization, Development, and the Global Cold War* (University of Massachusetts Press, Amherst, 2003) 25, 26.

[126]E Shills, The End of Ideology? (1955) 5 *Encounter* 55, 58.

[127]N Gilman, Modernization Theory, the Highest Stage of American Intellectual History, in, DC Engerman, N Gilman, MH Haefele & ME Latham (eds) *Staging Growth: Modernization, Development, and the Global Cold War* (University of Massachusetts Press, Amherst, 2003) 59.

the managing of the affairs of the countries.[128] A concrete and decisive step towards this U.S. type political and constitutional system in Pakistan was the 1958 *coup*.

2.9 1958—General Ayub's Coup (Dosso Case)

After the dissolution of the 1954 assembly as explained above, the second constitutional assembly came with a constitution instituting a parliament in 1956, but with more powers to the president. This constitution only lasted for two and a half years and no elections were held under it. Eventually there was a *coup* in 1958 and the abrogation of the 1956 constitution by the president, Iskander Mirza.

On 8 October 1958, President Mirza declared Martial Law. On 10 October 1958, the Law (Continuance in Force) Order was promulgated which was drafted by Snelson.[129] It restored the jurisdiction of all courts (along with writs of *Habeas Corpus, Mandamus* and *Certiorari*, however, not against Chief Martial Law Administrator), and directed the government to adhere "as close as possible to the late constitution".[130] The above order was challenged in the Supreme Court of Pakistan and decided in the *Dosso Case*. The Supreme Court, headed by Chief Justice Munir, upheld the Martial Law and the Law (Continuance in Force) Order.[131] The court, using Hans Kelsen's *General Theory of Law and State*, declared that a successful *coup d'etat* or a victorious revolution is an internationally recognized method of regime and constitutional change. Chief Justice Munir's position was that there can be a writ in the High Court on the basis of fraction of law but not on the basis of so called fundamental rights which are in the late Constitution of 1956.[132] For Munir, Amir-ud-din, Shahab-ud-in JJ, due to the phrase in the Order "the country should be run as nearly as may be in accordance with the late Constitution of 1956", means only structure and manner of government and not fundamental rights and the whole Constitution. How come, for them, an Order on one hand is abrogating a Constitution and on the other hand restoring it, that is, giving fundamental rights. Interesting fact is that Supreme Court was in a hurry to give legitimacy to this dissolution which was not even asked. It is pertinent to mention here that Cornelius disagreed about the consent of the Governor-General

---

[128] M Janowitz, *The Professional Soldier: A Social and Political Portrait*, (Free Press, New York, 1960). For literature emphasizing military's superiority as socio-economic modernizers, see SP Huntington, *The Political Order in Changing Societies* (Yale University Press, New Haven, 1968) 203, see A Stepan, *The Military in Politics: Changing pattern in Brazil* (Princeton University Press, Princeton & NJ, 1971) 9.

[129] As claimed by Munir CJ after his retirement in a newspaper article, see M Munir, Days I Remember, Pakistan Times, 11 November 1968 in Chaudhry, *supra* note 44, 87.

[130] *President's Order (Post-Proclamation)*, No 1 of 1958, *Laws (Continuance in Force) Order*, PLD 1958 Central Statutes 497.

[131] *The State v Dosso*, PLD 1958 SC 533.

[132] *Ibid* 535.

in the 1955 *Tammizudin case* but he agreed with the doctrine of necessity in 1958 in *Dosso case.*[133]

After few months in *Mehdi Ali Khan case*, though implicitly, Cornelius pushed fundamental rights as a substitute for the deficit of democracy caused in *Dosso case.* In the *Dosso Case*, Article II of the Order mandated the government to follow the late constitution, but not to restore fundamental rights. After nine months in *Mehdi Ali Khan's case*, the Dhaka High court issued a writ of Mandamus against the provincial government not to take *Waqf* properties as the right of communities to organize their religious institutions. In an appeal by the provincial government, the Supreme Court followed its previous decision in the *Dosso case* and reiterated that no law could be declared void merely because it came into conflict with fundamental rights.[134] Shahab-ud-din and Rehman JJ kept their position in *Dosso case.* Cornelius once again emphasized that the words that the country "shall be governed as nearly as may be in accordance with the late Constitution (of 1956)" is 'undervalued' He based his opinion on the observation of the last nine months and found no threat posed by fundamental rights in writs, other than preventive detention, to the paramount authority of the new regime.[135] In a way, Cornelius was trying to ease/minimize the anxiety of the military about fundamental rights. Cornelius wanted fundamental rights in the constitution to be present so that their existence could make them enforceable. For Munir, the Constitution is abrogated and not repealed. Sovereignty is not deriving its authority from the Constitution but from outside.[136]

Who dissolved the assembly and why? What new role was given to the judiciary after this outright exertion of hegemonic power to kick start modernization so as to reshuffle the class formations in Pakistan? To understand this we are to dialectically connect these decisions with changes in the structures outside these decisions.

2.9.1 Revolution/Evolution or Preventing 'Revolution'

The secondary literature suggests that President Mirza dissolved the 1958 assembly, and the courts justified it on the basis of doctrine of necessity.[137] But, who advised the president to dissolve the assembly? According to Ayub's diary (2007), CJ Munir was under the impression that General Ayub advised Iskander Mirza to do so. Later, during his exile, Mirza told Munir CJ (then retired) that Ayub was not consulted. Ayub was under the impression that Munir was responsible for that.

[133]Marri, supra note 89, 16.

[134]*Province of East Pakistan v Md. Mehdi Ali Khan*, PLD 1959 SC 387.

[135]*Ibid* 396.

[136]*Ibid* 413.

[137]ZK Maluka, *The myth of Constitutionalism in Pakistan*, (Oxford University Press, Karachi, 1995) 175.

Munir explained that he advised Mirza to allow elections to take place and let inevitable chaos develop so that he could declare emergency. Mirza was not sure he would be elected again and hence he abrogated the constitution.[138] For Munir, Ayub was not only behind the 1954 dissolution of assembly but the 1958 coup as well.[139] Mohammad Ali gave an interview to Shorish Kashmiri (that appeared in The Pakistan Times) wherein he said that Ayub was over-ambitious and conspired with Ghulam Muhammad and Mirza to diminish constituent assemblies. Of course, Ayub denied this in his diary.[140] Apart from Ayub's denial about any involvement, it is clear that Ayub was in the U.S. when the assemblies of 1954 were dissolved. Upon hearing the news, he wrote a full program of an alternative system.[141] He did not like the constitution and political system as the 1956 Constitution was a "hotch-potch of alien concepts" and brought confusion by distributing power between the Prime Minister and President and having no focal point of authority.[142] Even the Justice Shahab-ud-din Commission Report (Constitution Commission) [143] was against the dismissed legislature of 1958 as there was political interference in administrative matters rather than interference with the legislature. This caused failures of parliamentary democracy.[144] We see the nexus of civil-military bureaucracy and judiciary throughout this case. Though relevant and extensively debated, our quest has to go beyond Mirza's dishonesty, Ayub's ambitions, and Munir's wrong decision, to ask, why did they all agree to dissolve that assembly?

There was a strong decision by the hegemonic block (metropolitan bourgeoisie) under the leadership of U.S. imperialism to advance vigorously the modernization project in developing countries. The hegemonic class started bringing the fragmented and weak reigning under its control. Ayub was in U.S. at that time and Muhammad Ali Bogra an ambassador in the U.S. for several years came with American aid as prime minister from 17 April 1953 to 11 August 1955. Ch Muhammad Ali as prime minister (11 August 1955 to September 1956) extended reliance on hegemonic class very fast. After this H.S. Suhrawardy (13 September 1956 to 18 October 1957) as the Prime Minister attached great importance to SEATO and the Baghdad Pact and lent unqualified support to the West's policies in Hungary and Middle East.[145]

---

[138]C Baxter (ed) *Diaries of Field Marshal Mohammad Ayub Khan*: *1966-1972* (Oxford University Press, Karachi, 2007) 116.

[139]Munir, *supra* note 52, 92, see M Munir, Days I Remember, *Pakistan Times* (11 November 1968), in Chaudhry, *supra* note 44, 89.

[140]Baxter, *supra* note 138, 322.

[141]Khan, *supra* note 61, 188.

[142]*Ibid* 188, 54.

[143]This commission was formed by Ayub after his overthrow to propose a new political set up. It was headed by Justice Muhammad Shahb-ud-din and its members were Azizuddin Ahmad, Muhammad Sharif, Naseer A Seikh, Abu Sayeed Chowdhary, DM Barori, Arbab Ahmad Ali Jan, Aftabuddin Ahmad, Sardar Habibullah, and Obeid-ur-Rahman Nizam.

[144]Report of the Constitution Commission, 1961 (Karachi, 1962) 6.

[145]Munir, *supra* note 52, 84.

But all these arrangements to use civil and military bureaucracy by the hegemonic bloc was due to the thin mass base of the reigning class. Waseem explains that the Muslim League split into many groups, the last one being the Republican Party, which was formed in 1957. The Republican Party (180 members) and the Awami League (120 members) were the 'statist' parties, which dominated the legislature, and gave legitimacy to the parliamentary arrangement, without having a mandate from the masses. Indeed, the dominant political parties were reluctant to go to the masses, and were instead, born and reborn within the legislature.[146] The assembly was no more than a battlefield of the dominant parties. Between 1956 and 1957, 72 bills passed out of which 50 were ordinances.[147] The class base of the legislature was the landed elite with almost no capitalist class, at least in West Pakistan.[148] The main concerns of these parties were the control of the population and the discrediting of the Communist Party, rather than gaining legitimacy with voters.[149] The bureaucracy had even less concern with legitimacy. It wished only to acknowledge representatives who could control the population. This form of governance was easily justified by the U.S. approach to modernization, which supported a concept of elite democracy as an appropriate countervail to the upsurge of popular participation and democracy unleashed by anti-colonial struggles.

The reigning class, consisting dominantly of landlords from West Pakistan, were trying to unite under Liaqat Ali Khan and his assassination in 1951 deprived them of a leadership to bring other classes from East Pakistan under its hegemony and pose a challenge to imperialist hegemony or reach a better compromise. There had not been a majority party with a recognized leader in National Assembly.[150] The government changed six times in seven years after Liaqat. The Republican Party of landlords existed only in 1956 National Assembly under the leadership of Malik Feroz Khan Noon's government (December 1957 to October 1958). Under his leadership, the landed class justified the existence of landlordism and stopped land reforms.[151]

According to Waseem, the 1958 coup was not a military but rather a civilian arrangement to stop the 1958 elections. However, it did not carry any ideological content.[152] Newberg has also discussed the lack of serious ideological questions in

[146]Waseem, *supra* note 6, 118.

[147]M Ahmad, *Government and Politics in Pakistan* (Space Publishers, Karachi, 1970) 120.

[148]Habib Bank gave Rs. 80 million as a loan equal to half of the revenue, see Rehman, *supra* note 47. The statement of Industrial policy came in 1948. This was the beginning of a capitalist class. In 1950s, 99% growth was through Import Substitute Industrialization (ISI), see AR Kemal, Patterns and growth of Pakistan's Industrial Sector in Khan, *supra* note 48.

[149]Waseem (2007) thesis is that the bureaucracy cannot rule without legitimacy, and it did not trust that the political leadership could preserve the state's legitimacy, see Waseem, *supra* note 6, 87.

[150]Munir, *supra* note 52, 83.

[151]Munir, *supra* note 52, 89, 91.

[152]Waseem, *supra* note 6, 143.

Pakistan's constitution. In her analysis, the conflict is between the vice-regal system and the liberal conflict within the elite.[153] Chief Justice Munir, according to her, was secular but pro-establishment, whereas Cornelius was in favour of Islamic jurisprudence but was against the establishment. She concludes, "[a]lthough the regimes would change from civilian to military and from populist to authoritarian to dictatorship, the question they posed about democracy and equality were similar". That is why each regime with each new constitution only puts forward a "slightly revised role for the superior courts".[154] Newberg did not provide any details of Munir being secular or that Cornelius was religious. Similarly, she could not articulate the model of political development in the theory and practice of Cornelius and Munir CJs which connected to their decisions and writings. Above all, this is not particular to Newberg, quest for 'ideological' content definitely is confusing within the liberal framework or an 'institutionalist-functionalist' understanding. However, it can be explained in terms of class formation (as result of class struggle), a particular state form with an ideological content.

Departing from above analyses, the toppling of the 1958 election must be understood 'ideologically', as an attempt at the imposition of a controlled democracy. Key here is that the Communist Party of Pakistan (CPP), Progressive Writers Association (PWA) and Democratic Students Federation (DSF) had been banned; the communists had gone underground and taken refuge in the National Awami Party, and the NAP was definitely going to win the elections.[155] As explained above, the reigning class was fragmented and dispersed, unable to combat that challenge. By preventing the elections, the hegemonic imperialist class placed the juridico-bureaucratic structure as its seat of power ensuring the smooth steering of political development. This ensured that the communist movement would have no space from which to emerge.

The judiciary agreed with this arrangement. For Anwar-ul-Haq CJ the founding father Jinnah also praised 'evolution and not revolution'.[156] According to Newberg, Chief Justice Munir's persistent question during the hearing reflected serious worries about the prospect of violent upheavals in Pakistan. Interestingly, while mentioning the 1953 riots, Newberg ignores the *Pindi Conspiracy case* and the banning of CPP, PWA and DSF. Chief Justice Munir repeatedly pointed out that if there is no power of dissolution of the assembly, only revolution is left. In the *Maulvi Tamizuddin Khan* case, a concern was raised: what would be the position of

---

[153]PR Newberg, *supra* note 90, 10.

[154]*Ibid* 119.

[155]National Awami Party (NAP) was formed in 1957 in Dhaka. It was predominantly a Left wing party. NAP, in alliance with Awami League (a party of Bengali nationalism) was going to win the scheduled elections of 1959.

[156]S Anwar-ul-Haq, Quaid-i-Azam as a Constitutionalist, a paper read at the Third Jurist Conference held on 9 December, 1976 at Karachi, in Anwar-ul-Haq, *supra* note 28, 255.

the court if the assembly got inoculated by communist ideas? Chief Justice Munir's prompt response was 'Revolution with a capital R'. To this, the Advocate General responded 'Dissolution with a capital D'.[157] This clearly shows the concerns of the executive and judiciary in Pakistan.[158] Bureaucracy, according to Braibanti (1999) was very clear that "all were united, self-preservation if for no other reason, in their belief that the Civil Services of Pakistan-CSP was an elite group whose destiny, inherited from the ICS, was to govern Pakistan. Virtually all were opposed to radical reform".[159]

Chief Justice Munir also expressed these feelings on his retirement in the 1960s, saying the country was on the brink of a revolution and hence the court had to decide between anarchy and order. The bias of the Pakistani judiciary against the prospect of revolution was so extreme that one of the justices, who later became Chief Justice of the Supreme Court, Anwar-ul-Haq, announced while addressing the world delegates in Ghana that there is nothing revolutionary in his paper as no judge has so far been awarded the Nobel Prize for his revolutionary ideas.[160] For him, the changes in the existing laws in developing countries are an instrument of social revolution, "so as to forestall violent and abrupt changes".[161] The anti-communist ideas of Munir, Cornelius, S.A. Rahman CJs and other cold warrier jurists like A.K. Brohi, Sharifuddin Pirzada are discussed in the next chapter when they came strongly to the surface of intellectual combat seeing socialism as a successful political slogan in late 1960s and throughout 1970s.

The point made so far is that the 'ideological content' of the 1958 coup was to stop revolution,[162] a desire for a deeper and broader democracy that had been unleashed by anti-colonial struggle. Here, Chief Justice Munir and Justice Cornelius both stood against 'revolution' (socialist modernization) in spite of dissenting opinions. They stood for a state-formation of nation-building under capitalist modernization and a consequent model of 'political development', not for democracy versus dictatorship. For this, one is to look beyond the legal decisions to their ideas and involvement with 'modernization'.

Before we conclude this part, it is important to note here that other Commonwealth countries also 'benefitted' from the *Dosso case* as they were

[157]Newberg, *supra* note 90, 48.

[158]It is pertinent to note that up until this point, under the excuse of *Pindi Conspiracy* case, all the Communist Party leadership had already been arrested and in 1954 the Communist Party and its fronts like Progressive Writers' Association and Democratic Students Federation had been banned.

[159]Braibanti, *supra* note 104, 46.

[160]S Anwar-ul-Haq, Role of Law in a Developing Society, in, Anwar-ul-Haq, *supra* note 28, 83. This essay was a lecture delivered at the State House, Accra, on 7 October 7 1976 in connection with the Centenary Celebrations of the Supreme Court of Ghana.

[161]*Ibid* 92.

[162]Even if the anti-establishment/Left forces were not as strong, they did create fear in the elite. This was exaggerated in the overall cold war environment.

passing through similar problems in the nation-building project.[163] Nigeria faced the same type of military coups and used the same justification through the doctrine of necessity as Pakistan.[164] India used this justification during the emergency imposed by Indira Gandi.[165] Munir clearly used it as a legal principle of common law countries.[166] As far as the doctrine of necessity is concerned, Dieter Conrad notes that the political question was how the court should react to the suspension of the constitution and revolutionary changes in the constitution. For him, looking at cases in Commonwealth,[167] there are two basic types of cases; first are 'necessity' cases[168] and second are Kelsen cases.[169] Historically, for the writer, the doctrine of necessity was not a novel doctrine in Anglo-American and Continental European jurisprudence. British courts recognized the 1976 Revolution and German Reichsgericht recognized the November Revolution of 1918 as both these established the valid order.

But there was a need to have an arrangement more than the doctrine of necessity. The Ayub and Cornelius nexus brought this in Pakistan in the form of 1962 Constitution as a local variant of U.S. constitutional model during the decade of modernization in Pakistan.

---

[163]A list in this regard is given by Attorney General of Pakistan in *Begum Nusrat Bhuttoo v The Federation of Pakistan and others,* PLD 1977 SC 657. see L Wolf-Phillips, Constitutional Legitimacy in Pakistan 1977-82, in, WP Zingel, Stephanie Zingel, & Ave Lallemant (eds) *Pakistan in the 80s: Law & Constitution* (Vanguard, Lahore, 1985) 37, 70.

[164]P EhiOshio, Esq, Military Coups D' Etat in Nigeria: Rationale, Legality and Effects on Constitutionalism *PLJ* 1986 Journal Section 37, See D Conard, In Defense of the Continuity of Law: Pakistan's Courts in Crisis of State XIII *PLD* Journal Section (1985) 2.

[165]Emergency imposed by Indira Gandhi from 1975 to 1977 (21 months) under Article 352 (1) of the Indian Constitution.

[166]While commenting on *Nusrat Bhutto case* 1977, 22 years after the *Dosso case,* Chief Justice Munir made clear that he treated the doctrine of necessity as a common law principle applicable to all civilized governments. He rejected prefixes or suffixes of 'extra', '*supra*' with constitutional as all were authorized by the constitution, see Munir, *supra* note 52, 256, 271; See also, MM Stavsky, The Doctrine of Necessity in Pakistan, *16 Cornell Int' LJ* (1983) 341.

[167]Like *Madzimbamuto v Lardner- Burke of Rhodesia*; Discussions with reference to the Pakistani cases are also cited by Dieter Conrad, for example C Palley, The judicial process: U. D. I. and the Southern Rhodesian Judiciary (1967) *Mod L Rev* 263, see A de Smith, Constitutional law years in revolutionary situations *West Ont L Rev* (1968) 93, see also RWM Dias, Legal politics: norms behind the Grundnorm 26 *Cambridge LJ* (1968) 233, see also FM Brookfield, The courts, Kelsen, and the Rhodesian revolution 19 *University of Toronto Law* Review (1969) 326, see also RS Welsh, The function of the judiciary in a coup d'etat 87 *SALJ* (1970) 168, see also A Ojo The search for a Grundnorm in Nigeria-The Lakanmi case 20 *ILCQ* (1971) 117, see also JM Eekelaar, Principles of revolutionary legality in *Oxford Essays in Jurisprudence*, 2nd Series, (Oxford, 1973) 22, see also TKK Iyer, Constitutional Law in Pakistan: Kelsen in the courts 21 *Am J Comp L* (1973) 759, see Conrad, *supra* note 164, see LW Phillips, Constitutional Legitimacy in Pakistan 1977-82, in, Zingel, Zingel, & Lallemant, *supra* note 163, 123, 168 fn 2.

[168]*Special Reference* case (1955), *Mir Hasan* case (1969), *Asma Jilani* case (1972), *Begum Nusrat Bhutto* case (1977) as will be l cited and discussed in their order.

[169]Like the *Dosso* case.

2.9.2 *Ayub 'the Modernizer' and Pakistan as the Experimental Lab*

The late 1950s through the 1960s was the era of modernization theory taking root in Pakistan. It was led by Ayub politically and Cornelius judicially with the bureaucracy implementing modernization. According to Ayub, in his design of political development, people and their opinion were irrelevant and a "responsible government" should not be "prisoner of wayward public opinion".[170] Pakistan needed a strong, not popular government, Ayub argued.[171] His idea of 'basic democracy' (BD system) was to develop a controlled democracy with which the landed elite of Sindh and Punjab, as a reigning' class could also be controlled. In entering rural politics, he had to contend with the issue of land reform. Ayub stated that big land holdings impeded the free exercise of political institutions and could not flourish in democracy as landlords enjoyed protected constituencies. So in fixing a ceiling of landownership, the target was to build a strong middle class and land reforms as the '*Magna Carta of Rights'* for peasants. But private ownership was not to be destroyed.[172] He thus connected the democratic content of the new Constitution with land reforms.[173]

Munircalled it a 'controlled democracy'.[174] Ayesha Siddiqa argues that the threat of land reforms were a coercive tool to discipline the landlords.[175] I agree with this position but its theoretical explanation is that through the threat of these reforms, the juridico-bureaucratic structure got the consent of the reigning class for the hegemony of the metropolitan bourgeoisie. That is why these land reforms were halfhearted. Capitalist agriculture was part of modernization, and the landed class greatly benefitted from it. The state also created an industrialist class that had no political power but relied entirely on state bureaucratic power.[176] I argue that these three classes, plus the metropolitan bourgeoisie were the classes behind the state formation as led by Ayub. Ayub only targeted politicians who were part of the urban-based Jamat-e-Islami and the nationalist and communist alliance (National Awami Party).

How is the judiciary connected with this project of capitalist modernization in Pakistan? How were legal decisions, discourse, and the judiciary a crucial link in this project?

---

[170]Khan, *supra* note 61, 206.

[171]*Ibid* 213.

[172]I will evaluate this claim later.

[173]Khan, *supra* note 61, 87.

[174]Munir, *supra* note 52, 99.

[175]A Siddiqa, *Military Inc.: Inside Pakistan's Military economy* (Oxford University Press, Karachi, 2007) 75.

[176]H Alavi, Class and State in Pakistan, in, H Gardezi & J Rashid (eds), *Pakistan: The Unstable State* (Vanguard Books, Lahore, 1983).

2.9.3 Judiciary's Modernization 'Coalition'

Ralph Braibanti, a modernization theorist in the tradition of Huntington, met CJ Cornelius at a conference of the Southeast Asia Treaty Organization (SEATO) in 1958. He returned to Pakistan to become the Chief Advisor and Professor of the Civil Services Academy in 1960 in Lahore. At the time, he was on leave from Duke University and was on contract with United States Agency for International Development (USAID).[177] In his memoirs, he mentions Kyani CJ of West Pakistan High Court, Cornelius CJ, Nasim Hassan CJ, Mahmud Ali Qasuri and Rabia Sultana Qari from the judicial side and Mian Aminuddin (the first local head of civil services after 13 years of independence) and Agha Hamid (who succeeded Amiruddin).

When Braibanti returned to the U.S. in 1964, he gathered 26 scholars and government officials interested to work on Pakistani issues and launched the American Institute of Indian Studies. His students included Craig Baxter, Charles Kennedy, Afak Hayder and Lawrence Ziring. S.M. Haider was Braibanti's student and on his advice wrote a dissertation on the writ jurisdiction in Pakistan. He worked for the Law Reform Commission until his death. All above jurists and social scientists wrote extensively about judiciary and state of postcolonial Pakistan.[178] From Braibanti's account along with the speeches of A.R. Kayani and Cornelius CJ, one should not doubt the strong influence these jurists had on the civil and military bureaucracy leading modernization in Pakistan.

Chief Justice M.R. Kayani of Lahore High Court, who served as a judge from 1958 to 1962, headed the Civil Services Association for 7 years, which were crucial in terms of political and economic restructuring under modernization.[179] After him, Chief Justices S.A. Rahman and Shahabuddin headed the association, both from ICS. The judiciary was in a marriage of convenience with the bureaucracy in the first two formative decades (1947–1967) of Pakistan. Chief Justice Anwarul Haq (1970), hailing from CSP himself, mentioned how civil services produced men of judicial acumen like Shahabuddin, Cornelius, Rahman and Kayani.[180] The Chief Justice of the East Pakistan High Court, Amin Ahmad, also commented on the bureaucratic–judicial relation, explaining in 1970 that the Pakistani judiciary never interfered with the executive.[181]

Braibanti found that the Civil Services Academy was divided in two groups, old-line conservatives (pre-partition Indian Civil Servants) and new entrants

---

[177]Braibanti, *supra* note 104, xix.

[178]Discussion about their writings is in the coming chapters.

[179]See the presidential address delivered at the seventh annual dinner of the CSP Association in MR Kayani, Half Truths, in, MR Kayani, *The Whole Truth*, 39.

[180]S Anwar-ul-Haq (1970), Civil Service of Pakistan and its Critics, in, Anwar-ul-Haq, *supra* note 28, 301, address of welcome to the president of Pakistan, General Yahya Khan, on the annual dinner of West Pakistan Civil Services of Pakistan-C S P on 10 April 1970.

[181]JA Ahmad, Independence of Judiciary in Pakistan XXII *PLD* (1970) Journal Section 135, 138.

post-partition. Kayani CJ represented the old conservatives who considered themselves as custodians of the 'steel frame' of this service and, and hence unsupportive of reforms. Cornelius CJ was with new entrants wanting reforms to accommodate the needs of modernization. Kayani CJ wanted more civil services officers to join the judiciary[182] so as to make a liaison to correct the errors of administration.[183] Administration here represents popular ministries and politicians/administration[184] who were busy 'reforming' bureaucracy and Kayani resisting their undue transfers, appointments as officer on special duty—OSDs, and salaries in this process.[185] He strongly defended bureaucracy and held contempt for ministers.[186] For Kayani, the roots of political prejudices against civil services lies in the rivalry between bureaucracy as British period 'frame of imperialism' and political ambitions of politicians.[187]

On the other hand, Cornelius CJ was of the view that the CSP had been compartmentalized and was caste-structured.[188] As a result, it was not advancing beyond a certain level. He wanted it to be restructured, in order to be attuned with the political philosophy of the new state. Cornelius was part of a group of new reform-minded young Civil Service students, looking to establish a national character to the Service. He grafted Islam to the British-oriented structure as a way of bringing this national character. Kayani criticized, rather ridiculed, Government of Pakistan, Report of the Pay and Service Commission, 1962 written by Cornelius.[189] He showed how there was a connection between Cornelius report and the Constitution of 1962 by Ayub.[190]

How should the judiciary, being the dominant part of the bureaucracy, scrutinize the actions of the administration/politicians against bureaucracy? Justice Munir

---

[182]MR Kayani, Half Truths, in, Kayani, *supra* note 179, 34.

[183]MR Kayani, Not the Whole Truth, in, Kayani, *supra* note 179, 22, address of welcome to Major-General Sikander Mirza, President of Pakistan, at the 2nd annual dinner of C.S. P. Association on 17 March 1957.

[184]Comments of Justice SA Rahman in the foreword of MR Kayani, Half Truths, in, Kayani, *supra* note 179, iii; Kalyani strongly defended bureaucracy and contempt for ministers, see page 24.

[185]MR Kayani, Half Truths, in, Kayani, *supra* note 179, 12.

[186]MR Kayani, Not the Whole Truth, in, Kayani, *supra* note 179, 24, address of welcome to Major-General Skander Mirza, president of Pakistan, at the 2nd annual dinner of C.S. P. Association on 17 March 1957.

[187]MR Kayani, Half Truths, in, Kayani, *supra* note 179, 7.

[188]AR Cornelius, Equality of Opportunity in Public Service, in, Braibanti, *supra* note 108. This is also included in speeches as Appendices 10-15 in Braibanti, *supra* note 104, 466. This was an address before the Rotary Club of Lahore on 1 September 1961. This fact is described by Braibanti also in 1999, see Braibanti, *supra* note 104, 44.

[189]Presidential address titled "Use Your Intelligence Occasionally" delivered at the annual dinner of CSP Association on the 8 April 1961, the Nawab of Kalabagh being the guest of honour, see MR Kayani, Half Truths, in, Kayani, *supra* note 179, 38.

[190]An address delivered on 29 October at a dinner given by C SP Association titled "The Pay Commission and the Religious Consciousness of Islam, see MR Kayani, Half Truths, in, Kayani, *supra* note 179), 63.

believed in judicial restraint. The writ jurisdiction of the superior courts introduced in 1954 was retained in the 1956 Constitution. The power to issue writs of *habeas corpus, mandamus, prohibition, quo-warranto* and *certiorari* were vested with High Courts.[191] But the courts, even the Supreme Court, only used writ jurisdiction in those matters which were judicial in nature.[192] The first case was *Muhammad Saeed v Election Petitions Tribunal,*[193] where an effort is made to create a formula of judicial resistance by Munir. The *Tariq Transport Company case*[194] is an example of said judicial restraint. Chief Justice Munir made clear that pure administrative actions do not come under the control of the judiciary with the power conferred by Article 70 of the 1956 Constitution. Only actions of *ultra vires*, refusal to exercise jurisdiction and deviation from prescribed procedure, can come under judicial control. From 1955 to August 1962, 14,000 writs were filed in two High Courts and many reached the Supreme Court. This made Pakistan "the most litigious society in the world" at that time.[195]

Kayani wanted to develop writ jurisdiction in British tradition. He was aware of the power of writ jurisdiction and found it as the flowers of paradise.[196] For him, after 1955 *Tamizuddin Khan case,* writ was taken away but we brought it back.[197] These dynamics were commented upon in *Snelson's* case.[198] Mr Snelson's talk titled 'The Transitional Constitution of 1958' was distributed during his address to section officers in Secretariat Training Institute Karachi. He remarked that the High Courts, while exercising the prerogative writs, were interfering with the government and causing "chaos, disruption, friction, usurpation of function, uncertainty, and public confusion". These remarks were found to be in contempt of court by the Lahore High Court of Chief Justice Kayani. The Supreme Court of Cornelius CJ upheld the decision. Snelson was fined, which was later suspended by the governor. For Kayani, Snelson gave poor advice to suspend writ jurisdiction.[199] But Kayani's advice was resisted by his colleagues also. Justice Syed Ikhlaque Hussain, Justice West Pakistan High Court, while reflecting on this controversy around writ jurisdiction warned about restraints which judiciary should observe. He added that this power is discretionary not obligatory, it should be used judicially.[200]

---

[191]Articles 22, 163, 170 of the 1956 Constitution, see Khan, *supra* note 23, 108.

[192]*Tariq Transport Company v Sargodha Bhera Bus Service*2 PSCR (1958) 71. A decision by a Regional Transport Authority about granting a route to a bus company without authority came under review for *certiorari* and HC nullified the decision of RTA.

[193]PLD 1957 SC 91.

[194]*Tariq Transport Company v Sargodha Bhera Bus Service* 2 PSCR (1958) 71.

[195]Braibanti, *supra* note 104, 42.

[196]MR Kayani, Not the Whole Truth, in, Kayani, *supra* note 179, 41, 61, 87.

[197]MR Kayani, Not the Whole Truth, in, Kayani, *supra* note 179, 18.

[198]*The State v Sir Edward Snelson*, PLD 1961 Supreme Court 237.

[199]MR Kayani, A judge May Laugh, in, Kayani, *supra* note 179, 7, reply to farewell address by the Karachi High Court Bar Association, Nov 1962.

[200]SI Hussain, Justice West Pakistan High Court, Writ Jurisdiction of Superior Courts in Pakistan *PLD* (1958) Journal Section, 1, 7.

In 1960, after the retirement of three of the five judges of Munir's Court and with the new Constitution of 1962, the old terminology was abandoned and judicial review jurisdiction was re-defined in clear and precise terms in Article 98 which has continued in Article 199 of the present Constitution.[201] Cornelius gave a summary of development of writ jurisdiction in the *Merajuddin case*.[202] Elsewhere he stated that the British did not grant writ jurisdiction to the Indians, which was there for seven centuries. Rather, they used Confucian paternalism to rule through local rulers with uncontrolled power to "put up people right".[203] He acknowledged how superior courts in Pakistan developed it, particularly late CJ Kayani. But Cornelius was also in favour of *droit administerat if* with its *Conseil d' Etat* (administrative tribunals of French Administrative Law). Kayani ridiculed the concept of *Conseil d' etat* of Cornelius.[204] Furthermore, these disputes generally do not merely involve a question of fact or of law, but one of policy as well. Cornelius put forth such a proposal in the 1959 convocation of Punjab University Law College and then in 1960 at a Rotary Club function in Lahore, and finally in the form of a full analysis addressing the All Pakistan Lawyer's Association. He expressed appreciation for such a system in the *Farid Sons Ltd. Case*. It is pertinent that Cornelius did not find Supreme Court prerogative powers to confine public officials inappropriate as it had been found in Great Britain.[205]

S.M. Haider explained this scheme of A.R. Cornelius towards the administration tribunals in Ayub's era. According to Cornelius, the state's involvement in social development projects made doctrines and precedents of ordinary law inappropriate. If disputes arising from an increase in the role of the state were to go through ordinary courts, they would be chocked full. Whereas, S.M. Haider continued developing this concept of administrative tribunals, and succeeded to convince Bhutto. Nasim Hassan Shah was also a great admirer of this scheme.[206]

It is not irrelevant to know Haider's position on this development of writ jurisdiction to judicial review to administrative tribunals in relation to the requirements of modernization, nation-building and institutional restructuring in Pakistan. Quite in line with the functionalist position of Parson, influenced by Lucian Pye, Haider is very clear that Max Weber is applicable with vigour on

---

[201] S Ahmed Justice (2006) *Good Governance and the Role of Judiciary*, International Jurists Conference, Islamabad on 50th birthday anniversary of the Supreme Court of Pakistan in the year 2006, last visited 27 Nov 2013, <http://www.supremecourt.gov.pk/ijc/ijc.htm>.

[202] *State of Pakistan v Mehrajuddin,* PSCR 1959 SC 34.

[203] AR Cornelius, Public Administration and the Law, *PLD* (1964) Journal Section, 1, 6, 7, address to the participants of third advance management course of National Institute of Public Administration (NIPA), Karachi, on 30 November 1963; See also AR Cornelius, Writ Jurisdiction of Superior Courts, *PLD* (1964), Journal Section 73, speech delivered at Civil Services Academy, Lahore on 25 April 1964.

[204] As claimed by Ralph Braibanti, see Braibanti, *supra* note 104, 47.

[205] SM Haider, Plea for Administrative Tribunals: Scheme Visualized by Justice AR Cornelius, XXI *PLD* (1969) Journal Section 164, See *Farid Sons Ltd v Govt of Pakistan*, PLD 1961 SC 537.

[206] NH Shah, Droit Administratif-A Study, *PLD* (1964) Journal Section 45.

Pakistan bureaucracy.[207] Being an instrumentalist, he thought that public administration as an instrument- and most important is how "it is used and for what purposes".[208] CSP needed technocrats for modernization, but they were looked down upon by the general cadre of civil services officers.[209] To pacify Kayani's resistance, he argued that the administrative law emphasizes on function and not on the structure of the bureaucracy.[210] Cornelius' report for him is well known all over the world for its 'realistic and pragmatic recommendations'.[211] Though Cornelius' report seems to be against 'colonial rule' legacy in civil service, but showing its immediate connection with modernization exposes its neo-colonial nature. Other comments about his anti-colonial nature are just opposition to 'western' as a cultural instant of social formation and not the economic and political ones. To sum up, the judiciary has induced administrative reforms very effectively through a number of cases.[212]

The positions of both these justices, Cornelius and Kayani CJs leading and resisting reforms in civil services, respectively, in the era of modernization, were related to the place of bureaucracy in their respective model or understanding of political development. In Kayani's formation, bureaucracy was trusted as a colonial perception as well as the U.K. tradition where bureaucracy was dominantly from landed aristocracy and respectable. As opposed to this, Cornelius' formation seemed to be the pressure of modernization with his own grafting of 'Islam' and 'national' character on it. This distrust of state and bureaucracy and the so-called 'constitutional limitations' are very particular to U.S. model of political development.

So far book discussed the close relation of the judiciary with civil and military bureaucracy. The difference in Kayani and Cornelius CJs understanding was the reflection of how they wanted to address the demands for reforms under modernization. What is the place of democracy and in favour of fundamental rights in their models of political development? In the following section we are going to challenge the common liberal understanding that Cornelius CJ was pro-democracy and fundamental rights as compared to Munir CJ based on the *Tamizuddin case* and the *Dosso case* of 1950s and later Cornelius' rights cases like the *Moudoodi case* etc. against Ayub. Similarly, Kayani is portrayed as pro-democracy, as opposed to Ayub. We will see that all of them were against the legislature and people and their opposition to dictators was only to the 'degree of dictatorship'. They all wanted controlled democracy. Above all, rights in this formation by Cornelius were a substitute for democratic deficit.

---

[207]SM Haider, *Public Administration and Administrative Law* (Law Times Publications, Lahore, 1973) 37.

[208]Haider, *supra* note 207, 42.

[209]SM Haider, Administrative Modernization, A Design for in Pakistan Academy for Rural Development, Peshawar (1968) 189, in, Haider, *supra* note 207, 12.

[210]Haider, *supra* note 207, 134.

[211]Haider, *supra* note 207, 40; for complete evaluation of Cornelius report see page 90.

[212]Haider gave a full list of these cases, see Haider, *supra* note 207, 85.

2.10 Democracy and Fundamental Rights in Political Development: A Critical Appraisal of Munir, Cornelius and Kayani CJs

2.10.1 Presidential System Like U.S.: Elite Democracy or Controlled Democracy?

Ayub was an advocate of the presidential system and argued that even the founding father of Pakistan, Jinnah, did not want a parliamentary system. In light of this, he set up a Commission to deliberate on the issue in 1959, and promised to accept their recommendations. Justice Muhammad Shahbuddin, from the Indian Civil Services, headed the Commission; he later became Chief Justice of the Supreme Court (3 May 1960–12 May 1960) after Munir CJ. Hamid Khan presents the head of this Commission as a person with high integrity but one under severe pressure from the Ayub.[213] On the other hand, W.G. Choudhry stated that the Commission was free from any duress,[214] the Commission admitting the same.[215] The Constitution Commission of 1960 headed by Justice Shahabuddin, while in favour of a parliamentary form of government, recommended a presidential form of government like in the U.S. The reasons were parliamentary failures, due to the absence of well-organized parties. The outcome of the recommendations of the Commission was the constitution of 1962, which allowed a strong president and indirect franchise, quite contrary to the requirement of parliamentary system. Ayub called it "a blending of democracy with discipline—the two prerequisites to running a free society with stable government and sound administration".[216]

In the minds of the judiciary, like that of executive and bureaucracy, the idea was not the project of securing democracy but of planting a democracy that would slowly emerge. Cornelius' later court decisions can be better understood in their relation to the Basic Democracy system. According to him, the Basic Democracies Order of 1959 gave power to the people who were supportive of the 1962 Constitution, and would get rid of the colonial legacies of ancestry, wealth and class. This is the core of Cornelius' political theory.[217] He was expecting Churchill's to emerge from BD system.[218] There was nothing democratic in the BD system but apart from its explanation as a form of controlled democracy, its only

---

213 Khan, *supra* note 23, 138.

214 As claimed by Khan (2009), See Khan, *supra* note 23, 41, 136.

215 Constitution Commission Report (Government of Pakistan, Karachi, 1961) 2.

216 Broadcast on 1 March 1962 in Khan, *supra* note 61, 216.

217 AR Cornelius, Constitution of Pakistan *PLD* (1967) Journal Section, 78, The essay was an address to the Pakistan Council for National Integration, Dacca, 15 June 1967.

218 AR Cornelius, Power of the "word" in Context of National Leadership: Need for Expressing Fundamental Rights in Language of Islamic Scriptures, *PLD* (1965) Journal Section 37, 42, speech at the inauguration ceremony of Silver Jubilee function of the rotary club of Hyderabad on 13 February 1965.

connection with Cornelius seems administrative reforms modernization.[219] Cornelius also appreciated the most controversial constitution of 1962 as an 'Act of Faith'.[220]

The involvement of the entire population in political life in post-colonies was a serious issue for modernization scholars. This participation of the population in the social order in the form of 'popular sovereignty' is usually called power sharing, power diffusion, politicization, mobilization or participation explosion. According to Braibanti, the ruling elite had no concern about the quality of participation in regards to "literacy, responsibility, understanding of issues, to the quality of civic culture generally".[221] The only emphasis was on increasing participation. Participation as power sharing was good but "nevertheless, we cannot overlook the stress and crisis caused by accelerated power- sharing".[222] Braibanti is very clear, the collapse of systems of newly independent states are not caused by corruption or infiltration or even institutional weakness but accelerated participation. He called it 'demand-conversion crises'. The solution is either to control this demand-conversion crisis through the bureaucracy and increasing the strength of the judiciary to handle crises like in Pakistan or prevent them as in India. In India, according to Braibanti, demand is contained, diffused and spatially diverted by a competent single mass party.[223] Ayub and Cornelius in Pakistan faced the same problem.

How did Chief Justice Cornelius view democracy? He found that elections, which raise ideological differences, were dangerous, for there was the "virus of revolution just below the surface".[224] Socialism was not an option for him, as Muslims did not have freedom there. Though socialism in USSR provided consumer goods, the main issue was that Marxism/socialism is "totally divorced from religious belief".[225] Cornelius found the armed forces had a distinguished position among 'responsible' (not representative-my comments) sections of the community.[226] The Basic Democracy model of Ayub seems perfectly suited to his philosophy.

---

[219]AR Cornelius, Issues of Theory, *PLD* (1967) Journal Section, 104, paper read at the International Conference on Theoretical Problems of Administrative Reforms in Developing Countries held at the Rockfeller Foundation Villa Serbelloni, Bellagio, Lake Como, Italy.

[220]AR Cornelius, Spirit of the Pakistan: An "Act of Faith", *PLD* (1967) Journal Section 78, 90 speech at the Dacca Center of Pakistan Council for National Integration on 15 June 15 1967.

[221]R Braibanti (1964), The Role of Law in the Political Development of Pakistan, in, Braibanti, *supra* note 104, 95. This essay was first published in RR Wilson (ed) *International Comparative Law of the Commonwealth* (NC: Durham University Press, Durham, 1968).

[222]*Ibid.*

[223]R Braibanti (1964), The Role of Law in the Political Development of Pakistan, in Braibanti, *supra* note 104, 95. This essay was first published in Wilson, *supra* note 221.

[224]AR Cornelius (1978), Letter to Braibanti, in, Braibanti, *supra* note 104, 196, 198.

[225]AR Cornelius, Role of Religion in Social Welfare as Enjoyed by the Constitution, *PLD* (1965) Journal Section 127, 129, speech delivered at the inauguration of first in-service training course for social welfare offices at NIPA, Lahore, 7 July 7 1965.

[226]Cornelius, *supra* note 31, 11, address delivered at a gathering of Military officials at GHQ, Rawalpindi on 11 July 1962.

One should not be mistaken that Kayani CJ was against Ayub and hence was a democrat. He looked down upon the legislature, voters and the people and only CSP in leading the country for him.[227] In his political hierarchy there was contempt for the assembly. Courts are better and should exercise writ jurisdiction against administration/executive- who are politicians and technocrats. The Bar was worse than the administration in this formation.[228] We'll see how the bar was the most potent voice for participation, which annoyed juridico-bureaucratic structure. Kayani was not hopeful about the BD system, which was trying to bring "Churchills to the forefront".[229] Apart from Munir CJ's decisions against democracy, he believed that there could not be a participatory democracy due to lack of education etc. Therefore a form of government, which can promote growth, should be the priority that can bring conditions for the change in the form of government.[230]

To sum up, during modernization, all the jurists, including Cornelius, supported the notion of a controlled democracy—a version of U.S. liberal democracy with, indirect elections of the president, a strong presidential system like the U.S., bureaucracy leading modernization and judicial review vested in Superior Courts, and fundamental rights as a substitute for the deficit in the above controlled democracy.

2.10.2 The Cornelius 'Rights' Approach to Substitute for the Democratic Deficit?

This part of the book will attempt to understand the exaggerated difference of the Cornelius Courts with Ayub on the issue of fundamental rights, which is widely cited in regards to cases like the *Moudoodi case* and *Shorish Kashmiri case*.[231]

Ayub's modernization was liberal and some of its aspects were not liked by the Islamic forces, such as the family ordinance. Reacting to this, Ayub condemned the Jamaat-e-Islami leader, Maulana Abul Ala Maudoodi, and declared the Jamaat-e-Islami as an 'unlawful association' under section 16 of the Criminal Law Amendment Act, 1908 as amended by Ordinance of XXI of 1960. This declaration

---

[227]MR Kayani, Not the Whole Truth, in, Kayani, *supra* note 179, 12, 35.

[228]MR Kayani, Not the Whole Truth, in, Kayani, *supra* note 179, 43.

[229]MR Kayani, Not the Whole Truth, in, Kayani, *supra* note 179, 106.

[230]M Munir, Days I Remember, *Pakistan Times*, 11 November 1968 in Chaudhry, *supra* note 44, 94.

[231]Hamid Khan's (2009) analysis of Cornelius court is that his court kept its independence and gave a ruling to protect fundamental rights which set the path of future judicial activism, constitutional interpretation under judicial review, and due process of law, Khan, *supra* note 23, 187. According to SM Haider (1967), a balance was struck between public order concerns and individual liberty by the Cornelius courts while using judicial review of administrative tribunals, see SM Haider, Judicial Review of Administrative Discretion in Pakistan *PLD* (1967) Journal Section as cited by Newberg (1995), see also, Newberg, *supra* note 90, 106.

was challenged in the West Pakistan High Court, as well as by Maudoodi in the Dhaka High Court. The former dismissed the petition, whereas the latter accepted the petition and declared the notification to be without binding effects.[232] In appeals against both the decisions, the Supreme Court accepted Maudoodi's appeal and rejected the government's appeal unanimously.[233]

There are some other cases where the judiciary's defence of fundamental rights is exaggerated under the leadership of Chief Justice A.R. Cornelius, like in the *Malik Ghulam Jilani's* case, *Shorish Kashmiri's* case and *Abdul Baqi Balooch* case. Through these cases, according to Hamid Khan, a strong foundation of 'judicial review' and 'due process of law' was laid down by the courts of Pakistan.[234] During protests against the Tashkent Declaration,[235] many political leaders like Jilani, Nawabzada Nusrullah and Sardar Shaukat Hayat Khan were kept in detention under the Defence of Pakistan Rules and the Defence of Pakistan Ordinance of 1965. The West Pakistan High Court rejected their petitions. The Supreme Court, in its judgment, accepted Nawabzada's appeal and rejected that of Hayat and Jilani.[236] Here, the court laid down some broad principles and guidelines for cases of political detainees. Against the detention of a known journalist, Shorish Kashmiri, the High Court of West Pakistan accepted the petition and the Supreme Court upheld this judgment.[237] Abdul Baqi Balooch, as a Baloch activist and a strong opponent of Ayub, was under detention. West Pakistan High Court (Karachi Bench) rejected his appeal.[238]

These judgments defended against the arbitrary use of laws like the Defence of Pakistan Ordinance. But this does not explain what was really going on. Let us discuss the nature of rights in these cases as it evolved from courts proceeded by Chief Justice Munir to Chief Justice Cornelius. The 1956 constitution used the term 'fundamental rights' and these rights were justiciable.[239] On the other hand, the 1962 constitution did not use the words fundamental rights but included a few of these rights (speech, association and religion) in a chapter titled 'Principles of Law Making and Policy'; however, they were not justiciable. Later, with an amendment, the label 'fundamental rights' was given to these rights and their enforcement was assured through courts.[240] It was claimed as a form of the Bill of Rights by the Law

[232]*Tamizuddin Ahmad v The Government of East Pakistan* PLD 1964 Dhaka 795.

[233]*Maulana Abul Ala Maudoodi v Govt of West Pakistan*, PLD 1964 SC 673.

[234]Khan, *supra* note 23, 187.

[235]Ayub signed this declaration after the 1965 war with India and politicians presented this agreement as losing after winning the war.

[236]*Malik Ghulam Jilani v The Government of West Pakistan*, PLD 1967 SC 373.

[237]*Govt of Pakistan v Begum Shorish Kashmiri*, PLD 1969 SC 14.

[238]*Abdul Baqi Balooch v The Govt of Pakistan*, PLD 1968 SC 313.

[239]Articles 5(1), 5(2), 6, 22, 14, 16, 17, 15, 8, 10, 11, 18, 13, 20.

[240]*Constitution [First Amendment] Act*, 1963, According to Hamid, it was due to pressure of the people, restoration of political activities and the election of Moulvi Tamizuddin as speaker and Muhammad Ali Bogra as Prime Minister; (Remember Prime Minister Bogra was a staunch supporter of US type constitutional arrangements), see Khan, *supra* note 23, 157.

Minister, Chief Justice (Ret. as he then was) Munir. Placing it in a modernization design, we can understand that the judiciary had already been empowered to check the excesses of the administration or executive under Article 98, and through this amendment the legislature was made subordinate to courts.

First of all, the strong presidential design of the constitution half-heartedly wanted a legislature and now the grip around it was tightened by the juridico-bureaucratic design of fundamental rights. Second, this 'supremacy of judiciary' is a part of political but not economic modernization. This means that the judiciary was tied with a 'qualifying clause' not to interfere in economic modernization, which included the ordinances and regulation regarding land reforms, family ordinance, and other socio-economic concerns within the design of capitalist modernization. The interesting point to be noted here is the perceived contrast in the views of Chief Justices Munir and Cornelius around their approaches towards rights and democracy. Both were the part of the same project of political development from Ayub to Yahya. After retirement, Chief Justice Munir became the Law Minister for Ayub's government and Cornelius was the Chief Justice. Cornelius was law minister of the next dictator, Yahya Khan. Probably, S.M. Haider is the architect of certain position about Cornelius as the promoter of rights and democracy in Pakistan vis-à-vis Munir CJ which later is towed by Cornelius collectives in the years come. For him, Cornelius established the standards of 'reasonable restriction', 'reasonable suspicion' and 'reasonable satisfaction' in the *Mouddodi case*, *Jilani case* and above *Shaukat Ali case*.[241] Maybe, but the connection of fundamental rights with democracy in Cornelius formation as described by Haider and later Lombardi is problematic. Haider thought that Cornelius wanted the consent of the governed and that "the government should be by popular consent".[242] Similarly, toeing the same line, Lombardi tried to find some insights for the U.S. even in Cornelius's connection Islam and liberal democracy.[243] I have a different take on this issue.

First of all, the nature of rights in Cornelius's Court is not very different from that of Munir's Courts. In the *Dosso* case,[244] Cornelius believed that the natural rights theory in the absence of fundamental rights guarantees a positivist form in a constitution. He found rights apart from the 1956 constitution. Chief Justice Munir, on the other hand, relied on legal positivism, but did not refute Cornelius's concept of natural rights. What happens when the constitution is abrogated? Munir was of the opinion that these rights are fundamental, cannot be taken away and do not need the law. Justice Shahabuddin, Amiruddin Ahmad and Cornelius agreed on that point, but Cornelius wrote a separate opinion. He based his opinion on natural

---

[241]Haider, *supra* note 207, 13.

[242]Haider, *supra* note 207, 203.

[243]CB Lombardi, Can Islamizing a Legal System Even Help Promote Liberal Democracy?: A View from Pakistan, 7:3 *U St Thomas LJ* 649.

[244]*Supra* note 131.

rights but noted that when the constitution is not in force, there is concern about violation. This position is not very different than Munir's.

The difference between the Chief Justices became clearer in the *Mehdi Ali Khan* case. The courts retained the position in regards to fundamental rights established in the *Dossocase* and declined to review it.[245] Justice Cornelius accepted the presence of fundamental rights as natural rights in the *Dosso* case, but argued they were not justiciable. They could only be justiciable when present in a constitution. Chief Justice Munir was clear not to challenge the regime and allowed it to alter the state structure. Thus, the court accepted the presence of fundamental rights but absence of judicial powers. This shows the extent of the difference between Cornelius and Munir's courts. Even in the *Mia nIftikhar-ud-din* case,[246] courts refused their power to challenge the regime. In appeal, Justice Kaikaus accepted the plea of the government to amend and interfere with the fundamental rights and gave immunity to those acts from judicial scrutiny, stating, "[e]ven if the central government did contravene a principle of natural justice, its order would not be liable to challenge in a court".[247]

After the promulgation of the 1962 constitution, the Cornelius court began a review of cases involving justiciable rights.[248] S.M. Haider showed, by statistical analysis, how the rights cases based on natural justice doctrine increased under Cornelius courts after the 1962 constitution.[249] The first case was *Fuzlul Quader Chowdhury* wherein the court looked at the power of the president to amend the constitution. Ayub wanted his members of the executive body to speak in the National Assembly though they were not members, and hence he tried to amend the constitution accordingly. A member of the assembly moved the point in the Dacca High Court as to whether the president can make such amendments. The Dacca High Court held that the constitution should not be so easily changed.[250] The Supreme Court did not accept the appeal and Chief Justice Cornelius warned the government about the powers of the courts to judicially review any changes in the constitution.[251]

To sum up our departing position, the nature of the controversy was that the judiciary should act more as a custodian of the operational form of the Constitution than as the guardian of fundamental rights. Chief Justice Cornelius strongly defended the presidential form of the government against 'anomalous Parliamentary form' or a 'semi-Parliamentary form of Government'. For the judges, according to

---

[245]*The Province of East Pakistan v Md Mehdi Ali Khan Panni*, PLD 1959 SC 387.

[246]The Progressive Papers Ltd (PPL), a privately owned newspaper, was led by leading socialist writers like Faiz Ahmad Faiz, Syed Sibte Hassan, and Ahmad Nadeem Qasmi. It was taken under government control by Ayub.

[247]*Mian Iftikhar-ud-din v Muhammad Sarfraz*, PLD 1961 SC 585.

[248]see discussion in Tamizuddin Khan case and Dosso case.

[249]Haider, *supra* note 207, 178.

[250]*Muhammad Adbul Haq v Fuzlul Quader Chowdhury,* PLD 1963 Dacca 669.

[251]*Fuzlul Quader Chowdhury v Muhammad Adbul Haq* PLD 1963 SC 486.

the 'main fabric'[252] in the presidential form, a government minister should not be a member of the House, cannot have the right to vote, does not depend upon support of the assembly, nor are they responsible to the assembly. The point I want to make is that the Justice Cornelius, who later became the Chief Justice of the Supreme Court in cases regarding such rights, protected the presidential form of the government and the consequent necessary rights for democratic deficit in this form of government, and not the rights themselves.

Now let me move to the next level of evaluating these rights, that is procedural and substantive rights. The courts in the *Moudoodi case* and the *Sorish Kashmiri* case, according to Newberg, differentiate between procedural right of review and how the protection provided to substantive rights is possible with this review. Then, in *Ghulam Jilani, Fazlu lQauder Chowdhry*, and *Sirajul Haq Patwari* cases, the courts stood away from contestable substantive rights guarantees and only extended judicial review in formal sense. In a way, the judiciary stuck to procedural rights and refused to enter the domain of substantive rights, seeing that domain as an exclusive arena of legislature and politics.

Newberg objected to this 'deliberate judicial strategy' to use judicial review as "strange and twisted compact as any attempt to build democracy from authoritarianism without revolution must surely be",[253] and "courts put reform before revolution as an acceptable mode for political change".[254] Disappointed, Newberg came to the conclusion that "while an independent judiciary might be a prerequisite for the life and sustenance of a developing country, it could neither create the conditions for equity and development nor guarantee those results".[255] Newberg is correct here but this rubs against her problematic regret that the judiciary could not properly judge the state. The evidence so far shows that the judiciary (in the Cornelius tradition) aimed only to protect the presidential form of constitution and rights. Let us explore the nature of politics underlying these rights cases.

2.10.3 The Nature of Politics in Rights Cases

In order to add some structural context to this rights discourse, it is necessary to study the nature of the political and economic evolution behind Ayub's opposition. Islamists were among the 'cultural' opposition to the modernization project. During Ayub's regime, the All-Pakistan Women Association started a campaign against polygamy and for the right to divorce. The response was the *Family Laws Ordinance* of 1961. Its evaluation is a compromise between Ayub's liberal agenda and the religious opposition. The legal system was split: issues regarding the personal status

---

[252]Comments of AK Brohi on behalf of the respondent in the *Fuzlul Quader Chowdhury case.*

[253]*Ibid* 105.

[254]*Ibid* 106.

[255]*Ibid* 108.

of women such as marriage, divorce, inheritance and custody of the child were included under Islamic Law, whereas all other issues came under secular legal tradition.[256] Maulana Maudoodi, the founding leader of Jamaat-i-Islami, opposed the 'enlightened modernization' of Ayub. The government used the Political Parties Act of 1962 and the Criminal Amendment Act of 1908 to ban the party. Jamaat-i-Islami contested this decision in East as well as West Pakistan in criminal and civil petitions. The West Pakistan High Court dismissed the criminal petition,[257] but the East Pakistan High Court admitted the appeal.[258] The Supreme Court heard both in a joint appeal. The court upheld the rights of forming a political party and particularly the right to do the activities for which the party is formed. The court examined the nature of new ongoing political developments under Basic Democracy, a kind of guided and controlled democracy. The court looked at the cases in terms of rights, and how these rights allow political parties and their activities and the courts' role in protecting these rights. Courts were confronted between the controlled nature of democracy and the absolute nature of these rights. Cornelius was of the opinion of an independent judicial investigation into government complaints about Jamaat-i-Islami and hence, probably wanted a context for these absolute rights on which they could be evaluated and tested. The court did not accept this proposal. In the *Moudooi* case, not only was the right of judicial review of legislative acts was asserted by courts, but the principles in this regard were enumerated.[259] Thus, from a political analysis, the *Moudood icase* represented the mild opposition against Ayub by Islamists and an inclination of Chief Justice Cornelius towards Islamization. This may not be irrelevant to make connection of Mouddodi's model of political development and constitutional understanding with that of Cornelius and his collective. This does not mean political agenda and politics.

Leonard Binder elaborated Mouddodi's importance for the controversy he created over an Islamic constitution. Mouddodi sidelined the orthodox *ulema* and modernist secular politicians and forced the Constituent Assembly to consider four points which became the basis of Objectives Resolution in 1949. When Jinnah's speech to the Constituent Assembly left confusion,[260] Mouddodi came out with his four points of Islamic law and constitution in early 1948 in his address to law students. These four points became the basis of Objectives Resolution.[261] In his model of political development, 'nationalism' is the anti-thesis of Islam. The

[256]S Rouse, Liberation from Above or Within: Nationalism, Gender, and Space in Pakistan (March-April 2002) 97 *Against the Current* 14.

[257]Criminal Appeal No. 43, 1964.

[258]Civil Appeal No. 19-D, 1964.

[259]Braibanti, *supra* note 108, in, Braibanti, *supra* note 104, 153. This essay was first published in R Braibanti, (N. C. Duke University Press, Durham, 1966).

[260]For Martin Lau, Jinnah though a jurist, did not give a clear vision of the constitution of the new state. See M Lau, Pakistan: before 1947, in, Kazim Hassan et al. (ed), *Law in a World of Change: Selected essays in memory of Justice Sabihuddin Ahmed* (Pakistan Law House, Karachi, 2012) 167, 195.

[261]L Binder, *Religion and Politics in Pakistan* (Berkley: University of California, 1963) 103.

community had the right to rule, but through believers of Sharia and un-believers were not allowed to influence state policy. At the same time there was an *amir* (ruler), advisory council, and 'limited government' by elected representatives.[262] Readers will see these ideas common to the understanding of Cornelius collective comprising Hamoodur Rahman, A.K. Brohi, Sharifuddin Pirzada, and Khalid M. Ishaque. Opposition to this project is 'secular' Munir and Kayani but within liberal tradition. Sharifuddin Pirzada wrote in 1995 that Mouddodi relied on his book to challenge the banning of Jamaat-e-Islami in the *Moudoodi case*.[263]

Actual opposition to Ayub since 1958 came from the National Awami Party, which was an alliance of communists and nationalists. These two forces were resisting the state-building project of the juridico-bureaucratic structure as we have already discussed. So in the *Siraj Pitwari case*, the Cornelius court failed the test of fundamental rights as the attack was on the constitutional design and BD system. Chief Justice Cornelius and Justice Hamood-ur-Rahman of the Supreme Court defended the Basic Democracy (BD) system, while Chief Justice Murshad of the East Pakistan High Court reflected the unrest of East Pakistan. The division of provincial and legislative powers in the BD system and the executive were the issue in the *Sirajul Haq Patwari case* in East Pakistan High Court in 1965.[264] Chief Justice Murshad of the East Pakistan High Court made clear the separation of central and provincial powers in the 1962 constitution and argued that the Act of 1965 transgressed these powers. He relied on the *Fazlul Qauder Chowdhry* case and exercised the power of judicial review. The court decision strongly protected provincial autonomy. In an appeal in 1966, the Supreme Court of Chief Justice Cornelius reversed the judgment.[265]

I agree with the Newberg that, "when the court took on Ayub Khan, it was for his transgression of private rights, not the organization of his state".[266] But one can add that both of these are not separate, for we keep emphasizing 'more rights' in exchange for the lack of democracy. The Cornelius tradition of judicial review and rights discourse proved antithetical to the notion of a broader and deeper popular democracy, which could not accommodate other, small and oppressed nationalities. Actually, the Islamic 'national' spirit of Cornelius and his 'collective' could not accommodate the nature of contradiction involved in politics of suppressed nationalities. Justice Murshad resigned on 6 January 1967. Ayub received his resignation through the law minister and commented that he was brilliant but 'impulsive and unstable' and that he was very doubtful from the beginning of his success as a Chief Justice of East Pakistan.[267] Later, Chief Justice Murshad entered

[262]Binder, *supra* note 261, 91.

[263]See the preface of the second edition in 1995, in, SS Pirzada, *Evolution of Pakistan* (Royal Book Company, Karachi, 1963).

[264]*Sirajul Haque Patwari v Sub-divisional Officer, Chandpur*, PLD 1966 Dacca 331.

[265]*Province of East Pakistan v Sirjul Haq Patwari*, PLD 1966 SC 854.

[266]Newberg, *supra* note 90, 101.

[267]Baxter, *supra* note 138, 45.

Bengali politics and participated in the negotiations of the independence of Bangladesh.

A further test came for the Cornelius court in the *Roshan Khan* case.[268] Here, once again, the court was to decide between public order and individual rights. Chief Justice Cornelius was of the opinion that if a bona fide arrest is made, there is no question of individual rights and judicial review. Justice S.A. Rahman thought that executive action should be within constitutional and legal confines. Justice Hamood-ur-Rahman and Justice Kaikaus dismissed the case. Herein, the court hardly passed its own test established in the *Moudoodi case.*

But the judiciary failed the test in the *Malik Ghulam Jilani case.*[269] Ayub signed the Tashkent Declaration with India after the 1965 war. The opposition protested and arrests were made. The Lahore High Court considered police action justified in light of concerns of public order. The Supreme Court also upheld detention to prevent disturbance in public order but found the Lahore High Court's approach restrictive, as it should have looked into the reasonableness of the government action. The decision in the *Shorish Kashmiri* case[270] upheld its right to review executive actions that are arbitrary, unguided and uncontrolled. Two points are worth mentioning here, one that Shorish Kashmiri was a right wing anti-communist like Moudoodi of Jamaat, and secondly, Chief Justice Cornelius had now retired. Ayub's protective constitutional structure was deteriorating with his downfall.

Again in the *Agarthala conspiracy* case, the judiciary was tested around nationality politics. Mujeeb-ur-Rahman (who was leading the movement for Bangladesh), was accused of revolting and was taken into custody under DPR, along with 35 other individuals. Ayub's intention was to try such people under Court Martial. Ayub immediately called General Yahya and informed him that DPR had been destroyed by the Supreme Court at the behest of Cornelius, and Yahya should take them in military custody lest the High Court will let them go.[271] No one was convicted as the trial was not completed after Ayub Khan resigned. Mujeeb was tried by a special tribunal, headed by Chief Justice S.A. Rahman, and Chief Justices M. Khan and Muksumul Hakim of East Pakistan. The making of this tribunal under the 1968 Special Criminal Law Amendment (Special Tribunal) ordinance was challenged in High Court and refused.

The judiciary also supported Ayub in this most aggressive anti-communist act after the *Pindi Conspiracy case*. In the *Mian Iftikhar-ud-din* case, the Progressive Papers Ltd (PPL), a privately owned newspaper, was led by left-leaning socialists including landmark writers like Faiz Ahmad Faiz, Syed Sibte Hassan and Ahmad

---

[268]*The Government of Pakistan v Mrs Rowshan Bijaya Shaukat Ali Khan* PLD 1966 SC 286.

[269]*Malik Ghulam Jilani v The Govt of West Pakistan*, PLD 1967 SC 373.

[270]*The Government of West Pakistan. Begum Agha Abdul Karim Shorish Kashmiri* PLD 1969 SC 14.

[271]Baxter, *supra* note 138, 203.

Nadeem Qasmi.[272] The government removed the owners and director of the newspaper on the ground of 1952 Security of Pakistan Act.[273] The High Court accepted the order of the Govt under the *Dosso* case and *Mehdi Ali Khan* case.[274] S.M. Haider, being the main proponent of Cornelius' tradition of rights, accepted that the doctrine of natural justice "lost its prestine vigor" in this case.[275]

Newberg's analysis is worth summarizing to properly evaluate the rights discourse under Chief Justice Cornelius and later in a brief period of Chief Justice S.A. Rahman. For her, it was a mixed bag of decisions oscillating between judicial reviews of constitutional rights and accepting state limits on politics. Chief Justice Cornelius did not go beyond constitutional limits while defining natural rights. S.A. Rahman was more into positive rights and judging the law by its letters. On the civil liberties front, Cornelius was in favour of the Frontier Crimes Regulations, which were ruthlessly used by Ayub to suppress opposition, particularly for the nationalists and the communists in National Awami Party—NAP. Similar provisions were in the Criminal Code of West Pakistan. This means that rights protections and procedures are not guaranteed if not applied fairly.[276]

The analysis so far tried to establish how the debate and liberal analyses around the rights discourse in these cases hides the politics behind them (by omitting any analysis of class formations and class struggle), but also obscures what is going on with state apparatuses and their politics.

Chief Justice Cornelius's position on rights can also be understood from his speeches.[277] He criticized the universality of the United Declaration of Human Rights (UDHR) and its authoritative form and found that some of its Articles were explosive.[278] He rejected Article 21 of the UDHR, which declared the will of the people as the basis of authority of the government and this will is only made possible through free, secret voting in periodic general elections. Cornelius's objection to this was its validity as a human right being questionable and that people could be and had been happier and well governed under other modes of governance than democratic systems. He objected to the fact that the UDHR ignored a nation's right to choose its own form of government and ideologies

[272]Here again, Newberg (1995) did not comment on this ideological position of the newspaper and just mentioned that its publications were outspoken and against the government.

[273]*Security of Pakistan (Amendment) Ordinance*, 1959 (XXIII of 1959), *Security of Pakistan (Amendment) Ordinance* 1961 (XIV of 1961).

[274]*Mian Iftikhar-ud-din v Muhammad Sarfraz*, PLD 1961 Lahore 842.

[275]Haider, *supra* note 207, 176.

[276]Newberg, *supra* note 90, 104.

[277]AR Cornelius CJSC (Ret, as he then was), Islam and Human Rights, in, Braibanti, *supra* note 104, 278. Address delivered at the Pakistan Academy for Rural Development, Peshawar, 8 November 1977.

[278]*Ibid* 280.

(political and economic).[279] He went further and declared this type of democracy as divisive and in opposition to integration.[280] Article 19 (freedom of opinion and expression), Article 13 (freedom to leave the country) and Article 14 (right to seek asylum) were also contentious for him. For him, these Articles were averse to the concept of loyalty with country and community. In the Articles of the UDHR, Cornelius found "over-stress on the freedom of the individual citizen" at the price of the individual's obligations to the state or nation to which he or she belongs.[281]

Cornelius did not accept the U.S. human rights discourse. His view was that the inclusion of human rights in written constitutions was a local phenomenon of democracy and not necessarily based on the Magna Carta and the Bill of Rights of 1688 in England, for those were between kings and privileged nobles. Based on the work of A.K. Brohi, Cornelius made it clear that fundamental rights in the written constitution are meant to stop the interference of majority rule in individual matters, as the people are distrustful of legislative supremacy in newly independent countries. It seems that the greater rights in the hands of the courts were another form of stress on the already weak legislature, as in Pakistan.

As far as the relation of rights with popular democracy is concerned, the position of Chief Justice Cornelius is illustrative and very conclusive for our proposed analysis. It speaks for itself. For Cornelius, the rights in the constitution of newly independent countries like Pakistan are remedies "necessary for dealing evils that follow on each other, all stemming from the same source, namely, popular democracy".[282] For him, democracy based on the social contract and participation in representative government was an illusion. He wrote, "[t]he price of democracy is partisan politics".[283] Cornelius is very clear that developing countries had shown that self-government per se is no substitute for good governance. He claimed further that good government cannot be assured under self-government but only under autocratic rule.[284]

In a nutshell, we can see that the rights discourse of Cornelius courts stood behind the nation-building project in postcolonial development. Due to his religious inclination, he stood for the rights of the Right wing opposition. His rights discourse failed when the rights of the oppressed nationalities were presented. After reading his views on rights, we can see that he places rights above popular democracy. This is done under the veneer of Islamism. Let me show more closely the manifestation of Islam with a controlled liberal democracy. This way we can understand the rights discourse as a stopgap remedy for a democratic deficit. Let us add another cultural layer to this formation.

[279]*Ibid* 283.

[280]*Ibid* 281.

[281]*Ibid* 283.

[282]Ibid 287.

[283]*Ibid* 288.

[284]*Ibid* 291.

2.10.4 Islam and Jirga System in Nation-Building

The nation-building project under modernization in post-colonies lacked the cohesion that underpinned the West during the Industrial revolution.[285] To create this cohesion, Cornelius, in line with Liaqat's Objectives Revolution,[286] used Islam. In order to accommodate local hierarchies, the Jirga (in the North West Frontier Province) or the Panchayat (in Punjab-Sindh) was kept intact. This is the judicial system Cornelius had in mind under the Basic Democracy system. It is best illustrated in his essay about giving judicial responsibility to the people.[287] He concluded that the best arrangement would be a mix of the Jirga system and Islam.

First of all, he appreciated communal or village courts as they could dispose of cases without any expense and enforce a solution that was purely punitive or a deterrent. Imprisonment was needed only in cases of serious nature or public danger. He complained that British colonizers took away this judicial responsibility of the people suddenly, rather than in stages, as had been the case in England. Later, political responsibility was returned, though only partially, in the Reforms Act of 1919, but judicial responsibility was never returned to the people of India, for instance, the jury system was never tried in India.[288]

Ayub's Basic Democracy system, for Cornelius, was the only attempt made to return justice to the people.[289] Cornelius found an 'indigenous' justice system in the Panchayat system, which offered a design of a controlled democracy. He appreciated the Jirga system in the Northwest Frontier Crimes Regulation, which he had appreciated seven years earlier in the *Dosso case*.[290] At that time he valued the patriarchy in the Jirga system and kinship system as leading to less juvenile crimes. Similarly he found that "there are restraints imposed upon the freedom of behavior of women, which are effective to lessen the need for law to intervene for the purpose of checking excesses by both".[291] He admired the work of British legal

[285]Modernization was an imperialist project, while Enlightenment modernity was an indigenously European project, and contributed to the expansion of European colonization of Asia and Africa.

[286]The Objective Resolution was a part of the preamble of the Constitution and could not control the constitution. Later Zia made this Objective Resolution as the part of the constitution.

[287]Cornelius, *supra* note 31, 11.

[288]*Ibid.*

[289]*Ibid.*

[290]He gave the example of the Frontier Crimes Regulation enacted in 1872 by British deriving its history from Sir Olaf Caroe's book, "The Pathans".

[291]AR Cornelius (1965) CJSC, Crime and the Punishment of Crime, in, Braibanti (1999) 249, 259; speech delivered at the Third Commonwealth and Empire Law Conference in Sydney, Australia 27 August 1965.

commissions to codify these laws.[292] But, the critique of Cornelius remained, namely that the justice system was imposed upon the people and "did not derive from the life of the people themselves".[293]

Rather than looking at the culture of his own country and its people, he saw the roots of culture in the 'universality' of Islam and hence the Middle East.[294] He confused the concept of Islam with that of culture. His quest for the roots of the culture led him to "the external source of all legality", that is, *wahdat* (oneness of God) and Islam,[295] as opposed to his own claim of the law as growing out of the society, he found the sources of Muslim Common Law (Sharia) in 'advanced' middle Eastern Countries. The Iraqi ambassador pointed him to *Mujallah* and gave a copy. Cornelius started translating it in English.[296] This was an effort of the Turkish Sultans in the nineteenth Century to frame a general law of the Empire on the lines of the Napoleonic Code of France. *Mujallah* was abolished after the secular revolution of Atta Turk. Cornelius thought that this spirit was the basis of *Sharia* and was uncommon in our law as it was based on British Common law.[297] He went to the extent of favouring the amputation of hands as a deterrent, which according to him, could be done with a small surgery instead of by cutting the hand. He appreciated the Saudi system of criminal justice administration on the ground of deterrence. He also advocated the Jirga system, amputation, and Zakat.[298]

On the other hand, the Jirga system, for Braibanti, was a blending of the elite and popular will and spheres of juridical norms.[299] The Frontier Crimes Regulation of 1901 was not a 'return' to simple tribal justice, but according to Braibanti, the "institutional and normative adjustment" of tribal law and British criminal law.

---

[292]Communal courts, for him, were not at all organized. They worked in highly irregular fashion, and the conception of laws administered in these courts was not great. Four British law commissions were made with British personnel from 1834 to 1879 to codify these laws. He admired the work of British jurists who for 200 years had endeavored to figure out how the system should work. Cornelius, *supra* note 31, 8, address delivered at a gathering of Military officials at G H Q, Rawalpindi on 11 July 1962.

[293]*Ibid.*

[294]Cornelius, *supra* note 291, 249, 262, 63; speech delivered at the Third Commonwealth and Empire Law Conference in Sydney, Australia 27 August 1965.

[295]Justice Cornelius (1963) CJSC, *supra* note 23, 13.

[296]AR Cornelius, The Mujallah: Forward and the Hundred Maxims Rendered into English, *PLD* (1966) Journal Section 49, later Nasim Hasan Shah appreciated him as a highly developed legal system see NH Shah, Mujallah and its For-runners, *PLD* (1966) Journal Section 104.

[297]AR Cornelius (1968), Paramountcy of Islam: The Example of Majelle (Mujallah) of Turkey, in, Braibanti (1999) *supra* note 61 272, addressing the Karachi High Court Bar Association Dinner, 15 February 1968.

[298]AR Cornelius (1969) CJSC (Ret, as he then was), A Plea to Introduce Zakat, in, Haider, *supra* note 110, 360. Address in Peshawar, 2 May 1969.

[299]He based his opinion on the work of JND, Anderson, LC Green, and SA de Smith, The Frontier Crimes Regulation of 1901 was not a "return" to simple tribal justice, but according to Braibanti, "institutional and normative adjustment" of tribal law and British criminal law. Here normative content is more western then tribal. See Braibanti, *supra* note 104, 95.

Here, normative content is more western than tribal. One of the problems of a written constitution based on western values for nation-building was its confrontation with indigenous values.[300] This grafting of Islam onto the justice system paved the way for a state-Islamization by Zia in the 1980s and onward.[301]

Apart from this, did Cornelius really want to return justice to people? His slogan of "Justice of the People, By the People, for the People"[302] seemed a counter narrative of 'judicial democracy' as opposed to 'people's democracy. He placed judicial conscience above social and political conscious. Rejecting political conscious meant individual rights ranked superior to political and economic rights (rights of the people).[303] To make this proposition clearer, he stated in another speech that the law is made by the Legislature or Ordinance, but "it is only in the hands of Superior Judges, that such a rule takes the *authentic shape*, which is the hall-mark of *pure law*." [my emphasize] [304] But how do judges decide and where are the people in this picture? People only come, for him, as clarifying commercial, social, public interests in courts, then a spark from the light of God while delivering judgment as a manifestation of Divine purpose of the Universe. For him, fundamental rights in 1962 Constitution on *American pattern* were "for the implementation of the whole principles of the *Objectives Resolution*." [my emphasis].[305] He felt sorry that in Pakistan's superior courts, judges were facing hundreds of cases of fundamental rights but they did not understand them in the lights of Holy Scriptures of Islam. In that sense there is a conflict between foreign interpretation of these FRs and their true interpretation according to the dictates of Islam.[306] As opposed to foreign countries like U.S., who use in the expression 'moral responsibility' to differentiate it from natural justice which is based on religious conscience, Cornelius used natural rights theory.

To sum up Munir (1950s) and Cornelius (1960s) CJ courts, analysis in this chapter tried to debunk the famous liberal position that Cornelius CJ defended democracy and rights as opposed to Munir CJ. Analysis tried to show how Cornelius was against popular democracy and favoured of a very controlled democracy with a strong presidential system and limited electorate under BD

[300]*Ibid.*

[301]Braibanti (1999) found it a process that was "relatively insulated from politics." But we will see how this tradition continued as a part of juridico-bureaucratic structure.

[302]AR Cornelius CJSC, Justice of the People, By the People, for the People, *PLD* (1963) Journal Section 39, speech delivered at dinner meeting of the Rotary Club, Karachi, on 2 April 1963.

[303]Cornelius, *supra* note 302, 43; speech delivered at dinner meeting of the Rotary Club, Karachi, on 2 April 1963.

[304]AR Cornelius CJSC, Objectives Resolution and Duty of Man of Law: Need to Expand Law according to the True Philosophy of Pakistan, *PLD* (1965) Journal Section 45, Inaugural address at second law conference of SM Law College Karachi, 11 March 1965.

[305]Cornelius, *supra* note 304, 47, Inaugural address at second law conference of SM Law College Karachi, 11 March 1965.

[306]Cornelius, *supra* note 304, 49, Inaugural address at second law conference of SM Law College Karachi, 11 March 1965.

system. In this political formation, strong emphasis on rights is to address this democratic deficit. In the presence of a weak legislature, the judiciary's use of Islam as law in the name of Sharia and right of its interpretation above legislature added to this democratic deficit. Cornelius also included the patriarchy of Jirga system in his political and legal formation. To counter the pressure of land reforms and nationalist cum socialist forces, an alliance of Muslim clergy and feudals under Liaqat Ali Khan in the form of Objectives Resolution finally adopted an intellectual political discourse in the leadership of Cornelius. But this use of Islam led to confusion as per Munir CJ.[307] Cornelius' tradition had to be defensive in the face of rising socialism after the overthrow of Ayub in 1968 but it strongly continued under Chief Justices S.A. Rahman, Hamoodur Rahman and leading jurists like A.K. Brohi, Sharifuddin Pirzada, and Khalid M. Ishaq. I call this Cornelius collective. Resisting and overthrowing Bhutto in the 1970s, this tendency got an official legal and constitutional position under Zia dictatorship when parliamentary democratic constitution of 1973 was turned into a presidential one and the Objectives Resolution became the substantive part of the constitution along with other Islamization clauses (details to be followed in the next chapter). Later in the 1980s and 1990s, CJs Anwar, Haleem, Afzal Zullah, Nasim, Ajmal continued this quasi-liberal tradition. We saw that Munir and Kayani CJs, though gave decisions against legislature and fundamental rights, yet they were secular and liberal. As a whole, Munir and Cornelius CJs were within the liberal tradition of law standing together against socialist modernization, popular democracy, and deeper and broader participation of masses. Both of these CJs and the courts under them worked with the civil-military bureaucracy in advancing the hegemonic project of capitalist modernization. That is why I call it juridico-bureaucratic structure. But this project failed to stop popular participation and made modernization theorists like Huntington to re-evaluate the role of law in political development.

2.11 The Collapse of Modernization and Revisiting the Role of Law

For liberals, one of the many reasons for the downfall of Ayub was the inter-elite conflict.[308] As a whole, there were three problems with Ayub's modernization that led to its collapse: (1) The concentration of wealth as patronage was confined to industrialists; (2) Benefits only went to big landlords, and; (3) Ayub did not

[307]Munir, *supra* note 16, 50, 113.

[308]R La Porte, Succession in Pakistan: Continuity and Change in a Garrison State, 1969 *Asian Survey* 835, see F Ahmed, Structure and Contradiction in Pakistan, in, K Gough and H Sharma (eds) *Imperialism and Revolution in South, Asia* (Monthly Press Review, New York, 1973) 179, as cited by Waseem, *supra* note 6, 223.

accommodate the new middle classes in the political process.[309] As far as inter-elite struggles are concerned they are not violent and mostly take legal and constitutional forms. This is always only a situation that weakened the unity of the hegemonic bloc of the dominant classes and make possible for the subordinate classes to exert themselves. Ayub's policies, such as that which promoted the Green Revolution, resulted in growing class conflict. The rural inequality in terms of availability of cash, agricultural inputs, tube wells and tractorization was more visible and widespread as only the big landlords could afford these resources but not small farmers. The urban inequality was far greater than the rural one in real terms, at least in the industrial sector. The green revolution changed the landscape of social formation and gave birth to new subordinate classes, which changed the political landscape. Ayub's industrial policy was completely for industrialists, thus against workers. He brought forth the Industrial Dispute Ordinance, 1959, which made strikes impossible in public utility (sugar mills, textiles and many other sectors were included in the public utility). Instead of neutral labour courts having jurisdiction in industrial disputes, employer's representatives were made to sit on tripartite principle (employee and employer's representatives and a chairman). Above all, labour union leaders had no immunity from termination. These repressive policies resulted in the working class joining hands with students and un-employed, creating a major force against Ayub.[310] But the most vocal in these unrests were lawyers along with students. For Braibanti, the legal community was probably the most powerful elite group, outside government services in Pakistan.[311] He wrote, "[a]t the pinnacle of prestige were the barristers who studied in England at one of the Inns-of-Court".[312] The community also had "close identification with the ideology and techniques of modernization".[313] Another source of strength of the legal community was that most of the leading political leaders, including H.S. Suhrawardy of East Pakistan, Khan Abdul Qayyam Khan of the Frontier province, Mian Mumtaz Daultana and Mahmud Ali Qasuri were lawyers. Later in the country's development, however, it was possible to have too many lawyers in politics and hence the "consequent disproportionate emphasis on legal modes of thought as antithetical to the needs of development".[314]

Cornelius advised lawyers to stay away from politics. He gave an example of England, that those lawyers who are political were a class apart and fewer in numbers there.[315] Comments by the Bar Association on political matters irked Chief

---

[309]Burki (1980) as cited by Waseem, *supra* note 6, 223.

[310]Mohammad, *supra* note 14, 265, 272, 274.

[311]R Braibanti (1963), The Socio-Judicial Context of the Cornelius Era – 1950-70, in, Braibanti (1999), *supra* note 58, 108, 113. This essay was first published in Braibanti, *supra* note 108.

[312]*Ibid* 115.

[313]*Ibid* 119.

[314]*Ibid* 118.

[315]AR Cornelius, Unity of Lawyers in Essential Function of Law, *PLD* (1965) Journal Section 55, 56.

Justice Cornelius.[316] The erstwhile 'democrat' against Ayub, Chief Justice Kayani, had contempt for the bar vis-à-vis administration and bench because only the CSP had the right to rule in Pakistan in his proposition.[317] As opposed to this, S.M. Murshed, CJ East Pakistan High Court, though was in favour of the judiciary being granted an important position in regards to constitutional interpretation, yet warned against mistakes that the judiciary could make in this process. To correct this, he stressed the need of an active role of resistance by lawyers.[318] Ayub was also annoyed with the legal profession, which he found 'overmanned' but producing poor material.[319] He looked at the judges from a military perspective.[320] He selected three judges out of 11 and found practicing lawyers impressive, but session judges a poor lot. He wanted 'justice' instead of courts of law.[321] Supreme Court Chief Justice Fazal-e-Akbar requested and asked Ayub to give administrative powers to the Supreme Court over High Courts as High Courts were delaying decisions, granting stay orders automatically, even on false allegations about works on projects, leaving Fazal-e-Akbar helpless. Ayub told Fazal-e-Akbar that he wanted to grant these powers at the time of framing the constitution but 'legal pundits' found it against the independence of judiciary. Ayub then said that he made a supreme judicial body, which judges were reluctant to use. They would imprison and hang other people but dare not lift a finger against each other.[322] Before swearing in Supreme Court Chief Justice Hamood-ur-Rahman, he had separate talks about discipline in courts and bureaucracy, and about the language of Article 98 of the constitution, which gave unlimited powers to the courts. Ayub wanted to deal with it by legislation, otherwise he argued there would be utter lawlessness. But the cabinet advised him not to do so and to rather use security acts and provincial detention laws.[323]

Ayub was frustrated with lawyers because he argued that as a class they were ready to listen to any nonsense.[324] It was observed that the lawyers' role as gentlemen pursuing justice was no longer possible. The legal profession was close to a business and for some people was a 'dying institution'.[325] Chief Justice Anwar

---

[316]AR Cornelius, Speech at Annual Dinner of High Court Bar Association, PLD (1969) Journal Section, 107, 110. Addressing Karachi High Court Bar Association on June 1964, in R Braibanti, The Socio-Judicial Context of the Cornelius Era – 1950-70, in, Braibanti, *supra* note 104, 123. This essay was first published in Braibanti, *supra* note 108.

[317]MR Kayani, Not the Whole Truth, in, Kayani, *supra* note 179, 12, 28, 35, 124, 30, 141.

[318]SM Murshed Justice East Pakistan High Court, *PLD* (1964) Journal Section 81, 84, Speech delivered at the full Court Reference on 15 May 1964.

[319]After interviewing judges for the West Pakistan High Court, See Ayub Khan Diaries, *supra* note 105.

[320]Talking to the Lahore High Court Chief Justice Inamullah 1965-67, See Baxter, *supra* note 138.

[321]Addressing West Pakistan High Court Centenary by reception of HCBA, See Baxter, *supra* note 138.

[322]Baxter, *supra* note 138, 264.

[323]Baxter, *supra* note 138, 284.

[324]Response to Bhutto's speech, see Baxter, *supra* note 138, 282.

[325]W Farooqi, Dimensions of the Legal Profession, XX *PLD* (1968) Journal Section 73, 78.

ul Haq found that lawyers predominantly defended the established order, as their principal clients were mostly individuals with property or corporate owners.[326] On the opening ceremony of the High Court building, Ayub repeated the slogan that the rule of law and independence of the judiciary was not an issue but what was real was the suffering of the people due to the legal system. After the ceremony, the Chief Justice accepted that the legal profession had become sordid, and proposed an idea to appoint a legal advisor to guide litigants at the union council level. Ayub liked the idea but thought that lawyers would become further alienated from him.[327] What was Ayub's explanation?

Amjad Ali told Ayub that the problems he faced were due to the lack of inclusion of the intelligentsia and rising prices. Ayub responded that prices seemed comparable with other countries, whereas the intelligentsia did not feel participation without a direct vote.[328] This seems nuanced and compatible with the above analyses to understand political development and reflected the analyses in those days of dying capitalist modernization. The crux was popular participation and its expression under socialist modernization, which capitalist modernization under Ayub could not control. All the key commentators: Huntington, Braibanti, Cornelius and even Ayub, were aware of this. This realization is the key to understand the current emphasis of the centrality of law by good governance paradigm of the World Bank and institutionalists.

Law as a part of the modernization project[329] was in infancy when modernization came under crisis. This cast doubts on the role of law to the extent that Manzor asked "Is law dead?"[330] This raised concern about the role of law in political and economic development in Third World countries and hence demanded a social theory of law. Trubek's diagnosis was that the Eurocentric evolutionism and generalization in theory behind liberal legalism was a reason behind this fall.[331] Connected to this, according to him, was the creation of a strong central state under liberal legalism in modernization and the wish to govern social life by purposive rules.[332] For Trubek, this is statist legal instrumentalism, looking towards bureaucratic-administrative entities. He concluded that the economy and polity merged together to some extent in a developmental state. Law in an authoritarian regime for him is not supportive of democracy, rather the opposite. It resulted in the

---

[326]S Anwar-ul-Haq, Role of Law in a Developing Society, in, Anwar-ul-Haq, *supra* note 28, 96.

[327]Baxter, *supra* note 138, 258.

[328]Baxter, *supra* note 138, 93, 297.

[329]Trubek has cited an extensive list of the work in this area of law and development. Trubek, Towards a Social Theory of Law: An Essay on the Study of Law and Development, 82:1 The Yale Law Journal (1972).

[330]Manzor, The Crisis of Liberal Legalism 81, Yale Law Journal 1032 (1972) as cited by Trubek (1972), *ibid.*

[331]*Ibid* 1.

[332]As far as the relation of law and political development is concerned, he is convinced that the core conception is based on D Apter, *The Politics of Modernization (1965)* and S. Huntington *Political Orders in Changing Societies* see Trubek, *supra* note 329, 35.

legalization of politics and politics came in the hands of the specialized elite. As opposed to this type of functionalism, Trubek suggested that legal purposiveness itself is not enough to explain the relationship between law and politics.[333] So we need varying degrees of purposiveness in law and hence pluralist legal instrumentalism, which should be more competitive and representative. Trubek correctly critiqued the functionalism of Parsons, and the problems of liberal legalism. But to accommodate increasing competiveness and representation does not solve the problem. It seems that the problem identified by Trubek that the law stops representation—was found as a solution by institutionalists in the aftermath of collapsing modernization. Let me expand this argument.

Furthermore, the argument this book want to advance is that the 'institutionalism' (particularly legal institutions) came as a response to failed modernization and the consequences of increasing political participation. The behaviourial aspect of institutions was brought to functionalism to deal with the crisis of excessive participation. Based on Huntington's approach,[334] Braibanti was worried about the declining role of law in modernization project.[335] He argued political development treated the law in its institutional aspect and did not try to find functional or behavioural schools of jurisprudence. He did not agree with the dichotomy between institutions and functions and thought institutions perform functions and affect behaviour. There was a need for institutions as was emphasized by Huntington. For Braibanti, the decline of institutional study and importance of law was due to the expansion of political participation and popular sovereignty, which relies on extra-legal norms.[336] He accused social scientists of devaluing law through their involvement in social activism and physical agitation called 'confrontation politics' for immediate change. For him "agitation minimizes and eventually corrodes the vitality of law and institutions".[337]

The suppression of popular sovereignty and the restructuring of the center–periphery relation of Pakistan were the focus of Ayub's reforms. For this, as I have explained, he relied on controlled democracy and controlled participation. Ayub also noted that the attempt to bridge the gap between the state and society through the Basic Democracy system did not work. He wanted the science of social

---

[333]Trubek, *supra* note 329, 37.

[334]Braibanti also claimed that Huntington (who in turn used the criteria of Ward and Rustow, Emerson, Pye, and Eisenstad) is behind his analysis, see R Braibanti, The Role of Law in the Political Development of Pakistan, in, Braibanti, *supra* note 104, 82, 90, See Also SP Huntington. Political Development and Political Decay, XVII *World Politics* (1965) Journal Section 386.

[335]*Ibid* 84.

[336]In spite of the efforts of John Commons and Wesley Mitchel, Old Institutional Economics was a marginal theory until the 1960s. Until this time, Marxism and institutionalism were totally hostile. Kirsten Ford, "The Veblenian Roots of Institutional Political Economy", Working Paper No. 2011-07, Department of Economics Working Paper Series, University of Utah, 11.

[337]R Braibanti (1968), The Role of Law in the Political Development of Pakistan, in, Braibanti, *supra* note 104, 82, 87.

behaviour to develop first.[338] Social restraints are deeply embedded in habits of the people in accepted social arrangements. He correctly referred to these social arrangements as 'institutions'. For him, "[h]abits of thought and conduct are the most stubborn obstacles to development".[339] What can give stability in the meanwhile? For him, it was the constitution, law and the Supreme Court. He accepted that he could have lifted the emergency after the 1965 war was over and particularly after the judgment of the Supreme Court to insist on scrutinizing the emergency laws. He did not follow the courts and there emerged the rights cases as we discussed above. For Ayub, the Constitution was amended so that there was no need of Martial Law and emergency laws could be enough. Ayub thought about this but the law minister insisted on amending the law rather than the constitution, so the Supreme Court struck down those laws.[340] The political situation did not let Ayub amend the constitution, as the members of the parliament were scared of victimization and terrorization of agitators.[341] The point I want to make is that Ayub shared the same values and approach as that of Cornelius towards the citizenry. The difference was that Cornelius believed in conditional individual liberty to avoid social unrest, which Ayub did not understand.[342]

Braibanti called the problem of popular will and its accommodation in modernization the 'demand-conversion crisis'.[343] This needed a demand-diversion method. Some of this adjustment could be found in law and legal institutions. The political system tried to create ambiguity to blunt the demands of the presidential and parliamentary system in Pakistan and to create ambiguity around detention laws. The judiciary tried to decrease the ambiguity and helped the political system to adjust to demands. But, Braibanti was not sure how the law could increase or decrease ambiguity. Furthermore, the natural justice approach of the law as applied by the Pakistani judiciary helped in silencing these demands. In that sense, the political system is like a 12-cylinder engine with noisy tappets and a gummed-up cylinder and the natural justice approach of law is like foam on it, covering those noises, "quieting the noises and smoothing the ride".[344] Braibanti was scared of the risks of artificially removing law from its contextual tissues in this process. The reason behind his doubt could be that law, as a means of social change and engineering, had not yet been set up. The Law and Society Review had not yet

[338]Baxter, *supra* note 138, 93, 129, 297.

[339]Baxter, *supra* note 138, 93, 297, 322.

[340]This was the background of most of the "rights" cases in the Cornelius Courts.

[341]Baxter, *supra* note 138, 93, 297, 331.

[342]Interestingly, after his downfall, Ayub realized that he could have accepted the idea of civil liberties, see Baxter, *supra* note 138, 93, 297, 331.

[343]Burki (1998) also found that the 1960 s development created a divide deepening between the social and political realms, giving birth to a crisis of political participation. Ayub's political engineering (BD system) narrowed the political base while allowing social and economic development see Burki, *supra* note 34, 57.

[344]R Braibanti (1968), The Role of Law in the Political Development of Pakistan, in, Braibanti, *supra* note 104, 82, 100.

started.[345] My argument is that one should not assume the central role of law in this stage of modernization, but rather that it was the collapse of this phase of modernization led to the idea of using law and institutions to 'prevent' democracy. This was not clear to Braibanti at that time.

It is yet too early in the story to understand how legalism and institutionalism would pacify the rising lawyers and middle class in the years to come. In this chapter, I have argued that 'institutionalism' (particularly legal institutions) was a response to failed modernization. In the next chapter on the 1990s, we will see that institutionalism acted as a continuity of modernization in the age of globalization.

The analysis so far adheres to the view that the ethos of capitalist modernity (modernization in 1950–1960s) rested on an elitist democracy, which required controls on democracy. The law was a tool, only to support such capitalist economic and political (under) development. However, when capitalist modernization was challenged in postcolonial states in the 1970s, but the socialist bloc was also unstable, the architects of modernization theory now chose law (working through rules and institutions) as a response to the popular challenges. Capitalist modernization was to work through the imposition of legal, enforceable rules, where the spread of market economic and social values had failed. This was a new kind of modernization, which is pervasive to this day in our common understanding of the centrality of 'rule in law' in a democracy. Samuel Huntington and Douglas North were the architects of this new order.

With this background in mind, we will first show the place of law in the experiment of socialist modernity by Prime Minister Zulfikar Ali Bhutto in the 1970s. We will will then see how the law was re-deployed upon the demise of popular aspirations for a deeper democracy.

References

A Jalal, *Democracy and Authoritarianism in South Asia* (Sang-e-Meel Publications, Lahore, 1995).

A Jalal, *Self and Sovereignty: Individual and Community in South Asian Islam since 1850* (Routledge, New York, 2000).

A Jalal, *The State of Martial Rule: The Origins of Pakistan's Political Economy of Defence* (Vanguard/Cambridge University Press, London/Lahore, 1991).

A Ojo, The Search for a Grundnorm in Nigeria - The Lakanmi case, 20 *ILCQ* (1971).

A Siddiqa, *Military Inc.: Inside Pakistan's Military economy* (Oxford University Press, Karachi, 2007).

A Stepan, *The Military in Politics: Changing pattern in Brazil* (Princeton University Press, Princeton, 1971).

AD Smith, Constitutional Law Years in Revolutionary Situations, 7 *West Ont L Rev* (1968).

---

[345]Nov 1966 saw the first issue, see R Braibanti (1968), The Role of Law in the Political Development of Pakistan, in, Braibanti, *supra* note 104, 82. This essay was originally printed as a chapter in RR Wilson (ed) International and Comparative Law of the Common Wealth (NC, Duke University Press, Durham, 1968. The writer has modified the title of this essay.

BS Cohen, *Colonialism and its Forms of Knowledge: The British in India* (Princeton University Press, Princeton, 1996).

C Baxter (ed), *Diaries of Field Marshal Mohammad Ayub Khan: 1966–1972* (Oxford University Press, Karachi, 2007).

C Palley, The Judicial Process: U. D. I. and the Southern Rhodesian Judiciary, *Mod L Rev* (1967).

D Conrad, In Defense of the Continuity of Law: Pakistan's Courts in Crisis of State, in, *of Pakistan and others,* PLD 1977.

DA Washbrook, Economic Depression and Making of Traditional Society in Colonial India 1820–1855, 3 *Trans Royal Hist Soc* (1993).

DC Engerman, N Gilman, MH Haefele & ME Latham (eds), *Staging Growth: Modernization, Development, and the Global Cold War* (University of Massachusetts Press, Amherst, 2003).

DM Trubek, The Owl and the Pussy-cat: Is there a future of Law and Development, 25 *Wis Int'l LJ* (2007).

F Fanon. *Black Skin, White Masks* (Grove Press, New York, 1968).

F Fanon. *The Wretched of the Earth* (Grove Press, New York, 2004).

F Mohammed, Protecting Pakistani Labourers Post-Eighteenth Amendment: Recognizing Rights after the Devolution of Power, 9:2 *Loy U Chicago LJ* (2012).

F Robinson, *Separatism among Indian Muslims: The Politics of the United Provinces Muslims,* 1860–1923 (Oxford University Press, Delhi, 1993).

FM Brookfield, The Courts, Kelsen and the Rhodesian Revolution, 19 *University of Toronto Law* Review (1969).

H Alavi & T Shanin (eds), *Introduction to the Sociology of "Developing Societies"* (Monthly Review Press, New York/London, 1982).

H Gardezi & J Rashid (eds), *Pakistan: The Unstable State* (Vanguard Books, Lahore, 1983).

H Jalal & K Hasan (eds), *The Politics of the People- Awakening the People, Vol. Two, 1966–69* (Classic, Lahore, 1969).

H Khan, *Constitutional and Political History of Pakistan*, 2nd edn (Oxford University Press, Karachi, 2009).

H Zaheer, *The Times and Trial of the Pindi Conspiracy Case 1951: The First Coup Attempt in Pakistan* (Oxford University Press, Karachi, 1998).

HH Gerth & CW Mills (eds), *From Max Weber: Essays in Sociology* (Routledge/K Paul, London, 1970).

JM Dawood, *The Role of Superior Judiciary in the Politics of Pakistan* (Royal Book Company, Karachi, 1994).

KA Ali, Communists in a Muslim Land: Cultural Debates in Pakistan's Early Years, 45:3 *Mod Asian Stud* (2011).

L Binder, *Religion and Politics in Pakistan* (University of California, Berkley, 1963).

LA Khan, *Pakistan: The Heart of Asia: speeches by Liaqat Ali Khan* (Royal Book Company, Karachi 1989).

M Ahmad, *Government and Politics in Pakistan* (Space Publishers, Karachi, 1970).

M Hussain & A Hussain, *Pakistan: Problems of Governance* (Vanguard, Lahore, 1993).

M Janowitz, *The Professional Soldier: A Social and Political Portrait* (Free Press, New York, 1960).

SP Huntington, *The Political Order in Changing Societies* (Yale University Press, New Haven, 1968).

M Kaplan, Panopticon in Poona: An Essay on Foucault and Colonialism, 10:1 *Cult. Anthropol* (1995).

M Munir, CJSC (Ret, as he then was), *From Jinnah to Zia* (Vanguard, Lahore, 1979).

M Munir, CJSC (Ret, as he then was), *Highways and Bye-ways of Life* (Law Publishing Company, Lahore, 1978).

M Waseem, *Politics and the State in Pakistan*, 3rd edn (NIHCR, Islamabad, 2007).

MA Khan, *Friends not Masters: A Political Autobiography* (Oxford: London, 1967).

MKB Marri, CJBHC (Ret, as he then was), *A Judge May Speak* (Feroz Sons (Pvt) Ltd, Lahore, 1990).

NH Chaudhry, *Chief Justice Muhammad Munir: His life, Writings and Judgments* (Research Society of Pakistan, Lahore, 1973).

NH Shah, CJSC (Ret, as he then was), *Memoirs and Reflections* (Alhamra Printing, Islamabad, 2002).

Oxford Essays in Jurisprudence, 2nd series, (Oxford, 1973).

P Chatterjee, *The Nations and its Fragments: Colonial and Postcolonial Histories* (Princeton University Press, 1993).

PR Newberg, *Judging the State: Courts and Constitutional Politics in Pakistan* (Cambridge University Press, New Delhi, 1995).

R Braibanti, *Chief Justice Cornelius of Pakistan: An Analysis with Letters and Speeches* (Oxford University Press, Karachi, 1999).

RS Welsh, The Function of the Judiciary in a Coup d'etat, 87 *SALJ* (1970).

RWM Dias, Legal politics: Norms Behind the Grundnorm, 26 *Cambridge LJ* (1968).

S Anwar-ul-Haq, CJSC (Ret, as he then was), *Revolutionary Legality in Pakistan* (Pakistan Writers' Co-operative Society, Lahore, 1993).

S Toor, *The State of Islam: Culture and Cold War Politics in Pakistan* (Pluto Press, London 2011).

Shahid-ur-Rehman, *Who owns Pakistan*? (Mr Books, Islamabad, 1998).

SM Haider, *Public Administration and Administrative Law* (Law Times Publications, Lahore, 1973).

SM Haider, American Constitution and Assimilation of Modern Legal Norms in Pakistan, XL*PLD* (1988) Journal Section, 121, 126.

SR Khan (ed), *50 Years of Pakistan's Economy: Traditional Topics and Contemporary Concerns* (Oxford University Press, Karachi, 1999).

SS Pirzada, *Quaid-i-Azam Muhammad Ali Jinnah: As a Lawyer* (Nazaria-i-Pakistan Trust, Lahore, 2000).

TA Khan, *The Post-Colonial State in The Era of Capitalist Globalization: Historical, Political, and Theoretical Approaches to State Formation* (Routledge, New York, 2012).

TKK Iyer, Constitutional Law in Pakistan: Kelsen in the Courts, 21 *Am J Comp L* (1973).

WP Zingel, S Zingel & A Lallemant (eds), *Pakistan in the 80s: Law & Constitution* (Vanguard, Lahore, 1985).

ZK Maluka, *The myth of Constitutionalism in Pakistan*, (Oxford University Press, Karachi, 1995).

Chapter 3
Law Under Bhutto's Socialism (1970–1980s)

3.1 Judiciary Confronting Popular Democracy: 1968–1973

In the last chapter, we saw that a strong judiciary and rights discourse came as a response to a deficit in democracy under Ayub's strong presidential system. What is the place of law in a political model where there is popular and representative democracy (though not even deeper and broader)? Do people rush to their representatives and not the courts for justice? Is the legislature a protector of fundamental rights and not courts? The early years of Bhutto's regime, 1970–1973, give such an example. But liberal, let alone 'quasi-liberal' Cornelius tradition, analyses have very controversial and differing opinions about Bhutto. They have found his regime to be Bonapartist, or patrimonial, but not popular. He has been variously described as fascist,[1] a two-faced man,[2] and patrimonial ruler,[3] while his socialism has been referred to as Fabian socialism,[4] or naïve socialism.[5] For this latter tendency, Bhutto was a feudal, and he destroyed Ayub's modernity, which could have made Pakistan an Asian Tiger.[6] For Musharraf, Bhutto was a despotic leader and the worst thing that had yet happened to Pakistan.[7] Mushahid and Akmal, meanwhile, saw populism, liberal democracy and feudal despotism in Bhutto.[8] It is perhaps not sur-

---

[1]E Ahmad, Pakistan: Signpost to a Police State, *J. Contemp. Asia* (1974) 423, available at <http://www.bitsonline.net/eqbal/articles_by_eqbal_view_13B7A1E1.htm>, last visited 24 February 2014.
[2]S Taseer, *Bhutto: A Political Biography* (Ithaca Press, London, 1979) 193.
[3]GA Heeger, Politics in the Post-Military State: Some Reflections on the Pakistani Experience, *World Polit.* (1977) 254.
[4]SJ Burki, Is Pakistan's Past Relevant for Its Economic Future?, in, C Baxter & CH Kennedy (eds) *Pakistan: 1997* (Westview Press, Boulder, 1998) 17, 18.
[5]SA Burki, *A Revisionist History of Pakistan* (Vanguard, Lahore, 1998) 69.
[6]*Ibid* 71.
[7]P Musharraf, *In the Line of Fire: A Memoir* (Free Press, New York, 2006) 58.
[8]M Hussain & A Hussain, *Pakistan: Problems of Governance* (Vanguard, Lahore, 1993) 125.

M. Azeem, *Law, State and Inequality in Pakistan*, International Law and the Global South, DOI 10.1007/978-981-10-3845-7_3

prising that liberal intellectuals, like Newberg, also did not accept that the popularly elected government of Bhutto resembled democracy, even in its first years.[9] Hamid's analysis of Bhutto and his legacy shows how the Cornelius tradition viewed Bhutto. While admiring Bhutto's brilliance, he also found arrogance, impulsiveness and overarching ambitions.[10] Supreme Court Chief Justice Anwar-ul-Haq expressed these views clearly after his appointment as Chief Justice by Zia. He described a strain having been placed on the judiciary by the Bhutto regime.[11] Khalid M. Ishaque also hammered the "bureaucracy ridden welfare state" under Bhutto, which was causing greatest injustice under the cover of secrecy.[12] Chief Justice Sajjad Ali Shah evinces surprise that even being a barrister himself and with more than half of his ministers being lawyers, Bhutto could not help the judiciary in getting a better deal.

These views may be justifiable if Bhutto's regime is viewed in totality. However, if we break his period of governance into two, we can see that he had popular support at first. We will also see how Bhutto's party and its program have a contrasting relation of law and political development with that of Cornelius' tradition discussed in the previous chapter. With this established we can re-evaluate the case laws and legal struggles in Bhutto's early years.

3.1.1 The Rising Class and National Liberation Struggles and Changing Place of Law in Political Development

In the autumn of 1968, workers joined students and unemployed in all major cities of Pakistan until Ayub was overthrown in February 1969.[13] From Ayub's diary, which covers the period from the rise of Bhutto (1968–1970) till the 1971 liberation of Bangladesh, we can recognize the class forces of the time.[14] Ayub pointed out his fear of rising socialism as seen in fights between Suharto and Adam Malik; for him it meant a potential takeover by communism, even in a Muslim country.[15] He pointed out that the Red Shirts were creating problems in the Air Force,[16] and

---

[9]PR Newberg, *Judging the State: Courts and Constitutional Politics in Pakistan* (Cambridge University Press, New Delhi, 1995) 120.

[10]H Khan, *Constitutional and Political History of Pakistan,* 2nd edn (Oxford University Press, Karachi, 2009) 340.

[11]*PLD* (1977) Journal Section 253.

[12]KM Ishaque, Independence of Judiciary, *PLJ* (1975) Magazine Section 5, 15.

[13]Z Shaheed, *The Labour Movement in Pakistan: Organization and Leadership in 1970s* (Oxford University Press, Karachi, 2007); See also A Amjad, *Labour Legislation and Trade: Unions in India and Pakistan* (Oxford University Press, Karachi, 2001).

[14]C Baxter (ed), *Diaries of Field Marshal Mohammad Ayub Khan: 1966-1972* (Oxford University Press, Karachi, 2007).

[15]*Ibid* 129.

[16]*Ibid* 143, entry of Sep 1967.

feared a communist takeover by Bashani,[17] who had reached the countryside. Students and unions were also on his mind, fear that they would take over.[18] The landed elite came to Ayub, as well as the industrialists Adamjees and Hyesons,[19] whom he noted were shaky.[20]

Even in East Pakistan, though the national question seemed dominant, yet the socialists struggle and ideas were playing a crucial role. For Alavi, Mujib and Suhrawardy's Nationalist parties had their basis in the 'Sardari lineage' of rich landlords who were capable of controlling the votes until the independence of Bangladesh in 1971.[21] The success of the Awami League in the 1970 election was due to the fact that the rural elite jumped on the party's bandwagon.[22] But, since the early 1950s, there was another movement for the Bengali language led by grass-roots Left cadre. The movement echoed with the ideology of social justice and was marked with consciousness of the demands of workers and peasants.[23] This second tradition also contained the rural populist tradition of Bengali peasants led by Maulana Bashani (the working-class Maoist leader from East Pakistan). Ayub himself, as observed through his diary entries, was less concerned with Mujib than Bashani. For Alavi, socialists were intertwined in the Bengali language movement but remained distinct.[24] After the crackdown by the Pakistani army, the populist Marxist cadre in the first tradition joined the armed liberation struggle. This led to an intervention by India, "to forestall the liberation of Bangladesh by popular forces and to instal the Awami League elitist leadership in power".[25] The Marxist Left in East Bengal, according to Alavi, was on the forefront of an united armed liberation struggle in Bangladesh, along with sections of the Left in the Awami League.[26]

Bhutto, riding on this tide of working class upsurge, won 1970 elections. Joined by J.A. Rahim, Bhutto wrote the founding document of a new party, the Pakistan People's Party (PPP), in English in 1967.[27] Dr. Mubahsar Hassan and Hanif Ramay wrote the Urdu version wrote the Urdu version. The 1970s elections, the campaign and its results, are indicative of Bhutto's wide popularity, where in people were approached directly during the campaigning process, which was unique. The supremacy of the people, not that of the constitution, was a recurring theme in Bhutto's speeches. Additionally, the election results brought into political positions

---

[17]*Ibid* 328, entry of Sep 8, 1969.

[18]*Ibid* 333, 337, 343, 417, 418, entries of 02 and 07 October, and 02 Dec 2, 1969.

[19]*Ibid* 326, entry of Aug 30, 1969.

[20]*Ibid* 359, entry of Jan 26, 1970.

[21]H Alavi, The State in Post-Colonial Societies: Pakistan and Bangladesh, 74 *New Left Rev.* (1972) 59, 66.

[22]*Ibid* 79.

[23]H Alavi, Bangladesh and the Crisis of Pakistan, *Social Rev.* (1971) 289, 310.

[24]Alavi, *supra* note 21, 77.

[25]*Ibid* 80.

[26]Alavi, *supra* note 23, 294.

[27]Foundation Documents of the Pakistan People's Party, Lahore, November 1967.

little-known lawyers, engineers and other political novices. In Sindh, some large landowners were nominated on the condition that they would respect the PPP platform.[28] Horizontal solidarities among subordinate classes were struck based on class-consciousness. The party, furthermore, responded to regional issues, recognizing that in Punjab, class issues were dominant, whereas in Baluchistan, Sindh and East Pakistan, ethno-nationalist discrimination were serious concerns. Only in the NWFP did prior political regime hold sway.

A brief review of Bhutto's thought helps pinpoint his stance as clearly distinct from any of those who had preceded him, except possibly Jinnah. Bhutto found Western democracy to be responsible for considerable troubles left behind in decolonized countries. He argued that leaders of newly independent countries should have started with a clean slate and evolved a system from below. Against an elitist democracy, he believed that the right to vote should not be based on property or education.[29] He wanted a substantive democracy as opposed to a formal one and commented that democracy could not arise out of inequality, like that which existed in India.[30] Bhutto attacked the Basic Democracy system of juridico-bureaucratic Cornelius-Ayub nexus as having "nothing democratic in it",[31] calling its supporters as "Brahmins of this country".[32] For him, economic objectives could not be abandoned. Furthermore, he argued, "we want democracy as well as socialism".[33] He wanted a socialist economy,[34] with socialist modernization as 'objective sciences' like mathematics.[35]

Bhutto also saw the importance of delinking centre–periphery relations for the countries of Asia and Africa[36]; and the importance of connecting with the other nations of the world including the communist, Islamic or emerging nations of Asia, Africa and Latin America. Bhutto was opposed to Ayub's closed western bloc, and the Islamic world of the Cornelius tradition. Even during his time with Ayub, he understood not to unnecessarily extend principles of attachment to the U.S. in lieu

---

[28]SA Hussain, *The Discourse and Politics of Zulfikar Ali Bhutto* (Macmillan, London, 1992) 80.

[29]ZA Bhutto (1968), Political Situation in Pakistan, in, H Jalal & K Hasan (eds) *Zulfikar Ali Bhutto* (1969)*: The Politics of the People: Awakening the People, 1966-69*, vol 2 (Classic, Lahore, 1969) 89, 91, Pamphlet, April, 1968.

[30]Bhutto (1967), My Debut in Journalism, *supra* note 29, 22, 28. The Pakistan Observer, Dacca, 12 January, 1967.

[31]Bhutto (1968), Role of Women, *supra* note 29, 51, 55, an address to PPP Women Workers Lahore, January 29, 1968.

[32]Bhutto (1968), Starting with a Clean Slate, *supra* note 29, 43, 46, an address to the Muzaffargarh Bar Association, January 17, 1968.

[33]Bhutto (1969), The Struggle Continues, *supra* note 29, 186, 193. Speech at a Meeting, Peshawar, November 5, 1968.

[34]Bhutto (1968), Starting with a Clean Slate, *supra* note 29, 43, 45. Address to the Muzaffargarh Bar Association, January 17, 1968.

[35]*Ibid* 43, 47. Address to the Muzaffargarh Bar Association, January 17, 1968.

[36]ZA Bhutto (1965), Asian African Solidarity, in, *The Quest for Peace: Selection from Speeches and Writings 1963-65* (Classic, Lahore, 1965) 31, 38. Address at the Afro-Asian Seminar, Lahore, Feb 11 1965.

of China and the U.S.S.R.[37] Yet, he claimed that he also did not wish to delink from the West.[38] He noted that the economic successes of the U.S. were due to its vast resources and a small population. Pakistan has a large population and fewer resources, so the U.S. model could not work.[39]

As far as ideas about law and judiciary are concerned, Bhutto, distancing himself from Cornelius, Munir and Ayub's coup tradition, stated that the *coup d'etats* in Pakistan were not revolutions "as those who were ousted were brought back".[40] Revolution and *coup d'etat* are different for him, with revolution having a "motor of ideals in it". A coup gave the impression that it has solved the problem, though it did not. So, instead of the status quo or coup, he argued that one should favour revolution,[41] that revolution could produce socialism, as in that age only two systems were possible, capitalism or socialism.[42]

Bhutto was of the opinion that in 1954, people were unaware of their rights, leadership was weak, and resistance came in the form of a writ petition (in the *Moulvi Tamizzuddin* case). However, dictatorship could not be destroyed filing writ petitions. Ayub was overthrown by the people, not a writ petition, which served as a warning for dictators of the future.[43] We learn from Bhutto's speeches that he thought it was an inalienable and fundamental right of the people to participate in governing.[44] People can surrender some of their rights for a collective purpose. A regime can win the cooperation of the people if individual rights are protected, or, in an ideological state where civil liberties are suspended until the achievements of high ideological objectives/ends are met. An authoritarian system can work, but the people must believe in the objectives so that they can sacrifice their rights.[45] He rejected the West's criticisms of the leaders of poor countries in this regard.[46] He also warned lawyers to mend their ways, that one day they would have "to appear before the court of the people".[47]

---

[37]*Supra* note 28, 108.

[38]*Ibid* 37.

[39]Bhutto (1968), Why People's Party?, *supra* note 29, 153, 154. Speech at Party Meeting, Peshawar, October 27, 1968.

[40]Bhutto, A New Class of Landlords, *supra* note 29, 80, 82. Address at Larkana Bar Association, March 12, 1968.

[41]Bhutto (1968), Political Situation in Pakistan, *supra* note 29, 89, 91. A Pamphlet, April, 1968.

[42]Bhutto (1968), Revolution Brewing, *supra* note 29, 159 at 160. Speech at Ismalia College, Peshawar, October 28, 1968.

[43]Bhutto (1969), Why Ayub Fell?, *supra* note 29, 232, 234. Address at the District Bar Association, Hyderabad, June 26, 1969.

[44]Bhutto, Address to Nawabshah Bar Association, *supra* note 29, 161, 63.

[45]The examples are when Nehru faced famine, he asked for cooperation from the people but he did not accept terms against India's national interest. Same was Nasser facing a ban on the supply of wheat, see Bhutto (1967), On Accusation by the Ayub Regime, *supra* note 29, 38, 39. Address to Young Lawyers' Circle, Lahore 25 February 1967.

[46]Bhutto (1965), The Role of Great Powers, *supra* note 29, 24, 25. Address to the Foreign Press Association, London, May 6, 1965.

[47]Not the Cornelius court (my comments), see Bhutto (1968), The Government, *supra* note 29, 119. Address at Sind Convention, Hyderabad, September 21, 1968.

Before the 1970 election, Bhutto gave a full departure of his constitutional scheme from the prevailing Cornelius tradition. His distancing from Cornelius was an indication of his disagreement with this juridico-bureaucratic structure and its institutional arrangements. Cornelius served in Yahya's regime as the Minister of Law. When Yahya requested Cornelius and G.W. Chaudhry of East Pakistan to draft a new constitution in 1971, Bhutto, then Foreign Minister and President, objected to this assignment and called Cornelius a "Dhimmi"[48] who could not write the constitution of a Muslim State. After this, Cornelius refused to support Bhutto in seeking support from the Christian countries for the release of prisoners of war in India.[49] However, more important to understand is how do both, Cornelius and Bhutto, differ in their political and constitutional understanding.

In Bhutto's constitutional scheme, presented before the 1970 election, the forthcoming constitution would have its particular bias, which is the expression of class forces by which it is fashioned.[50] Yet, the constitution and referendum cannot bring about 'structural changes'.[51] Similarly, there is not a single thought about the judiciary acting as a check on restraint on legislature and executive. Rather, people not courts are the protectors of the Constitution here.[52] Bhutto's constitutional scheme strongly rejected presidential system like in the U.S., declaring it a "militaristic state without being military dictatorship".[53] Demand for a presidential system for him was a demand for dictatorship.[54] Whereas Ayub's, as well as the Constitutional Commission report by Justice Shahabuddin, rejected the option of a parliamentary system on the grounds of there being too many political parties, Bhutto reasoned there were too many parties due to the democratic process.[55]

Bhutto also departed from Ayub and the Cornelius tradition in idea of the imposition of Islam. Bhutto argued that Ayub should not have suppressed indigenous cultures, rather, he should have "encouraged the flowering of a variety of cultures within our state to enrich the development of a synthesized national culture".[56] Bhutto emphasized the need of a synthesis of modernity and tradition[57] as opposed to the grafting of Islam on liberalism as done by the Cornelius tradition. In

[48] A non-Muslim citizen of an 'Islamic state.'

[49] R Braibanti, *Chief Justice Cornelius of Pakistan: An Analysis with Letters and Speeches* (Oxford University Press, Karachi, 1999) 18.

[50] JA Rahim, *Outline of a Federal Constitution for Pakistan* (Pakistan People's Party Political Series No. 4, Lahore, 1969) 22.

[51] Rahim, *supra* note 50, 9.

[52] Rahim, *supra* note 50, 21.

[53] Rahim, *supra* note 50, 51.

[54] Rahim, *supra* note 50, 52.

[55] Rahim, *supra* note 50, 61.

[56] ZA Bhutto, *The Great Tragedy* (Pakistan People's Party Publication, Karachi, 1971) 3.

[57] Bhutto (1965), *supra* note 36, 31, 39. Address at the Afro-Asian Seminar, Lahore, 11 February 1965.

fact, his political style indigenized and nativized Pakistani politics through the participation of people for the first time in it.[58]

After Ayub, and before Bhutto, Cornelius joined Yahya as a law minister, S.M. Haider, as a true continuity of Braibanti and Cornelius, kept promoting Cornelius' legal formation as a combination of Islam and U.S. liberal legal system.[59] He elaborated, in more detail, how judicial review was developed under Cornelius courts *to curb and veto the majority* [my emphasis].[60] He advocated the first articulated case of Cornelius's position on rights vis-à-vis Munir. This extensive account tried to prove his position as being closer to the U.S. system.[61] This description uncritically became a trend within legal circles in Pakistan and was later continued by Justice Nasim Hassan Shah, Hamid Khan and current legal academics like Lombardi.[62] He strongly pushed the idea of administrative tribunals of Cornlius and wrote a full book.[63] He invited Cornelius for talks in influential circles.[64] After Cornelius, S.A. Rehman and Fazal-e-Akabar served as Chief Justices of Supreme Court for 96 and 166 days, respectively, and finally Hamood-ur-Rahman became Chief Justice of the Supreme Court and was intended to give a new level of 'original thinking' in 1969 to trend of Islamization initiated by Cornelius.[65]

The above trend had to stop on the face of Bhutto's popular democracy. Bhutto's perception of the role of politics and law was entirely different than that of Ayub

---

[58]Hussain, *supra* note 28, 254.

[59]SM Haider used US Supreme Court decisions on racial segregation of Blacks. SM Haider, Equality before Law and Equal Protection of Laws as a Legal Doctrine for the Prevention of Discrimination and Protection of Minorities, *PLD* (1971) Journal Section 65.

[60]SM Haider, Judicial Review and Public Administration in Pakistan, *PLD* (1969) Journal Section 98; SM Haider, Contribution of Mr. Justice A. R. Cornelius to the Expansion of Judicial Review and Public Liberties, *PLD* (1970) Journal Section 39; SM Haider, Evolving Doctrine of Judicial Review in Pakistan, *PLD* (1969) Journal Section 157.

[61]SM Haider, Judicial Review, Natural Rights and Legislative Action, *PLD* (1970) Journal Section 66.

[62]CB Lombardi, Can Islamizing a Legal System Even Help Promote Liberal Democracy?: A View From Pakistan, 7:3 *U. St. Thomas L.J* (2010) 649.

[63]SM Haider, Contribution of Mr. Justice AR Cornelius to Administrative Law, *PLD* (1969) Journal Section 55; SM Haider, Plea for Administrative Tribunals: Scheme visualized by Mr. Justice AR Cornelius, *PLD* (1969) Journal Section 164; SM Haider, French Administrative Law: A Mode, *PLD* (1970) Journal Section 25. He advocated how Cornelius advanced this idea in 1960 onward; SM Haider, A Framework of Administrative Law for Pakistan, *PLD* (1970) Journal Section 98. Finally, he wrote a book to develop this idea fully. SM Haider, Public Administration and Administrative Law (Law Times Publications, Lahore, 1973).

[64]AR Cornelius, Speech at the Inauguration of International Seminar on Administrative Law, Journal Section, *PLD* (1971) Journal Section 30; AR Cornelius, Fundamental Rights under Shari'at, *PLD* (1970) Journal Section 144, an address delivered at the first orientation course in Administrative Law instituted by the Ministry of Law, and conducted by Dr. S. M. Haider of Pakistan Academy for Rural Development.

[65]H Rahman, Significant Features of Islamic Jurisprudence & Need to Re-establish Tradition of Original Thinking, *PLD* (1969) Journal Section 48, a speech delivered at the reception of the International Muslim Jurists Organization, Karachi on January 01, 1969.

and Cornelius. Whether Bhutto believed it or not, he was responding to people's restlessness, the subaltern classes (a mix of class and ethno-nationalist groups[66]), who gradually rose beginning from mid-1960s.

To conclude, the political developments since Ayub's overthrowing in 1968, the policies of Yahya reflects how he tried to counter the imbalance created by capitalist modernization of Ayub. He promoted 'social justice and egalitarianism' to prevent concentration of wealth and hence, promulgated a Control and Prevention Ordinance 1970.[67] Yahya immediately gave a labour policy recognizing that workers had not received a 'fair deal' under the previous regime and passed an Industrial Relations Ordinance in 1969.[68] Yahya immediately purged 300 high level bureaucrats,[69] and also curtailed the powers of the judiciary through *Jurisdiction of Courts (Removal of Doubts) Order, 1969*.[70] Through a presidential order, *Judges (Declaration of Assets) Order, 1969*, judges of the superior courts were ordered to declare their assets before the Supreme Judicial Council on a prescribed form.[71] Justice Fazle Khan of Lahore High Court resigned and Justice Shaukat Ali was removed from the service on the recommendation of Supreme Judicial Council.[72] Yahya brought back the Cornelius Report of 1962 (which was critical of the old type of bureaucracy) and published it. Similarly, he appointed Cornelius to be in charge of the Pay Commission. He agreed to democratic institutions, political parties and elections.

Though Yahya's coup was similar to Ayub's in term of the continuity of the power structure, and though it was also bloodless,[73] it was not tolerated by the juridico-bureaucratic structure, which was quite comfortable with Ayub. Yahya instituted a parallel judicial structure, which the courts also vigorously opposed. Yahya established special and summary military courts and any appeal in High Courts and the Supreme Court could not override the orders of these courts.[74] Added to this was Pakistan's defeat in the 1971 war under the leadership of Yahya, which led to the independence of Bangladesh.

In 1971, Bhutto inherited a smaller country (as Bangladesh had now seceded) and 'a baffled people'.[75] He emphasized economic change more than political

[66]*Ibid.*

[67]T Kamran, *Democracy and Governance in Pakistan* (South Asian Partnership-Pakistan, Lahore, 2008) 70.

[68]F Mohammed, Pakistani Labourers Post-Eighteenth Amendment: Recognizing Rights after the Devolution of Power, 9:2 *Loy. U. Chi. L.J.* (2012) 265, 274.

[69]CH Kennedy, *Bureaucracy in Pakistan* (Oxford University Press, Karachi, 1988) 77.

[70]*Jurisdiction of Courts (Removal of Doubts) Order*, 1969, and Presidential Order 3 of 1969, PLD 1969 Central Statutes 119.

[71]*Judges (Declaration of Assets) Order*, 1969; PLD 1969 Central Statutes 120.

[72]*President v Justice Shaukat Ali*, PLD 1971 SC 585.

[73]M Waseem, *Politics and the State in Pakistan*, 3rd edn (NIHCR, Islamabad, 2007) 234.

[74]*Supra* note 70.

[75]ZA Bhutto, *The Third World: New Directions* (Quartet Books, London, 1977) 14.

change so as to break with economic inequality.[76] Pakistan was forced to "squeeze centuries into decades" but not through a 'pernicious doctrine'[77] of functional inequality,[78] rather through economic strength as there is no power without economic strength.[79] Within days of Bhutto assuming office, the passports of 22 business families were confiscated and two main industrialists, Ahmad Dawood and Fakhruddin Valika, were shown handcuffed on TV. According to Lawrence J. White, Bhutto 'nationalized' ten industries within weeks in January 1972 arrest two leading Pakistani industrialists.[80] The landed class now faced land reforms based on principles of rationalization and Bhutto's labour, education and health reforms became directed by rational policies.[81] The labour policy was the continuity of Noor Khan's policy. On 10 March,[82] and later on 12 March 1972, 1300 civil servants[83] were dismissed, retired or reduced in rank. These actions were not reviewed in any court of law. Bhutto retired 43 top rank officers from the three armed forces in four months. On 4 March 1972, Commander-in-Chief of the Army, Lt. General Gul Hasan and Air Marshal Rahim, the head of the Air Force, were dismissed. Bhutto brought the command structure of the military under the Prime Minister. Bhutto lifted Martial Law on 20 April 1972 after putting an interim constitution in place. This constitution was parliamentary in nature, with the president as supreme commander of the forces. The President could promulgate ordinances only when the National Assembly was not in session. In the first six months, between December 1971 and May 1972, Bhutto had controlled the potentially hostile centres of power.[84]

This situation of Yahya's humiliated departure after the defeat in the 1971 war with India and Bhutto's popularity gave birth to the *Asma Jilani case* and *Zia-ur-Rahman case* which showed the relation of judiciary with this transitional and unprecedented period of popular democracy in Pakistan.

---

[76]*Ibid* 20.

[77]*Ibid* 22.

[78]*Ibid* 22.

[79]*Ibid* 86.

[80]LJ White, *Industrial Concentration and Economic Power in Pakistan* (Princeton University Press, Princeton, 1974) 3.

[81]Waseem, *supra* note 73, 302.

[82]*Martial Law Regulation 114*, 1972, *Removal from Service (Special Provisions) Regulation No. 114*, 1972, PLD 1972 Central Statutes 387.

[83]572 from Sindh, 251 from Punjab, 109 from NWFP, 393 from the center, while none from Baluchistan.

[84]Hussain, *supra* note 28, 119.

3.1.2 Asma Jilani Case: For Democracy or Just Against a Dictator?

Asma Jilani case is celebrated by liberal and quasi-liberal doctrinal analyses as a victory of the judiciary against a dictator, in favour of democracy. The 'Cornelius tradition' under the leadership of Supreme Court Chief Justice Hamood-ur-Rehman was facing a new political situation. Newberg's claim is that the courts were 'unprepared' for Bhutto.[85] I disagree. They were fully ready to confront Bhutto but the *Asma Jilani* and *Zia-ur-Rahman* cases were indicative of the transitory nature of politics, which was marked with popular democracy. Trained under the juridico-bureaucratic mindset of 'controlled democracy' and 'constitutional limits' courts were cautious, reluctant and could not understand the changing politics and what legal tools were required.

The facts of the case were that Malik Ghulam Jilani was detained under the Defence of Pakistan Rules, 1971 which was rescinded and substituted by Martial Law Regulation No. 78. Asma Jilani, the daughter of the detenu, challenged this order. The government maintained the position that the court has no jurisdiction to entertain the petition under Jurisdiction of Courts (Removal of Doubts) Order, 1969 by Yahya. Through this Order, the jurisdiction of the courts was ousted. The Sindh High Court gave similar a decision in a case challenging the detention of Altaf Gohar. Both cases came before the Supreme Court in an appeal. The Supreme Court had a chance to reflect on *the doctrine of necessity* and Kelsen's theory and found it to be an inappropriate law. The Court also declared that as Ayub had no power to hand over power to Yahya under the Constitution of 1962, Yahya had illegally usurped the power, Provisional Constitutional Order 1969[86] was illegal, and hence the jurisdiction of the courts was not ousted.[87]

What was the actual target of Hamood-ur-Rehman CJ; Yahya, doctrine of necessity in Dosso case, or Jurisdiction of Courts (Removal of Doubts) Order, 1969 by Yahya? To know this, we are to transcend this liberal analyses' dichotomy of democracy versus dictatorship particularly around this case. Calling Yahya 'a usurper' by the CJ seems a simple reflection of the general hatred people had for Yahya after losing the 1971 war against India. But particular to this hatred in Hamood-ur-Rahman CJSC is his exposure to the criminal role of Yahya and his military generals in the war of 1971 because Hamood-ur-Rahman headed the commission to inquire in this matter, which was declassified after 40 years. If we look into the timeline of the Commission's Report, it is clear that recording of the evidence started from February 1, 1972 and it finished on 26 April 1972. Hamoord-ur-Rahman wrote this Report till 8 July 1972, whereas the Asma Jilani case was decided on 20 April 1972. So, clearly the decision of Asma Jilani case was

[85]Newberg, *supra* note 9, 132.

[86]*Provisional Constitution Order, (1969)*, PLD 1969 Central Statutes 41.

[87]*Asma Jilani v Government of the Punjab*, PLD 1972 SC 139.

made based on the report by CJ Hamoor-ur-Rehman, Anwar-ul-Haq CJLHC and Tufail Ali Abd-ur-Rahman CJSHC. The decision was not the tip of the anger which the verdict of the Commission Report had, that is, to publicly try Gen. Yahya, Gen. Hamid, Gen. Pirzada, Gen. Umar, Let-Gen. Hussan, Maj-Gen. Mitta for being a party to a criminal conspiracy to illegally 'usurp power'.[88]

Now coming to the validity of Kelsen's theory and doctrine of necessity, Sharifuddin Pirzada objected that the decision in *Dosso case* was against the principles of natural justice theory. This pitted Munir's positivist reliance on Kelsen's theory against Cornelius' tradition of natural law. CJ objected the very positivist nature of Hans Kelsen's theory which was made universal by Munir CJ. In that sense, according to the court, CJ Munir made two errors, he thought that Kelsen's theory was universal (though it was hypothetical in the words of A.K. Brohi in this case). Second, Munir CJ misapplied this theory on Pakistan.[89] For Hamood-ur-Rehamn CJ, positive theory places authority in the political sovereign. Similarly legal realism, like positivism, is the will of state made through courts. As opposed to this, natural law finds its authority in moral principles, which the Cornelius tradition had replaced by Islam and hence 'sovereignty belongs to Allah' (Objectives Resolution). Hamood-ur-Rahman, while attacking Kelsen's doctrine of necessity as a grundnorm, placed the controversial Objectives Resolution as the new grundnorm, which, according to him, was never abrogated and he warned, "it cannot be".

Important to understand is that Hamood-ur-Rahman did not reject the doctrine of necessity but the way it was understood and applied by CJ Munir using the tradition of common law. Rather, Hamood-ur-Rahman CJ followed the role of the American courts when they adjudicated upon the validity of the acts after suppression of the rebellion in the Southern States. Courts did not undo the acts of the usurper necessary to peace and order and affecting property and contractual rights because it could result in disastrous consequences. Ignoring the doctrine of necessity in that could have disastrous consequences. The method employed by the CJ was that courts should first conclude whether the acts of the usurper were illegal, then courts should bring doctrine of necessity to aid this situation to help the public. So, the principle will be principle of *condonation* and *not legitimation*.[90] This means that all businesses be closed, not to be opened, and the order should be restored according to the objectives mentioned in the Objectives Resolution. What the court should not do is to help the usurper entrench its power further and violate the rights of the citizens.[91] However, this decision sent two wrong messages to the legislature

[88]The Report of Hamood-ur-Rehman Commission of Inquiry into 1971 War: As Declassified by the Government of Pakistan (Vanguard, Lahore, 2001) 352.

[89]*Supra* note 87, 181.

[90]*Supra* note 87, 204.

[91]*Supra* note 87, 207.

as well as to the subordinate courts; one that courts are to decide all the acts of the usurper under the principle of condonation and that the controversial Objectives Resolution is the grundnorm. This misunderstanding gave birth to the *Zia-ur-Rahman* case.

3.1.3 Zia-ur-Rahman Case: A Judicial Retreat on the Face of Popular Democracy

The decision in the *Asma Jilani* case left a doubt in the minds of the legislature that each and every act by Martial Law would be 'condoned' by the courts. Bhutto's civilian Martial law government did not challenge this decision but it nullified the judgment by bringing Article 281 in the constitution, which validated all Martial Law Orders and Regulations and debarred the court from adjudicating upon them. Bhutto arrested his political opponents—Mukhtar Rana (a member of National Assembly and a very popular mass leader), Altaf Hussain Qureshi and Dr. Ijaz Hussain Qureshi (editors and publishers of *Urdu Digest,* respectively), and Majib-ur-Rahman Shami (editor of the weekly *Zindigi*).[92] The arrests were challenged through several writs filed by the relatives of the arrested in the Lahore High Court a hearing was held on 6 July 1972. The Lahore High Court, specially Justice Afzal Zullah (who later became Chief Justice of Supreme Court in early 1990s extending Cornelius tradition around Public Interest Litigation), 'correctly' understood the message of the Supreme Court in the *Asma Jilani case*. The court declared the Objectives Resolution as supra-constitutional, wherein sovereignty belongs to Allah. But instead of declaring the legislature exercising this sovereignty as trustee, the court went further and declared itself as the trustees of the people and Almighty, having the power to judicially review. The court then made clear that the legislature is not allowed 'tinkering' regarding this judicial power.[93] All the judges struck down Article 281 of the Interim Constitution.

An elected assembly found this judgment to be a clever attempt to undermine the Legislature. The debate included the view that the judiciary cannot question the policy of the government nor could it strike down the constitution. Substantive provisions of the constitution could not be controlled by its preamble or even by the Objectives Resolution. The purpose of appeal by the state in *Zia-ur-Rahman case* in the Supreme Court was to make clear the boundaries and limits of courts. The Advocate General emphasized the omnipotence of the Legislature, like the British Parliament, where courts do not have authority to challenge it. The entire *Ziu-ur-Rahman* judgment by the Supreme Court was a retreat by the judiciary. After

[92]Right wing leaders.

[93]*The State v Zia-ur-Rahman and others*, PLD 1973 SC 49, 63.

defining the scheme of separation of power under a written constitution, Hamood-ur-Rehman CJ made clear that "a Legislature, under written constitution, possesses the same power as "omnipotence" as the British Parliament".[94] The Chief Justice further made clear that the Supreme Court is not above the constitution, rather a creature of the constitution and the constitution gives it a right to interpret the constitution, which is a judicial power different than jurisdiction which is territorial and hierarchy to adjudication.[95] Coming back to the Objectives Resolutions, the Chief Justice made clear that Objectives Resolution is not a supra-Constitutional document, not enforceable as such, and *Asma Jilani case* did not declare Objectives Resolution as *grundnorm*.[96]

Because the Chief Justice was obsessed with Yahya in the *Asma Jilani case*, political questions regarding current regime were missing, that is, resumption of power by an elected, representative and popular leader. In this appeal, while describing how the political situation is changed, Hamood-ur-Rahman CJ gave legitimacy to the Legal Framework Order-LFO and to the regime. For him, Bhutto was the "elected representative of the people", the National Assembly was validly constituted, and the "Interim Constitution is a valid constitutional document".[97] All liberals Hamid, Newberg did not like this aspect of the decision, meant to give legitimacy to Bhutto. Munir CJSC (ret. as he then was) not only pointed out the mis-statements by Hamood-ur-Rehman CJSC, but also defended his reliance on Kelson's theory in his decision of *Tamizuddin Khan* case.[98] Munir, very correctly, was doubtful about the 'legality' of Bhutto but was very sure of Bhutto's 'popularity'. Here, one can add that apart from the legal theoretical adventure of Hamood-ur-Rehman, this was the 'popularity' that gave legitimacy to Bhutto, which the court simply reiterated.

Does this really mean that Hamood-ur-Rahman believed in democracy, supremacy of the legislature by not considering Objectives' Resolution as the *grundnorm* and, above all, was he a democrat? For this, we are to consider his model of political development from his writings and speeches.

In his model of state formation, Hamood-ur-Rahman CJSC wanted *Khalafit* with a body of persons (Turkish Grand Assembly after the regime of last *Khalifa*), which could elect a Council of Regency which would later elect the *Khalifa*. The *Majlis-e-Shoora* (parliament) could become a modern legislature but *cannot legislate about what already is decided in Quran and Sunnah* [my emphasis].[99] These legislators, for him, were not to be tied to any political party or their programs and were not beat the mercy of the head of the state. They were to be of special qualification with

---

[94]*Ibid* 66.

[95]*Ibid* 69.

[96]*Ibid* 61.

[97]*Ibid* 76.

[98]M Munir, *Highways and Bye-ways of Life* (Law Publishing Company, Lahore, 1978) 258.

[99]Rahman, The Concept of State in Islam, *infra* note 100, 214, an address delivered at a Sham-e-Hamdard function 1980 as well as at the Pakistan Administrative Staff College, Lahore.

knowledge of the teachings of Islam and technocrats. He made clearer that this model was not like Anglo-Saxon parliamentary model of U.K. but close to the presidential system of the U.S. He was in favour of giving a constitutional role to the military.[100]

While serving as a judge of the Supreme Court under Cornelius' justiceship in the 1960s, he dreamed of the "Kingdom of God on Earth".[101] He did not hesitate to join Zia as his constitutional advisor after the overthrowing of Bhutto. Relating his speeches of this period with Zia's Islamization gives us a clear indication that he was one of the important minds behind these controversial Islamic law amendments, which violated the human rights of minorities and women.[102] Anyhow, freedom of individual, for him, was limited to 'orderly' or 'controlled freedom'.[103] A.K. Brohi, while addressing the inaugural ceremony of the annual governing body meeting of All Pakistan Women's Association in 1966, had regretted that the role of women taking care of children is given up.[104] Hamood-ur-Rahman also reminded women of their 'primary responsibility', as explained by Brohi, above.[105]

To sum up this part, Hamood-ur-Rahman and his model of political development was quite in line with Cornelius' tradition of 'controlled democracy', with a strong president and the judiciary as a restraint on his powers as protectors of human rights. The decision in the *Asma Jilani case* was the reluctance and caution of the proponents of this tradition in the face of popular democracy. The announcement of democracy as an 'institutional change' from the courts was not necessary because peoples' mobilization and *structural changes* underway were louder than courts. Cornelius' tradition in judicial office, as well in the bar, waited for the Bhutto to lose support to come up with their model of political development.

---

[100]H Rahman, *Reflections on Islam* (Islamic Book Foundation, Lahore, 1983) 173.

[101]Rahman, The Kingdom of God on Earth, *supra* note 100, 36, a presidential address read at Iqbal Day function held under the auspicious of the Central Iqbal Committee in April 1967.

[102]Rahman, Muhammad (Peace Be Upon Him): The Last Prophet of Allah, *supra* note 100, an address read at an Eid-e-Milad-un-Nabi function held at the Assembly Chambers Lahore in January 1979.

[103]Rahman, The Rule of Law and Civil Rights in Islam, *supra* note 100, 176, a speech delivered at a Symposium arranged by the Civil Rights Forum on April 03, 1974.

[104]AK Brohi, Women and Family in an Age of Affluence, in, K Ahmad (ed) *Islam in the Modern World*, 2nd edn (Publishers United Ltd., Lahore, 1975) 125.

[105]Rahman, The Position of Women in Islam, *supra* note 100, 239, a presidential address at a conference of the Federation of Business & Professional Women Club, Karachi on August 15, 1975.

3.2 Democratic Deficit Under Bhutto and the Return of Strong Judiciary: 1973–1977

3.2.1 Judicial Reaction to Bhutto's Socialism

Bhutto put the judiciary 'in its place' through his plan of socialist modernization. He nationalized basic industries through the Economic Reforms Order, 1972 on 2 January, 1972.[106] The Supreme Court and High Courts could not question any of the provisions of this constitution and no injunction could be granted against anything done under this Order. The Land Reforms Regulation 1972 was promulgated on 11 March 1972, which also barred the courts from challenging its provisions and injunctions against any act under this regulation.[107] The management of schools and colleges was taken over under another Martial Law Regulation and the jurisdiction of the courts was completely ousted.[108] In order for the implementation of his socialist restructuring of the economy, Bhutto also reshuffled the bureaucracy by the Removal from Service Regulation dated 10 March 1972.[109]

Bhutto's new 1973 constitution had socialist orientation. The relevant clauses were Article 3, which laid down the principle of, "from each according to his ability" to each "according to his work"; Article 253, which was against the concentration of wealth and placed a limit on property one could own; and Article 34, giving full participation of women in all spheres of life. The Constitution also provided fora right to property under Article 23, subject to restrictions for many social objectives without fair compensation.

The courts could not grasp that the procedure of the law was no longer supreme, that popular will was. There was no need to check every legislative action by the judiciary, as the legislature was popular. The judiciary did not have to look for an excuse to intervene against executive actions. There was a need to rethink the purpose of the government, the new emerging foundations of the state and the place of legislature in it. But 'class' was a new idiom or term of art for the judiciary. There was a collective opposition by chief justices and lawyers in Cornelius' tradition against socialism in general and Bhutto's 'Islamic socialism' in particular.

Toor has argued that retired Supreme Court, Justice S.A. Rahman (a close colleague of Cornelius) was an 'established Cold Warrior' who actively countered

---

[106] *Economic Reforms Order*, 1972, President's Order I of 1972, PLD 1972 Central Statutes 86.

[107] *The Land Reforms Regulation*, 1972, *Martial Law Regulation No. 115*, 1972, PLD 1972 Central Statutes 388.

[108] *Martial Law Regulation No. 118*, 1972, PLD 1972 Central Statutes 441. The courts were not happy with this and then, in 1987, reacted to this nationalization. In *Board of Foreign Mission of Presbyterian Church v Govt of the Punjab*, PLJ 1987 SC 464, the SC found that in the nationalization of the high quality education provider institutions only the management of the schools is transferred and not the property.

[109] *Supra* note 82.

Bhutto's 'indigenous' version of 'Islamic Socialism'.[110] Chief Justice Munir, though secular and liberal, responding to socialism's rising demand during Ayub's last period, corrected the 'masses', that equality before law does not mean that the entire wealth of the country should be equally divided, irrespective of 'qualification' and participation in the production.[111] He found Islam and socialism two contradictory words.[112] For him Marx and Engels were utopians.[113] Chief Justice Shahabuddin (3 May 1960 to 12 May 1960) was worried that the youth was attracted towards Western and communist ideas.[114]

This prejudice continued in later superior court judges during and after Bhutto. For Chief Justice Anwar-ul-Haq (23 September 1977 to 25 March 1981), class struggle and class-consciousness were a "class prejudice" and the best way to get rid of this class prejudice was to legislate like England and achieve a welfare state.[115] Chief Justice Nasim found the economic reforms of Bhutto "radical to the extreme".[116] Chief Justice Sajjad Ali Shah (4 June 1994 to 2 December 1997) called Bhutto's socialist economic reforms as 'extreme measures' to resuscitate the economic life of the country.[117] Chief Justice Ajmal Mian (23 December 1997 to 30 June 1999) started visiting prisons in the mid-1980s. While on such an inspection tour of a Qazi Court of District Turbat, he saw a young man with a red scarf around his neck who entered the court, did not greet anyone and did not seek permission from the Qazi. The Qazi told Chief Justice Ajmal (as a Chief Justice of Baluchistan High Court) that he was a court clerk and one of the many young people from Baluchistan who went to the U.S.S.R. 'illegally' for further education and were

---

[110]AK. Brohi (Allah Buksh Brohi), was a known jurist and was also involved as a prosecutor in *Pindi Conspiracy case*. See AK Brohi, Reflections on Islamic Socialism, in, H Mehdi (ed) *Essays on Pakistan* (Progressive Publishers, Lahore, 1970); AK Brohi, Iqbalian Ijtihad and the Concept of Islamic Socialism *Iqbal Rev.* (1968) as cited by S Toor, *The State of Islam: Culture and Cold War Politics in Pakistan* (Pluto Press, London, 2011).

[111]M Munir, Change-over and Thereafter, in, NH Chaudhry (ed) *Chief Justice Muhammad Munir: His life, Writings and Judgments* (Research Society of Pakistan, Lahore, 1973), published in Pakistan Times of 3 March 1969.

[112]Munir, *supra* note 98, 228.

[113]Munir, CJSC (Ret, as he then was), Stateless and Classless Society, *supra* note 111, 173, published in Pakistan Times on 23rd and 24th January 1972.

[114]M Shahabuddin, *Recollection and Reflections: Being a Summary View on Religion and Social Life in the Sub-continent of Indo-Pakistan* (PLD Publishers, Lahore, 1972) 177.

[115]S Anwar-ul-Haq, CJSC (Ret, as he then was), You can Legislate against Prejudice, *infra* note 229, 357, 359.

[116]NS Shah, *Memoirs and Reflections* (Alhamra Printing, Islamabad, 2002) 166.

[117]SA Shah, CJSC (Ret, as he then was), *Law Courts in a Glass House: An Autobiography* (Oxford University Press, Karachi, 2001) 57.

'taught' communism. Chief Justice Ajmal admonished the young clerk and "tried to impress upon" the young clerk that he should be respectful to the elders and to the courts.[118]

While the reluctant and cautious Cornelius tradition in judicial office was looking at a weakening Bhutto who was loosing popular support, the strongest intellectual and legal reaction against Bhutto's socialism was by leading jurists A.K. Brohi and Khalid M. Ishaque. A.K. Brohi disliked the concept of 'Islamic socialism' in so-called intellectual circles during late 1960s. For him, in this combination 'Islamic' though substantive, was degraded into becoming an adjective of "socialism".[119] Later in 1970, he attacked Bhutto's party program with Islamic socialism.[120] He emphasized that we do not need the concept of social organization, production and distribution from socialism because there are no words like capitalism and socialism in Holy Quran.[121] To see socialism winning he proposed law as a means for peaceful change. He rejected the Marxist concept of law in that it serves a status quo.[122] When socialism became a reality in the early 1970s under Bhutto, being apologetic, he wanted it close to the labour party in England rather than like Lenin's. Nationalization without compensation was 'expropriation' which is *Haram* in Islam and against inviolable rights of property.[123] For him the 'Muslim' way is the middle way between communist and capitalist ideologies, that is, between everything for the state and complete liberty of the individual.[124] But when we read his understanding of political development, which seems as though he was the main ideologue behind the Cornelius tradition, this simply is neither the freedom of the capitalist society nor distribution of the socialist society. This became evident under Zia's dictatorship in the 1980s, which was the practice of the

[118]A Mian, CJSC (Ret, as he then was), *A Judge Speaks Out: An Autobiography* (Oxford University Press, Karachi, 2004) 80.

[119]Brohi, The Concept of Islamic Socialism, *supra* note 104, 94, an address on Iqbal Day celebrations on 23 April 23, 1967.

[120]Brohi, The Concept of Islamic Socialism, *supra* note 104, 99, an essay contributed to the *Daily Press* in 1970.

[121]Brohi, The Concept of Islamic Socialism, *supra* note 104, 105, an essay contributed to the *Daily Press* in 1970.

[122]AK Brohi, Law as an Instrument of Peaceful Change, *PLD* (1970) Journal Section 8, a lecture delivered at Banker's Staff College, Karachi on December 1, 1969.

[123]Brohi, The Concept of Islamic Socialism, *supra* note 104, 111, an essay contributed to the Daily Press in 1970.

[124]Brohi, Quintessence of the Islamic Way of Life, *supra* note 104, 44, an address delivered at the All-Pakistan Islamic Studies Conference, held at the University of Peshawar on March 28, 1964.

philosophy of Cornelius tradition (details to follow). Similarly, another influential jurist in Cornelius tradition,[125] Khalid M. Ishaque, gave a detailed critique of the economic system in socialism.[126]

3.2.2 *There Is a Need of Check on the Legislature*

Seeing a parliamentary system with supremacy of the legislature, the Cornelius tradition presented their alternate model, which they had developed since the Ayub–Cornelius period. Before the 1973 constitution, Khalid M. Ishaque in 1972 warned that borrowed constitutions do not work. Constitutional limits, for him, were necessary on the power of the public functionaries and rule of law is such a limit. He further made clear that law here is Sharia and hence these constitutional limits are available in Islam defined by Sharia and Allah.[127]

Later in 1975, the Cornelius tradition produced a detailed reminder on the need for the judiciary to curb the legislature. The military was demoralized after their 1971 war defeat and the judicial arm was in search of a balance of power. The best piece of writing chronicling this fact is the 1975 work of Khalid M. Ishaque. He was a Senior Advocate of the Supreme Court and an eminent jurist and scholar of law and Islamic studies. He found the judicial arm of the state curtailed, all the powers had been concentrated in the executive and there was no counterbalance either in the legislature or judiciary. Ishaque complained about the exclusion of the jurisdiction of the courts from social disputes and the creation of administrative tribunals. He was annoyed with the judicial restraint of the courts so as to avoid confrontation with the executive. He pushed the courts to become the final protector for the people, as found in the constitution. He found that there was greater suffering under Bhutto than the colonial period, and blamed British precedents for this.

According to Ishaque, the judiciary's aversion to adjudicate upon policy matters during Bhutto's regime was flawed and was not followed by libertarian countries

---

[125]A number of judges of the superior courts came from the chamber of the writer. Justice Abdul Qadir Sheikh, Justice Amir Raza, Justice Nasir Aslam Zahid, Justice Majida Rizvi, Justice Nizam Ahmad, Justice Sabihuddin Ahmad, Justice Ghulam Nabi Soomro, Justice Mujeebullah Siddiqui, Justice Amir Hani Muslim, and Justice Mushtaq Memon. The writer's father was DIG of Bombay Sind Presidency before partition. At the age of 32, he was appointed Additional Advocate General of West Pakistan in 1958, and Advocate General in 1964. He became the project Director of Islamic Research Institute and was the member of Council of Islamic Ideology (1969-72) and again from 1977-80 (which is Zia regime, and note that he had no such post during Bhutto's regime). He taught *Seerut-un-Nabi* (the life of the prophet, a trend as one of Zia's steps to promote Islamization) during 1976-77 in Sind University. The writer was clearly embedded in the Cornelius tradition.

[126]For example, KM Ishaque, *Islamic Principles of Economic Management* (Economist Research Unit, Karachi, 1982).

[127]KM Ishaque, *Constitutional Limitations: An Essay on Limits on Exercise of Political Power* (Pakistan Publishing House, Karachi, 1972) 1.

like the U.S. and France. He also did not like the sovereignty of the parliament. He wanted it to be under rule of law, meaning, the 'Objective Resolution' which had subordinated the sovereign parliament under Allah. For him, Bhutto's period mirrored the U.K., and Pakistan should move to a more U.S. type of system where the courts were the final arbitrator. He did not like state intervention in economic activity and accused such state intervention as always excluding the jurisdiction of the courts. He criticized legislations which were passed only to gain popular votes, legislation that promoted welfare oriented goals but was indifferent to individual needs.[128]

3.2.3 Recall for a Presidential System

The 1973 constitution promoted "parliamentary democracy with a vengeance".[129] A.K. Brohi has given an account of popular disenchantment with parliamentary democracy.[130] He cited Lord Hailsham's critique of parliamentary democracy in England[131] and declared it valid for all parliamentary democracies, on the grounds that the political requirements and economic necessities of the modern state have 'outpaced' the growth of its parliamentary institutions. The solution, for Brohi, was a "non-sovereign law-making" body in place of an omnipotent parliament which could judicially review the federal structure of the federation. He supported a pure "*centrally directed line*". For him, parliamentarians should support their government. On the basis of this, he concluded, "serious thought should be given to the remodelling of government on the presidential pattern". He rejected Ayub's presidential system as "*having the worst features of both the parliamentary democracy as well as of the presidential type*". He brought Justice Shahabuddin's report as a reference, which supported a presidential system of governance over a parliamentary system of governance. Brohi also gave a few suggestions to amend the constitution so as to bring it closer to the American style of constitution.[132] A.G. Chaudhry also claimed that the 1973 Constitution had the defect of not maintaining

[128]*Supra* note 12, 7.

[129]CM Shafqat, Constitutional Development in Pakistan, *PLJ* (1984) Magazine Section 41, 55-56. The writer is not only skeptical about this constitutional position of the president, but is sarcastic about it. At the time of writing, he was a Law Consultant at Cornelius, Lane & Mufti in Pakistan. This law association and its tradition is directly linked to Cornelius CJ.

[130]A.K. Brohi was the lawyer of Zia (Federation), Yahya Bakhtiar was appearing on behalf of Bhutto. A. K. Brohi was made Federal Minister for Law and Parliamentary Affairs by Zia.

[131]L Hailsham, *The Listener* (October 21, 1976).

[132]AK Brohi, Disenchantment with Parliamentary Democracy, XXIX *PLD* (1977) Journal Section 81.

the balance of power between the three organs of the state (which, he says, is why Bhutto seized all the power) as in England under Mrs. Thatcher and the period of the 20 months emergency in India under Indira Gandhi.[133]

The judiciary in Pakistan was not asking for a balancing role, it was cautious on the face of popular support for Bhutto. To put it correctly, the Chief Justice of Pakistan in 1973 made it clear that the power of judicial review in the Constitution of 1973 did not mean supremacy of the judiciary over the executive or legislature. In the face of wide-ranging changes, the judiciary in Pakistan was facing a dilemma of identity. Courts in Pakistan, according to Justice Kamal Mustafa, decided to perform a function in-between two extremes. The courts never tried to assume the functions of the parliament.[134] But we will see that this was a temporary position of the judiciary. As soon as Bhutto lost popular support, the idea of the democratic deficit emerged, and the judiciary assumed a central role in granting rights to fill the deficit.

3.2.4 Rights Under the Bhutto Regime: Confrontation or a Substitute for Democratic Deficit

In the Constitution of 1973, and in politics around this period, Bhutto tried to regulate and confine the powers and jurisdiction of the superior courts. He was clear that no court should have any jurisdiction except that which was conferred, or would be conferred in the future on it by the constitution or by or under any law.[135] Bhutto, through the Fourth Amendment, forbade the courts from making orders against preventive detention. No debate was held in the assembly about this.[136] The sum of the amendments made by Bhutto was to remove the perceived hurdles on his path of reforms. His opponents defined this as uncontrolled powers[137] and by critics as "removing legislature and judicial oversight from his personal and party program".[138] For Newberg, the process of modernization of Baluchistan, through the abolition of the Sardari system of large land holdings, was done in a 'heavy-handed manner'. She concludes that, "both sides were right and wrong".[139] Note that, in

[133]AG Chaudhry, Undesirability of Parliamentary Democracy, *PLJ* (1995) Magazine Section 99. He wrote this essay in the background of his dissatisfaction with the parliamentary democracy in 1990s in Pakistan, which was polluted with horse-trading and political defection as a result of patronage.

[134]KM Bhukhari J, The Role of Judiciary in a Developing Country, XXVIII *PLD* (1976) Journal Section 5, 6, a paper read at the Pakistan's Jurists Conference, 1975. The writer was a justice of Lahore High Court at that time.

[135]Article 175(2), *The Constitution of Islamic Republic of Pakistan*, 1973.

[136]*Constitution (Fourth Amendment) Act* 1975, *Act* LXXI of 1975, PLD 1975 Central Statues 337.

[137]Khan, *supra* note 10, 317.

[138]Newberg, *supra* note 9, 139.

[139]*Ibid* 141.

this analysis, personal and party programs are presented as negative, as opposed to the very highly placed doctrinal ideals of law.

Supreme Court Chief Justice, Hamood-ur-Rahman stated in 1975 that the court avoided judicial interpretation that might create confrontation with the legislature; rather, the courts tried to protect the rights of the citizens.[140] He was clear that democracy alone could not guarantee liberty; it needed the rule of law.[141] The place of judiciary in the constitutional scheme of 1973 was the same as that of previous constitutions. However, no other power and jurisdiction was given to the courts except those given in the constitutional scheme (Article 175(2)), in an effort to avoid 'judicial activism'.[142]

The difference of positions on rights and politics between Bhutto and Hamood-ur-Rehman CJ and his other Cornelius collective jurists is illustrative in a live encounter of speeches. In the Second Jurists conference titled "Law as an instrument of peaceful change in developing countries", Bhutto and Hamood-ur-Rehman CJSC were present. The President of Pakistan Bar Association, Yahya Bakhtiar, requested Bhutto to lift the emergency because the Defence of Pakistan Rules were being misused in some cases.[143] Bhutto very confidently articulated his case of fundamental rights in relation to political development. He emphasized on the jurists to examine the questions of law with constant reference to Pakistan's social and economic problems. There is no equality before law if there exists glaring social and economic inequalities.[144] Giving examples of land reforms and nationalization of industry, Bhutto emphasized the necessity of radical changes by a representative government to enable even the unprivileged to arrest and enjoy their fundamental rights. Bhutto rejected fundamental rights as philosophical absolutes and for him "they flow from, and are not prior to social justice".[145] He blamed those against his radical reforms as supporters of *laissez faire* and against progressive thought. Hamood-ur-Rehman CJSC, in his presidential address in the same conference, accepted that following *laissez faire* we should not ignore social elements. But, at the same time, being offensive, he pointed out that we should not ignore individuals altogether as is done by philosophies of totalitarianism.[146] He further added that in our zeal of welfare state (which Bhutto

---

[140]H Rahman, CJSC, Presidential Address to Second Pakistan Jurist Conference 09-12 January 1975, *PLD* (1975) Journal Section 8.

[141]H Rahman, CJSC, My Concept of Rule of Law and Civil Rights, XXVI *PLD* (1974) Journal Section 84, 85.

[142]This declining power of the judiciary is evident from *Ch Zahoor Elahi, MNA v the State,* PLD 1977 SC 273, where the Justice Yaqub Ali accepted the exclusion of jurisdiction of court over offences under amendments in Defence of Pakistan Rules in 1976. Cases illustrating this situation are *Sher Ali and others v Sheikh Zahoor Ahmad*, PLD 1977 SC 545; *Niaz Ahmad Khan v Province of Sind and others*, PLD 1977 Karachi 604.

[143]*PLD* (1975) Journal Section 1, 2.

[144]*PLD* (1975) Journal Section 4, 5.

[145]*Ibid.*

[146]*PLD* (1975) Journal Section 8, 9.

claimed), we cannot crush the freedom of the individual. There is "no room for despotism under rule of law".[147] Later, expanding on the rule of law, law is Sharia and Quran for him and the courts are to interpret it etc.

As soon as Bhutto lost popular support, Hamood-ur-Rehman started relying on old juridico-bureaucratic structure and therefore tools to address this democratic deficit devised during Cornelius period. In the *Liaqat Ali Case*, Liaqat Ali, the son of Abdul Hamid Khan Jatoi Member National Assembly, was detained without serving the reasons of detention. The question before the court was that in cases of detention, whether the subjective satisfaction of the executive authority is enough and is immuned from judicial examination based on the *Liversidge case.*[148] Or the executive detaining authority should have some objective material, which can satisfy a reasonable person as to the necessity for such orders of detention, the Court decided in favour of the latter.[149] The court followed the rules of detention systematically developed under Cornelius and later Hamood-ur-Rehaman CJs in the *Ghulam Jilani* cas*e*, *Baqi Baluch* case, *Shorish Kashmiri* case and later *Haider Bux Jatoi* case.[150] In the *Abdul Hamid* case, the court went in further detail, merely stating the grounds of detention are not necessary but what is necessary is to discuss facts also.[151] In *Nawab Begum* case, the Court further bound the government to not only inform the detenue of the grounds for detention along with the detention order, but the same should be communicated to him as well.[152] All these cases were connected with the language controversy in Sindh in the month of July 1972 leading to the destruction of properties and bloodshed. In a very important political case of a politician Abdus Sattar Khan Niazi, the High Court granted bail to the petitioner in cases which were registered against him, and the grievance of the state was that the High Court did not even know the nature and number of those cases. The court strongly protected those provisions which required the detention authority to produce the detenue before the magistrate and Review Board. In this case, the prosecutor took five months to produce a list of seven cases before the court.[153]

The judiciary adjusted slightly and stepped back in *F.B. Ali* case.[154] This case made clear the status of emergency provisions and the scope of the Army Act. The Petitioner challenged the validity of Ordinance 3 and 4 of 1967. This Ordinance amended certain classes of Sections 2 and 59 of the *Pakistan Army Act, 1952* to

---

[147]*PLD* (1975) Journal Section, 8, 10, 11.

[148]*Liversidge v Sir John Anderson,* L R 1942 AC 206.

[149]*Liaqat Ali v Govt of Sind and another,* PLD 1973 Karachi 78, 93.

[150]*Govt of West Pakistan v Haider Bux Jatoi,* PLD 1969 SC 210.

[151]*Abdul Hamid Khan v The District Magistrate, Larkana*, PLD 1973 Karachi 344, 351.

[152]*Nawab Begum v The Govt of Punjab (Home Secretary) and another*, PLD 1974 Lahore 344, 346.

[153]*Abdus Sattar Khan Niazi v The State*, PLD 1974 Lahore 324.

[154]Here some army officers, planning an aborted coup against Bhutto, were tried by a military court. They came before the LHC and SC on the ground that they were retired and should not be tried by the military courts. SC refused relief and stated that ordinary courts should not interfere with military courts. See *infra* note 151.

include seduction, etc. The Petitioner's position was that no statute in U.S. can be framed to try civilian in times of peace. The courts opinion was that the *Pakistan Army Act* and its 1967 amendment do permit the trial of the civilian in times of peace.[155] In this amendment, the persons who tried to seduce and subvert the loyalty of army personnel will be tried under the Army Act and, for CJ, this was clearly connected with the defence of Pakistan. The courts refused equal protection of law on the basis of uniformity of procedure because it may be different for different classification of people. The court agreed with the scope of the military courts (which Bhutto established to deal with the unrest) but upheld its own powers. It relied on the judgments in the *Fazlul Quader Choudhry* and *Siraj-ul-Haq Patwari* cases. This was at a time when a number of cases regarding the detention of politicians were coming into the courts. The Courts' responsibilities to protect the rights of the citizens like in the case of *Malik Ghulam Jilani case* were reinforced.[156] Along with detailed guidelines, the Supreme Court made the points clear, that detention should be based on reasonable ground, objective criteria and consideration. Second, detentions are open to judicial review.[157] The courts were also strictly instructed to observe due process of law.[158]

But that was not easy for the Chief Justice. While agreeing with the CJ, an interesting case is mentioned by Gul Muhammad J. like a reminder. This case can be seen as indicating supremacy of the Legislature. Summary facts of the case were also told by Mohammad Gul J. The High Court had declared that the fee taken under *West Pakistan Cotton (Control) Act, 1959* was illegal and directed twice in writs for it to be refunded. Bhutto's government amended the law retrospectively to nullify the affects of these writs. The Council for the cotton mills in the Supreme Court made a plea that the judgments of the High Court were the end products of the constitutional jurisdiction whereas validating ordinances by the Legislature was sub-constitutional legislation. The Supreme Court refused to accept this argument because it could strike at the very root of the power of the Legislature. It would also

[155] *F B Ali v the State*, PLD 1975 SC 506, 521.

[156] This case is discussed in chapter three of this book. It was a detention case of many politicians in a protest against Taskent Declaration. Lahore High Court found the detention orders *bona fide*, whereas SC accepted the appeal of Nawabzada Nusrullah Khan, but rejected that of Sardar Shoukat Hayat Khan and Jilani. See *Malik Ghulam Jilani v The Govt of West Pakistan*, PLD 1967 SC 373.

[157] Some other important cases of this nature were *Zafar Iqbal v Province of Sind and 2 others*, PLD 1973 Karachi 316; *Abdul Hamid Khan v the District Magistrate, Larkana and 2 others*, PLD 1973 Karachi 344; and *Liaqat Ali v Government of Sind through Secretory Home Department*, PLD 1973 Karachi 78.

[158] *Khan Muhammad Safdar v the State and another*, PLD 1974 Lahore 200; and *Mrs. Habiba Jilani v the Federation of Pakistan through secretary, Interior Ministry*, PLD 1974 Lahore 153.

throw into serious disarray the pivotal arrangement of the three organs of the state in the Constitution. The remedial or curative legislation by the Legislature is also the end product of the constitution.[159]

3.2.5 *Legislature's Reaction*

Bhutto's political opponents continued using the courts, however, Bhutto responded strongly. The legislature passed an amendment in the Criminal Procedure prohibiting granting of bails before trials.[160] This was followed by the Fourth Amendment in the constitution in 1975.[161] The High Courts were ordered to stop interfering in the executive's detention orders, and from matters of stay of recovery, assessment or collection of public revenues. On 1 September 1976, the Fifth Amendment brought changes in the transfer terms of the appointment of judges, separation of the judiciary from the executive, and the establishment of separate courts for Sindh and Baluchistan. Its main feature, however, was restrictions on the grant of interim bails.[162]

The debate in the Assembly is helpful in order to understand the differences brought about by the Fifth Amendment. Federal Education Minister, Abdul Hafeez Pirzada, a known jurist, complained about the encroachment of the judiciary upon the functions of the legislature and the executive. While emphasizing the coexistence of the three organs of state, Bhutto (himself a Lincolns Inn graduate) made clear that independence of the judiciary does not mean supremacy or sovereignty of the judiciary. Sovereignty, according to him, lies in the legislature elected by the people. He argued that the judiciary should be subordinate to law and should not try to become a parallel legislature or executive.[163] This episode of confrontation with the judiciary coincided with Bhutto's losing popularity, using state apparatuses against people,[164] and law and rights replacing this democratic deficit.

[159] *Messrs Mamukanjan Cotton Factory v The Punjab Province and others*, PLD 1975 SC 50.

[160] *Code of Criminal Procedure (Amendment) Ordinance*, 1975, PLD 1973 Central Statutes 57; *Code of Criminal Procedure (Amendment) Act* 1976 (Act XIII OF 1976), PLD 1976 Central Statutes 175 – Section 498A was added to the Code of Criminal Procedure.

[161] *Constitution (Fourth Amendment) Act,* 1975 (Act LXXI of 1975), PLD 1975 Central Statutes 337.

[162] *Constitution (Fifth Amendment) Act*, 1976 (Act LXII of 1976), PLD 1976 Central Statutes 538.

[163] As discussed by Hamid Khan, though in a negative tone. See *supra* note 10, 298.

[164] *The Constitution (Third Amendment),* 1975, Act XXII of 1975, PLD 1975.

3.2.6 *Liberal Rights, But No to Ethno-nationalism—The National Awami Party Case*

By a notification, No. SRO-176(1)/75 issued on 10 February 1975, the government of Pakistan banned the National Awami Party (NAP) alleging that the party was operating "in a manner prejudicial to the sovereignty and integrity of Pakistan". The Party was also alleged to be carrying out terrorist activities, including the killing of PPP senior minister of the NWFP province, Hayat Mohammad Khan Sherpao.[165] On February 24, 1975, a reference was filed in the Supreme Court by the government under Section 4 of the *Political Parties Act*, 1962. The court held that the National Awami Party was acting in a manner prejudicial to the sovereignty and integrity of Pakistan.[166] In the *NAP case*, the judiciary agreed to put reasonable restrictions on fundamental rights when they come in conflict with state security. The Supreme Court's verdict in the *NAP case* was followed by an Ordinance as an amended Political Parties Act to ban NAP leadership to qualify for Members of National Assembly or Member of Provincial Assembly. A Special Tribunal on anti-state activity was established and bail in such cases was disallowed.

It should be noted that this decision did not mean that the courts were favouring Bhutto. The NAP controversy was an ethno-national question in which the courts had a unitary position. The most important aspect of the decision is how the court separated nation from nationality. NAP's position, as per the statement submitted by Wali Khan, was that Pakistan is a Nation but is composed of five nationalities having their own distinct 'language' and 'culture'. Commenting on the issue of the ideology of Pakistan, he declared that a state as such has no ideology and political forces give it an ideology. In that sense, Islam was the Muslim League's ideology and the PPP has given it a different ideology of socialism. Cornelius tradition's jurist Sharifuddin Pirzada was the *amicus curie* in this case. The Court reproduced exactly this position in his writings as well as that of A.K. Brohi. Whereas, Munir CJ first time heard the word 'ideology of Pakistan' in 1962. This was Sharifuddin Pirzada, who in 1963 carved out the evolution, genesis and etymology of Pakistan from legal documents and constitutional missions under the British.[167] While he was proud that Moudoodi used his book in the famous *Moudoodi* case to defend the ban against his party Jamaat-e-Islami,[168] now Pirzada was prosecuting the ban of another party. Similarly, jurist Brohi was against the 'Gospel of nationalism', for him the new modern state emerged after the disintegration of Christian Europe under the Pope and hence has no spiritual orientation and he

---

[165]*Infra* note 166, 77, 86.

[166]*Islamic Republic of Pakistan v Abdul Wali Khan*, PLD 1976 SC 57.

[167]SS Pirzada, *Evolution of Pakistan* (Royal Book Company, Karachi, 1963).

[168]SS Pirzada, *Evolution of Pakistan, 2nd edn* (Royal Book Company, Karachi, 1995) PREFACE.

cursed protestentism for this. *Khilafat* (just like the Pope had been in Europe) for him was a return to that 'spiritual' life of the Muslim World.[169] He gave culture a subsidiary role. Culture is particular which is subordinate to 'universality' of Islam.[170] The court in the *NAP* case followed the same line of arguments. For the court, the Muslims of India claimed that they were a separate nation than Hindus and hence wanted a separate country to live according to the Quran and Sunnah. Therefore, for the Chief Justice, to say Pakistan was not one 'nation' but several 'nationalities' having different culture, ethnicity, etc. was to deny the very basis of Pakistan. The Chief Justice added, "The concept of nationalism is opposed also to the fundamentals of Islam which preaches that entire *Muslim Millat* is one nation under one *Khalifa*". [emphasis is mine] Muhammad Gul J went to the extent that NAP leaders were trying to emulate Mujibur Rehman, who separated Bangladesh from Pakistan.[171] For Burki (1998), Jinnah emphasized the social and cultural differences of Muslims with Hindus in India over religious differences. Pakistani leaders, however, could not understand the social and cultural differences of Bengalis and insisted on religious similarities and that Islam could fashion a nation out of Balochis, Muhajirs, Pathans, Punjabis and Sindhis.[172] Amnesty International criticized this decision of the Supreme Court, and Yahya Bakhtiar reacted strongly declaring the 'political organization' having bias against Pakistan. He condemned Amnesty International report for 1975–76 which claimed there to be 38,000 political prisoners in Pakistan.[173]

To sum up, Bhutto's early period after 1970 was a period of popular democracy. The courts could not exert themselves against this class formation and stepped back. The *Asma Jilani* and *Zia-ur-Rahman* cases were representative of this transition. Around 1975, Bhutto lost popular support, forcing him to rely on the military, the bureaucracy and the judiciary. The common story of the courts confronting Bhutto with the importance of rights is the story of a lack of democracy and not the strength of judiciary. Even the nature of these rights were in Cornelius tradition by the same stream of judges. They tried to push the Objectives Resolution but had to step back. Still, the religious opposition was so strong that Bhutto had to accommodate them and declare Qadiani's as non-Muslims and had to ban alcohol.[174] This opposition came so strongly that it turned the tide of political

---

[169]Brohi, Islam Meets the Challenge of Modernism, *supra* note 104, 87, a lecture delivered at the Pakistan Military Academy Kakul in 1979.

[170]AK Brohi, What is Islamic Culture?, in, *A Faith to Live by* (National Hijra Council, Islamabad, 1984) 201, an address delivered at the Fifteenth Century Hijra National Conference on History and Culture, Islamabad, Pakistan (July, 03, 1980).

[171]*Supra* note 166, 181.

[172]Burki, *supra* note 5, 5.

[173]Reply Yahya Bakhtiar while addressing to the advocates at Lahore on 28 October, 1976, PLD 1976 Journal Section 270, 274.

[174]AU Qasmi, *The Ahmadis and the Politics of Religious Exclusion in Pakistan* (Anthem Press, London, 2015).

development for many decades to come in Pakistan. Its strength was the decision of the hegemonic class to back it at the height of the cold war, that is, the invasion by the U.S.S.R. in Afghanistan and Iranian Revolution of 1979 and hence Pakistan as a frontline state.

3.2.7 *Bhutto's Downfall: Countering the 'Suppression Explanation'*

Bhutto's complicated era is reduced to suppression when analyzed by the Right,[175] and the betrayal of socialism when analyzed by the Left. Bhutto's downfall has been linked to the alienation of the middle class and to campaigning by the opposition alliance (Pakistan National Alliance). Waseem suggests that Bhutto's regime should be characterized as an intermediate regime, representing both the old elite and the newly aspirant lower middle class.[176]

We are to go beyond this description to grasp the relation of law with democracy in Bhutto's last years (1975–77), with a more dynamic analysis. Let us first agree that the first genuinely populist leader of Pakistan was Bhutto.[177] However, Bhutto was not able to deliver sufficiently to the working class or the middle classes, due to the resistance of the old juridico-bureaucratic state structure.

Opposition towards Bhutto first came from the Civil Services of Pakistan; business people, industrialists, landlords and retired military officials. A party-based opposition was formed by landlords in the United Democratic Front under the leadership of Pir Pagaro, a big landlord of Sindh province. The National Awami Party came under the influence of autonomists (ethno-nationalists) and some urban radicals. At the same time, landlords moved into the PPP and hence, their opposition was weakened.

PPP ticket holders in the 1977 elections were from big landed families as opposed to the middle class candidates of the Pakistan National Alliance. Forty of the 100 previous MNAs of the PPP were refused party tickets.[178] The Bhutto regime showed a bias towards the small-scale industry, trading and merchant classes.[179] State patronage by Bhutto could only co-opt the salariat segment to some extent while traders and merchants who were in the secondary and tertiary layers of

---

[175]Khan, *supra* note 10, 293.

[176]Waseem, *supra* note 73, 346.

[177]But the question can be asked: why the working class also turned against Bhutto? According to Kamran Asdar Ali "hopes [of the working class] were raised as Bhutto assumed control of the country." KA Ali, The Strength of the Street Meets the Strength of the State: The 1972 Labour Struggle in Karachi, 37 *Int. J. Middle East Stud.* (2005) 83, 89.

[178]S Mujahid, *The 1977 Pakistani Election* as cited by Waseem, *supra* note 73, 332.

[179]S. Akbar Zaidi, *Issues in Pakistan's Economy* (Oxford University Press, Oxford, 2005) 105.

production were not integrated.[180] Thanks to nationalization, there were jobs that were used at the discretion of the regime to accommodate supporters and to remove opponents.[181] During the first two years of Bhutto's rule, bureaucrats were bypassed, but Bhutto indulged them after nationalization,[182] bringing the bureaucracy under political supervision or oversight.[183] While responding to the accusation that he misused civil services, Bhutto responded that bureaucrats holding high political offices during his regime were chosen through elections. Above all, he explained that in a multiparty democratic system, watertight segregation was impractical. In the U.S., the party fills top administrative posts, he argued. Similarly, in the parliamentary system, civil services and the other services are not considered islands running parallel to the governments—"the myth of segregated, neutral civil servant was needed by colonialism". The neutrality and facelessness was fraudulent.[184] In the first 2 years, Bhutto tried to undermine the military but later used it. Raza had advised Bhutto that the military has a permanent place on the political scene of Pakistan and not to eliminate it.[185]

Why did Bhutto not strengthen the legislature and the party, but rather relied on the bureaucracy and military? Legislators were mostly absent, even with a two-third majority, the legislature could hardly pass any bill. Ministers were absent when issues concerning their departments were raised. Bhutto's presence always made attendance better but he himself neglected the legislature.[186] The party was rife with factions.[187] By 1976, the provincial governments were placed under Nawab's and the landed aristocracy, and conservatives dominated the PPP.[188] This divided the party and left no choice for Bhutto but to rely on the state machinery.

---

[180]AS Akhtar, *Overdeveloping State: The Politics of Common Sense in Pakistan, 1971-2007* (Submitted to SOAS, University of London for the degree of PhD, 2008) 164.

[181]Hussain, *supra* note 28, 125.

[182]Waseem, *supra* note 73, 310.

[183]See SJ Burki, Twenty Years of the Civil Service of Pakistan: A Re-evaluation, 9 *Asian Surv.* (1969) 239; HA Rizvi, *Military, State and Society in Pakistan* (Macmillan, Basingstoke, 2000); Kennedy, *supra* note 69.

[184]ZA Bhutto, *If I am Assassinated* (Classics, Lahore, 1979) 54.

[185]R Raza, *Zulfikar Ali Bhutto and Pakistan, 1967-77* (Oxford University Press, Karachi, 1977).

[186]Hussain, *supra* note 28, 205-207.

[187]In Punjab, there was fight among the Ramay and Khar groups in 1972. In 1970, Khar and Rao were rivals. There were bloody clashes among peasants and landlords and employers and workers. Sheikh Rasheed lost control and Khar was brought in. After much cruelty, Khar was removed and Ramay was brought in, but Khar soon started factionalism. He went to the extent of contacting opposition parties. The same thing happened in Sindh.

[188]Hussain, *supra* note 28, 212.

3.3 Juridico-Bureaucratic Cornelius Tradition Restored (1980s)

In the 1977 elections, the Pakistan People's Party won four-fifths of the seats of the National Assembly, but there were allegations of rigging in the polls. A strong agitation against Bhutto arose on the streets and he declared a partial Martial Law in Karachi, Lahore and Hyderabad under Article 245 of the Constitution. The Martial Law was challenged before Lahore High Court and a full bench declared the Martial Law unconstitutional.[189] Between 4 and 5 July 1977, the Chief of the Army Staff, General Zia-ul-Haq, imposed Martial Law in the country. He did not abrogate the constitution but held it in abeyance.[190] This was different than the previous two Martial Laws imposed by Ayub and Yahya wherein the constitutions of 1956 and 1962 were abrogated. The powers of the High Courts and Supreme Court to issue writs under Article 199 were taken away. Later, these courts were allowed to have writ jurisdiction except against the Chief Martial Law Administrators or Martial Law Administrators working under him.[191]

The judiciary welcomed Zia without resistance, with the sole exception being Supreme Court Chief Justice Yakub, who had been given an extension in his job by Bhutto. Zia met with Chief Justice Yakub the same night of Bhutto's overthrowing on 5 July 1977. The Fifth and Sixth Amendments by Bhutto had increased the age of retirement of judges so that Supreme Court Chief Justice Muhammad Yakub could be retained at his position. Zia, through his Chief Martial Law Administrators order, withdrew this extension because Yakub had admitted the case filed by Bhutto's wife against the overthrow.[192] Consequently, the Supreme Court Chief Justice Muhammad Yakub stood retired. The next Supreme Court Chief Justice appointed was Anwar-ul-Haq, who had been denied this position for six months due to Bhutto's amendment. Four High Court Chief Justices were appointed governors of respected provinces and they happily moved. Writ jurisdiction of the High Courts and Supreme Court was restored within two days of taking a new Oath on Provisional Constitutional Order, which all the judges took. Two Chief Justices forced three judges of the Lahore High Court and two judges of the Supreme Court appointed by Bhutto to take the Oath using Supreme Judicial Council.

While renowned jurists and advocate Hamid was 'shocked' by the way the judiciary fell into the lap of Martial Law,[193] I am not so surprised. It was a forceful and quick return of the quasi-liberal institutional setting under Ayub and Cornelius. This tendency and class formation stayed alive during Bhutto as pointed out above. The end of the 1970s was the height of the cold war and the hegemonic class

---

[189] *Dervesh M. Arbey, Advocate v Federation of Pakistan*, PLD 1977 Lahore 846.

[190] *Proclamation of Marshal Law*, July 05, 1977, PLD 1977 Central Statutes 326.

[191] *Laws (Continuous in Force) (Amendment) Order*, 1977, PLD 1977 Central Statutes 325.

[192] *Laws (Continuance of Force) (Fifth Amendment) Order*, 1977, PLD 1977 Central Statutes 441.

[193] Khan, *supra* note 10, 342.

backed this class formation to overthrow Bhutto. I find that the judiciary found it as an ideal period in terms of its centre–periphery relations (in the height of its relations with the U.S. in the Cold War) to establish the constitutional set up like the U. S. This model includes a strong president, judicial review to take care of fundamental rights, and the Objectives Resolution as the substantive part of the constitution, which had not even been available to Cornelius courts. This judicial period was different than Ayub's only in the sense that Ayub tried modernization with a liberal face whereas Zia implemented capitalist modernization with an Islamic veneer. According to Ishrat Husssain, Zia's period further continued with modernization and was a success.[194] Grafting of Islam was the only 'shortcoming' of the 'Cornelius tradition' under Ayub, which Zia did not hesitate to do. Judges sat on tribunals with Brigadiers to disqualify politicians. Supreme Court Chief Justice Anwar-ul-Haq acted as president during Zia's absence on foreign tours. Judicial review was being used consciously and cautiously. Relief was found in about 10% of the cases brought before the superior courts.[195]

A full Supreme Court bench, consisting of nine judges, began hearing the *Nusrat Bhutto* case in 1977,[196] which challenged the coup. The position of the Federation presented by its counsel, A.K. Brohi, was that Martial Law is not imposed to displace the constitutional authority but to bridge and return the country to the constitutional path. Similarly, newly appointed Attorney General Sharifuddin Pirzada also explained that the Chief of the Army Staff had not usurped the state power but he had ousted the usurper, who was elected through massively rigged elections.[197] Apart from the sophistory of these arguments, these two jurists were against Martial Law and Yahya's coup in the *Asma Jilani case*, giving theoretical basis to the then Chief Justice Hamood-ur-Rehman. As per justices Waheeduddin and Dorab Patel, not the judgment of *Asma Jilani case* but the findings of *Reference of His Excellency the Governor-General* of 1955 are applicable in this situation.[198] The crux of the judgment was that the new legal order is for a limited period and for a limited purpose. Only a few parts of the old order are held in abeyance on the ground of state necessity. When are the elections after this short period? The Supreme Court did not give a definite time but believed in the solemn pledge given by Zia to seek a mandate and have free elections.[199] Supreme Court justices

[194] I Hussain, *Pakistan: The Economy of an Elitist State* (Oxford University Press, Karachi, 1999).

[195] Khan (1999), *supra* note 11, 343.

[196] *Begum Nusrat Bhuttoo v Chief of the Army Staff and Federation of Pakistan*, PLD 1977 SC 657.

[197] *Ibid* 673.

[198] *Ibid* 723, 740 respectively; Reference of His Excellency the Governor-General, PLD 1955 FC 435.

[199] *Ibid* 723.

Muhammad Afzal Cheema and Nasim Hassan Shah found the doctrine of necessity as *salispolulisupremalex* (necessity makes prohibited things permissible) valid within Islamic jurisprudence.[200]

For Dieter Conrad, the judicial verdict will not significantly alter the course of events in revolutionary change cases. So the courts are to decide whether to resign or continue working under the regime. The Supreme Court has to look at these matters from the perspective of constitutional legitimacy but has a day-to-day administration of justice. So arises a need of deliberate restraint or giving legitimacy to the regime. The path adopted by the courts was based on a principle of limited dictatorship (which included the doctrines of necessity, implied mandate, the principle of minimum recognition, etc.).[201] Using a liberal framework of 'constitutional governance', Tayyab Mahmud found this decision, along with other decisions like *Dosso* case, doctrinally inconsistent, judicially inappropriate and a politically timid response.[202] Yet this characterization is another form of looking at the judiciary as a 'neutral' and 'autonomous' institution facing events under pressure. It does not reveal how the courts themselves are the part of the juridico-bureaucratic structure. As already pointed out, the decision in the *Asma Jillani* case against the dictator did not stand on the shoulders of the judiciary, rather it was the mass support that led the way to a decision like this. Similarly, the decision in the *Nusrat Bhutto* case was one for state formation, which could handle the rising tide of the Cold War. Analysis in this book does not consider it sufficient to describe the courts as pragmatic by Conrad. Continuity of our ongoing analysis in its historical trajectory will show how this decision was the strong revival of state formation under Ayub–Cornelius with class formation discussed below.

3.3.1 Rehabilitating the Old State Structure

General Zia resurrected the old juridico-bureaucratic structure, with the military leading it. He disengaged some of the landed elite from the PPP with little effort. Soon, the landed elite was evicting tenants. Zia's economic and administrative policies and anti-nationalization stance pleased business. The family of Nawaz Sharif (who later became Prime Minister), which had suffered from nationalization in 1972 and had lost Ittefaq Steel Industries, now rose up again in the 1980s due to the patronage of Zia. Punjabi industrialists replaced Gujarati industrialists.[203]

[200] *Ibid* 724, 762 respectively.

[201] D Conrad, In Defense of the Continuity of Law: Pakistan's Courts in Crisis of State, in, WP Zingel, S Zingel & A Lallemant (eds) *Pakistan in the 80s: Law & Constitution* (Vanguard, Lahore, 1985) 123, 145.

[202] T Mahmud, Praetorianism and Common Law in Post-Colonial Settings: Judicial Responses to Constitutional Breakdowns in Pakistan, *Utah L. Rev.* (1993) 1225, 1228.

[203] Shahid-ur-Rahman, (1997) *Who owns Pakistan*, available at <http://www.scribd.com/doc/125960792/Who-Owns-Pakistan>, last visited Nov 21, 2013.

The Zia regime was also the first truly military regime in Pakistan with the military as his constituency, with many direct benefits to them.[204] Government officials made personal contacts with military officers and inducted many of them into the civil services. The bureaucracy welcomed Zia and Chief Justice Anwar-ul-Haq headed a Civil Service Commission to recommend policy measures, his report was full of conservative measures.[205] This Martial Law regime was accompanied with the strongest ever hold by the metropolitan bourgeoisie (hegemonic class) on this military as seat of power in light of the Cold War, which was at its height after the invasion by the Soviet Union in Afghanistan.

Even a short period of people's aspirations under Bhutto had tremendous potential. There was a need to roll this back completely. There was no major change in labour law and economic policy by Zia but suppression unleashed against PPP was used to roll back the labour.[206] Whether the PPP wanted the Left behind it or not but the Left was behind PPP. The period from 1977 to 1985 was a period of exclusion, marginalization and exploitation of the subalterns.

3.3.2 Rolling Back Popular Democracy to the Extent of "Judicial Murder" of Bhutto

The Zia regime suppressed the subordinate classes, ensured that popular forces could not influence state policy and hence eliminated their potential to capture the state.[207] It went to the extent of committing the 'judicial murder'[208] of Bhutto. Bhutto was charged with the murder of Nawab Muhammad Ahmad, father of Ahmad Raza Kasuri, on November 1974, he was implicated in this case under abetment. The case was directly moved to the Lahore High Court and a five-member bench headed by Maulvi Mushtaq conducted the trial. The other judges were Ziauddin Paul,[209] Aftab Hussain, who was very close to the Chief Justice and two other judges who were very weak.[210] The High Court, vide its judgment in this case dated 18 March 1978, convicted all the accused for criminal conspiracy and murder, sentencing them to death.[211] In an appeal against this

---

[204]A Siddiqa, *Military Inc.: Inside Pakistan's Military Economy* (Oxford University Press, Karachi, 2007) 149.

[205]Report of the Civil Services Commission 1978-79 (Government of Pakistan, Islamabad, 1979).

[206]Establishment killed between 150-200 workers in colony textile for asking a bonus of three months. A Baqir, *Pakistan's Chicago: 1978 Massacre at Colony Textile Mills*, available at <http://www.viewpointonline.net/component/content/article?id=1750:pakistans-chicago-1978-massacre-at-colony-textile-mills>, last visited April 18, 2016.

[207]Akhtar, *supra* note 180, 41.

[208]As Benazir called it. See *infra* note 218, 389.

[209]Known for his hostility against Bhutto and an old Muslim League supporter.

[210]Khan, *supra* note 10, 335.

[211]*State v Zulfiqar Ali Bhutto and others*, PLD 1978 Lahore 523.

conviction, a bench of nine judges of the Supreme Court, with an opinion of four to three, supported the High Court decision.[212] Bhutto was hanged by the military in spite of a plea for clemency by Kurt Waldheim (Secretary General of U.N.), President Jimmy Carter of the U.S., Prime Minister Pierre Trudeau of Canada, Chancellor Helmut Schmidt of West Germany, President Giscard d'Estainge of France and Prime Minister James Callaghan of the U.K. The hanging took place on 4 July 1979 at 2 am in the morning at Rawalpindi Central Jail.

It is well known that it was not a fair trial from the beginning till the end.[213] An appeal against the order of the Lahore High Court was heard by a full bench of nine judges of the Supreme Court headed by Chief Justice Anwar-ul-Haq. Bhutto raised the issue of a biased trial, which was rejected by the Chief Justice.[214] The judgment was four to three. The review petition against this judgment was dismissed on 24 March 1979 unanimously by all the seven judges of the Supreme Court.[215]

The role of the judiciary in this 'judicial murder' needs explanation to fully expose what occurred. After the premature retirement of the Chief Justice of Lahore High Court, Sardar Iqbal, Maulvi Mushtaq was supposed to be the next Chief Justice of the respective court. However, Bhutto had appointed Justice Aslam Riaz as Chief Justice, superseding seven other judges including Justice Maulvi Mushtaq. After Bhutto's overthrow, Zia obliged Justice Maulvi Mushtaq by making him Chief Election Commissioner and Acting Governor of Punjab as well as acting Chief Justice of Lahore High Court. Bhutto called him "a man known to be after my blood".[216] Bhutto explained the roots of this enmity. Justice Maulvi Mushtaq met Bhutto after he became president in the early 1970s and revealed his ambition to become Chief Justice of Lahore High Court. Instead, after a few months, Justice Sardar Muhammad Iqbal was made Chief Justice of Lahore High Court by Bhutto. Maulvi Mushtaq expressed his resentment and suggested to the Punjab Chief Minister to put a "shot through the head" of Bhutto. Mushtaq Ahmad faced a second blow when Justice Aslam Riaz Hussain was made Chief Justice of Lahore High Court. After Zia's coup, however, he was invited and made Chief Justice of Lahore High Court as well as Chief Election Commissioner during the trial of Bhutto.[217] Maulvi Mushtaq's appointment as Chief Justice of Lahore High Court and as Chief Election Commissioner consolidated the "mockery of the separation between the executive and the judicial branches of the government".[218]

---

[212]*Zulfiqar Ali Bhutto v The state*, PLD 1979 SC 53, All the judges in favour were from Punjab and three dissenting judges were from the other provinces.

[213]Khan, *supra* note 10, 335.

[214]*Zulifqar Ali Bhutto v State*, PLD 1979 SC 53.

[215]*Zulifqar Ali Bhutto v the State*, PLD 1979 SC 74.

[216]Bhutto, *supra* note 184, 37.

[217]Bhutto himself told this story. See *Ibid.*

[218]B Bhutto, *Daughter of the East: An Autobiography,* 2nd edn (Simon & Schuster, London, 2007) 120.

During the trial, Zia published a white paper and accused Bhutto for rigging the 1977 elections. He presented him as 'modern Machiavelli' and Bhutto in turn called his 'White Paper' a 'white lie'.[219] Bhutto did not expect justice from courts but from the people of Pakistan,[220] not believing in this trial. The courts even criticized his lack of faith in Islam. In this regard the comments by Hamid (2009) are very important "they (comments of the judges) only reveal the mindset of the judges and betray their innate dislike for Bhutto and his style of governance".[221] This statement is very peculiar to reducing the Bhutto regime to a style of governance. Rather than substantive differences in Bhutto's economic reforms and agenda as explained in the first part of the chapter. All the accused were sentenced to death.[222]

3.3.3 Zia's Constitutional Engineering: Fine Tuning of the Juridico-Bureaucratic Structure

The judiciary was careful not to use judicial review against Martial Law. A constitutional amendment, Article 212-A, was added in the constitution to establish military courts. This actually gave constitutional recognition to the already existing military courts and empowered them to the extent that no High Court could grant any injunction, and make an order against them. So, the Supreme Court was deprived of the fruits of judicial review, which it secured in *Nusrat Bhutto* case.

The courts continued to use rights against the regime, for instance, the *Mumtaz Bhutto* case.[223] In this case, two members of the PPP were detained under Martial Orders no. 12, which excluded the jurisdictions of the High Courts and the Supreme Courts to challenge these detentions. Yahya Bakhtiar's argument was that fundamental rights are available whereas Messrs A.K. Brohi and Sharifuddin Pirzada rejected the presence of fundamental rights. It is considered a sound judgment against the military. It challenged detention without trial as an arbitrary act of the executive. After that, courts started reviewing the decisions and actions of military courts.[224] Then, with consecutive constitutional amendments, the High Courts and the Supreme Court were completely deprived of any action against Martial Law

[219]Bhutto, *supra* note 184, 6.

[220]Bhutto, *supra* note 218, 145.

[221]Khan, *supra* note 10, 336.

[222]*State v Zulfikar Ali Bhutto*, PLD 1978 Lahore 523.

[223]*Mumtaz Ali Bhutto and another v The Deputy Martial Law Administrator, Sector I, Karachi and 2 others*, PLD 1979 Karachi 307, 335.

[224]Mr. Justice M. Dilawar Mahmood's judgments, in, M Farani (ed) *Tyranny and Justice in Pakistan* (1993)*: A selection of the Judgments of Mr. Justice M. DilawarMahmood delivered against Martial Law Orders* (Idara Mutalia-e-Tareekh, Lahore, 1993); *Syed Essa Noori v Deputy Commissioner, Turbet and 2 others*, PLD 1979 Quetta 188; *Satar Gul and another v Martial Administrator, Zone "B", NWFP, Peshawar and 2 others*, PLD 1979 Peshawar 119; *Anwar Ali v Chief Martial Law Administrator and 3 others,* PLD 1979 Karachi 804.

authorities.[225] Nonetheless, this was not enough for Zia. He made wholesale constitutional amendments through a Provisional Constitutional Order (PCO) on 25 March 1981. It was like taking a hammer to the powers of Judiciary.[226] This Provisional Constitutional Order was challenged in the Lahore High Court and easily upheld by a divisional bench, without going into the details of the case.[227] This Order was a humiliation or a restructuring of the judiciary, but according to Chief Justice Anwar-ul-Haq (he stood retired), this constitution did not hold support of the people as its character has changed,[228] it was called a "coup within coup".[229]

Sajjad Ali Shah J (who later became CJ of the SC 1994–1997) took the Oath under Zia's Provisional Constitutional Order. His reasoning is similar to that of Nasim Hassan Shah J (who also later became CJ of the SC 1993–1994). Senior judges at that time, according to Sajjad J, thought that the Provisional Constitutional Order was using the word 'law' to defend everything under the purview of law. Another argument the conservative judiciary made was that the judiciary could be better protected from within and by not allowing the handpicked judges to fill the judiciary.[230] Yet, if someone does not consider the interplay of structural relations between the judiciary and the civil-military bureaucracy, he/she cannot stop him/herself from the shock, like that which Hamid had about "the way the judiciary fell into the lap and ultimately the trap of the Martial Law".[231] Rodney W. Jones suggests that the new political leadership came from the lower and middle class who were more conservative and politically less sophisticated than president Ayub.[232]

Analysis in this book has two alternate explanations of what was going on. One is that the intensified class struggle and close presence of the metropolitan bourgeoisie in the light of Afghan war and Iranian revolution (1979), made the dominant classes (the 'historic bloc') react strongly, as opposed to during Ayub's regime. So this was not a matter, more or less, of the sophistication of the middle classes. In terms of class struggle, the climax was reached in the period from Bhutto's overthrowing (1977 to 1981–1982). During this time, fragmented left forces, the PPP Left and the nationalist forces (the pro-Moscow National Awami Party) fought

---

[225] *Constitutional (Amendment) Order,* 1980, PLD 1980 Central Statutes 89; *Chief Martial Law Administrator - CMLA Order,* 1979, *Order Number 72,* October 20, 1979, PLD 1979 Central Statutes 568; *Chief Martial Law Administrator - CMLA Order,* 1980, *Order number 77,* June 02, 1980, PLD 1980 Central Statutes 152.

[226] *Provisional Constitutional Order,* 1981, *CMLA's Order 1 of* 1981, PLD 1981 Central Statutes 183.

[227] *Tajjamal Hussain Malik v Federal Govt of Pakistan,* PLD 1981 Lahore 462.

[228] Interview of Justice Anwarul Haq, *The Muslim* (08 March, 1985).

[229] S Anwar-ul-haq, *Revolutionary Legality in Pakistan* (Pakistan Writers' Co-operative Society, Lahore, 1993) 31.

[230] Shah, *supra* note 117, 122.

[231] Khan, *supra* note 10, 342.

[232] RW Jones, The Military and Security in Pakistan, in, C Baxter (ed) *Zia's Pakistan* (Vanguard, Lahore, 1985) 71.

tooth and nail in a war against U.S. imperialism, but unfortunately under the leadership of Benazir Bhutto. When the class struggle was defeated, the period of 1985–1988 saw the restoration of a presidential system like that was formed under Ayub. Meanwhile Benazir Bhutto, unlike her father, accepted the hegemonic class and democracy was restored with a limited role of Benazir Bhutto, but, this changed the 1973 constitution altogether into a presidential system.

3.4 Revival of the Constitution of 1973 Order, 1985-RCO: A Perfection of the U.S. Type Presidential System and Islam of Cornelius Tradition (1985–1988)

From 1973–77, Bhutto made seven amendments but Zia promulgated 26 constitutional amendments by 1985, when Martial Law was withdrawn and democracy was restored. Out of those amendments, the 8th amendment, that is, Revival of the Constitution of 1973 Order-RCO of 1985 made as many as 65 amendments in the constitution. Furthermore, the insertion of the Objectives Resolution 1949 as a substantive part of the constitution (Article 2-A) amended 60 Articles of the constitution, and added five new Articles and six new clauses. After that, the quasi-democratic regime of Juneju (1985–1988) made the 8th amendment, which was followed by the 10th and 12th amendment.

According to A.G. Chaudhry, this total of 36 Amendment Acts and orders hardly left any Article of the constitution untouched.[233] These amendments made the constitution the creator of the worst kind of presidential system. Now, the cabinet had to work to advise the president and not the other way around. The president could promulgate emergency ordinances, and was the supreme commander of the Armed Forces; he also had full authority on financial and political matters. Above all, the president could dissolve parliament in instances of national interest.[234] Zia's amendments were found valid in the *Yaqoob Ali case*[235]; with the dissenting opinion of Justice Hussian Mirza was a cry in the desert.

After the extreme act of Bhutto's 'judicial murder', Zia imposed Islam as the final nail in the coffin of popular will. Women were reduced to 'half' status through the Hadood Ordinance and very suppressive punishments were included in the criminal code. It terrorized the poor, who were the victims of these harsh

[233]AG Chaudhry, Balancing the Constitution, *PLJ* (1994) Magazine Section 137.

[234]Article 58(2)(b) through 8th amendment in the Constitution of Islamic Republic of Pakistan, 1973.

[235]*Yaqoob Ali v Presiding Officer, Summary Military Court, Karachi*, PLD 1985 Karachi 243.

punishments.[236] According to Waseem, Islam was helpful for the manipulation of power, to claim a right to rule, and was not a new factor indicating a change in politics.[237]

The Objectives Resolution[238] was part of the preamble of the 1973 constitution but in 1985, Zia made it a substantive part of the constitution by adding Article 2-A (*Revival of the Constitution of 1973 Orde*r, 1985). All of this was not an accident or the creation of one person, Zia, but was the continuity of political developments in 1950–1960s under the juridico-bureaucratic structure of Ayub–Cornelius and were perfected under Zia. Below is the brief of the decisive role played by all the jurists of Cornelius tradition.

After Bhutto was overthrown, new Chief Justice, S. Anwar-ul-Haq in his speech mentioned that Bhutto's period was one of extraordinary stress and strain on judiciary. The attitude of the executive was "aggressive, judges were insecure".[239] Mushtaq Hussain, newly selected Chief Justice Lahore High Court, while addressing the full court reference to welcome his appointment, endorsed the above statement.[240] A known jurist Aamir Raza A. Khan, being the president of LHC bar Association, called Bhutto's period as a "constitutional and legal tyranny". He did not hesitate to thank Mushtaq Hussain for guidance and counselling in the troubling time of the later half of 1976.[241] This simply means there was full coordination among all these 'legal' actors against Bhutto during the last years of his troubled rule.

Retired Chief Justice of Supreme Court, Hamood-ur-Rahman, being Zia's advisor for constitutional and parliamentary affaires, announced that from merely talking about Islamic system, we had started taking some preliminary steps. To guide this process, he gave a full concept of state in Islam having sovereignty, liberty, justice, fraternity, democracy and accountability.[242] Anwar-ul-Haq CJSC sitting there also thanked 'Khauda' for Sharia and Sunnah coming in Pakistan, but

[236]The worst punishment was lashes and only the poor were given the punishment. Musharraf observed this while serving as Martial Law Administrator as Lieutenant Colonel and he requested Major General Rafi Alam not to lash poor people. Musharraf, *Supra* note 7, 63.

[237]Waseem, *supra* note 73, 390.

[238]The Objectives Resolution was passed by the first Constituent Assembly of Pakistan after independence in March 1949. According to this resolution, sovereignty belongs to Allah (God Almighty) and He delegates this authority to the State of Pakistan, which will be exercised by the representatives of the people. Judiciary used this article to enable itself to judicial activism for Islamic right to justice (examples are *Akbar Ali v Secretary, Ministry of Defence, Rawalpindi,* 1991 SCMR 2114; *Hakim Khan v Government of Pakistan*, PLD 1992 SC 595; *Sakina Bibi v Federation of Pakistan,* PLD 1992 Lahore 99). The point to be noted here is that judiciary played on the discourse of Islam by the military to control the masses. Secondly, it was the same tool as Cornelius wanted. That is why I called the judiciary under Zia as part of the Cornelius tradition.

[239]S Anwar-ul-Haq, At Full Court Reference on His Elevation as Chief Justice, Journal Section, *PLD* (1977) Journal Section 253, 254.

[240]*PLD* (1978) Journal Section 41, 42.

[241]*PLD* (1977) Journal Section 260; Full Court Reference on the Elevation of Mushtaq Hussian as CJLHC on 17/1/1978, *PLD* (1978) Journal Section 48.

[242]*PLD* (1979) Journal Section 1, 10.

he was worried that its fruits were not seen in the society. Then he moved to the trend of that time, citing verses of the Holy Quran and giving their references.[243] Next year Chief Justice Anwar-ul-Haq also assured that all the justices of SC are 'whole heartedly' in favour of the enforcement of Sharia laws in Pakistan.[244] The same year Sharifuddin Pirzada announced that the British tradition of calling judges 'My Lord' would be stopped and judges of Lahore High Court decided to wear Sherwani's and Arabic Choogha.[245] He found all this Islamization as a continuity from Jinnah to Zia, establishing an Islamic state in Pakistan.[246] Under this intellectual umbrella, Zia changed substantive areas of laws with Islamic provisions, established Shariat Courts, Shariat Faculty, Law Commission and Council of Islamic Ideology of Pakistan, and enacted Huddood Law, Zakat and Ushr Order, Zakat and Tax Concessions.[247] New CJ Haleem not only welcomed Zia's Islamization, but pointed out how external (probably western and communists) un-Islamic elements were present and their hazardous effects were to be eliminated at the same time.[248] Chief Justice of Lahore High Court, the son of Pakistan's national poet Allama Iqbal, made clear that Zia's Islamization was not advancement in a new direction but a conscious attempt to realize the hopes of the Muslim of the sub-continent. For him it is connected with Islamic resurgence (the idea of Islamic renaissance given by his father) after the disillusionment of Muslims from capitalist *democratic order* as well as Marxism (my emphasize).[249] A.K. Brohi, as Rector of Islamic University,[250] started service training of judges, prosecutors and legal practitioners to implement Huddood and Sharia laws.[251] The point which needs to be stressed is that all this submission of the judiciary and jurists to Zia was not an accidental or mishap, but the continuity and perfection of the political design advanced by Cornelius and his colleagues. What discontinued was a desire of the subalterns for a deeper and broader democracy. To address that deficit of democracy quasi-liberal Cornelius tradition had a louder rights discourse.

---

[243]S Anwar-ul-haq, CJSC, Speech at the Judicial Year 1979-1980 Ceremony, *PLD* (1980) Journal Section 52, 54.

[244]S Anwar-ul-haq, Speech at the Inaugural Year 1980 on 27-9-1980, *PLD* (1980) Journal Section 137, 139.

[245]Speech by Sharif-ud-din Pirzada, *PLD* (1981) Journal Section 59, 60.

[246]S Pirzada, Addressing at the Death of Munir CJ and Rebutting His Position that Jinnah Wanted a Secular State, *PLD* (1981) Journal Section 78, 81.

[247]Dr Tanzil-ur-Rehman, Implementation of Shari'ah in an Islamic State - The Case of Pakistan, *PLD* (1981) Journal Section 87.

[248]M Haleem, CJSC, Speech at the Commencement of the Judicial Year 1981-82 on October 03, 1981, *PLD* (1981) Journal Section 26.

[249]J Iqbal, CJLHC, Islamization in Pakistan, *PLD* (1984) Journal Section 65.

[250]Islamic University was the idea of Brohi and he played a role as the founder rector of the university to implement the idea see Haleem CJSC, speech at the Full Court Reference of SC on the Demise of Brohi, *PLD* (1988) Journal Section 64, 66.

[251]SA Hussain, Inaugural Speech, *PLD* (1982) Journal Section 42.

3.5 Public Interest Litigation (PIL): A Deficit for Democracy, Dying Working Class Politics and the Emergence of Middle Class

There is plenty of mainstream 'uncritical' literature on Public Interest Litigation (PIL) in Pakistan. The rise in the rights profile is commonly credited to Supreme Court Chief Justice Haleem and Nasim Hasan Shah.[252] It is considered to have started from the landmark *Benazir Bhutto cases*.[253] Another view is that PIL existed before the *Benazir Bhutto case* of 1988, but was not acknowledged or given a formal status.[254] Some associates of Cornelius suggest that he should be treated as the first PIL lawyer in Pakistan,[255] but Werner Menski disagrees. He accepts Cornelius was a 'postcolonial jurist' who wanted to make the Supreme Court of Pakistan the 'edifice of justice'. Yet, Cornelius was not in favour of opening the courts, allowing them to become activist courts, as is the case with PIL. Rather, he supported the French system of administrative tribunals as self-cleansing mechanisms for bureaucracy. His approach was to trust the bureaucracy, whereas PIL begins with a presumption of distrust of the executive and legislature.[256]

I disagree with Werner Menski, because he reduced PIL to a legal technique for opening the courts for the public by loosening of locus standi. Secondly, rather than the court as part of state structure, his position advanced a neutral and unbiased judiciary which was 'distrusting' of the executive and the legislature. This analysis also lacks a coherent understanding of legal development alongside political development in their historical trajectory. In the continuity of my ongoing analysis, I consider PIL as a part of the overall political project of state formation initiated and continuously pushed by the Cornelius collective, which was accomplished in a legal and constitutional formation under RCO of 1985. In its particularity, as already mentioned, this was a hybrid of Islam and the U.S. type liberal legal system. That is, a strong presidential system and a strong judiciary for the protection of rights to address this democratic deficit. The judiciary's rights and judicial review,

---

[252]AR Alam, Public Interest Litigation and the Role of the Judiciary, International Jurists Conference, Islamabad, Pakistan (2006) 2 <http://www.supremecourt.gov.pk/ijc/ijc.htm>, last visited Nov 27, 2013; AR Alam, The Public Interest Litigation in Pakistan, Menski, Alam & Raza, *infra* note 254, 22.

[253]*Benazir Bhutto v Federation of Pakistan*, PLD 1988 SC 416.

[254]MK Raza, Reviewing the Law of Public Interest in Pakistan, in, W Menski, AR Alam & MK Raza (eds) *Public Interest Litigation in Pakistan* (Platinum Publishing limited, Lahore, 2000; and Pakistan Law House, Karachi, 2000) 64, 86.

[255]That seems to be the position of Nasim and Hamid. Their claim is that leadership of CJ Cornelius established the basis of the independence of the judiciary, and gave rulings about fundamental rights and civil liberties. This movement gave birth to judicial activism, liberal interpretation of the constitution and strengthened concepts of judicial review and due process of law. See Khan (2009), *supra* note 11, 187.

[256]W Menskie, Public Interest Litigation: A Strategy for the Future. The Fourth Cornelius Memorial Lecture, Menski, Alam & Raza, *supra* note 254, 106, 108.

though derived from the liberal tradition as a concept, gained strength from the Objectives Resolution and authority of the judiciary to interpret law (Quran and Sunnah). I call it the *quasi-liberal* project. The hegemonic class, under the leadership of U.S. imperialism, badly needed the military as a seat of power and religious parties in Afghan *Jehad*. By 1985, the reigning class was reorganized under this hegemony by the juridico-bureaucratic structure. There were few new things around 1985 and onward. First of all, the organized working class' resistance was destroyed; added to this was the rise of the middle class due to money sent by gulf emigrants. The rising middle class was less interested in socialism and consequently, a welfare state, and more in legal and constitutional rights. Finally, an important factor was that by 1985, Benazir Bhutto had accepted the hegemonic class and succeeded to convince the U.S. about her loyalties. This allowed her to come back to Pakistan and lead a faction of the reigning class. This is the background of the famous Benazir Bhutto PIL cases where she was granted relief by the juridico-bureaucratic structure. Below is a detailed account of all this understanding.

3.5.1 Benazir Bhutto *Cases*

In the first case, Benazir challenged certain amendments in the Political Parties Act (III of 1962) by Zia. By these amendments, Zia made it compulsory for political parties to get registered before participation in elections. Benazir Bhutto found these amendments violative of the fundamental rights enshrined in Article 17 (freedom of association) and Article 25 (equality of citizens) of the 1973 Constitution, and she was given relief. Chief Justice Haleem wrote the judgment and gave a detailed account of the principles and philosophy of PIL. Justices Muhammad Afzal Zullah and Nasim Hassan Shah were also present, who are important because they promoted PIL in the first half of the 1990s after Haleem CJSC's retirement. Though all agreed with the judgment of the case, the positions of Haleem CJSC and that of Afzal Zullah and Nasim JJ should be considered separately. Whereas the former started PIL dominantly on liberal footings, the later used PIL under Islamic rhetoric in the Cornelius tradition.

Haleem CJSC wanted to combine fundamental rights and directive principles of state, that is, to use fundamental rights to implement the principles of policy. For this he devised a new technique of using Article 184(3) of the Supreme Court writ jurisdiction without an 'aggrieved party', which was essential in adversarial proceedings. For this, the court can dispense with the traditional rule of locus standi for PIL. Chief Justice Haleem did not let Benazir Bhutto's petition wait on the High Court's decision, and stated that procedural rules should be relaxed in cases dealing with fundamental rights. Article 184(3) did not identify which procedure should be followed.[257] Two years before this judgment, Haleem CJSC had laid down the full philosophy of PIL in his speech in 1986.[258] He stood for a "new theory of liberal legalism" which University of Wisconsin Professor Trubek and Galanter had presented—*law as an aid to overall development of society.*[259] He wanted to avoid 'mechanical jurisprudence' and move to human welfare oriented law (not welfare state-my comments). He was interested in interdisciplinary understanding, that is, studying the *impact of sociology on law* and new concepts of property and to new concepts of compensation. Doing this, for him, made lawyers appreciate the value of *liberal training*, which includes a spirit of inquiry and analysis, informed by a sense of obligation to society. Through the above inquiry, *law can be integrator of ecological, cultural, social, economic, institutional and political dimensions of a given society*. This means resolving social conflicts through the application of "flexible rules of law" and these can promote human welfare.[260] He further made clear the role of law in this era was from principles *of pragmatism and realism*, even using the term "*legal social engineering*" for all this.[261] Then he described the technique to make these ends meet, like judicial activism, and defined the term as "a device by which judges exercise their law-making power through the application of the doctrine of precedents, the innovation of the concept of public policy, the infusion of law with the principles of equity and the beneficial interpretation of the statutes and of the constitution".[262] By emphasizing certain parts of his philosophy, I have tried to show that the dominant roots of PIL philosophy in Haleem are in liberal legalism, pragmatism, legal realism, law and society and sociology of law.[263] Grafting of Islam on all this in Haleem's view is very mild; but in his formation the judiciary had occupied the position of an "arbitrator between government and people, in regard to public and private rights".[264] This simply means politics does not represent the people. There is an assumption of one 'public' standing against the government. While invoking this PIL, the judiciary is "not yielding to the every shifting impulse of the popular will",[265] that is, no to popular will. The judiciary here seems like just another unelected institution in place like the military, further curbing the already limited elected voice of people in a liberal democracy.

---

[257]*Supra* note 253.

[258]M Haleem, Law, Justice and Society, *PLD* (1986) Journal Section 205.

[259]Haleem, *supra* note 258, 207.

[260]Haleem, *supra* note 258, 208.

[261]Haleem, *supra* note 258, 211.

[262]Haleem, *supra* note 258, 209.

[263]He seems very well aware of new trends in law, development and society. For example, he called the concept of human rights as the concept of new world order. See M Haleem, CJSC, The Domestic Application of International Human Rights Norms, *PLD* (1988) Journal Section 92, a paper read at the Judicial Colloquium held under the auspices of the Commonwealth Secretariat, London at Banglore (India) during 24 to 26 Feb 24-26 1988.

[264]Haleem, *supra* note 258, 210.

[265]Haleem, *supra* note 258, 220.

In the Benazir Bhutto case judgment, Justice Muhammad Afzal Zullah gave a cautionary note that political parties should not misuse this right of politics against Pakistan, which for him is 'Islam'.[266] Nasim also relied on the position of Cornelius CJ, S.A. Rahman and Kaikaus in the *Mouddoodi* case in tradition of Cornelius collective. In that sense Newberg is right that this decision is similar to *Moudoodi's* case.[267] But the legal position presented by these two judges had a different trajectory and mission during Zia's regime and in the years to come.

3.5.2 PIL, Islam and Judiciary's Rise

Whereas the analysis in this book will connect the rise of PIL with the dying welfare developmental state under modernization around 1990 in the next chapter, the roots of its very particularity nature in Pakistan are state formation after the RCO of 1985, which we described above as a hybrid of Islam and U.S. type liberal legal system with a strong president. Supreme Court Justices Muhammad Afzal Zullah, Nasim Hassan Shah, Chief Justice Azad Jammu and Kashmir Raja Muhammad Khurshid Khan, Chief Justice Federal Shariat Court Gul Muhammad Khan and jurists like Khalid M. Ishaque systematically developed and elaborated on the special role which the judiciary could acquire by its powers of judicial review under the new Objectives Resolution as a substantive part of the constitution in RCO, that is, authority to interpret law (Quran and Sunnah).

Even before Haleem CJSC, two speeches by Khalil-ur-Rehman Khan, Judge Lahore High Court, in 1983 are very illustrative of the new institutional role of the judiciary vis-à-vis legislature and civil bureaucracy working for the executive (strong military president Zia). He stated that the bureaucracy is weak against the political majority and lacks authority, resulting in dissatisfied citizens coming to the courts. Therefore, there was a need to separate the judiciary from the executive.[268] He wanted the rule of law and rejected the idea of French Conseile d' esate, calling it, "New Despotism", in the words of Lord Hawart, that is, the idea of effective legal control of the administrative agencies through the courts of law.[269]

In that sense, the return to democracy for the judiciary, after 1985 RCO, was not a restoration of prestige of political representatives or supremacy of the legislature. Rather, that was a strong role of judiciary under a strong president. Chief Justice Azad Jammu and Kashmir, Raja Muhammad Khurshid Khan, declared that the judiciary "enjoys the exclusive privilege to construe, interpret, and apply the law and to see that no law made by the Legislature offends the injunctions of Islam".[270]

[266] *Supra* note 253, 542.

[267] Newberg, *supra* note 9, 204.

[268] K Khan, JLHC, Administrator and the Citizens, *PLD* (1983) Journal Section 190, 192.

[269] K Khan, JLHC, Judicial Review of Administrative Action, *PLD* (1983) Journal Section, 183, 185, 190.

[270] RMK Khan, CJAJK, Fifth Jurists Conference: (Fourth Session) Presidential Address, *PLD* (1986) Journal Section 217, 219.

This is similar to natural law and natural rights controlling the important agency of the government, in the words of Sir Edward Coke. Chief Justice Raja felt sorry that in England, supremacy of the Legislature could not be challenged, the courts could only interpret and apply the law made by the Legislature. Therefore, he advised that we follow American traditions, where the Supreme Court can strike down a legislation which is beyond the law-making power of the Congress, or state Legislature.[271]

To this liberal U.S. like legal formation, Chief Justice Federal Shariat Court, Gul Muhammad Khan, added the special position of judiciary due to Islamic changes in the law, particularly the Objectives Resolution under Zia. First, he iterated how the 1973 constitution created a Council of Islamic Ideology to guide provincial and national assemblies for the Islamization of law. However, its function was merely recommendatory or advisory. Later in 1979, Zia created the Shariat Benches in the High Courts, which could judicially review laws against the recommendations of Council of Islamic Ideology or in case of delay in considering its recommendations by the government. For Chief Justice FSC, this power was so important that many Chief Justices of High Courts decided to become the members of the said Shariat Benches.[272] Later in 1980, the Federal Shariat Court was created which was given sou motu power in 1982. It was made clear that this power of judicial review in Shariat Benches of High Courts and FSC was very precious. Why? For Chief justice Gul, Islamic scholars made laws, which were binding on rulers in older times. But now, legislators who may not have sufficient knowledge of Islam were making laws. Therefore, the above-mentioned judicial review and sou motu powers in High Courts Shariat benches as well as the FSC can be used to challenge the un-Islamic nature of those laws.[273] He further emphasized how the RCO 1985 had made the Objectives Resolution as the substantive part of the Constitution by adding Article 2-A, and this, for him, brought 'material changes' in the situation. He did not have any confusion about the development of this legal 'material change'. He mentioned the *Asma Jilani case* where Hamood-ur-Rehman CJSC tried to make the Objectives Resolution as the grundnorm of the Constitution. He did not want to share this power of judicial review with any other organ of the state because this was against the legal system in Islam. So the high court should, according to the CJ, declare a law un-Islamic and grant interim relief.[274] Proposed analysis in this book is continuously bringing to the notice of the reader that this 'Islamic judicial review' was not alone in its own. Rather, all the jurists of the Cornelius collective pitted it against the supremacy of the legislature of U.K. type and tried to prove it in line with the strong position of the judiciary in the U.S. style legal system. For Shariat Court Chief Justice Gul Muhammad Khan, there was no supremacy of the legislature in the U.K. in the beginning and the Parliament governed by the supreme

[271] *Ibid* 221.

[272] GM Khan, CJFSC, Islamization of Laws in Pakistan, *PLD* (1986) Journal Section 249, 262.

[273] Khan, *supra* note 272, 264.

[274] Khan, *supra* note 272, 267.

common law which was not statutory, written and man-made law but the law of the God and natural law. To make his point clearer, he stated that this old age of natural law in England like the current age of dominance of Quran and Sunnah in Pakistan.[275] What else?

Another authority for the supremacy of the judiciary in legal and political state formation under Zia came from Khalid M. Ishaque. For him, the judge was not an umpire under Islamic law. Rather, the Legislature in the Islamic system has a 'secondary status' to that of the judiciary because it can reject the legislative laws if they conflict with Quran and Sunnah.[276] Nasim Hassan Shah JSC, applauded the application of the Objectives Resolution by the Shariat Court and later in a concurrent judgment by the Shariat Appellate Bench, where the power of the government to remove a senior civil servant from his office was declared unlawful by the courts. In his judgment, the Chairman Shariat Appellate Bench of the Supreme Court remarked, "[m]an having been born in the image of Allah cannot be permitted in matters of judgment to do injustice". He was amused that these were not the words of a public figure or a religious leader but of a Chairman of the Shariat Appellate Bench of the Supreme Court.[277] By the way, the juridico-bureaucratic structure under Zia was pretending no less than the clergy. Reciting the verses of the Holy Quran in speeches became a fashion, *Iqbali at* as thoughts of the poet Iqbal about the renaissance of Islam became a fashion to give this tendency a philosophical touch.[278] When objections arose against this undue emphasis being given to religion those days, Justice Nasim Hassan Shah reacted strongly.[279] This was not an accident or the design of Zia alone, the judiciary not only led but also defended the Islamization of laws in Pakistan.[280] Charles H. Kennedy and Martin Lau correctly pointed out this role of a strong judiciary using the idiom of Islam but Kennedy presented it at a very descriptive level with a set dichotomy of liberalism versus Islam, whereas Lau showed it empirically at a definite juncture.[281] Whereas,

---

[275]GM Khan, CJFSC, English Courts Followed God's Law, A Speech Delivered at Barrister's Dinner at Karachi on 28-1-1988, *PLD* (1988) Journal Section 245.

[276]KM Ishaque, The Moral Basis of Islamic Law: How does it Operate? *PLD* (1987) Journal Section 141, 142.

[277]NH Shah, JSC, Justice and Islam, *PLD* (1988) Journal Section 1; NH Shah, The Objectives Resolution and its Impact on the Administration of Justice in Pakistan, *PLD* (1987) Journal Section 186.

[278]NH Shah, Role of Iqbal in the Creation of Pakistan, *PLD* (1983) Journal Section 209.

[279]NH Shah, A Speech Delivered on the Convocation of Kinnaird College, Lahore on 7 March 1985.

[280]Raja Muhammad Khurshid Khan, CJAJK on Fourth Azad Jammu & Kashmir Judicial Conference on 8 April 1985.

[281]CH Kennedy, Islamization and Legal Reforms in Pakistan 1979-1989, 1 *Pacific Aff.* (1990) 62; CH Kennedy, Repugnancy to Islam - Who Decides? Islam and Legal Reforms in Pakistan, 4 *Int'l & Comp. L.Q.* (1992) 769; CH Kennedy, Pakistan's Superior Courts and the Prohibition of Riba, in, RM Hathaway & W Lee (eds) *Islamization and the Pakistani Economy* (Woodrow Wilson International Center for Scholars, Washington, 2004); M Lau, *The Role of Islam in the Legal System of Pakistan* (Martinus Nijhoff Publishers, London, 2006).

analysis in this book is trying to show the historical trajectory of the rise of the judiciary and the use of the 'ideology' of Islamic law in league with a U.S. type of liberal legal system adding to the marginalization and exclusion of subalterns.

This way, by 1988, the Cornelius tradition was able to announce how the Supreme Court in Pakistan was exactly like the U.S. in style of leadership.[282] Secondly, how could have the U.S. constitution and related legal norms have assimilated in Pakistan.[283] As already named, it was a 'quasi-liberal legal' project in Pakistan carried forward by the Cornelius collective. Whereas Afzal Zullah CJSC and later Nasim Hassan Shah carried this project with the rise of PIL in the early 1990s, there emerged a 'liberal legal' project under the leadership of Benazir Bhutto and the old defeated left in the late 1990s and throughout the 2000s under good governance.

While the juridico-bureaucratic structure along with the ruling feudal and capitalist elite was restructuring during Zia regime, Benazir Bhutto became the leader of the Pakistan People's Party. She revived her relation with her closest ally in the power structure, that is, the landed elite. The Movement for the Restoration of Democracy (MRD) was one of the landed classes with some Leftist support.[284] The landlord class, according to Benazir Bhutto in 1988, provided logistics like tractors and trucks to transport supporters and supplied better communication technologies.[285] Her excuse for taking the money is simple, that the PPP had always been a multi-class party and a coalition of many different socio-economic groups, namely "[m] arxists, feudal landlords, businessmen, religious minorities, women, the poor".[286] According to Waseem, the small and middle business class did not support the MRD.[287] Ayesha Jalal (1994) called it a "politics of compromise", that is, the interest of the landed class as well as the state can be the same but not necessarily all the time.[288] The MRD bore fruit and the landed class was capable of reemerging in the 1985 elections.[289] There was no fear of land reforms because in

[282]SM Haider, A Comparative Review of Supreme Court Leadership in United States of America and Pakistan, *PLD* (1988) Journal Section 54.

[283]SM Haider, American Constitution and Assimilation of Modern Legal Norms in Pakistan, *PLD* (1988) Journal Section 121.

[284]Bhutto, *supra* note 218, 165, 168.

[285]Bhutto, *supra* note 218, 242.

[286]Bhutto, *supra* note 218, 267.

[287]Waseem, *supra* note 73, 394.

[288]A Jalal, The State and Political Privilege in Pakistan, in, A Banuazizi & M Weiner (eds) *The Politics of Social Transformation in Afghanistan, Iran and Pakistan* (Syracuse University Press, Syracuse, 1994).

[289]In non- party elections of 1985, landlords won 66% of the national seats (158 out of 238) and, in 1988, landlords won 76% (156 out 207) seats. See S Shafqat, Democracy and Political Participation in Pakistan, in, S Mumtaz, JL Racine & I Ali (eds) *Pakistan: The Contours of State and Society* (Oxford University Press, Karachi, 2003).

1981, the Federal Shariat Court was created and declared land reforms un-Islamic in the *Qazal Bash Waqf case*,[290] becoming a hurdle for any popular movement in relation to land distribution.

Unlike her father, Benazir Bhutto enlisted the help of the U.S., viewing its policy of standing against Soviet aggression in Afghanistan as the correct approach. Her only complaint was that the U.S. had supported General Zia.[291] She naively claimed that it was the CIA that was involved with Zia which was separate from the U.S. state. Lacking popular support, she was left only with a rights discourse to challenge Zia. Based explicitly on Locke, Rousseau, and John Stuart Mill, she insisted on the guarantee of the rights in her understanding of the nature of state and society. Her model of change was thus starkly within a liberal set of terms.[292]

The point that proposed analysis want to prove in the following pages is that once Benazir made a class compromise, the state was ready to accommodate her as soon as the hegemonic class accommodated her. The judiciary also granted her relief. The courts were ready to accommodate Benazir Bhutto against Zia until the end of 1987. The cases arising from this situation are considered as the judiciary's new phase of judicial activism around PIL. Let us look at this era more closely.

3.6 The Rise of Liberal and Quasi-liberal (Islamic) 'Legalism' and the Dying Working Class Struggle

The question before us is, why was 'legalism' acceptable for all class formations as a form of political development in the late 1980s and throughout 1990–2000s? Particularly, why did the rising 'liberal' middle class, as well as 'quasi-liberal' (in terms of ideological contestation) support this project? This question demands one to figure out the relation of the state patronage, political/class struggle ('political

[290]*Qazalbash Waqf v Chief Land Commissioner, Punjab, Lahore and others*, PLD 1981 FSC 23. In an appeal against this decision, in the *Qazalbash Wakf* case, the Supreme Court also declared land reforms un-Islamic see *Qazalbash Waqf v Chief Land Commissioner, Punjab, Lahore and others*, PLD 1990 SC 99. An appeal against this case is pending now on the grounds that the Supreme Court wrongly decided the issue in the *Qazalbash Wakf* case. The main ground raised is that there was an erroneous assumption of jurisdiction, that is, "it has affected Article 17 and Article 51 of the Constitution, rendered Article 24(3) (f), and Article 253 (1) and redundant and nugatory, and affected the jurisdiction of this honourable court [S. C.]." This simply means, according to the appellant, that the jurisdiction was wrongly assumed by the appellate court. The appellant's counsel called it a 'reluctant' judgment because out of five judges, one judge dismissed the appeal, one expressed reservation on the assistance provided to the court, and one judge only declared a few provisions as un-Islamic.

[291]B Bhutto, *Wither Pakistan: Dictatorship or Democracy?* Dr. Iqbal Narejo (ed) (Al-Hamd Publications, Lahore, 2007) 35, 67.

[292]She described her struggle similar to that of Corazon Aquino against Ferdinand Marcos, indicating that the U.S. should help her like it was helping Aquino.

society') and 'legalism' of 'civil society' (in which takes us straight to this discourse as promoted in the 1990–2000s).

Akhtar (2008) used Antonio Gramsci's ideas of hegemony, historical bloc and common sense to develop a historicized theory of the postcolonial state. He attempted to dialectically look at the relationship of accumulated power and capital, and emphasized their logic and practice in wider society. He observed that the intermediate classes[293] and the religio-political movements/clerics are part of the ruling coalition.[294] The intermediate classes in Pakistan, according to Akhtar (2008), owe their economic power to the deepening of capitalism and derive their political influence from their access to the state.[295] He added that the understandings of how intermediate classes are structurally a part of the ruling coalition and in turn how subordinate classes are tied to this coalition through intermediate classes,[296] all through patronage. Subordinate classes are not tied in personalized market relations with intermediate classes but through patronage and also in exploitative conditions.[297] Subordinate classes are also connected with this patronage through the lower bureaucracy and if they resisted, they were punished. The court and police at the lower level were to control dissent so as to protect patronage. So these intermediate classes, according to Akhtar (2008), isolate the historical bloc from counter-hegemonic challenges.[298] As a result, "the structure of power remains exclusive despite the great objective changes in the wider society".[299]

First of all, there is a need to understand the proper use of the term 'patronage'. Anthropological use of the term has a technical meaning, which is an interpersonal relationship between 'patron' and 'client' like in peasant societies. In political science meanings, it refers to the ways that are used by party politicians to distribute public jobs or special favours in return for getting votes. This means purchasing political activity and responses,[300] in that sense, it is very much connected to the legislature. The problematic aspect of Aasim's explanation is that patronage

---

[293]Akhtar's study is based on Harriss-White, Barbara (2003), see B Harriss-White, *India Working: Essays on Society and Economy* (Cambridge University Press, Cambridge, 2003). Intermediate classes are internally differentiated across the dimensions of urban and rural, organized and unorganized, wage labourand self-employed. See Akhtar, *supra* note 180, 160.

[294]The military-bureaucratic oligarchy and three propertied classes - landlords, industrialists (the indigenous bourgeoisie), and foreign capital (metropolitan bourgeoisie).

[295]He differentiates between clientalism and patronage. Patronage is the exercise of the power of the patron unchallenged by dependents. Clientalism meant the dependent can negotiate and secure more benefit from the patron. Akhtar drew this distinction from C Clapham, *Private Patronage and Public Power: Political Clientelism in the Modern State* (St. Martin's Press, London, 1982).

[296]Examples of intermediate classes are *Arti*, transporter, contractors.

[297]Landless wage labour, workers of small industry are included in this category. See Akhtar, *supra* note 71 at 169.

[298]Akhtar, *supra* note 180, 169.

[299]He concluded this on the basis of struggles in districts of Okara and Charsada.

[300]A Weigrod, Patronage and Parties in Political Structure: Patrons, Patronage, and Political Parties, 10:4 *Comp Stud Soc Hist.* (1968) 377.

explained here seemed a deliberate attempt of the state (military) to kill the politics of resistance. For him, from 1977 to 1985 (Zia's regime), coercion from the military along with legal and constitutional arrangements was not enough, and hence, military rule effectively devised the politics of patronage to replace politics of confrontation. This meant that the state delivered political and economic power. This preposition stands on the state's 'rationality' (though not good) and its 'will' to give or not to give patronage. The state in these analyses acts as a 'subject' that is not neutral (though it should be). Thus, a specific state formation is not just the product of class formation and politics; rather certain state formation is creating all kind of class formations and struggles. This is a very descriptive nature of the affairs. How to conceptualize it? Let us first correct this causal relation.

It is true that a new middle class emerged in the 1980s. The remittances of those who had migrated to the Arab world for employment and the increase in the service sector,[301] and informal economy became connected with big industrialists through patronage links, particularly in Central Punjab. Gulf migrant families are the dominant explanation of the popularity of Zia.[302] According to Burki, Zia belonged to groups of urban middle class professionals (actually the groups which resented Bhutto). Based on this, Burki said that Zia knew the pulse of 'middle Pakistan'.[303] These classes came in local body elections and later Federal and Provincial non-party-based elections. In 1979, Zia's local bodies undermined the Pakistan People's Party national politics through the localization of politics. In the 1985 non-party base elections, 52.9% registered voters cast their vote. Voters connected through patronage were pulled out by the candidates who were rival landed factions. These elections were without issues or ideologies. Similarly in the 1987 local body elections, the Muslim League backed 40% of candidates and they were all fearful of disqualification. The remaining 60% were contesting elections under a rigged system. The PPP lost.

Putting the legislature back into state formation, we will see how patronage in a horizontal and vertical direction binds the Prime Minister as a head of the legislature within state formation in the late 1980s and early 1990s. Horizontally he/she had to hold all the legislators, or they would defect. Vertically legislators were to bind intermediate classes in a 'hegemonic bloc' of the three fundamental classes as explained in chapter two of this dissertation. So, the dynamics of class formation are responsible for patronage. On the other hand, the explanation of patronage as an excuse for the non-existence of 'politics of resistance' by Akhtar ignores the structural issue, which is the non-representation of the working class in all of these state formations. Any change in this particular state formation needs struggle within class formations and the key is class struggle. Class struggle is buried in Aasim's prevailing 'politics of common sense'.

---

[301] 40% of total labour force (Government of Pakistan, 2007).

[302] JS Addleton, *Undermining the Centre: The Gulf Migration and Pakistan* (Oxford University Press, Karachi, 1992) 23.

[303] Burki, *supra* note 5, 79.

We should grasp that the legislature (made up of the reigning landed and capitalist class and, through it, the new entrant intermediate classes as the part of 'historical bloc') contributes to state formation. Furthermore, it is not a matter of 'access to the state' (the way patronage is usually explained) with the state conceived as outside the classes. This mistaken position leads to solutions from 'civil society' to go to the state and fix it through the rule of law or the control of corruption. Rather, the middle class is the part of class formation embedded in certain modes of production and which needs class struggle to change the class formation. This can explain the working class struggle, and its effects on consequent class formations (of the 1950s, 1960s and 1970s) gave birth to a politics of resistance and a consequent ideology in Bhutto. Its results were 'welfare' through the state. The demise of the politics of resistance was not because of Bhutto or Zia or the military only, but because of the inability of the working class or its representative Left to project its politics. Patronage did not stop the politics of resistance, rather the absence of politics of resistance has resulted in the current class formations and class struggle, and hence patronage has been allowed to grow.

How come the 'intermediate class' as a part of the 'historical bloc' expresses its own politics (or is accommodated) in a contradictory relation with landed, capitalist and metropolitan bourgeoisie? To understand this, first of all, let us depart from the conception of class on economic criteria very particular to American political science. Instead of taking intermediate classes outside or alongside classes, we can look at their positions in the economic and production spheres and particular politics and we can assume that they are a part of the petty bourgeoisie. At an ideological level, they believe in individualism, the status quo and fear of revolution, the myth of 'social advancement' and aspirations to bourgeois status, a 'neutral state' above classes and political stability. They also have a tendency to support a 'strong state'.[304] Based on this, we have seen how these aspirations are addressed by a presidential system like that of the U.S. with safe political advancement in 1960–1980s in relation to three fundamental classes to stop working class participation. The only contrast was Bhutto's era of 'politics of resistance' (with its focus on the support of the working class). After this period, both the Cornelius project as well as Benazir Bhutto's liberal project, along with the newly emerged petty bourgeois (1980s), chose 'legalism' and 'constitutional' struggles. Macroeconomic populism was replaced by macroeconomic stability.[305] The following chapters, focusing on the 1990s and 2000s, will demonstrate the rising role of the judiciary within this transition.

---

[304]N Poulantzas, On Social Classes, in, J Martin (ed) *The Poulantzas Reader: Marxism, Law, and the State* (Verso, London/New York, 2008) 186, 198.

[305]As Ishrat Hussian, the governor of the state bank put it. For him, countries which experienced 'populist' episodes were poor in macroeconomic policy, see Husain, *supra* note 194, 358.

References

AS Akhtar, *Overdeveloping State: The Politics of Common Sense in Pakistan 1971–2007*, SOAS, 2008.

A Amjad, *Labour Legislation and Trade: Unions in India and Pakistan* (Oxford University Press, Karachi, 2001).

A Jalal, The State and Political Privilege in Pakistan. In: A Banuazizi & M Weiner (eds), *The Politics of Social Transformation in Afghanistan, Iran and Pakistan* (Syracuse University Press, Syracuse, 1994).

A Mian, CJSC (Ret, as he then was), *A Judge Speaks Out: An Autobiography* (Oxford University Press, Karachi, 2004).

A Siddiqa, *Military Inc.: Inside Pakistan's Military Economy* (Oxford University Press, Karachi, 2007).

A Weigrod, Patronage and Parties in Political Structure: Patrons, Patronage, and Political Parties, 10:4 *Comp Stud Soc Hist.* (1968).

AK Brohi, *A Faith to Live by* (National Hijra Council, Islamabad, 1984).

AU Qasmi, *The Ahmadis and the Politics of Religious Exclusion in Pakistan* (Anthem Press, London, 2015).

Bhutto, *Daughter of the East: An Autobiography,* 2nd edn (Simon & Schuster, London, 2007).

C Baxter & CH Kennedy (eds), *Pakistan: 1997* (Westview Press, Boulder, 1998).

C Baxter (ed), *Diaries of Field Marshal Mohammad Ayub Khan: 1966-1972* (Oxford University Press, Karachi, 2007).

CB Lombardi, Can Islamizing a Legal System Even Help Promote Liberal Democracy?: A View From Pakistan, 7:3 *U. St. Thomas L.J* (2010).

CH Kennedy, Islamization and Legal Reforms in Pakistan 1979-1989, 1 *Pacific Aff.* (1990).

CH Kennedy, Repugnancy to Islam - Who Decides? Islam and Legal Reforms in Pakistan, 4 *Int'l & Comp. L.Q.* (1992).

DI Narejo (ed), *Wither Pakistan: Dictatorship or Democracy?* (Al-Hamd Publications, Lahore, 2007).

GA Heeger, Politics in the Post-Military State: Some Reflections on the Pakistani Experience, *World Polit.* (1977).

H Alavi, Bangladesh and the Crisis of Pakistan, *Social Rev.* (1971).

H Jalal & K Hasan (eds), *Zulfikar Ali Bhutto (1969): The Politics of the People: Awakening the People, 1966-69,* vol 2 (Classic, Lahore, 1969).

H Khan, *Constitutional and Political History of Pakistan,* 2nd edn (Oxford University Press, Karachi, 2009).

H Rahman, *Reflections on Islam* (Islamic Book Foundation, Lahore, 1983).

I Hussain, *Pakistan: The Economy of an Elitist State* (Oxford University Press, Karachi, 1999).

J Martin (ed), *The Poulantzas Reader: Marxism, Law, and the State* (Verso, London/New York, 2008).

JA Rahim, *Outline of a Federal Constitution for Pakistan* (Pakistan People's Party Political Series No. 4, Lahore, 1969).

JS Addleton, *Undermining the Centre: The Gulf Migration and Pakistan* (Oxford University Press, Karachi, 1992).

K Ahmad (ed), *Islam in the Modern World,* 2nd edn (Publishers United Ltd., Lahore, 1975).

KM Ishaque, *Constitutional Limitations: An Essay on Limits on Exercise of Political Power* (Pakistan Publishing House, Karachi, 1972).

KM Ishaque, *Islamic Principles of Economic Management* (Economist Research Unit, Karachi, 1982).

LJ White, *Industrial Concentration and Economic Power in Pakistan* (Princeton University Press, Princeton, 1974).

M Farani (ed), *Tyranny and Justice in Pakistan (1993): A selection of the Judgments of Mr. Justice M. Dilawar Mahmood delivered against Martial Law Orders* (Idara Mutalia-e-Tareekh, Lahore, 1993).
M Hussain & A Hussain, *Pakistan: Problems of Governance* (Vanguard, Lahore, 1993).
M Lau, *The Role of Islam in the Legal System of Pakistan* (Martinus Nijhoff Publishers, London, 2006).
M Munir, *Highways and Bye-ways of Life* (Law Publishing Company, Lahore, 1978).
M Shahabuddin, *Recollection and Reflections: Being a Summary View on Religion and Social Life in the Sub-continent of Indo-Pakistan* (PLD Publishers, Lahore, 1972).
NH Chaudhry (ed), *Chief Justice Muhammad Munir: His life, Writings and Judgments* (Research Society of Pakistan, Lahore, 1973).
P Musharraf, *In the Line of Fire: A Memoir* (Free Press, New York, 2006).
PR Newberg, *Judging the State: Courts and Constitutional Politics in Pakistan* (Cambridge University Press, New Delhi, 1995).
R Raza, *Zulfikar Ali Bhutto and Pakistan, 1967-77* (Oxford University Press, Karachi, 1977).
RM Hathaway & W Lee (eds) *Islamization and the Pakistani Economy* (Woodrow Wilson International Center for Scholars, Washington, 2004).
S Anwar-ul-Haq CJSC (Ret, as he then was) *Revolutionary Legality in Pakistan* (Pakistan Writers' Co-operative Society, Lahore, 1993).
S Mumtaz, JL Racine & I Ali (eds) *Pakistan: The Contours of State and Society* (Oxford University Press, Karachi, 2003).
S Taseer, *Bhutto: A Political Biography* (Ithaca Press, London, 1979).
S Toor, *The State of Islam: Culture and Cold War Politics in Pakistan* (Pluto Press, London, 2011).
SA Burki, *A Revisionist History of Pakistan* (Vanguard, Lahore, 1998).
SA Hussain, *The Discourse and Politics of Zulfikar Ali Bhutto* (Macmillan, London, 1992).
SA Shah, CJSC (Ret, as he then was), *Law Courts in a Glass House: An Autobiography* (Oxford University Press, Karachi, 2001).
SM Haider, *Public Administration and Administrative Law* (Law Times Publications, Lahore, 1973).
T Mahmud, Praetorianism and Common Law in Post-Colonial Settings: Judicial Responses to Constitutional Breakdowns in Pakistan, *Utah L. Rev.* (1993).
The Report of Hamood-ur-Rehman Commission of Inquiry into 1971 War: As Declassified by the Government of Pakistan (Vanguard, Lahore, 2001).
W Menski, AR Alam & MK Raza (eds), *Public Interest Litigation in Pakistan* (Platinum Publishing Ltd., Lahore, 2000; and Pakistan Law House, Karachi, 2000).
WP Zingel, S Zingel & A Lallemant (eds), *Pakistan in the 80s: Law & Constitution* (Vanguard, Lahore, 1985).
Z Shaheed, *The Labour Movement in Pakistan: Organization and Leadership in 1970s* (Oxford University Press, Karachi, 2007).
ZA Bhutto, *If I am Assassinated* (Classics, Lahore, 1979).
ZA Bhutto, *The Great Tragedy* (Pakistan People's Party Publication, Karachi, 1971).
ZA Bhutto, *The Quest for Peace: Selection from Speeches and Writings 1963-65* (Classic, Lahore, 1965).

Part II
Law Under Neo-Liberal Development: Rights for Democratic Deficit (1990–2008)

Chapter 4
A Strong Judiciary in a 'Weakening State' (the 1990s)

In the 1990s and 2000s, the judiciary evolved through a number of stages. It began with the separation of power (1989–1990), went on to a period of asking for the independence of the judiciary (1991–1994) and then focused on issues surrounding the appointment of judges (1996–1998). In the early 2000s, the supremacy of the constitution was constructed (1999–2006), while changes in the latter half of the decade meant that the supremacy of the judiciary was prioritized (2007), and, finally, I argue, a 'judicial dictatorship' was established (2008). This chapter will explain this progression as linked to a changing state that was dynamically responding to developing class formations.

4.1 Class Formations Under Neo-liberalism

4.1.1 The Start of Neo-liberal Globalization and the Rise of New Institutionalism

With the 1970s came global economic stagnation, the toll of the Vietnam war, the 1972 oil shock and the abandonment of the gold standard by the U.S., which resulted in significant material and ideological shifts, debates and conflicts. The promotion of non-Western (non-capitalist) development with top-down development thinking began to lose priority.[1] The eventual response was neo-liberalism,

[1] O Tornquist, *What is Wrong with Marxism: On Capitalists and State in India and Indonesia* (Manohar, New Delhi, 1989). He studied Indian and Indonesian non-capitalist development strategies and outcomes. Vivek Chibber (2003) found that in India, the state intervention was purely supportive, doling out subsidies and offering protectionism to emerging sectors and gradually the capitalist class started gaining influence over the state, see V Chibber, *Locked in Place: State-Building and Late Industrialization in India* (Princeton University Press, Princeton, 2003).

M. Azeem, *Law, State and Inequality in Pakistan*, International Law and the Global South, DOI 10.1007/978-981-10-3845-7_4

on the one hand, and post-development in development thinking, on the other.[2] The former attacked the state in the name of market-led development and the latter did so in the name of anti-development.

Samuel Huntington translated the collapse of modernization as a problem with human behaviour,[3] and the New Institutionalism school of thought began to adopt the same assumptions.[4] Huntington found the dichotomy of modern and traditional as asymmetrical where modernity is abstractly defined to create a category of tradition.[5] He rejected the idea of a liberal universalistic cultural model; modernization and development do not necessarily produce cultural westernization.[6] He suggested replacing modernization with a 'neutral' shift, and advised the U.S. not to promote modernization as a counter to communist revolution, but rather, to follow the rules of stability. Why did he do this?

American political life was in chaos in the 1960s. Huntington and others found the norms of this period excessively liberal and wanted the re-imposition of authority, both at home and abroad. The chaos arose from 'an excess of democracy', according to Huntington, and so a higher degree of government was needed, that is, more imposition of the will of the government on the people.[7] The World Bank moved to a 'Basic Needs' approach instead of large infrastructure projects, such as those under President Robert McNamara.[8] It is not irrelevant to mention here that one of the main proponents of this approach was Finance Minister of Pakistan, Dr. Mahboob-ul-Haq. In a nutshell, modernization was dead by the

---

[2]M Rahnema & V Bawtree (eds) *The Post-Development Reader* (Zed Books, London, 1977).

[3]As we have discussed while concluding chapter three (1960s) with reference to Ralph Braibanti and Huntington, see R Braibanti (1968), The Role of Law in the Political Development of Pakistan, in, R Braibanti, *Chief Justice Cornelius of Pakistan: An Analysis with Letters and Speeches* (Oxford University Press, Karachi, 1999) 82, 90, see also SP Huntington, Political Development and Political Decay XVII *World Politics* (1965) 386.

[4]For Douglas North, the neoclassical model has a dilemma. On the one hand, there is a rational self-interested individual and on the other hand there is a need to control this self-interest, which itself gives rise to free rider problems, and hence a need of a Hobbesian model of state. This needs some constraints on behaviour, which is provided through institutions. These constraints are norms, but there are also constitutional rules fundamental to maintain property rights. So "a theory the structure of (and change in) political and economic institutions must incorporate a theory of ideology", to further the development of transactional cost theory, and to resolve the free rider problem. See DC North, *Structure and Change in Economic History* (W.W. Norton & Company, New York & London, 1981) 203, 44, 18, 55, 32.

[5]SP Huntington (1970), The Change to Change: Modernization, Development and Politics, in, CE Black (ed), *Comparative Modernization: A Reader* (Free Press, New York, 1976) 25-60

[6]SP Huntington, The West: Unique, not Universal 75:6 *Foreign Affairs* (1996) 28, 37.

[7]SP Huntington, *Political Order in Changing Societies* (Yale University Press, New Haven, 1968) 1-8.

[8]N Gilman, Modernization Theory, The Highest Stage of American Intellectual History, in, David C Engerman, Nils Gilman, Mark H Haefele & Michael E. Latham (eds) *Staging Growth: Modernization, Development, and the Global Cold War*, (University of Massachusetts Press, Amherst, 2003) 47, 70.

1980s. Yet, for a while, it lived in truncated form and had an explicit revival around the 1990s. The salient structure of the old building was not ready to collapse.[9]

Modernization returned with American hegemony as "the unstated, undefended, but nevertheless omnipresent liberal vision of historical change". This hegemony was spearheaded and firmly defended by the Japanese-American Hegelian philosopher Francis Fukuyama.[10] Lucian Pye, while addressing the American Political Science Association in 1989, gave the verdict that the collapse of communism was proof that the modernization theory was right.[11] The point I want to make is that globalization and neo-liberalism were the continuity of the modernization project.[12]

4.1.2 1990s: The State for the Market and not for the People

The metropolitan bourgeoisie were the first to push the idea of a non-interventionist state. The reigning theory was that 'trade openness', or free trade, was conducive to industrialization and development.[13] The policy reforms of this time are commonly termed as the Washington Consensus.[14] The thinking was that only a 'market' with individuals responding to price signals, and thereby "allocating resources to their most productive use", could eliminate the difference between developed and underdeveloped countries. The market could hence bring an end to the traditional development path of underdeveloped countries with its stages of growth, 'take off' and industrialization.[15] As a result, local state formations faced pressure for restructuring from International Financial Institutions that promoted the withering

---

[9]C Lasch, *The True and Only Heaven: Progress and its Critics* (WW Norton & Company, New York, 1991) 162.

[10]Gilman, *supra* note 8, 47, 73.

[11]LW Pye, Political Science and the Crisis of Authoritarianism: The Vindication of Modernization Theory 84:1 *Am Polit Sci Rev* (1990) 3, 19.

[12]Though modernization was a particular response to the Cold War, I argue that it continued pushing the capitalist path of development and modernity.

[13]M Shafaeddin, Does Trade Openness Favor or Hinder Industrialization and Development? Technical Group meeting, Geneva, Switzerland (March, 16–17, 2006) <http://mpra.ub.uni-muenchen.de/4371/1/MPRA_paper_4371.pdf>.

[14]The Washington Consensus was described by John Williamson (2004) as deregulation, decentralization, liberalization and hence with no need for a state for development, see J Williamson, The Washington Consensus as Policy Prescription for Development, a lecture in the series 'Practitioners of Development' 2004, World Bank (13 January 2004), last visited 22 June 2008. <http://web.nps.navy.mil/~relooney/3041_WashingtonConsensus_2.pdf>.

[15]D Kennedy, The 'Rule of Law', Political Choices, and Development Common Sense, in, David M Trubek & Alvaro Santos (eds), *The New Law and Economic Development: A Critical Appraisal* (Cambridge University Press, Cambridge, 2006) 129.

away of the state.[16] Marxist theorists rejected this diminishing of the state approach,[17] for the theories of the weakening state paid little attention to the difference between the states of the North or the South. Further, North–South integration was presented as a win–win situation, whereas for critical and Marxist theorists, this was patently false. Marxist theorists posited the Washington Consensus as a new restructuring phase of the world economy, and accumulation of capital along with a new international division of labour, which resulted in the re-colonization of the developing countries and exploitation of workers (in export processing zones). The changes were perceived as quantitative and transitory, not qualitative, for the extractive and imposed exploitation of capitalism was the same. States continued to play their role in the capitalist economy, with tight borders kept intact for the protection of national capital. Marxists posited that the nation-state in the third world, while weak as compared to the imperial powers, was strong against its people.[18]

4.1.3 Changing State Formation and Class Formation in Pakistan

In Pakistan, scholars diverged widely in their understanding of the character of the changing state in the 1990s and 2000s. Mushahid and Akmal argued that qualitative changes were apparent in politics at the end of the 1980s, with a decline of Left–Right polarization, greater affluence and national self-assurance.[19] As such, they reiterated the 'End of Ideology' thesis (their views on the judiciary to follow). For Ayesha Siddiqua, the relationship among different state institutions affects the capacity of the state to deliver, and hence can determine relatively how strong or weak the state is.[20] In established and institutionalized democracy, multiple interests are accommodated and the state is considered strong, internally and externally. For Cheema, bureaucracy was rule-based until Ayub in terms of patronage to large

---

[16]Susan Strange (1995) describes a 'defective state' to meet the needs of globalization and call this phenomenon the 'erosion of the state'. The weak state idea has been projected by both neo-liberals and much post-development thinking. For neo-liberals, the third world state is too weak to institute a market for multinational capital, both in developed as well as developing economies. Post-developmentalists are critical of state because of its repressive role towards subaltern and marginalized and are against any role of the state in their alternate models. See S Strange, The Defective State, 124:2 *Daedalus* (1995) 55.

[17]L Panitch, The New Imperial State, 2 *New Left Rev* (March/April 2000), 5.

[18]For Amin-Khan (2012), most of the post-colonial states are "firmly ensconced in implementing neoliberal policies", see TA Khan, *The Post-Colonial State in The Era of Capitalist Globalization: Historical, Political, and Theoretical Approaches to State Formation* (Routledge, New York, 2012) 67.

[19]M Hussain & A Hussain, *Pakistan: Problems of Governance* (Vanguard, Lahore, 1993) 50.

[20]A Siddiqa, *Military Inc.: Inside Pakistan's Military Economy* (Oxford University Press, Karachi, 2007) 31.

industrialist groups. It became 'non-rule-based' from the Bhutto's period onward, with the state distributing patronage at the local level and hence, proving to be a weak state.[21] Furthermore, Cheema found considerable change in the state's ability to affect social formations. From this, A.S. Akhtar deduces that the importance of bureaucracy has increased to distribute patronage,[22] distribution through the lower bureaucracy used to control the politicians on patronage. This development for A.S. Akhtar does not *weaken* the state per se [emphasis added by the writer]. Oligarchy's dominance was restored within a decade. A.S. Akhtar also believes that the state is losing a source of its power to affect or direct change. For Hasan, the state structure remains unchanged in spite of changes in social formation.[23] He looked at how the operation, management and implementation of the fiscal system, structure and governance of the Pakistani state did not reflect any demographic, social, cultural and economic changes.[24] Addleton describes how, during the 1970s and 1980s, gulf migration undermined the Pakistani state's ability to centralize economic decision-making.[25] This resulted in the insulation of oligarchy and the dominant classes from counter-hegemonic challenges. In this view, the state is not weakened, but has in fact negotiated change in such a manner so as to consolidate its power.

These theories have not looked at Pakistan sufficiently within the wider geopolitics in which it is located. In this wider context, the metropolitan bourgeoisie increased its grip on the economy through International Financial Institutions. The ruling class, though in control of democratic institutions, was not hegemonic, and many of the deals were brokered according to the priorities of International Financial Institutions, sometimes with interim Prime Ministers to make quick fixes in the economy and polity.[26] After the failure of each democratic regime in the 1990s, a caretaker prime minister, from the World Bank or IFIs, was appointed. After the dissolution of Nawaz Sharif's assembly, the Vice President of the World Bank, Moeenuddin Ahmad Qureshi, was appointed as caretaker Prime Minister from 13 July 1993 to 19 October 1993. Similarly, after the dissolution of Benazir Bhutto's government in 1996, Regional Vice President of the World Bank for Caribbean and Latin America, Shahid Javed Burki became caretaker Finance Minister (1996–97 for 67 days). That was not enough; hence, during Musharraf's

[21]A Cheema (2003), State and Capital in Pakistan: The Changing Politics of Accumulation, in, Ananya Mukherjee Reed (ed) *Corporate Capitalism in Contemporary South Asia: Conventional Wisdoms and South Asian Realities* (Palgrave Macmillan, Basingstoke, 2003) as cited by AS Akhtar, Overdeveloping State: The Politics of Common Sense in Pakistan 1971–2007, SOAS, 2008 159.

[22]*Ibid* Akhtar, 74.

[23]A Hasan. *The Unplanned Revolution: Observations on the Process of Socio-economic change in Pakistan* (City Press, Karachi, 2002) as cited in Akhtar, *supra* note 21, 159.

[24]*Ibid.*

[25]JS Addleton, *Undermining the Centre: The Gulf Migration and Pakistan.* (Oxford University Press, Karachi, 1992).

[26]For a very detailed account of this unfortunate aspect of the history of Pakistan, see Shahid-ur-Rehman, *Pakistan: Sovereignty Lost* (Mr Books, Islamabad, 2006).

regime, Executive Vice President of Citibank Shaukat Aziz was elected (actually 'selected') as Prime Minister (from August 20, 2004 to November, 2007). The state was indeed weakened with the entry of International Financial Institutions, Structural Adjustment Programs, and their related conditionalities, as well as by being denied control of resources. Furthermore, unequal and uneven development raised the additional crisis of how to gain control of people who were increasingly discontented. The growing poverty put pressure on the fragile democratic polity. The state's administrative authority, which is linked to its cohesiveness, was weakened or compromised due to the deepening of capitalism, with the new middle class emerging as a contender of power. The encroachment of capitalism was also marked with an unorganized economy outside the formal economy and polity. New local spheres of power, like the regional political party Muttahida Qaumi Movement (MQM), as well as NGOs, also became contenders of power.

A.S. Akhtar saw this middle class as co-opted by the already defined historic bloc. As already discussed in the last chapter that it is not quite so simple, and moreover, he never defines the dominant class within the hegemonic bloc, or how state formation and the liberal project was affected. In proposed explanation here, the Pakistani state was structurally dependent on the metropolitan bourgeoisie (through their International Financial Institutions), and it became more dependent on it under rising neo-liberalism. The civil society of the late 1990s allied with legalism and constitutionalism, thus acting as a check on the corrupt 'political elite' until the end of the 1990s—but all of this was within the priorities of the hegemonic bloc. Forthcoming analysis will now demonstrate this by analyzing the judiciary, its decisions and particular legal discourses around the separation of power, the appointment of judges, the independence of the judiciary, and the loud rights discourse under Public Interest Litigation (PIL) that emerged through the 1990s.

4.2 Judiciary in Transitional Governance (1988–1990)

4.2.1 Class Formation: Which is the Hegemonic Class?

Mushahid and Akmal point out that the U.S. worked hard in the 1988 transition away from pro-American dictatorship towards pro-American democracies such as the Philippines, South Korea and Panama. Arnold Raphael met Zia on 29 May 1988, just an hour before dismissing Prime Minister Juneju (and died with him in an airplane accident). Ghulam Ishaq Khan met Robert Oakley[27] for five hours

[27]He came to Pakistan as US Ambassador in August 1988 after the death of Lewis Raphel in an airplane crash. In this crash, Pakistan's President Zia was also killed.

before dismissing Benazir Bhutto.[28] Zulfikar Ali Bhutto found the U.S. to be a destabilizing factor for his regime. Benazir Bhutto found the U.S. to be important to stay in government, but feared that the Western intelligence elite was comfortable with the Generals and not her, and looked at her as the daughter of a socialist firebrand,[29] despite little reason for this suspicion.

Benazir Bhutto sent a team of experts to London to study how the Prime Minister's office at 10 Downing Street worked.[30] She admired Thatcher[31] and in her 1988 party manifesto, promoted the idea of privatization. She wished to break the dominance of public sector units by giving impetus to the private sector.[32] She did not find this motivation inconsistent with her father Bhutto,[33] and some writers even claimed the lack of ideology in her politics.[34] It should not be surprising for us, therefore, that in spite of impressive growth, Pakistan opted for a Structural Adjustment Program, though it did not economically need the program, and other liberalization measures.[35]

---

[28]Hussain & Hussain *supra* note 19, 39, 156.

[29]B Bhutto, *Daughter of the East: An Autobiography,* 2nd edn (Simon & Schuster, London, 1988, 2007) 403.

[30]Bhutto, *ibid* 398.

[31]SN Bhutto, a rebel son of Bhutto, accused Benazir Bhutto having a soft corner for Thatcher in the 1980s, but she refused the comparison saying that Thatcher was right wing giving the example of high unemployment. Later she got impressed with how Thatcher's policies created a middle class whose actual centre was privatization. According to herself, she launched the program of privatization for the first time in South Asia and Middle East. See *ibid* 283.

[32]She felt proud that deregulation happened under her leadership and Pakistan was integrated into the global economy as one of the emerging markets. Her successes are the introduction of the private banks, and financial institutions comprising stock market, Central Revenue Department, making State Bank autonomous, and reforming corporate law. See B Bhutto (1999), I am Determined not to let Down those who Believe in a Democratic, Modern, Moderate, Muslim State, in, *Benazir Bhutto: Speeches and Statements* (Musavaat Publications, Lahore, 2006) 16, address at SDPI Seminar, Islamabad, 5 March 1999.

[33]According to Benazir Bhutto, her father followed socialism as route to economic emancipation and she was following deregulation for the same goal. For her information replaced ideology as the idiom of action, see B Bhutto, in, Dr Iqbal Narejo (ed) *Wither Pakistan: Dictatorship or Democracy* (Al-Hamd Publications, Lahore, 2007) 119, 239.

[34]Wilder (1998), Waseem (2007) on the basis of elections. Their results show how the wide ranging and ideological politics before 1970s is converted into very functional and localized politics. For Wilder (1998) *biradari* or kinship is the main the reason for voters, but this is connected with patronage networks as the candidate can deliver patronage to supporters. Similarly, Waseem (2007) found the loss of ideology as a reason for less vote turn out in 1988 elections [at 429]. According to him Benazir Bhutto replaced Islamic socialism with social democracy [at 140]. Disappointed from no ideology, Pakistan People's Party and Pakistan Muslim League are presented, respectively, as Left and Right of the centre parties [at 436], see M Waseem. *Politics and the State in Pakistan* (NIHCR, Islamabad, 2007), see also AR Wilder, *The Pakistani Voter: Electoral Politics and Voting Behaviour in Punjab* (Oxford University Press, Karachi, 1999).

[35]I Husain, *Pakistan: The Economy of an Elitist State* (Oxford University Press, Karachi, 1999) 300.

To sum up, the post-1988 era was a 'Period of the Return to Democracy' and an 'Era of Structural Adjustment'[36] as well as one of 'Competitive Democracy'.[37] Let us now examine struggle in state formation.

4.2.2 The Cornelius Tradition in the Judicial Office

The 'political governance structure' left by General Zia for Benazir Bhutto, who was appointed as Prime Minister in 1988, might be summed up by the phrase "Ali Baba may be gone, but the forty thieves remain".[38] Section 58(2)(b) of the Constitution was a powerful tool through which the president could dissolve the National Assembly. The structures, institutions and dominance of the military in the country remained intact. Above all, the judiciary was accustomed to Zia's set-up and had been long connected with the Cornelius tradition[39] of judicial thinking through jurists like Supreme Court Justice Nasim Hasan Shah and Afzal Zullah.[40] Meanwhile, its counterpoint, that is the legislature, was tied up in the web of patronage and riven with political defection.

Zia dissolved Juneju's assembly on 29 May 1988.[41] He died on 17 August. Nobody challenged this dissolution. Only after his death was the dissolution of assembly challenged in Lahore High Court.[42] The court did not find reasons that could be used to dissolve any assembly. Is the power to dissolve assemblies 'discretion' or the 'opinion' of the president? Does it need 'subjective' or 'objective' satisfaction of the president? The court decided that this power was not the 'whim' or 'will' of the president and "absolute, unchallengeable, and unlimited power is not available to an individual however high place he may occupy".[43] But no relief was granted, as dissolution meant the death of assembly. The counsel was asked to cite an example of the assembly ever having been restored, and they could not provide

---

[36]SA Zaidi, *Pakistan's Social and Economic Development: The Domestic, Regional and Global Context* (Rupa Co, New Delhi, 2004) 22.

[37]SJ Burki, *A Revisionist History of Pakistan* (Vanguard, Lahore, 1998) 86.

[38]Nusrat Bhutto commented while addressing in Larkana on 10 November 1988, see Bhutto, *supra* note 29, 388.

[39]It is just that the old guards, Brohi and Pirzada, who brought legitimacy to the Ayub era, were also significantly involved in promoting *the doctrine of necessity* when Zia overthrew Bhutto. The judiciary during the Bhutto era was altered, yet its post-1958 vestiges remained. In my analysis, the Cornelius tradition is a particular kind of state formation, as defined at the end of Chap. 3. It required a strong presidential system, rights to compensate for the democratic deficit, and it used the idiom of Islam as a centrifugal force for nation-building. I term it a *quasi-liberal project*.

[40]He called Cornelius his mentor.

[41]See the order on pages 756–7, *Muhammad Sharif v Federation of Pakistan* PLD 1988 Lahore 725.

[42]JM Dawood. *The Role of Superior Judiciary in the Politics of Pakistan* (Royal Book Company, Karachi, 1994).

[43]*Khawaja Muhammad Sharif v Federation of Pakistan* PLD 1988 Lahore 725, 757, 759.

any such example. In hearing an appeal, the Supreme Court decided the matter in the *Haji Saifullah Khan* case.[44] The court did not allow the use of Section 58(2)(b) for dissolution of assemblies as an absolute discretion without reasonable grounds, and hence made it subject to judicial review. These 'bold reversals' from 'usurper's position' in both the *Asma Jilani* case and Juneju's assembly dissolution case only came about when the persons concerned were not in power. Post-Zia courts checked the validity of the dissolution order of each ground on merit, but this 'merit' was open to interpretation.[45] For Charles H. Kennedy, the post-Zia courts' activism resulted in an ambiguous system of "mixed presidential-prime ministerial authority".[46] My argument is that this state formation represents a continuity of a juridico-bureaucratic structure in the Cornelius tradition under Nasim that wanted a strong president, but with a judicial check on it. This does not mean a strong legislature vis-à-vis the president. As far as the traces of prime ministerial component are concerned, that was the struggle of the legislature against a rising judiciary.

During her first regime, Benazir Bhutto was hostile towards Supreme Court Justice Nasim, as he was the only remaining judge who had convicted her father. Benazir Bhutto thought Nasim a 'murderer' of her father, for she thought of her father's conviction as 'judicial murder'.[47] She removed him from the chairmanship of the Pakistan Cricket Control Board, and Justice Nasim responded with judicial indifference. He thought that he gave the judgment on merit and, moreover, Bhutto's lawyer did not respond.[48] Bhutto also refused to sit at the same table as Justice Nasim (he was second most senior judge of the Supreme Court at that time) during the groundbreaking ceremony of the Supreme Court building, which was held on 25 October 1989.[49] Benazir Bhutto's conflict with her father's detractors was clearly visible and extended well beyond a particular individual.

Benazir Bhutto granted clemency and commuted all death sentences of persons sentenced by both military and civilian courts to life imprisonment, on 18 December 1988 under Article 45 of the constitution. This was to benefit the Pakistan People's Party workers, who were brutally suppressed during Zia's regime. The Lahore High Court found these Prime Ministerial orders repugnant to the Article 2-A of the constitution. The court went to the extent of stating that only heirs of the deceased can commute, remit or pardon sentences in matters of *Hudood, Qisas* and *Diyat*, and the president had no powers in this regard.[50] This

---

[44]*Federation of Pakistan v Haji Muhammad Saifullah Khan* PLD 1989 SC 166.

[45]CH Kennedy, Presidential-Prime Ministerial Relations: The Role of the Superior Courts, in, CH Kennedy & Raul Bakhsh Raise (eds) *Pakistan: 1995–96* (Vanguard, Lahore, 1995) 17, 20, 24.

[46]*Ibid*, 27.

[47]Bhutto, *supra* note 29.

[48]NH Shah Chief Justice SC (Ret as he then was), *Memoirs and Reflections* (Alhamra Printing, Islamabad, 2002) 199, 193, 308.

[49]SA Shah Chief Justice SC (Ret as he then was), *Law Courts in a Glass House: An autobiography* (Oxford University Press, Karachi, 2001) 160.

[50]*Mst Sakina Bibi v Federation of Pakistan* PLD 1992 Lahore 99, 123.

protective attitude of the judiciary towards Zia's legacy was displayed very openly in the decision of the dissolution of Benazir Bhutto's Assembly. Zia's legacy, which is considered in terms of political continuity, I have shown its intellectual formation in Cornelius collective in 1980s.

4.2.3 The Dissolution of the Benazir Bhutto Assembly Case

On 6 August 1990, President Ishaq used Article 58(2)(b) of the constitution to dissolve the national assembly (as well as provincial assemblies) under the charges of corrupt practices, political defection (horse trading), encroachment on provincial powers, nepotism, deteriorating law and order, ridiculing the judiciary, and undermining civil services.[51] A full bench of the Lahore High Court upheld the order of dissolution of assembly,[52] criticizing the assembly for not completing legislative work. During 20 months, 50 ordinances or bills were presented before the assembly; only fifteen were passed and 35 did not proceed and were allowed to lapse. The dissolution of the Sindh Provincial Assembly was also challenged, as was the judgment of the Sindh High Court.[53] The Supreme Court upheld the judgment of the Lahore High Court by a majority.[54] The first important aspect of this judgment is the observations of Justice Shafi-ur-Rehman against political defection. The second is the dissenting views of Justice Abdul Shakoor Salam, who did not agree with the grounds of dissolution, and Justice Sajjad Ali Shah, who found the order of dissolution of the assembly mala fide, but did not find relief in restoration as the election had already been held and a new government was in place (as had happened in *Haji Saifullah case*).

When the dissolution of the provincial assembly of the North Western Frontier Province (NWFP) was challenged in the Peshawar High Court, a surprising verdict came. A full bench of the Peshawar High Court accepted the petition and declared the impugned order *ultra vires* of the constitution, without lawful authority, and therefore of no legal effect. The court also restored the assembly and cabinet.[55] The problem with Chief Minister *Sherpao's case* in the decision of Peshawar High Court was that it was based on technicalities, though his position might be called principled. The point here was that there were structures to correctly dictate the rules of the game. Within a few minutes, the judgment was presented before a single bench of the Supreme Court in Peshawar, which suspended the operation of

---

[51]The only difference between Ishaq and Zia was that Zia only gave four reasons to dissolve the assembly whereas Ishaq gave 13 along with voluminous files prepared by Ministry of Justice and Parliamentary Affairs, see Kennedy, *supra* note 45, 21.

[52]*Ahmad Tariq Rahim v Federation of Pakistan* PLD 1991 Lahore 78.

[53]*Khalid Malik v Federation of Pakistan,* PLD 1991 Karachi 1.

[54]*Khawaja Ahmad Tariq Rahim v Federation of Pakistan* PLD 1992 SC 646.

[55]*Aftab Ahmad Khan Sherpao v The Governor of NWFP* PLD 1990 Peshawar 192.

the judgment. A full bench of the Supreme Court later upheld this.[56] One of the concerns of the Supreme Court was the political defection, which affected the representative character of the assembly. The Supreme Court judges who did not uphold the decision of Peshawar High Court were Ajmal Mian and Nasim Hasan Shah.[57] Belonging to the Cornelius tradition, Nasim along with Ajmal tried to be viewed as defenders of 'democracy' to a fraction of the ruling class in the years to come.

What happened to those Peshawar High Court judges who restored the assembly? The President responded by not promoting Chief Justice of the Peshawar High Court Sardar Fakhre Alam, nor Supreme Court Justice Inayat Elahi Khan. In addition, Nazir Ahmad Bhatti was sent to the Federal Shariat Court as a punishment, and Justice Qazi Muhammad was blocked from becoming a permanent judge. The dissenting judge was, meanwhile, made a permanent judge.[58] Even a cursory analysis of these judgments can show us how the judiciary fully supported the constitutional and political arrangement of the juridico-bureaucratic structure of Zia's legacy. But declaring these decisions as explicitly political does not add much to our analysis. Let us evaluate some of the allegations or excuses for the dissolution of the assemblies from a class perspective.

4.2.4 Did the Legislature Not Legislate or Were There Legislative Hurdles?

One of the allegations against the legislature was that it did not legislate. However, the fact of the matter was that the legislature could not legislate, as the Pakistan People's Party government did not have representation in the senate. The senate was elected under Zia in 1985, a time when the Pakistan People's Party did not participate in elections. As a result, only 15 ordinances and bills out of 50 could be presented in parliament. The National Finance Commission could not operate as the opposition by the Pakistan Muslim League-N was strong in the largest province of Punjab and was denying access to the central government. The court could not understand the basic inadequacies within the constitutional structure, as the wholesale amendments by Zia (in the early- to mid-1980s) had converted a parliamentary system into a presidential system. Furthermore, these were also the inadequacies of the division of political power during a time of transition regarding the governance of the country.

---

[56]*Federation of Pakistan v Aftab ahamd Khan Sherpao* PLD 1992 SC 723.

[57]*Ibid.*

[58]H Khan, *Constitutional and Political History of Pakistan,* 2nd ed. (Oxford University Press, Karachi, Khan 2009) 411.

4.2.5 Political Defection: A Weak Democracy in a 'Strong State'

The next allegation was that Benazir Bhutto had bought members of the legislative opposition. A vote of no confidence was moved against Benazir Bhutto on 1 Nov 1989, which was defeated and political chaos erupted. Benazir's government bribed and bought the opposition members; those who defected were rewarded with ministries and loans from the nationalized banks. In the *Humayun Saifullah Khan* case,[59] the question of political defection came before the Supreme Court. The judiciary was not only reluctant to address this issue, but thought it to be a domain of the legislature.[60] Though the dissenting judge, Ajmal Mian, declared later that floor crossing thrived, flourished and polluted the political culture of Pakistan, the Supreme Court did not decide this issue in 1990.[61] Wilder made it clear that the Pakistan People's Party was greatly weakened by the practice of patronage started by Zia and could be manipulated by the bureaucracy.[62]

While the rigging of elections is generally mentioned as a problem, patronage is not, because it is an indispensable part of South Asian democracy.[63] For example, Benazir Bhutto and Nawaz Sharif gave land worth an approximate of Rs. 166 million to their friends.[64] In order to check that discretion, in August 1993 Moeen Qureshi promulgated an Ordinance and brought that distribution under a committee, though Benazir Bhutto did not let this Ordinance become a law.[65] In 1993 and 1994, 100 members of the Punjab Assembly and two members of the North Western Frontier Province (NWFP) defected. Presidential ordinances of 1990, 1991, and 1993 were put forward to stop floor crossing but could not pass, as they were not placed before the parliament. 'Parliamentarianism' for Benazir Bhutto was merely a headcount in the assembly.[66] The decision in the case challenging the dissolution of Benazir Bhutto's assembly, however, merely judged it as a deviation from an 'ideal type' of democracy.

---

[59] *Humayun Saifullah Khan v Federation of Pakistan and two others* PLD 1990 SC 599.

[60] A bench comprising Justice Shafi-ur-Rehman, Justice Abdul Qadeer Chaudhry, Justice Rustom S Sidhwa and Justice Ajaml Mian heard the case and did not declare Section 8-B of the Political Parties Act 1962 as *vires* of the Constitution by a majority of 3 to 1. Ajmal Mian J in his dissenting opinion wrote that legality of Section 8-B of the Act will encourage floor crossing.

[61] A Mian Chief Justice SC (Ret as he then was), *A Judge Speaks Out: An autobiography* (Oxford University Press, Karachi, 2004) 217.

[62] Wilder, *supra* note 34 132.

[63] M Khan, Patron-client networks and the economic effects of corruption in Asia, 10 *EJDR* (1998) 15.

[64] D Kux, *The United States and Pakistan 1947–2000: Disenchanted allies*, (John Hopkins University Press, Baltimore, 2001) 324.

[65] Interview of Ayesha with Moeen Qureshi in Siddiqa, *supra* note 20, 105.

[66] M Waseem, Pakistan Elections 1997: One Step Forward, in, C Baxter & CH Kennedy (eds) *Pakistan: 1997* (Westview Press, Boulder, 1998) 1, 9.

4.2.6 Appointment of Judges (1988–1990)

Questions around the appointments of judges had come before the judiciary in the *Haji Saifullah Khan* case.[67] Zia had dissolved Prime Minister Junejo's government but did not appoint a caretaker Prime Minister. With Zia's death, Pakistan was 'deprived' of a president, prime minister and provincial assemblies.[68] This state of vacuum continued until Benazir Bhutto took office in 1988. The question in the *Haji Saifullah Khan case* was in regards to the legal status of all the governmental actions that took place during that period.

The Supreme Court declared the office of Prime Minister necessary, and its absence led to the altering of the character of the constitution to become a presidential system rather than a democracy.[69] What about the appointments of 30 judges of superior courts during this period? On March 1989, the ruling Pakistan People's Party issued a notice suspending appointments of judges during the period of the caretaker government. The courts reacted to this and instructed the government to retract its notice.[70] The government insisted on removing three judges.[71] These judges could not work for a week until the matter was resolved in a review petition, heard by a bench of four judges, whereas 11 judges heard the actual petition. In this review, the judges were reinstated.[72] For Newberg, the quick conclusion was that the Pakistan People's Party had reacquired its reputation for meddling with the justice system.[73]

Articles 177 and 193, read with Article 48, made it clear that the president, on the advice of the Prime Minister, should make the appointment of judges, and hence the president had no discretionary powers. In the *MD Tahir* case, the Lahore High Court had given the verdict that consultancy with the Prime Minister in these appointments was not mentioned in Article 193.[74] The Federal Government challenged that decision and a full bench of 11 judges of the Supreme Court heard the case. The judiciary was divided with 7 to 4 in favour of the Prime Minister. There was a great deal of pressure on the judiciary to side with the president.[75] Due to this uncertainty, Benazir Bhutto, during her first term in the office of Prime Minister, could not make any appointments in the judiciary.

---

[67]*Federation of Pakistan v Haji Muhammad Saifullah Khan* PLD 1989 SC 166.

[68]Kennedy, *supra* note 45, 17, 19.

[69]*Federation of Pakistan v Haji Muhammad Saifullah Khan* PLD 1989 SC 166.

[70]*Muhammad Akram Sheikh v Federation of Pakistan* PLD 1989 SC 229.

[71]*Federation of Pakistan v Muhammad Akram Sheikh* PLD 1989 SC 229 & *Haji Muhammad Saifullah v Federation of Pakistan,* 1989 PLD SC 690.

[72]*Muhammad Akram Sheikh v Federation of Pakistan* PLD 1989 SC 229.

[73]PR Newberg, *Judging the State: Courts and Constitutional Politics in Pakistan* (Cambridge University Press, New Delhi, 1995) 210.

[74]*M D Tahir v Federal Government,*1989 Civil Law Cases, 1369.

[75]Khan, *supra* note 58, 410.

The tug of war between the Prime Minister and the president can explain the importance of the appointment of judges' issue. The judiciary was divided on the president reference in 1989. Lawyers who were present during the proceedings were shocked by the remarks judges made in regards to each other. The judiciary could not decide the matter as the president and the Prime Minister entered into a compromise around the issue.[76] In MD Tahir's appeal in the Supreme Court, Sharifuddin Pirzada represented the president and Yahya Bakhtiar represented the federal government as Attorney General. A compromise was struck between the Prime Minister and the President, and it was decided that the appointments would be made by the 'mutual consent' of both.[77] Till this time, the judges were unclear about their role in the appointment of judges but only on the concept of separation of power. Only after 1989 did the judiciary began to claim the appointment of judges as their sole right. The point I tried to establish is that, until 1989, the judiciary was not the sole claimant of the appointment of the judges, as it became in 1995 in the *Judges* case.

4.2.7 Not the Unconstitutional Act but Constitution Itself was a Problem

The judiciary protected Zia's constitutional set-up in the *Haji Ahmad* case and *Abdul Mujeeb Pirzada* case. The Pakistan People's Party was left with no option except to challenge the 8th Amendment to change the character of the constitution.[78] The topics discussed in the *Haji Ahmad* case are representative of the nature of this short-lived transitional democratic government of Benazir Bhutto. After the 8th Amendment had been implemented in 1985, many acts were done under the constitution, including the elections of 1988, so it was difficult to declare this amendment unconstitutional. An interesting aspect in this case is the courts' attempts to avoid the controversy as a sensitive political question and not the subject of adjudication. The court stated that regardless of whether the 8th Amendment was passed according to the constitution or not can be adjudicated by the court, but the division of power between the President and Prime Minister should not be adjudicated by the court but resolved by the parliament. The lesson that Supreme Court Chief Justice Ajmal Mian tried to teach was that "the courts cannot replace the constitution making place of sovereign elected bodies".[79] The judiciary could not keep this in mind in the coming years. The main case in this

[76]The matter was disposed of in *Secretary, Ministry of Law, Justice and Parliamentary Affairs, Islamabad v MD Tahir* SCMR 1990 189, see Mian, *supra* note 61, 119.

[77]Shah, *supra* note 49, 143.

[78]*Haji Ahmad v Federation of Pakistan and 88 others*, Constitutional Petitions D-76, 163, 168 of 1989.

[79]Newberg, *supra* note 73, 214.

regard was the *Abdul Mujeeb Pirzada* case.[80] It is pertinent to note again that until this point (1989), the judiciary was not claiming superiority over the legislature, as it started to do in the late 1990s. Whereas on the one hand, the judiciary was trying to protect the juridico-bureaucratic set-up of the Cornelius tradition, at the same time it was slowly strengthening itself through Public Interest Litigation (PIL). I will discuss this later in this chapter.

4.3 The First Regime of Nawaz Sharif (1990–93): Separating the Powers in a Weakening State

In 1990, Nawaz Sharif defeated Benazir Bhutto and emerged with a two-third majority in the assembly with the help of the juridico-bureaucratic structure, particularly a coalition formed and funded by the Inter-Services Intelligence (ISI) and led by President Ghulam Ishaq Khan.[81] Whereas Nawaz's appeal was a promise of economic reform and to make Pakistan an Asian tiger, which were popular slogans of 1990–91, his economic plan was deregulation, privatization and deep market economic reforms. He drew up the Protection of Economic Reforms Ordinance, 1991, followed by two more ordinances in 1991 and 1992.[82] All the Ordinances were finalized in an Act of the Parliament on July 1992 called the Protection of Economic Reforms Act, 1992.[83] Benazir Bhutto, as the leader of the opposition, did not accept the results of the election and confronted the Prime Minister and

[80]*Abdul Mujeeb Pirzada v the Federation of Pakistan and other* PLD 1990 Karachi 9, later this matter came in *Mahmood Khan Achakzai & others v Federation of Pakistan & others*, PLD 1997, SC 426. Abdul Majeeb Pirzada was a politician and wanted to become a senator. The Senate was a bottleneck for Pakistan People's Party to move any legislation. There were many other petitions which were pending challenging many issues of the constitution due to overarching effects of the amendment. Justice Ajmal Mian is of the view that SC upheld this view taken by him as Chief Justice SHC in the *Mahmood Khan Achakzai*case, see for comments of Justice Mian, *supra* note 61, 109.

[81]Human Rights Case No. 19/1996, etc. A*ir Marshal (Retd) Muhammad Asghar Khan Applicant (s) v Gen Ret. Mirza Aslam Baig*, etc. It had been established in the case that the then president of Pakistan, Ghulam Ishaq Khan, in league with COAS General Aslam Baig, and intelligence head General Asad Durrani, established an 'Election Cell' 'illegally'. Mr. M Younas A Habib, the Chief Executive of Habib Bank Ltd, provided Rs 140 million belonging to public exchequer, out of which an amount of Rs. 60 million was distributed to politicians. See for short order dated 19 October 2012, last visited 28 February 2014 Online: <http://tribune.com.pk/story/453773/asghar-khan-case-short-order-full-text/>.

[82]*Protection of Economic Reforms Ordinance*, 1991, (Ordinance XXVI of 1991*) PLD* (1991) Central Statutes 494, *Protection of Economic Reforms Ordinance*, 1991 (Ordinance XXXIX of 1991), *PLD* (1992) Central Statutes 55, *Protection of Economic Reforms Ordinance*, 1992 (Ordinance III of 1992), *PLD* 1992 Central Statutes 166.

[83]*Protection of Economic Reforms Act*, 1992, (Act XII OF 1992) *PLD* (1992) Central Statutes 250.

president. She had to face references against her for disqualification.[84] However, these references were of no use except to harass her about the imprisonment of her husband, Asif Zardari.

Benazir Bhutto could not have brought any change in the judicial structure in her last tenure, due to the reasons mentioned above, and could only show her resentment. As a product of the Zia period, Nawaz easily won support of the juridical establishment. His support came from the senior most Supreme Court Justice Nasim Hasan Shah, who later became the Chief Justice of the Supreme Court during Nawaz's first tenure, Supreme Court Justice Rafiq Tarar and Supreme Court JusticeAjmal Mian, who continued to show their support in the years to come. This group represented a 'quasi-liberal', legal, petty bourgeoisie project in the Cornelius tradition. What was new was the formation of a 'liberal' legal project, which I am going to explain below. Before this, we should not forget, both of these projects were part of a class formation under the metropolitan bourgeoisie's advancing neo-liberalism. The reigning classes were represented by two fractions (under Nawaz's Muslim League and Pakistan People's Party). So, particular legal developments (tools for judicial activism like separation of power and particularly Public Interest Litigation (PIL)) can be explained as a crisis within these class formations.

4.3.1 Contours of the 'Liberal Legal Project' in Pakistan

Based on the declining role of the state under neo-liberalism, the 'intellectuals' redefined the role of the state and law in Pakistan using a tendency I call a '*liberal project*' with legal interventions that I term as a '*liberal legal project*'. The intellectuals included a wide range of the liberal left who were disenchanted with the socialist experience as well as the Pakistan People's Party, but continued to fight democratic struggles through emerging NGOs. Their mandate was to cut the excesses of neo-liberalism, as well as to restructure the state, society and democracy. Their critique did not fit perfectly within the poststructuralist stance (a response opposing the thrust of formal legal institutions). They could not present 'local' or tradition as an alternative because that was represented by a quasi-liberal tradition of Cornelius in terms of some grafting of Islam on a liberal Constitution. Under these circumstances the liberal project and its associated liberal legal project could not develop a full critique of neo-liberalism. This resulted in vulnerability of this project to be dominantly co-opted by neo-liberalism in the form 'social' of good governance in 2000s.[85]

[84]*Parliament and Provincial Assemblies (Disqualification of Membership) Order*, 1977. President's (Post-Proclamation) Order 17 of 1977, PLD (1978) Central Statutes 17.

[85]Meaning incorporating social concerns into the agenda of market and development reforms, in the form of a Comprehensive Development Framework (CDF), see R Kerry. The Future of Law and Development: Second-Generation Reforms and the Incorporation of the Social, in, David M Trubek & Alvaro Santos (eds) *Law and Development Theory and the Emergence of a New Critical*

The pioneering collective for this new mandate was the Sustainable Development Policy Institute, which was under the leadership of Tariq Banuri.[86] In the early 1990s, this tendency had a full plan, based on Alexis de Tocqueville 150 years earlier, that the transfer of power to elective officials must take place simultaneously with the transfer of power to judicial officials. All 'successful' societies have 'strong and independent' judiciaries, the intellectual collective argued. This 'vision' puts forward a full package of judicial reforms, with judges being paid high salaries.[87] The plan also needed democratic decentralization, which for Banuri was impossible without strong and effective judicial institutions at the local level.[88] He argued this case based on the collapse of the socialist pattern of national organization, which were the world's major centralized political and economic management systems. Banuri saw that there was enthusiasm for decentralization, which was critical of the "state-centered view of the world".[89] Redefining the role of the state could be done through institutional change and institutional reforms, particularly legal ones. This included changes to bankruptcy laws, environmental laws and the law to ensure the independence of the State Bank of Pakistan.[90]

This liberal project practically supported judicial activism through Dr. Faqir Hussain (a main proponent of Public Interest Litigation (PIL), who helped the Supreme Court in its PIL intervention), who declared it a revolution with origins in the American and British legal systems.[91] Dr. Pervaz Hassan was on the board of Governors of the Sustainable Development Policy Institute and he brought forward the *Shehla Zia case*. Pervaz Hassan placed Dr. Banuri on different judicial commissions.

The quasi-liberal project under the Cornelius tradition already dominated the state, particularly in the judiciary as already pointed out. Common to the 'quasi-liberal' and 'liberal' projects (under the two-party system of Nawaz Sharif's Muslim League and Benazir Bhutto's Peoples Party, respectively) was the centrality of law. Both were also adherent to neo-liberal project conditionalities.[92] This

(Footnote 85 continued)

Practice (Cambridge University Press, Cambridge, 2006), see also JD Wolfensohn, A Proposal for a Comprehensive Development Framework, online: <http://web.worldbank.org/archive/website01013/WEB/0__CO-87.HTM>, last visited 9 May 2014.

[86]A Harvard graduate (1986) deep in the 'sustainable development' paradigm of the IFIs. He provided advice to United Nations, the World Bank, ADB, Sida, EU, SAARC, USAID, and DFID.

[87]T Banuri, *Democratic Decentralization and the Judiciary* (SDPI, Research Report, Islamabad, 1992) 22. This plan bore fruit in 1999 with Asian Development Bank legal reforms project.

[88]He compared five countries around the world from the perspective of centralization and decentralization (UK, US, India, Pakistan, Japan.). See *Ibid* 4.

[89]*Ibid* 4.

[90]The Eight Five Years Plan: Basic Framework for Justice in Pakistan, SDPI- Policy Paper Series 5, Islamabad (1993) 11.

[91]Dr F Hussain, Public Interest Litigation, SDPI Working Paper Series 5, Islamabad (1993 1.

[92]The same economic policies were from both the parties, see Husain, *supra* note 35, 357.

made the judiciary an arena of struggle for contending fractions of the same class formations. The judiciary was thus a problem, as well as a solution emerging from the changing class formation under neo-liberalism in 1990s. Human rights, decentralization and constitutionalism, as new institutional arrangements, were substitutes or forms of class struggle or used to accommodate subalterns. This is the class formation and changing structural relation under neo-liberalism within which we are to evaluate the state formations and the rising role of the judiciary.

There is no doubt that the role of the judiciary was changing. Mushahid Hussain and Akmal Hussain identified that the judiciary had to adjust to new realities. Before this, the judiciary as a political institution was conservative, upheld the status quo and reflected a conservative mood. It now needed to play a role *above and beyond the call of duty*. Mushahid Hussain and Akmal Hussain called on the judiciary to protect democracy, in light of the failure of politicians and politics to do so, and to keep itself clean from 'plot and pajero culture'. Up until that time, writers found the judiciary clean, compared to other institutions.[93] There was also pressure to fashion changes in law so that economic conditions of the people could change.[94] "The performance of the judiciary"[95] slowly became a new indicator, or hope for the development of a country, not the Human Development Index (HDI).

The point to remember is that both the above projects were allied with the rising petit bourgeoisie in bar politics and within the judiciary. They were also connected with the exclusion of the working class. Following is the elaboration on these two points.

4.3.2 *Separation of Power and Independence of the Judiciary: A Gap in Parliamentary Democracy*

For A.G. Chaudhry, the executive did not wish for a separation of powers.[96] This was the inherent defect of the parliamentary form of government in the British tradition.[97] The presence of service tribunals, special courts, military courts, as well as administrative courts in Pakistan, in fact, made it clear that judicial power was

---

[93]Hussain & Hussain, *supra* note 19, 54, 57.

[94]Shah, *supra* note 48, 300; speech delivered in Delhi in SAARCLAW conference on 28 January 1994.

[95]A Mian (1990) Chief Justice SHC (as he then was), Independence of Judiciary, XLII *PLD* (1990) Section Journal 8, 11; a paper read at a seminar in Lahore organized by the Center for the Independence of the Judges and Lawyers (CIJL), The International Commission of Jurists (ICJ), The Ministry for Law and Justice, Government of Pakistan and the Human Rights Commission of Pakistan, on 9 November 1989.

[96]AG Chaudhry, Understanding of Parliamentary Democracy, *PLJ* (1995) Magazine Section, 99.

[97]*Ibid* 103.

not confined to the judicial organ of the state itself, and could be conferred by the executive as well as the legislature. It was accepted that legislation could nullify a judgment. In this context, in the 1973 constitutional scheme, only judicial review could protect against tyranny.[98]

As the judiciary in the 1990s was clearer that its future was with the U.S. in a unipolar world, Justice Ajmal Mian insisted that the constitution be based on the trichotomy of power, as was the case with the U.S. constitution.[99] He was the main architect of the separation of power position in 1990 when he was Chief Justice of the Sindh High Court, and accordingly, he wrote the judgment in *Sharif Faridi case*.[100] Ajmal Mian argued the separation of power as a 'modern' concept; in ancient times all the three powers were vested in one person, the Monarch or chief of the tribe.[101] He extended this view further that the separation of power not only ensures freedom from interference from the executive but from "all other pressures, considerations, and prejudices".[102]

Article 175(3) in the 1973 constitution, which pertains to the separation of power, was invoked in the case as self-executing, and one that did not need legislative regulation for the judiciary to uphold it.[103] Then Supreme Court Chief Justice Haleem commented that Ajmal was intending to take over the government. Chief Justice Ajmal replied that he intended to do so with the kind support of the Supreme Court Chief Justice, which was a milestone towards the independence of judiciary.[104] In appeal, Nasim, who was then Justice of the Supreme Court, played an important role in finalizing the matter and was appointed as chairman of the committee, by the Supreme Court Chief Justice, to figure out how to implement the judgment. Benazir Bhutto did not implement the decision. In 1996, some steps were

---

[98]AG Chaudhry, Judicial Power and Jurisdiction in Context of Basic Structure of the Constitution, *PLJ* (1995) Magazine Section 149, 172.

[99]A Mian Justice SC (as he then was), Separation of Judiciary from the Executive *PLD* (1993) Journal Section 54, 55, Presidential address delivered at Sindh High Court Bar Association Karachi on 19 November 1992.

[100]*The Province of Sindh v Sharaf Faridi* PLD 1994 SC 105; In 1973, the constitution clause (3) in Article 175 declared that "the judiciary shall be separated progressively from the executive within three years from the commencing day". Later, 3 years were extended to 5 and after the Martial Law of 1977 process could not be completed until 1987. Finally in *Sharaf Faridi case*, the court declared the above constitutional clauses as 'self-operating' and asked the government to complete the separation judiciary from the executive.

[101]Mian, *supra* note 95; a paper read at a seminar in Lahore organized by the Center for the Independence of the Judges and Lawyers (CIJL), The International Commission of Jurists (ICJ), The Ministry for Law and Justice, Government of Pakistan and the Human Rights Commission of Pakistan, on 9 November 1989.

[102]*Ibid* 11.

[103]See the dissenting view of the Justice Qazi JSHC in the *Sharif Faridi case.*

[104]Mian, *supra* note 61, 114.

taken through an Ordinance,[105] but it took another year for it to become an Act of Parliament.[106]

On the other hand, Khoosa[107] is of the opinion that separation of power is an ideal and has never been achieved anywhere in the world, rather, such rigorous segregation is sometime inconsistent. Therefore, it should be according to the practical requirements of the countries. Its roots are colonial, but its reason is the current constitutions of newly independent countries following the Westminster model. In the 1970s, according to Khoosa, steps taken by Bhutto, "swung the balance in favour of legislators",[108] but then legislators began to assert authority beyond their legitimate scope. The judiciary began restricting each organ of the state to curb its limits.

The judiciary was becoming self-conscious of its place in the new state formation in local and global class formation. The concept of separation of power was linked to the issue of the judiciary's independence, a point that linked to the appointment of judges[109] in the years to come. Behind the linear evolvement of these legal formations was 'legalism' of a quasi-liberal and liberal project alike as a class formation. Out of this quasi-liberal project emerged the rising judiciary under Public Interest Litigation (PIL) in the early 1990s.

4.3.3 Bar's Politics: Constitutional Politics and Rising Petit Bourgeoisie

An analysis of the rise of the judiciary in the 1990s is incomplete without explaining the increasing role of the bar. This was important because it was the ground for 'legalism', which was linked to the rising middle class. The rise of the middle class in the 1980s, as explained above and in the last section of chapter three, was also accompanied with an apparent depoliticized version of politics. Politics were based on local (instead of national) issues and loyalties based on *biradari* (kinship, caste, clan). Bar associations were no exceptions. The 'political group' in the bar (hailing from Lahore and Punjab) was such an example—the lawyers in this group joined hands based on *biradari* to get support from the ruling party, led by Zia in that case. For example, the *Arian* caste group was led by Mian

[105]*Legal Reforms Ordinance*, (Ordinance XL of 1996) PLD 1996 Central Statutes 300.

[106]*Legal Reforms Act*, 1997 (Act XXIII of 1997, PLD 1997 Central Statutes 402; A detailed account of separation of judiciary from the executive is found in MP Awan, Separation of Judiciary: Bit by Bit, *PLD* (2001) Journal Section 99.

[107]J ASK Khosa, Legislature, Executive and Judiciary: Conflicts and Cohesion, *PLJ* (1994) Journal Section 65; A paper read at Third SAARC LAW Conference held in New Delhi, India on 30 January 1994.

[108]*Ibid* 67.

[109]As claimed by Mian, *supra* note 99, 55; Presidential address delivered at Sindh High Court Bar Association Karachi on 19 November 1992.

Asrar and A. Karim Malik (brother of Justice Khalil Ramday). Similarly, the *Jutt* caste group was led by people like Ashraf Wahla and Dr. Khalid Ranjha. They were themselves affiliated with the Muslim League and the conservative Jamaat-e-Islami.[110]

In this context, A.S. Salam and others formed a group called the 'professional group' during Z.A. Bhutto's regime. The group opposed right wing politics and promoted liberalism, democracy and progressiveness. The Pakistan People's Party supported it via members like Fakhrunnissa Khokar and Latif Khoosa. Wasi Zafar and Hamid Khan were young lawyers in that group. Later in the Zia period, this group distinguished itself from former groupings, and came forward as a representative of a new middle class politics. It proclaimed itself as 'professional' and against 'political influence' on the bar, but it was actually against 'big' politics.

In the era of the 'end of ideology', this group became a hub for patronage seeking, with vacillating groups of *biradaris* in the bar. Its success was based on gaining positions in judiciary, as well as attorney general offices and legal advisories in the state institutions and even law ministries for the upper class lawyers, as there grew an increasing demand for technocrats in neo-liberal formations. The politics of this bar was part of the new state formation. The best is to explore this argument through the trajectory and influence of lawyer Hamid Khan.

Hamid Khan became a representative of the rising petit bourgeoisie during the Zia regime. He developed under the Cornelius tradition, and wanted more lawyers in the legislature, noting the legislatures' lack of competency. He remarked that five out of the first eight Prime Ministers were lawyers. Yet, he was worried that lawyers were now coming from the middle classes and could not compete in elections.[111]

Nepotism was a chief concern. Hamid Khan spoke out very strongly against the hegemony of the judiciary in terms of appointments. According to him, Chief Justices, like the executive and legislature, were involved in appointing their relatives, and other favourites, to judicial offices of the Attorney General or Assistant Advocate Generals. During the Zia period (1979–1985), judges put their relatives first in judicial offices and then in the superior judiciary. During the Juneju regime (1985–88), for the first time, unknown and even unseen lawyers were appointed. The practice of appointing acting Chief Justices and others continued. Furthermore, the loyalties of the judiciary were bought through gifts of plots of land.[112]

Hamid was equally critical of the legislature and executive.[113] He found that the legislature incompetent, bureaucrats made laws in haste and the Pakistan Law

---

[110]Interview with Pervaiz Anayat Malik, 14 December 2012.

[111]H Khan (1992), The Role of the Bar in Promotion of Human Rights, Civil Liberties and Legal Aid, in, H Khan (ed) *The Judicial Organ: Speeches and Articles* (Freedom Forum for Human Rights and Development, Lahore, 1999) 42, 43, 44; a welcome address on the second session of the Centenary celebrations of Lahore High Court, 25 November 1992.

[112]H Khan (1994), Judiciary-institution in decay, *ibid* 66. This also appeared in daily *The Nation* in two instalments, 14–15 October 1994.

[113]H Khan (1992), Judiciary: A Bastion of nepotism and favouritism, *supra* note 111, 9, also published in daily *The News* in two instalments on 23 and 30 May 1992.

Commission favoured judges. For him, democracy should be about consensus and not confrontation or disagreement. He stated that the legislature was a hangout for smugglers, dishonest politicians and former bureaucrats. In this context, he sided with the judiciary regarding any challenge to this juridico-bureaucratic structure.

He targeted the creation of special courts through the 12th Amendment.[114] Prime Minister Nawaz Sharif, during his first tenure, made special courts for the trial of heinous offences, which were gruesome, sensational or shocking to public morality (and thereby could threaten his drive for foreign investment).[115] There were also allegations of political harassment under these laws.[116] Hamid Khan responded that special courts are a form of "no confidence in the regular courts". He also stated that the roots of law and order issues are politico-socioeconomic structures and unless unemployment, distribution of land, as well as over population and illiteracy are addressed, laws and special courts cannot help.[117] Thus he defended the existing judicial system.

In the 1990s, after the return of the Pakistan People's Party, an opposing 'liberal project' emerged, reflecting the politics of the Pakistan People's Party in the bar. They argued that the 'professional' group was only 'professional' in its aim to capture the profession and judiciary. For 'liberals,' connected with the Peoples Party, professional group lawyers were professionals in terms of their practice as mostly company lawyers and nothing else.[118] But the Pakistan People's Party was unable to break the influence of the Cornelius tradition (Hamid Kahn's professional group) in bar politics until the 2000s.

4.3.4 *What About the Working Class in the 'Liberal' and Quasi-liberal Project?*

Where was the working class in this rising politics of legalism and constitutionalism by both liberal and quasi-liberal projects? The best way to explore this is by looking at the legal treatment of the issues of privatization, liberalization and free market inequalities which directly affected the working class. When Benazir Bhutto

[114]*Ibid* 15, see also H Khan (1992). Special Courts for Speedy Trial, *supra* note 111 17, also published in the *The Nation* on 3 August 1992.

[115]*Terrorist Affected Areas (Special Courts) Ordinance*, 1991 (No XXIV of 1991) and then the *Speedy Courts for Speedy Trial Ordinance,* 1991 (No. XXV of 1991). The judges appointed were qualified for the appointment as a judge of HC, and were appointments made by government after consultation with Chief Justice. Appellate court was combined SC and HCs with three judges, one from SC and two judges from HCs. Here important point to be noted is that the government has the right to decide which cases were supposed to be sent to these courts.

[116]*State v Syed Qaim Ali Shah* PLJ 1992 SC 625.

[117]Khan, *supra* note 111, 20, also published in daily *The Nation* on 3 August 1992.

[118]Interview with Mian Hanif Tahir Advocate, Former President, People's Lawyers Forum, Punjab, 13 December 2012.

decided to privatize 113 small industries in 1989, 'liberals' like Omar Asghar (a left social democrat and a main proponent of the project of decentralization in late 1990s) advised the workers to accept the government's privatization package. Later, workers leader Yaqoob, along with the leadership of the All Pakistan Small Enterprises Union Association (APSEUA),[119] met with Farooq Laghari (the then General Secretary of the Pakistan People's Party who later became president of Pakistan during the second tenure of Benazir) to seek help against Nawaz regime's privatization policies. Laghari strongly advocated for privatization and forced the union to accept such a deal.[120] The response was the same from the nationalist Awami National Party. All Pakistan Small Enterprises Union Association (APSEUA) was left with the option of a 'legal' struggle, though Yaqoob stated that "we were not trained and owners were crooks with their legal advisors".[121]

The judiciary and liberal project were responding to this absence of the working class in state and legal formations through Public Interest Litigation, constitutionalism and the rule of law. In a nutshell, the working class became 'structurally restrained', and the class formation became dominated by 'ruling classes' and the 'legalism' of emerging petty bourgeoisie. The judiciary was the least concerned about the workers, as a class. When Nawaz Sharif invited 3500 army personnel to the struggle at Water and Power Development Authority (WAPDA) to ban the union, the workers were not granted judicial relief.[122] Similarly, when privatization of the Kot Addo power plant was challenged through advocate Asghar Gill, the court decided against the workers.[123] Why were the workers never the subject of the very romanticized version of PIL in Pakistan, other than the show case litigation of the *Darshan Masih* case? This needs to invoke the analysis of the very class bases of PIL in Pakistan in both its 'liberal' and 'quasi-liberal' versions in its particularity.

4.3.5 Public Interest Litigation: A New Level of the Juridico-Bureaucratic Structure in the Cornelius Tradition

Public Interest Litigation emerged in the wake of are treating welfare state, and as a new form of critique of democracy and legislature (in my view, in contempt of politics). It allowed the judiciary to exert itself against a weak legislature. The first

[119]Muhammad Yaqoob was the leader of All Pakistan Small Enterprises Union Association (APSEUA).

[120]Interview with Muhammad Yaqoob, 17 July 2010.

[121]Interview with Muhammad Yaqoob, 17 July 2010.

[122]Workers went to Supreme Court through Abid Hasan Minto but the SC rejected the petition. Interview with Khursheed Ahmad, General Secretary Pakistan Workers Confederation dated 4 September 2010.

[123]*Ibid.*

official consolidation of this discourse was in the Quetta Declaration (August 14, 1991). Later a scheme was published.[124] Regrettably, boards were set up in few districts on a 'trial and error' basis, but could not succeed due to a lack of commitment at the local level and a lack of resources.[125] The courts continued their work.

The Quetta declaration included about 35 PIL cases, which soon became 600.[126] In the *Darshan Masih* case,[127] the court sought fit to respond to a simple telegram from bonded labourers to free them, and so a letter was treated as a petition. Supreme Court Chief Justice Afzal Zullah mentioned Fundamental Rights under Articles 9, 11, 14, 15, 18 and 25 of the constitution to invoke the writ jurisdiction of the Supreme Court under article 184(3). The Chief Justice inquired of the matter in his chambers asked help from the bar and the police and ordered an inquiry by the Advocate General of Punjab. In his orders, he banned bonded labour, without a complainant or accused or adversarial nature of litigation in the court. Superior courts began to declare that the need for a petitioner was immaterial, and made a case between the court and the respondent.[128] Sometimes courts did not even allow the petitioner to leave the petition.[129] High Courts stepped in and began *suo moto* actions,[130] as in instances of when women were being burnt by 'defective stoves'.[131] Other such cases were the *Student Politics* case,[132] the *Ameer Bano* case,[133] the *Rashid Ahmad Khan* case,[134] and the *Shirin Munir* case.[135] The perspective of this phenomenon is in the next section.

---

[124]A scheme for the Protection of Human Rights of all Classes of Society in the Country (Amended in the light of Memorandum of proceedings of Judicial Conference, held at Quetta (See *PLJ* (1991) Magazine 151 which gave the scheme. Quetta Declaration was on 14 August 1991. Declaration derived its authority from Articles 2A, 4, 5, 7 to 40, 184(3), 187, 189, 190, 199, 201, 203, Chapter 3A of Part VII of the Constitution and the Objective Resolution and was a full multi-layer scheme from national to local level.

[125]MK Raza, Reviewing the Law of Public Interest in Pakistan, Menski, *infra* note 151, 64, 72.

[126]NH Shah Justice, Public interest litigation: As a means of social justice *PLD* (1993) 32.

[127]*Darshan Masih v the State* PLD 1990 SC 513.

[128]Like in *Al-Jehad Trust v Manzoor Ahmad Wattoo* PLD 1993 Lahore 875, 876.

[129]*Pervaiz Elahi v Province of Punjab* PLD 1993 Lahore 595, 655.

[130]In Re: (Suo Motu Notice) PCrLJ (1990) 1231 noticed miserable conditions of the prisoners in juvenile Jail, Landhi, Karachi.

[131]In *State v Senior Superintendent of Police* PLD 1991 Lahore 224, Muhammad Munir J Lahore High Court took a suo motu action and investigated families, etc.

[132]*M Ismail Qureshi v M Awaais Qasim* 1993 SCMR 1781.

[133]*Mst Ameer Bano v SE Highways* PLD 1996 Lahore 592. Here the court lifted a ban on hiring employees.

[134]*Rashid Ahmad Khan v. President of Pakistan*, PLD 1994 SC 36. The court gave a judgment on a loan defaulter but noted that there are no policy guidelines for the writing off of bad loans. The court ordered the State Bank to form a policy on that issue.

[135]*Shirin Munir v Government of Punjab* PLD 1990 SC 295. The court attacked the unfair quota system of medical colleges though it was not prayed. The case was not a writ petition.

PIL as a rise of judiciary: PIL was not a coincidence, but a phenomenon connected to the rise of judiciary in a weakening state and retreating welfare state, and the judiciary was aware of this rise. Justice Aslam Riaz of the Supreme Court, on his retirement, pointed out that in this extraordinary phase of our history, we can rely on the judiciary to achieve political stability as a third party/force.[136] Similarly, Justice Javed Iqbal, disappointed from the democracy of Bhutto and dictatorship of Zia, pinned hopes on the judiciary to save Pakistan.[137] Chief Justice Haleem of Supreme Court, in the presence of Benazir Bhutto pointed out that this is the era of '*constitutionalism*', and the Supreme Court is *the protector and defender*' of the Constitution and rule of law. He emphasized the pivotal role of the *rule of law* for '*constitutional democracy*' and the Supreme Court as "under an obligation to observe the law".[138] His analysis clearly placed the court at the centre of political and social change.[139] Being 'liberal', Benazir Bhutto, in her reply, repeated the same concepts of 'American Constitutionalism'. She connected 'liberal democratic norms' with the above concepts, reducing the gap between politics and law. She perfectly represented the emerging liberal 'legalism' of politics.[140]

Though Justice Haleem started PIL more in a liberal fold, yet it turned more towards the Islamic tradition under the Chief Justices Afzal Zullah and Nasim Hasan Shah. Chief Justice Afzal Zullah rejected foreign influences of common law and law of nature on PIL.[141] Apart from the *Zia-ur-Rehman* case, roots of his own thinking can be traced in the cases of 1970s like *Haji Nizam* case.[142] He used the concept of Basic Structure of the constitution, which for him is of Islamic character. He made references to the Quran, general norms of society and the 'Islamic Common Law' as opposed to the 'Common Law' of England. Later, Chief Justice Nasim Hasan Shah continued with PIL in this Islamic colour, but reluctantly so.[143] Women were agitating against Hudood laws and courts, for Nasim, have tried to 'soften' the rigour of some of the provisions of Hudood laws.[144]

---

[136]PLD 1989 180, 183; speech at his retirement.

[137]PLD 1989 190, 194; speech at his retirement.

[138]M Haleem, Chief Justice SC, welcome address at the ceremony of SC building, *PLD* (1990) Journal Section 1, 2.

[139]*Ibid* 3.

[140]B Bhutto, Reply to Chief Justice Haleem's speech at the ground breaking ceremony of SC building, *PLD* (1990) Journal Section 4.

[141]Ghulam Ali v Ghualm Sarwar Naqvi PLD 1990 SC 1.

[142]Haji Nizam khan v Additional District Judge, Lyallpur PLD 1976 Lahore 930.

[143]Some relevant decisions of Nasim are Sardar Ali v Ghulam Sarwar PLD 1990 SC 1 (right of inheritance to women is given- Nasim put Islamization against customary law), *Mst. Sahi Bibi v Khalid Hussain* 1973 SCMR 577 (gave right of Khula to women even if husband is not agreeing, that is, the woman is not forced to live with him), *Shirin Munir v Govt of Punjab* PLD 1990 SC 295 (exclusive admission to women in medical colleges); See also *Begum Rashida Patel v Federation of Pakistan* PLD 1989 FSC 95.

[144]NH Shah JSC, Legal Aid to Women PLD 1990 Journal Section 74, 77, see NH Shah, Rights of Women before Courts of Law *PLD* (1990) Journal Section 80.

Though the judiciary was strengthening itself in the garb of PIL, pivoting it on Islam, yet it was not without pressure from the 'extremist' inside the judiciary and bar pressing hard reliance on Objectives Resolution (Khosa, Tanzil-ur-Rehman, etc.). Asif Saeed Khan Khoosa (who later became justice of Supreme Court) regretted that the potential of Article 2-A is not properly realized for establishing a legal order. Courts, for him, have been deciding against the strength of 2-A. This was happening even after the strong reliance by Justice Tanzil-ur-Rehman on 2-A for a 'crusade' against 'Riba' and the *Family Laws Ordinance*, 1961 and the welcome of Nasim Hasan Shah for an Islamic Legal Order as 2-A.[145] He wanted to remove those provisions of the Constitutions, which were a hindrance to the realization of Article 2-A. For him, the Council of Islamic Ideology (Article 227(2)) and the Federal Shariat Court (Article 3-A) were monopolizing Islamization and courts were not upsetting these provisions of the Constitution, rather placing Article 2-A at a level of that of an ineffective preamble. He went to the extent of inciting the courts to use the new door of 'judicial activism'. He did not hesitate to state that if certain provisions of the courts were to be held in abeyance due to 'necessity' (means in *Nusrat Bhutto* case), why could not the inviolable obligations of Islamization be allowed by courts. He gave the examples of two cases with pride where the courts used Article 2-A 'effectively'; one, Article 53 placing limits on property, is denuded in *Waqaf Qazilbash* case and second, Article 45 (president power to pardon) declared void in the *Skina Bibi* case.[146]

On the other side were 'liberals' as an off shots of Left, with a great tradition of resisting Zia's Islamic legislation against women, minorities, etc. In dialectical relation, this liberal project was more forceful, riding on the wave of neo-liberalism of the hegemonic class unleashed by globalization and Benazir Bhutto in power representing a faction of the reigning class. Students from SOAS and Harvard were bringing analyses to justify PIL differently than U.S., influenced by India but Islam in Pakistan in its particularity.[147] Dr. Faqir Hussain found the roots of PIL in the U.S. and British tradition with indigenous variations.[148] Asif Saeed Khan Khosa, pushing Article 2-A to use Objectives Resolution for Islamization, became scared of its use in suo motu cases in PIL. For him, this use of Islam is to overlap or defy the specified 'limits' of the constitutional scheme of a Muslim state. This reliance on Islamic provisions and then reluctance is very particular to Khosa and Nasim Hasan Shah, as happened in *Hakim Khan* case (detail to follow). Other objections by Khosa against the use of suo motu in PIL were, one, that the court itself becomes

145 ASK Khoosa, The Ineffective Effect of Article 2-A, Constitution of Pakistan, *PLD* (1990) Journal Section 50, 56.

146 *Ibid.*

147 MH Khan, The Concept of Public Interest Litigation and its Meaning in Pakistan *PLD* (1992) Journal Section 84, 85.

148 Dr. F Hussain, Joint Secretary Pakistan Law Commission, Public Interest Litigation in Pakistan *PLD* (1993) Journal Section 72, 73.

a complainant; two, the defendant is at a disadvantage because the court already has a position; three, the judge should not acquire the role of a reformer.[149] Dr. Faqir reacted to this and tried to justify the genesis and evolution of *locus standi*.[150] Later, towards the end of the 1990s, Menski started 'indigenizing' PIL in 'South Asian' tradition.

Public Interest Litigation in the Wake of the Retreat of the Welfare State: Werner Menski has linked the rise of Public Interest Litigation with the demise of the welfare state.[151] Public interest, as opposed to public welfare, was the new norm and even if an order was passed for public welfare, but is in violation of the state or against the basic norms of justice, it cannot be protected.[152] He approved of the fact that South Asian judges refused to dream about absolute equality. It is not surprising that exactly at this time, the land reforms of 1972 and 1977 were declared as un-Islamic.[153] As a quasi-substitute, public interest litigation was necessary, to make some promise of equality. Finally, the judges were the 'ultimate arbitrators' to decide what was Public Interest Litigation and what was not.[154]

Apart from Menski's understanding, the judges thought that they were using law for the welfare state.[155] Actually, the judges reinterpreted the welfare state as not for free education and health but for life, liberty, honour and protection of property. This is where the judiciary is needed and only the judiciary has the 'calibre' to do this.[156] Judges might have refused to dream about 'equality' as promised by the welfare state and claimed by Menski and one can romanticize the 'rhetoric' of judges representing public interest, but for workers the demise of available meagre welfare state was not good news. In Pakistan, PIL against a weak democracy in a weakening state of 1990s created further stabilizing effect.

Public Interest Litigation as a Substitute of Democracy and a Critique of Legislature: The main supporters of Public Interest Litigation found democracy to

---

[149]ASK Khosa, Suo Motu Exercise of Writ Jurisdiction *PLD* (1993) Journal Section 87, 96.

[150]Dr F Hussain, Access to Justice *PLD* (1994) Journal Section 10.

[151]W Menski (1997), Public Interest Litigation: A strategy for the future. The Fourth Cornelius Memorial Lecture, in, Werner Menski, Ahmad Rafay Alam & Mehreen Kasoori Raza (eds) *Public Interest Litigation in Pakistan* (Platinum Publishing Limited & Pakistan Law House, London & Karachi 2000) 112.

[152]*Anwar Muhammad Khan v Director of Industries and Mineral Development* PLD 1994 Lahore 70, 92.

[153]Federal Shariat Court declared land reforms un-Islamic in 1981 in *Qazal Bash Waqf v Chief Land Commissioner, Punjab, Lahore* and others PLD 1981 FSC 23. In an appeal against this decision, Supreme Court also declared land reforms un-Islamic in *Qazalbash Wakf case*, see PLD 1990 SC 99.

[154]W Menski (2000), Introductory Over View of Public Interest Litigation in Pakistan; Past Future, *supra* note 151, 12.

[155]See proceedings of the seminar on law reforms which was titled "Law, Justice and Welfare State" organized by Pakistan Bar Council, speech of Saeeduzzaman Siddique JSC, *PLD* (1999) Journal Section 97.

[156]Justice (Ret) KM Samadani, Law, Justice, and Welfare State, *PLD* (1999) Journal Section 132, 132.

be connected with constitutionalism. Internationally and locally, human rights issues were now centre stage.[157] But democracy meant politics, so how far can Public Interest Litigation go to uphold democracy? There is clear evidence that Public Interest Litigation went on to undermine the legislature.

The judiciary in Pakistan was trained in the juridico-bureaucratic structure of the Cornelius tradition, and thus to engage in political issues. As already discussed, the Objectives Resolution undermined the legislature by putting above it the undefined laws of *Sunnah* and *Sharia*. Justice Majid invoked an inquisitional jurisdiction as opposed to an adversarial or accusational one, and hence made litigation possible by an aggrieved person who has no personal interest but needs the welfare of the general public.[158] He used Sections of 3, 4 and 5 of the *Enforcement of Shariah Act*, 1991, which he called the "statutorily recognized supreme law of the land". He said there is no provision in the constitution for the accountability of the state functionaries, and hence *Sharia* filled this gap. This aspect of Public Interest Litigation and its association with Article 2-A had always posed the danger of further undermining an already undermined legislature. In the early 1990s with the beginning of Public Interest Litigation, the Cornelius tradition forcefully defended Article 2-A and its related Objective Resolution after the decision in the *Hakim Khan case*.[159] The court in this case declared that the Objective Resolution of Article 2-A was not a beacon of light for legislation. It simply means that "Article 2-A changes nothing". As opposed to this, Sardar Sher Alam Khan argued that this provision is unique in the history of the constitution and had made the Quran and Sunnah above man-made law and legislation. Furthermore, according to him, the court has the power to judicially review Article 2-A and not the legislature.[160]

The pioneer and main proponent of PIL in Pakistan, Dr. Faqir Hussain, found that the parliamentary system could not work in our democratic culture and met with meta-legal and extra-legal strokes. Politicians were mainly responsible for this.

---

[157]Hussain, *supra* note 150, 20; The writer was the Joint Secretary Pakistan Law Commission. The point to remember is that exactly during this period SDPI Tariq Banuri wrote on the same topic and Dr Faqir Hussain's writing is included in his book.

[158]*Al-jehad Trust and another v Mian Ahmad Nawaz Wattoo and 8 others* PLD 1993 Lahore 875; Mian Ahmad Nawaz Wattoo was the Chief Minister of Punjab.

[159]*Hakim Khan v Government of Pakistan* 1992 PLD SC 595; this case was decided by Dr Nasim Hasan Shah, Shafi-ur-Rahman Saad Saood Jan, Abdul Shakrul Salam and Muhammad Afzal Lone JJs SC. Dr Nasim Hasan JSC wrote the decision and others agreed. Where the court declared that the Objective Resolution after becoming the substantive part of the constitution by Article 2-A could not guide them to formulate such provisions for the constitution.

[160]Comments of Sardar Sher Alam Khan. He quoted a writer from the Cornelius tradition, Khalid M Ishaq's unpublished essay, *Islamization Business of Legislature Only?* And emphasized judicial review rather than legislative review guarding the limits of Allah by courts. So, according to this view, all disputes between individuals and public authorities are the natural characteristics of judicial power in Islam. Khalid M Ishaq made it clear that the constitution in Islamic state does not create judicial power; it only distributes it. This seems that the judiciary should create its judicial power, and distribute it through constitution by interpreting it. See SS Khan Advocate, *The Role of Judiciary and Objective Resolution: A Plea for Reappraisal of Hakim Khan Case* (Institute of Policy Studies, Islamabad, 1994) at 17.

The reason for this is the "poor standard of calibre and intellect of our parliamentarians".[161] Horse trading, for him, was a new thing for European and North American politics. In Pakistan, politicians were busy supervising development projects, sanctioning loans, plots and seeking appointments in service, etc. instead of law making, which was their primary responsibility. How does one control them? Instead of self-governing mechanisms of parties as in the U.K., he suggested a U.S. type of statutory regulations with qualifications for candidates.[162]

The court went on to ban student politics as part of its drive to correct the ills of democracy,[163] which had already been done by Zia during his regime. The same day, Supreme Court Chief Justice Afzal Zullah passed an order to remove restrictions on the marriage of airhostesses of Pakistan International Airlines (PIA) and nurses in the military hospitals. Public Interest Litigation increasingly showed ambivalence towards addressing social discrimination, while it targeted political and economic challenges.

There was a second strand of opinion that Public Interest Litigation should be separate from politics. There was concern of public interest being misused,[164] as these types of cases are of personal interest and predominantly of political nature. It was argued that they were filed when the petitioner was in opposition or had another agenda that was not in public interest.[165] Public Interest Litigation brought by impoverished people was being used for political ends and the decade to come was a witness of this. However, the judiciary was, overall, committed to the political dimensions of Public Interest Litigation.

Public Interest Litigation as a substitute for the State: The definition of the state is found in Article 7.[166] The judiciary "interpreted itself to be the part of the state".

---

[161]Dr F Hussain, Electoral System of Pakistan: Suggestions for Refrom, *PLD* (1994) Journal Section 86, 87.

[162]*Ibid* 93.

[163]In *M Ismail Qureshi v M Awaais Qasim,* 1993 SCMR 1781, the petition was brought by one person against another but the courts decided to interfere and held an inquiry out of that case. Hearing arguments from the students, teachers as well as politicians, they decided to ban student politics. Zia had done this to suppress dissent among students and the Pakistan People's Party government had just restored the right to dissent in 1988.

[164]Example are *Benazir Bhutto v President of Pakistan* PLD 1998 SC 388, and *Asad Ali v Federation of Pakistan* PLD 1998 SC 161. List of cases given are *Ittefaq Foundry v Federation of Pakistan* PLD 1990 Lahore 121, *Pervez Elahi v Province of Punjab,* PLD 1993 Lahore 595, *Al-Jehad Trust v Manzoor Ahmad Wattoo,* PLD 1993 Lahore 875 and *Sabir Shah v Shad Mohammad Khan* PLD 1995 SC 66.

[165]MK Raza (2000), Reviewing the Law of Public Interest in Pakistan, in, W Menski, Ahmad Rafay Alam & Mehreen Kasoori Raza (eds) *Public Interest Litigation in Pakistan* (Platinum Publishing Limited & Pakistan Law House, London & Karachi, 2000) 98.

[166]Article 7 of the 1973 Constitution of Pakistan; "Definition of the State. In this Part, unless the context otherwise requires, 'the State' means the Federal Government, Majlis-e-Shoora (Parliament), a Provincial Government, a Provincial Assembly, and such local or other authorities in Pakistan as are by law empowered to impose any tax or cess".

The responsibilities of the state were felt and taken up by the judiciary.[167] It also used the rights discourse as protection against the state and as enforceable by the courts.[168] Thus, the judiciary was filling policy gaps along with newly created spaces by restraining the state and state institutions. For example, in *Fazal Jan v. Roshan Din,* 1990 PLD S. C. 661, Afzal Zulla Chief Justice Supreme Court ordered that women should be given free legal aid, rather than decide through legislation or policy. The height of this newfound power can be seen in the *Shehla Zia* case.[169]

Before 1988, Chief Justice Haleem's judicial activism as a state-directed judicial activism to direct the state to perform the duties owed to the citizen. Afterwards, this role was extended from checking the violations of individual rights to directing the Prime Minister and executive to implement policies.[170] The law no longer focused on the maintenance of peace and order, but on providing social justice.[171] The government was equated with the state and the 'government' extended right down to the smallest civil servant who was abusing power.[172] All this was around the idiom of rights.

Official Advocacy of PIL and Nature of Rights: The foundation of Rights in Chap. 1 of Part II of the Constitution of 1973 of Pakistan is described as having its origin from the Bill of Rights of the U.S. Constitution, the 1789 Declaration of Rights of Man and Citizen of the French Revolution, the Irish Constitution of 1935 and the Universal Declaration of Human Rights of 1948. It also has traces from the philosophies of Locke, Rousseau, the theory of natural law and English Common Law and the economic theory of individualism, that is, *Laissez Faire.*[173] Khan claimed that the roots of Public Interest Litigation can be found in the U.S. system.[174] Menski, on the other hand, claimed its origin as purely South Asian.[175] My position is that in Pakistan, Public Interest Litigation developed very strongly within the ambit of western legal discourse of rights and constitutionalism. A poor grafting of Islam on Western ideals was done in the late 1980s, which continued in early 1990s under the Chief Justices Afzal Zullah and Nasim. This was a

[167]Khosa, *supra* note 149.

[168]AG Chaudhary, Definition of the State *PLJ* (1994) Magazine Section, 232, 233.

[169]*Fazal Jan v Roshan Din* PLD 1990 SC 661, see *Shehla Zia* case, Shehla Zia v WAPDA PLD 1994 SC 693.

[170]Like in *Shehla Zia case*, where Principles of Policy were made justiciable (Article 9 of right to life) by the SC, and hence the courts to play a role.

[171]Shah, *supra* note 48, 123, 130.

[172]W Menski, Introductory Over View of Public Interest Litigation in Pakistan: Past and future, in, Menski et al. (ed) supra note 125 8.

[173]AG Chaudhary, Definition of the State *PLJ* (1994) Magazine Section 232, 232.

[174]Khan, *supra* note 149, 84, see also MH Khan, *Public Interest Litigation: Growth of the Concept and its Meaning in Pakistan* (Pakistan Law House, Karach, 1993).

[175]W Menski, Introductory Over View of Public Interest Litigation in Pakistan: Past and future, *supra* note 151, 18.

momentum of the old Cornelius tradition. Later, in the late 1990s and 2000s, the dominant mode of PIL was liberal, with the changed position of the hegemonic block for war against terror and using the military as a seat of power to curb this terrorism.

In spite of this type of rights discourse in the early 1990s, the last genuine critique of rights discourse came from A.G. Chaudhry, which tried to cut across the liberal boundaries. Based on the UN Conference on Human Rights 1993 held in Vienna, he criticized the UDHR that 20 out of 30 articles were about civil and political rights, while five covered economic, social and cultural rights. The focus on individual political freedoms like the right to vote and hold public office, along with rights like free speech and assembly were derived from Western jurisprudence and liberal thought.[176] He argued that the UDHR "proclaims to have elevated the principles of government of Western civilization to the international level".[177]

According to the writer, the summary implementation of the abstract concepts of human rights was being pushed by the Western Governments, NGOs and human rights activists, especially in the United States, without cultural, social, political considerations. Chaudhry notices that "for many in the West, the end of the Cold war was not just the defeat or collapse of communist regimes, but it was the supreme triumph and vindication of Western system of governments and their values." There has been a tendency since 1989 in the West to measure all states by what the West regard as 'democracy'; "The hard core of rights that are truly universal is smaller than many in the West profess"; "they do not realize that poverty, insecurity, and instability breads human rights abuses, while wealth creates security and stability".[178]

I present this critique to draw a contrast with the uncontested UDHR in the 'liberal' project of the 1990s. I agree with A.G. Chaudhry's critique, but also want to examine the limits of change within and through the constitution, and the limits of the rights discourse and practice of PIL. Whereas A.G. Chaudhry had been a 'constitutionalist' who believed that socialism will come through enforcement of the constitution, he was clear that though the UDHR "recognizes in unmistakable terms the supremacy of individual rights to free speech and political expression, it lays great emphasis on the economic and social rights of the people. In view of these provisions, we have our own standard of Human Rights".[179]

---

[176]AG Chaudhry (1994), Conceptualization of Human Rights, *PLJ* (1994) Magazine Section, 1, 2; The writer is talking about the UN Conference on Human Rights 1993 held in Vienna where the Western countries accused Asian countries of undermining the idea of universality of Human Rights.

[177]*Ibid.*

[178]*Ibid* 5.

[179]*Ibid* 5.

4.3.6 Dissolution of Nawaz's Assembly (1993)

There was a fresh dispute between the Prime Minister and the president regarding the appointment of the Chief of the Army Staff. On April 1993, president Ishaq dissolved the National Assembly, accusing it of maladministration, corruption, nepotism, terrorizing opposition and use of official resources for political ends.[180] The order of the dissolution was challenged in the Supreme Court and a full bench of 11 judges, headed by Nasim Hassan Shah, accepted the petition by a majority of ten to one. The dissenting judge was Sajjad Ali Shah.[181] This seems to be a very courageous decision, but the 'rules of the game' were dictated elsewhere. The restoration did not last for more than two months, for a deal was brokered between the president and Prime Minister through the military, and both resigned! According to Supreme Court Justice Sajjad, Supreme Court Chief Justice Nasim was determined to restore the assembly and made a statement that he was not like Chief Justice Munir and he would give good news to the nation.[182] Nasim Hasan Shah boasted that an overthrown government was back to power through the judiciary for the first time in the known history of the democratic and civilized world.[183] The legislature itself noted that it was sitting in session because of the Supreme Court.[184]

To sum up, a structural analysis of the features of politics and judicial changes in the early 1990s shows that the replacement of the minimal welfare state and privatization was accompanied with two effects on the class formation. There was a new 'compromise' within the 'power bloc' going through undefined, complex mediations. The crisis of the state was the crisis of the new arrangement around privatization and consequent opportunities for the hegemonic metropolitan bourgeoisie, as well as bitter competition among different fractions of the reigning landed and capitalist class. Privatization and neo-liberalism brought an increasing inequality, which placed more pressure on the state to deliver what the market was still not able to allocate. The legislature's open courts (*Khuli Kachehri* of Nawaz)[185] or the judiciary's populist PIL was a poor substitute in this context.

---

[180]The text of the order is reproduced on page 572–575 of *Muhammad Nawaz Sahrif v President of Pakistan* PLD 1993 SC 473.

[181]*Muhammad Nawaz Sahrif v President of Pakistan* PLD 1993 SC 473.

[182]Shah, *supra* note 49, 176, as cited from *Jang Karachi* dated 12 May 1993.

[183]NH Shah CJSC, "Supremacy of Constitution"-Recent Developments *PLD* (1994) Journal Section 34, 47.

[184]The remarks of the Prime Minister Nawaz after the restoration of the assembly in 1993 while the session of the parliament resumed as quoted by Justice Nasim Chief Justice SC (ret) in his autobiography; See Shah, *supra* note 48, 106.

[185]In similar fashion, Prime Minister Nawaz Sharif started publicly visiting sites of domestic violence, patted the heads of victim, and produced the slogan that justice should be provided at the door step and should be cheap and quick, see *jehan Zulm wahan Nawaz Sharif* (wherever there was cruelty, Nawaz Sharif would be there to redress). Sajjad, a justice of SC, started acquitting the accused and for this was silently removed by the Chief Justice SC. He made the observation in the

4.4 Benazir Bhutto's Second Term (1993–96): The Judiciary and Democracy Confrontation

In her 2nd tenure (from 1993 to 1996), Benazir Bhutto attempted to fix institutional loopholes and the pitfalls of her first regime (1988–90). She was lucky to have General Kakar and wanted him to continue due to increasing extremism in the military, but he refused. To please the army, she supported the formation of the Taliban's control of Afghanistan but later insisted on breaking relations the group and warned that 'strategic depth' would become a 'strategic threat'. When Kakar retired and Javed Ashraf was transferred from the Inter-Services Intelligence (ISI), it was considered the 'death-knell' for Benazir Bhutto's second government.[186] The second loophole was the 8th Amendment, or what she termed as allowing the possibility of a "military-backed coup with constitutional dressing".[187] Hence, she elected Farooq Laghari to be the president of Pakistan from her own party.

It was hard enough to maintain an alliance with unbridled allies let alone control them when in the opposition. Benazir Bhutto's weak government tried to survive by encouraging political defection of the opposition. She gave residential plots and lands to members of assembly. Fifty-five opposition members were among the applicants for plots in the capital city of Islamabad. When this was challenged in the Lahore High Court, Justice Munir A. Sheikh rejected M.D. Tahir's writ, an advocate against the granting of plots to members of assembly, on the grounds that if the lawyers and journalists can have plots, why not the members of assembly?[188] Expressing real opposition, on 9 June 1996, the *Sunday Express London* reported that Benazir Bhutto had bought a £2.5 million mansion in Britain. Meanwhile, the IMF saw corruption as a big hurdle to raising revenue in Pakistan. Aid donors were unhappy over government reluctance to curb the menace of corruption and accused the government of fudging figures. They put pressure on the IMF to go public over the level of corruption in Pakistan.[189]

(Footnote 185 continued)

appeal of *Sabiha* case that the new publicity was sensationalizing them and was affecting the investigation in favour of one party. See Shah, *supra* note 49, 362.

[186] *Supra* note 29, 420, 242.

[187] *Ibid* 408.

[188] *The Daily Pakistan*, 14 May 1996 8.

[189] *The Nation*, 23 June 1996.

4.4.1 Appointment of Judges: The Democratic Regime Exercising Constitutional Power?

Given the range of decisions, Benazir's regime felt challenged. In these circumstances, the control of the judiciary was needed to hold the power of the state. The restoration of the Nawaz government was a clear indication of the judicial institutions emerging power. When Benazir Bhutto herself dissolved the provincial assembly of the North Western Frontier Province (NWFP), it was challenged in the Supreme Court, which accepted the petition by a majority of seven to two.[190] Again on 5 September 1995, the president imposed emergency in the province of Punjab to get rid of the undesired Chief Minister Wattoo, the Lahore High Court again accepted the petition in its judgment of 30 October 1996.[191]

Benazir Bhutto could not trust anyone at the highest post of judicial hierarchy, so she sought to appoint those who had decided favourably for her regime. Chief Justice Saad was not confirmed, rather Sajjad was appointed as the Chief Justice of the Supreme Court in 1994, possibly since Sajjad was one of the two dissenting judges when her regime was dissolved in 1990 and he had observed that the purpose of the dissolution was just to get rid of the Pakistan People's Party. Sajjad himself thought that in India and elsewhere there was no problem with political appointments in judiciary.[192]

With Sajjad as Chief Justice of the Supreme Court, the government of the Pakistan People's Party removed the Chief Justices of the High Courts to strengthen its hold on the judicial system of the provinces. Chief Justices against the regime were removed or transferred to Federal Shariat Court (FSC), kind of a demotion. The Chief Justice of the Sindh High Court and Nasir Aslam Zahid accepted these transfers, while the Chief Justice of the Lahore High Court refused. Two Supreme Court judges were sent to take their places as Acting Chief Justices. One of them was Muhammad Ilyas of the FSC who was earlier denied as Chief Justice of the Lahore High Court by Nawaz and was sent back as Chief Justice Lahore High Court. The Peshawar High Court (PHC) was also headed by an acting Chief Justice. With only three acting Chief Justices in three High Courts, the government had full control of the judiciary, because acting Chief Justices could not give strong decisions against the regime.

Next were the political appointments in the High Courts. The Sindh High Court and Lahore High Court were full of recent political appointees, with 9 and 20 new appointments of judges, respectively. According to Hamid, only six High Court judges could hardly qualify as judges, and eight or nine could not appear in High Courts as advocates.[193] The Supreme Court had 7 ad hoc judges against 10

---

[190]*Sabir Shah v Federation of Pakistan* 1994 PLD 1994 SC 738.

[191]*Manzoor Ahmad Wattoo v Federation of Pakistan* PLD 1997 Lahore 38.

[192]Shah, *supra* note 49, 199.

[193]H Khan (1998), Government and Judiciary 1994 to 1997: the Crisis of State, *supra* note 111, 133, also published in seven instalments in daily The News, 2,3,4,11,13, and 15 March 1998, and *PLJ* (1998) Magazine Section 66.

permanent judges. The Acting Chief Justices were acting as Benazir Bhutto's stamps for those appointments.

How was Benazir Bhutto using the ad hoc judges? The first service by Sajjad was to adjourn the appeal in the *Pir Sabir Shah* case on the request of the Federal Government and without notice to the appellant. The majority decision was seven to five. Six ad hoc judges supported the Chief Justice, and the minority was constituted of five permanent judges. In November 1994, the Pakistan Bar Council condemned the appointments in the superior courts as not being based on merit. It also condemned the appointment of acting Chief Justices in the High Courts and the ad hoc judges of the Supreme Court. The Sindh High Court Bar Association and Karachi Bar Association went on strike; they were supported by the opposition but were attacked by the police.

The democratic government of Benazir Bhutto thus exercised its own 'constitutional powers', even though the Chief Justice was to be consulted on judicial appointments under Article 177(1), 193(1) and 203-C(4) of the Constitution and his opinion should be given due significance and weight. What if he was not consulted? Khosa went to the extent of saying that not consulting the Chief Justice was unconstitutional and to not fulfil this obligation was high treason. Under Article 47(1) the president can be impeached for this. But should the Supreme Court rewrite the constitution where there is a flagrant abuse of executive power? This is what it in fact did in the *Judges*' case.

4.4.2 *Judges' Case: Appointment of Judges Is not the Right of a Democratic Regime*[194]

In August 1994, 25 judges were appointed to the Lahore High Court in one sweep and again on 10 April 1995, notification of the appointment of nine judges came without any considerations of the recommendations of the Chief Justice of the Supreme Court.[195] The response to this was the *Judges*' case. Sajjad himself was involved in this despite his own political appointment, and called Supreme Court Justice Ajmal to help him.[196] The purpose was to correct the image of the judiciary. One of the major features of the judgment was to stop the appointment of ad hoc judges and acting judges against the permanent places of Supreme Court and High Courts, respectively; if it was to be done then it should be done permanently within 90 days. Permanent vacancies in the judiciary should be filled within 30 days, and

[194]Cases where judiciary talked about independence of judiciary, separation from the executive and then qualification for the appointment of judges are *Govt of Sindh v Sharif Faridi* PLD1994 SC 105, *Al-jehad Trust v Federation of Pakistan* PLD 1996 SC 324 & *Malik Asad Ali v Federation of Pakistan* PLD, 1998 SC 161.

[195]See for details Shah, *supra* note 50, 227.

[196]Mian, *supra* note 61, 176.

except for reasons to be recorded by the president, the senior most judges should be Chief. A Supreme Court judge should not be sent as acting Chief Justice to the High Courts. The Acting Chief Justices should not be considered as constitutional consultees. Consultation should be meaningful and purposive and consensus oriented, and the opinion of the Chief Justices in the consultation is binding on the executive except for strong recorded and justifiable reasons on behalf of the executive. The requirement of 10 years practice does not mean enrolment, but actual practice/experience. The appointment of Chief Justices of the High Courts to FSC should be with their consent.

Before moving ahead, it is better to outline a critique of the case. There were the judges' own interests at play, and there were constitutional and statutory interpretations made, which were beyond recognized principles. The invalidity of the appointment of judges on the advice of Acting Chief Justice was not extended to critiquing the appointments made during Zia's regime. In addition, one provision of the constitution was held to supersede another, which was unusual in the annals of constitutional law, and a provision of the constitution was held to be inoperative and ineffective.[197] In terms of personal dynamics, Supreme Court Chief Justice Sajjad was uncomfortable whenever the question of the senior most judge to be appointed as Chief Justice arose, as he had informed Benazir Bhutto that there were in fact three judges senior to him before his own appointment.[198] Justice Manzoor Hussain Sial told Ajmal not to insist on this point; otherwise Sajjad would compromise with the government. Furthermore, Supreme Court Chief Justice Sajjad wrote his judgment on the basis of Ajmal's judgment but deprived him of credit.[199]

The federal government did not want to proceed with the *Judges*' case. Sajjad faced pressure from government quarters to adjourn these cases *sine die* as requested by Benazir Bhutto on several occasions.[200] When he refused, 'deliberate revenge' was taken against the Supreme Court Chief Justice and he was reminded about the personal favours he received from Pakistan People's Party government.[201] On 19 March 1996, a day before a short order, Pakistan People's Party government confirmed ten additional judges to the Lahore High Court and seven additional judges to the Singh High Court. Benazir Bhutto ridiculed the judiciary publically in the press and parliament. Even while the *Judges'* case was under hearing, while addressing the District Bar Association of Jacobabad and Nasirabad on 4 April 1996, Benazir Bhutto claimed that she had the constitutional authority to appoint

[197]H Khan (1998), Government and Judiciary 1994 to 1997: the Crisis of State, *supra* note 111, 138, also published in seven instalments in daily The News, 2,3,4,11,13 March, and also in *PLJ* (1998) Magazine Section 66.

[198]Mian, *supra* note 61, 179.

[199]*Ibid* 189.

[200]It means Justice Sajjad Chief Justice SC was so easily approachable and did not live a secluded life as was the requirement of a powerful emerging power broker and player. See Shah, *supra* note 49, 240.

[201]See for detail Shah, *supra* note 49, 214.

Supreme Court Chief Justices and Chief Justices of High Courts. She went to the extent of stating that she could appoint any member of the said bar for those posts.[202]

Hamid Khan, on behalf of the Pakistan Bar Council, showed extreme disappointment that the judge's case order was not implemented. The Pakistan Bar Council also declared in its meeting that advice of the Prime Minister is necessary for the appointment of the judges in a parliamentary form of government. Chief Justice Sajjad did not appreciate this and refused Hamid Khan's help but accepted S.M. Zafar as *amicus curiae* in the case.

It was clear that the judiciary needed independence. Refusing a ride with the democratic government in structural tension within the state structure left only one option, that is, to strengthen the old juridico-bureaucratic structure. President Laghari, alongside his former colleagues from the 1968 Civil Services of Pakistan, was in the president house, and the independence of the judiciary was fought through the establishment. The point to remember here is that before, this judiciary always sided with the establishment, but as a junior partner. This time the judiciary sought the help of the establishment for its own independence. According to Benazir Bhutto, Sajjad was promised the Interim Prime Ministership by the President in this controversy.[203]

There were clear differences between the Prime Minister and the president.[204] Wahabul Khari, Advocate Supreme Court (ASC), filed a writ petition asking the president to appoint judges, as the advice of the Prime Minister was not required. On 21 September 1996, the president moved a reference, asking the Supreme Court "whether the advice of the Prime Minister under Article 48(1) of the constitution was mandatory for the appointments of the Chief Justices and justices of the superior courts".[205] Sajjad was of the opinion that the advice of the Prime Minister is not necessary for the appointment of the judges. But Supreme Court Justices Ajmal and Saeeduzzaman were of the opinion that the Prime Minister cannot be excluded in a parliamentary form of government and other judges were also of the same opinion, as was the Pakistan Bar Council (PBC).[206]

On 8 June 1996, a committee of Chief Justices in Murree decided that five judges from the Sindh High Court, three from Peshawar and nine from the Lahore High Court would be laid off.[207] In an order on three review petitions and reference no. 1/1996 of the government, the Chief Justice demanded the record of confirmation of those additional judges of the Lahore High Court and Sindh High Court,

---

[202]NH Shah Chief Justice SC (Ret as he then was in 1997), Judiciary in Pakistan: A Quest for Independence, in, C Baxter & CH Kennedy, *Pakistan: 1997* (Westview Press, Boulder, Colorado, 1998) 76.

[203]Bhutto, *supra* note 29, 421.

[204]Reasons usually given are the interference of Benazir Bhutto's husband Zardari in the affairs of the country and the death of her brother, Murtaza Bhutto.

[205]President's Reference No. 2 of 1996.

[206]Mian, *supra* note 61, 209.

[207]Shah, *supra* note 49, 273.

who were confirmed one day before the short order. The Prime Minister appealed the judgment of the *Judges*' case but had to withdraw when Chief Justice Sajjad insisted upon staying on the bench for the appeal. Benazir subsequently, partially, implemented the judgment. Permanent Chief Justices were provided to the High Courts within 30 days, ad hoc Supreme Court judges were relieved, and some High Court judges who were not appointed on merit were laid off.

4.4.3 Dissolution of Assembly at the Altar of Independence of Judiciary

Sajjad, according to his own account, had no motive in the *Judges*' case except the rule of law,[208] but the result was the dissolution of Benazir Bhutto's assembly (1993–1996). On 26 September 1996, Laghari dismissed Benazir Bhutto's government, using Article 58(2)(b) of the constitution, under the charges of corruption, inability to maintain law and order, accusing the presidency and the state agencies in the murder of her brother, deliberate delay in the implementation of the judges' judgment, humiliating the judiciary, violation of fundamental rights and nepotism. Benazir Bhutto and the speaker of the national assembly, Yousaf Raza Gilani, challenged the dissolution. As opposed to a full bench, the offended Chief Justice formed a seven-judge bench and with a majority of six to one upheld the order of the President.[209]

Since four democratic governments had now been dissolved due to the 8th Amendment,[210] it was under challenge in some petitions. The offending Chief Justice decided to hear these cases before the case of dissolution of assembly in the Benazir Bhutto case. The Supreme Court, after due consideration, upheld the validity of the 8th Amendment.[211]

The bar also resisted the appointment of judges by the executive as it reduced the judicial organ of the state to merely a department of the government.[212] The judgment in the *Judges*' case was welcomed as it restored the confidence of the

[208] Shah, *supra* note 49, 268.

[209] *Benazir Bhutto v Farooq Ahamd Laghari* PLJ 1998 SC 27.

[210] Article 58 (2) (b) of the 1973 Constitution of Pakistan through which the President can dissolve the legislative assembly.

[211] *Mahmood Khan Achakzai v Federation of Pakistan* PLD 1997 SC 426.

[212] H Khan (1996), Mr. Justice Manzoor Husain Sial—an epitome of a judge, *supra* note 111, 73, see also H Khan, "Opening of Judicial Year 1996–9, Lahore High Court" address as Vice Chairman Pakistan Bar Council, in, *supra* note 111, 84; In this address, Hamid Khan informed about the dangers of misuse of this power.

public in the judiciary, and hence, its impact was healthy. Still, the story was not over, as it was noted by Hamid Khan that judicial consultees could not be trusted as they had a history of giving favours to their relatives and colleagues.[213]

4.4.4 'State Capture': Disenchantment with the Washington Consensus and Subalterns

Benazir Bhutto observed the 'state capture' by juridico-bureaucratic structure. At the same time, the metropolitan bourgeoisie observed the 'state capture' by the local elite (reigning class) in developing countries, including Pakistan and raised the issue of 'corruption' in developing countries. From this point onwards, 'civil society' with its 'liberal project' came as a watchdog on the corrupt political elite. Crumbs for subalterns (through basic needs development projects) were also not reaching the desired layers to pacify them, resulting in disenchantment with market economy.

In these circumstances, critique of the 'liberal project' (NGOs-non-governmental organization) had twofolds. On the one hand, it wanted to cut the excesses of the Structural Adjustment Program, particularly its *ad hocism*. It attacked the International Monetary Fund and World Bank's Structural Adjustment Programs as neo-liberalism, a "naïve nineteenth century (European liberalism)" and gave a call for pro-poor initiatives.[214] Later, when these policies were implemented, this project pointed out how this human development is not part of economic development. That is why what is given through social action program is sucked back through indirect taxes under structural adjustment. How did the cuts on health and education expenditures affect people? Structural Adjustment Programs is anti-people and anti-state in one breath.[215] On the other hand, it wanted social development through NGOs as political elite was corrupt.

Benazir Bhutto's Social Action Plan (from 1993 to 1996) had been criticized for *ad hocism*, the community's ability to handle projects, and the inability of the federal and provincial governments to fund the recurring costs of development projects.[216] When the case for the dissolution of Benazir Bhutto's government came before the Lahore High Court, the justices found that the *People's Works Program* violated Article 97. Rs. 8 billion was allocated for it without legislative backing,

[213]H Khan (1996), Mr. Justice Manzoor Husain Sial- an epitome of a judge, *supra* note 111. This was an address of Hamid Khan as a Vice Chairman, Pakistan Bar Council in the reference on the retirement of Mr. Justice Manzoor Husain Sial, 24 March 1996.

[214]A Zaman, Eradicating Poverty in South Asia by the Year 2002: Issues in a New International Dialogue with Donors, Working paper series# 14, Islamabad (1993) 4.

[215]J Bennett, Structural Adjustment and Social Development: A Agenda for the Poor, Research Report Series# 17, Islamabad (1998) 6, 8.

[216]M Mahmood, A Model for Social Development Based on the Community, Policy Paper Series#20, Islamabad (1993) 2, 5.

meaning that the 'liberal' project and the judiciary alike were critical of the political elite. So in the years to come, the discourse of the centrality of courts, legalism and hopes placed on civil society, in both liberal and quasi-liberal projects, allowed for joining hands with metropolitan bourgeoisie.

4.5 Nawaz Sharif's Second Term (1997–1999)

4.5.1 Independence of the Judiciary to Judicial Activism: Confronting Democracy 'Actively'

In the light of the rising worries of state capture by IFIs, President Laghari and his appointed caretaker Prime Minister, Meraj Khalid, raised the slogan of accountability before the 1997 elections. Benazir Bhutto's democratically elected government faced allegations of corruption by her own party nominated president Laghari, and ex-speaker of the National Assembly.[217] This resulted in a new emphasis on accountability.[218] It is to be remembered here that the famous philanthropist of Pakistan, Edhi, told the caretaker Prime Minister that the accountability process is a waste of time. He urged the Prime Minister to focus on the socioeconomic development of the country.[219]

But the decision to focus on corruption came due to pressure from outside. Transparency International once again ranked Pakistan second in 1997 for corruption.[220] On 22 October, at the end of his 5-day visit, World Bank president James D. Wolfensohn addressed a news conference along with Finance Minister Sartaj Aziz. He asked the Government of Pakistan-GOP to control corruption, and offered help to reform the judicial system. He blamed the weak judicial system for being unable to check corruption.[221] It is not surprising that the same year, Transparency International declared Pakistan the second most corrupt country in the world; the caretaker Prime Minister admitted his failure in proving corruption.[222]

The Election Commission asked the legislatures to submit their asset statements.[223] A list of loan defaulters was published to stop some legislators from participating in elections. The State Bank of Pakistan gave this list to the Election Commission, which made it public. Where jurists were giving legal constitutional recipes for control of corruption like strict observation of Article 62 of the

[217]According to Miraj Khalid, ex-speaker of the assembly, all members of the government are corrupt except for President Laghari. *The Daily Khubrain* (6 March 1996).

[218]Statement of Wasim Sajjad, Chairman Senate. *The Nation* (12 March 1996).

[219]*Dawn* (27 November 1996).

[220]*The Muslim* (3 July 1997) 8.

[221]*The Muslim* (23 October 1997) 1.

[222]*The News* (24 December 1996).

[223]*Dawn* (1 July 1996).

constitution, there were also voices of not using judicial forums as laundries for washing dirty personal and political linen especially where the political sovereign (voter) has given its verdict.[224] The point I want to make here is that the focus of this anti-corruption campaign was politicians. When Nawaz targeted the bureaucracy, the judiciary quickly reacted to stop it.

4.5.2 Old Juridico-Bureaucratic Structure Reacting to Democracy

In the 1997 election, Nawaz Sharifwon was with a two-third majority. His first act was to get rid of the notorious 8th Amendment without any discussion in the assembly.[225] It is interesting that just a few months ago, the judiciary had declared this amendment valid. Similarly, political defection (or horse trading) was a serious problem in assemblies and Nawaz, through the Fourteenth Amendment, prohibited this practice on 3 July 1997. This decision was again made without discussion in the assembly.[226] Now, Nawaz Sharif was safe 'constitutionally' and 'politically', but this was not enough protection.

Soon, Nawaz Sharif was involved in a controversy with the judiciary on the issue of interfering with the bureaucracy. He was questioned for openly handcuffing officers of the Water and Sanitation Agency in Faisalabad, who were later released by the courts, as no charges were registered against them; for establishing separate courts for combating terrorism; and on the issue of the appointment of judges. Nawaz Sharif used an accountability campaign against the bureaucracy and military in an effort to strengthen himself. However, this campaign did not work.

The case of *Usman Farooqi,* a steel mill chairman prosecuted for the importation of pig iron, was of political importance due to Zardari's involvement being husband of Benazir Bhutto. Justice Amanullah, appointed to the Singh High Court by Benazir Bhutto, granted him bail.[227] The Capital Development Authority chairman, Shafi Sehwani, was also granted interim bail.[228] The Prime Minister pleaded for no bail in corruption cases.[229] The sacking of Naval Chief Mansur-ul-Haq (taken up in the *Mansur-ul-Haq* case) under allegations of irregularities and wrongdoings in the Agosta 90-B deal was another important case, a rare happening in the country's history.[230] The Navy denied the charges and declared that French submarines were

---

[224]Justice ASK Khosa, Cleaning the Fountainhead: A Constitutional recipe for elimination of corruption *PLJ* (1996) Journal Section 126, 142.

[225]*Act 1 of 1997* PLD 1997 Central Statutes 323.

[226]*Act XXIV of 1997* PLD Central Statutes 324.

[227]*Dawn* (6 March 1997).

[228]*The Frontier Post* (25 March 1997).

[229]*Dawn* (4 March 1997).

[230]*The Nation* (25 April 1997).

selected on merit.[231] Air Chief Marshal Khattak had to refuse kickbacks in a $2.66 billion Mirage deal to quell rumours.[232] After this, Chief of Army Staff Jehangir Karamat ordered a stop to the media trial of army officials.[233]

This was the environment in which Nawaz presented the *Ehtesab Bill* (which made measures to restore accountability) in the assembly. The government supported the amendments that any person arrested on charges of corruption would not be granted bails for 2 years.[234] The opposition protested, but the National Assembly passed the amended bill.[235] The opposition considered this bill "overwhelmingly discriminatory, arbitrary, and selective",[236] and 'blind legislation'.[237] The Human Rights committee of the Pakistan Bar Council, headed by Chairman Rana Ijaz Ahmad Khan, rejected the *Ehtesab Act*, 1997 and requested the president to hold a referendum on it. The initiator of accountability in Pakistan, Meraj Khalid (the ex-caretaker Prime Minister) declared that accountability was futile, as the rulers had not risen above political considerations.[238] President Laghari urged Nawaz Sharif to review the *Ehtesab Act* and the Prime Minister assured the president that he would modify the Act in view of public criticism about some of its controversial clauses.[239]

A full bench, headed by Chief Justice of the Lahore High Court Sheikh Riaz Ahmad, heard the case against the *Ehtesab Act*, 1997. The Lahore High Court dismissed the petition on the ground that article 248(2) of the constitution exempted the president and the governors to be held under criminal litigation while in office.[240] The validity of Ehtesab Ordinance was upheld on 17 Feb 1997.[241] Meanwhile, Prime Minister Nawaz Sharif publicly arrested and handcuffed three officials of the Faisalabad Development Authority.[242] The government issued a list of 554 corrupt officials that had been compiled by the Prime Minister secretariat.[243] Seven grade 22 officers were among the 87 were suspended.[244] The judiciary

[231]*The News* (24 April 1997) 8.

[232]*The News* (9 April 1997).

[233]*The Daily Khubrain* (27 April 1997).

[234]*The Muslim* (3 April 1997) 5.

[235]*The News* (30 May 1997) 1.

[236]I Alam, *The News* 4/6/97 6.

[237]R Rabbani, Pakistan People's Party senator, leader of opposition in the Senate, *The Frontier Post* (4 June 1997) 4.

[238]*Dawn* (9 June 1997).

[239]*The Nation* (19 September 1997) 1.

[240]*The Nation* (3 December 1996).

[241]*Dawn* (18 February 1997).

[242]*The News* (11 March 1997).

[243]*The News (6* April 1997).

[244]*The News* (10 April 1997).

launched a campaign against the arrests of these bureaucrats. The arrests themselves were considered political victimization, the judiciary argued that the arrested bureaucrats were either close to the opposition, Pakistan People's Party, or were not obeying the political orders of Nawaz Sharif.[245]

4.5.3 Resisting a Parallel Judicial System of Special Anti-Terrorist Courts

The fervour for an independent judiciary was so high that newspapers published that the judiciary was the 'Courthouse of the Government', and it was needless to burden it with a prefix of independent.[246] I have already discussed that the second front of the struggle against the judiciary was the establishment of new anti-terrorist courts.[247] On 13 August 1997, *the Anti-Terrorism Bill* was passed. Writ petitions were filed in the High Courts against this law, and when such an appeal was dismissed it came to the Supreme Court for leave to appeal. Notices were issued to the Attorney General. Nawaz's position was that the law was necessary, giving examples of such existing laws in England meant to deal with the Irish Republican Army terrorism issue, and pointed to the Terrorist and Disruptive Activities Act in Indian Kashmir. Supreme Court Chief Justice Sajjad could not decide on the issue as he went on a direct strike with the Prime Minister. Later, the court in the *Mehram Ali* case by Chief Justice Ajmal Mian decided the issue.[248]

The judiciary attempted to stop the parallel judicial system again when Nawaz called the military to assist the civil power against unrest in Sindh. On 20 October 1998, the federal government promulgated an ordinance titled the Pakistan Armed Forces (Acting in Aid of Civil Power) Ordinance 1998. Under this, military courts that did not grant bails were set up in Sindh for speedy trials. The Supreme Court declared the military courts unconstitutional in an appeal on 17 February 1999. The Supreme Court declared that the cases be heard by special courts (which had already been tuned to the existing judicial system) and guidelines were laid down for the trial of the cases. Later, in 1998, the Courts/Tribunals run by the executive without the control of the High Courts were found under Article 203 to be in violation of the requirements of the constitution.[249]

---

[245]*The Frontier Post* (15 April 1997).

[246]GH Abbasi Advocate, Independence of Judiciary *PLD* (1998) Journal Section 88, 89.

[247]Hamid Khan's reason was that Nawaz Sharif just wanted to accommodate Pakistan Muslim League-N's members as special judges, see H Khan *supra* note 197, 138.

[248]Reference: *Mehram Ali case,* Mehram Ali v Federation of Pakistan PLD 1998 SC 1445; The SC found several provisions of the Act unconstitutional and violations of fundamental rights. The SC was given (actually acquired) the right to appeal under this Act in this judgment and made possible its shape within the already existing judicial system. In a way, it did not let the parallel judicial system to exist.

[249]Mehram Ali v Federation of Pakistan PLD 1998 SC 1445, see also 1998 SCMR 1156.

4.5.4 Tools Beyond Judicial Means: From Suo Moto to Social Investigation and the Organ for 'National Integration'

The growth of judicial power was apparent beyond its opposition to parallel courts. The Judiciary began taking *suo moto*[250] notices on the killings of people in Karachi on the premise that the federal, as well as provincial governments, had failed to control the situation.[251] Chief Justice Sajjad took similar stepson the issue of religious sectarian killing in Lahore, in a hearing in his chamber on 1 July 1997. He even summoned leaders of both sects to the hearing as well as their organizations, namely Sipah-e-Sahaba (a Sunni sect organization) and Sipah-e-Muhammad (a Shia sect organization). Apart from the judiciary's own 'tacit active approval' of sectarian violence, prosecution and intimidation of minority sects,[252] it also failed to understand the reasons for the emergence of socio-religious movements and sectarianism.[253]

4.5.5 Appointment of Judges: The Judiciary's Exclusive Right

Chief Justice Sajjad recommended five judges for appointment in the Supreme Court. Under the judgment in the *Judges*' case, the Prime Minister was to accept this recommendation or give reasons for not accepting in writing. One of the judges in the list had decided a few cases against the Prime Minister's Ittefaq Group of Industries while he was in opposition. Another judge had been a Federal Secretary

---

[250]Latin phrase meaning 'on its own motion'. Legal actions taken by the judiciary against any unjust and wrong doing in the state and the society.

[251]Shah, *supra* note 49, 380.

[252]According to Tayyab Mahmud, the sectarian violence, prosecution and intimidation of minority sects are increasing with the tacit active approval of public authorities including judiciary as they are validated by superior judiciary. He relied on *Dard and others v Pakistan*, Criminal Appeal 149/89. The pronouncement of the SC in the *Dard Case* 3 July 1993 was disturbing for it upheld Ordinance XX of 1984 prohibiting Ahmadis to publically practice and declared it as crime, see T Mahmud, Protecting Religious Minorities: The Courts' Abdication, Kennedy, *supra* note 45, 83; See also O Siddique & Z Hayat, Unholy Laws & Holy Speech: Blasphemy Laws in Pakistan - Controversial Origins, Design Defects and Free Speech Implications 17 *Minn. J International L* (2008) 303.

[253]For Robert Nicholas (1998), the socio-religious movements were the result of socially disrupted wars and wide open trade which Pakistani state interrupted in the mid-1990s. He called it the "the micro-politics of protests" on the basis of Migdal's state-in-society outline, see R Nicholas, *Challenging the State: 1990s Religious Movement in the Northwest Frontier Province*, Baxter, *supra* note 202, 1, 25; See also M Ahmad, Revivalism, Islamization, Sectarianism and Violence in Pakistan, Baxter, *supra* note 202.

within Benazir Bhutto's government. Instead of approving the appointments, the Prime Minister issued a notification to reduce the number of judges in the Supreme Court from 17 to 12, as it was in 1986. Supreme Court Chief Justice Sajjad told the president that the strength of the Supreme Court could only be reduced if its jurisdiction is reduced.[254] The workload of the High Courts had increased many folds due to new laws such as the *Ehtesab Act*, *Drugs Act*, and the *Control of Narcotics Substances Act*. Furthermore, the judiciary was not letting any cases under the purview of these laws go through other judicial channels. The Chief Justice suspended the notification and the Prime Minister had to follow suit. The validity of this order, dated 21 August 1997, was challenged in the court but withdrawn by the government on 16 September 1997.

Yet, the Supreme Court Chief Justice himself did not follow the *Judges'* case ruling. He did not appoint the senior most judges from the Sindh High Court, Lahore High Court and Peshawar High Court, and vacancies were not filled within 30 days, but according to the schedule of the Chief Justice. Now, only two parties were left in the appointment of judges, that is, the bench and the bar, which was led by Hamid Khan. After the *Judges*' case, the elected government was reduced to rubber-stamping the recommendations of the Supreme Court Chief Justice. Since the judges were picked from the bar or the lower judiciary, this created a tension between the bench and the bar. Chief Justice Sajjad was appointing only service judges, whereas Hamid Khan was demanding that lawyers be appointed as judges.[255] Nawaz Sharif wanted the right to appoint judges back. We have already discussed that the judiciary was resentful of any parallel judicial systems such as the anti-terrorist courts and special speedy trial courts. Below is the climax of this controversy.

4.5.6 Challenging the Supremacy of the Legislature

Under the leadership of Supreme Court Chief Justice Sajjad, the judiciary seemed determined to play an important role as, he noted, "Pakistan was passing through a very critical stage"[256] and therefore it was necessary to find the legislature as not legislating.[257] Speeches made by the Prime Minister and Chief Justice at the South Asian Association for Regional Cooperation in Law (SAARCLAW) conference in Karachi from 3 to 5 October 1997 were clearly indicative of this struggle for supremacy between the judiciary and the legislature.

---

[254]Shah, *supra* note 49, 395.

[255]H Khan (1998), Government and Judiciary 1994 to 1997: The Crisis of State, *supra* note 111, 143.

[256]Shah, *supra* note 49, 401.

[257]The legislature had not legislated and had issued 200 ordinances and imposed taxes of the amount of Rs 2 billion without the approval of the parliament, see Shah, *supra* note 49 260.

A three-member bench headed by Chief Justice Sajjad suspended the operation of the Fourteenth Amendment against political defection.[258] The Prime Minister called it 'illegal' and 'unconstitutional' and a violation of the supremacy of the parliament. Based on these speeches, contempt of court proceedings was initiated by the court against the Prime Minister. The Prime Minister appeared twice before a bench of five judges headed by Chief Justice Sajjad, but Sajjad did not drop the contempt proceedings. To counter this, the Parliament passed a Contempt of Court Bill (an amendment) wherein contempt could be appealed before another bench of the remaining Supreme Court judges, and the execution of the punishment could not happen for a 30-day period pending the appeal. President Laghari did not sign this bill as Chief Justice Sajjad restrained him to do so as the President asked the court whether he should sign it or not, though this was not required!

The Supreme Court, led by Chief Justice Sajjad, then took up the Inter-Services Intelligence (ISI) case for hearing. The ISI was alleged to have spent money to bring Prime Minister Nawaz Sharif to government in the 1990s. This was a clear indication of the intent to disqualify the Prime Minister, but also the beginning of a fight within the judiciary that had not yet learned how to work consistently. A two-judge bench of the Supreme Court in Quetta entertained a petition against the appointment of the Chief Justice. The bench referred this case to the Chief Justice to form a large bench. On 27 November, a five-member bench of the Supreme Court, headed by the Chief Justice himself, suspended the order of the Quetta bench by 4–1. Members of parliament heckled the Chief Justice in the courtroom. This was a day before the commencement of contempt proceedings against the Prime Minister.

A bench headed by the Chief Justice began hearing the contempt case on 28 November 1997. In order to prevent this hearing, members of the ruling party, ministers, parliamentarians and members of provincial assemblies stormed the Supreme Court building. The Chief Justice wrote a letter to the president requesting the army to protect him, also requesting that references against the Supreme Court justices of the Quetta and Peshawar registries be sent to the Supreme Judicial Council. The next day, two separate cause lists were circulated for 1 December, one by Supreme Court Chief Justice Sajjad of five judges and the second by a Chief Justice Saeeduzzaman Siddiqui of 10 judges. Each Chief Justice annulled the administrative orders of the other.

A group of retired judges was also active, led by Ret. Supreme Court Chief Justice Nasim Hasan, who restored Nawaz's government in 1993. They viewed the judicial activism of Supreme Chief Justice Sajjad as extending from fundamental rights violation to entering the domain of politics. Hasan warned the courts that they had curtailed executive powers but that Nawaz was elected with powerful support and that he may put his weight behind the appointment of judges.[259] He argued that this could result in bizarre consequences and the scope of the judiciary should be

[258]Nawaz Sharif stopped floor crossing through this amendment. *Constitution (Fourteenth Amendment) Act*, 1997, Act XXIV of 1997, PLD Central Statutes 324.

[259]Baxter, *supra* note 202, 73.

confined to wrongs done to the citizens.[260] Supreme Court Justice Rafiq Tarar[261] was involved as well, calling Supreme Court Chief Justice Sajjad a 'judicial terrorist', and influenced a number of judges against Justice Sajjad.[262] He was rewarded with the Presidency of Pakistan for his role.

The climax of this crisis of state came when Jehangir Karamat, Chief of Army Staff, called a conference of Corps Commanders, as the President and Prime Minister requested him to act as an arbitrator. General Musharraf (as he then was) insisted that the elected government should stay in power. The Corps commanders decided to send a message to Sajjad 'to behave himself'.[263] President Laghari resigned and on 23 December 1997, a 10-member bench announced the appointment of Supreme Court Chief Justice Sajjad as void, as his appointment violated the principle of seniority. Hamid Khan opined that both the judges and the legislators were wrong. This was a drama with no hero.[264] This may be true, but what the analysis in this book is trying to show is a linear rise of the judiciary since 1990. The judiciary did not become weak after the removal of Supreme Court Chief Justice Sajjad, and, relatedly, the supremacy of the legislature was not established. Below is the explanation for this.

4.5.7 1998: *Supremacy of the Parliament?*

Nawaz got rid of Article 58(2)(b) of the constitution through the 13th Amendment. Now, the president could not dissolve the elected assembly and Nawaz called it this amendment as the supremacy of the parliament.[265] Was this true on the face of a strong judiciary? Before 1990, the dominant view was that the judiciary could not legislate or question the wisdom of the legislature,[266] though in reality the legislature also could not amend the constitution under Article 70 by adopting procedure laid down in Articles 238 and 239, that is, the law should not be inconsistent with fundamental rights, or be repugnant to the injunctions of Islam. The doctrine of basic structure denied the right of the people to amend the constitution through their

---

[260]NH Shah Chief Justice SC (Ret as he then was), *Memoirs and Reflections* (Alhamra Printing, Islamabad, 2002) 128.

[261]His famous decision was when he held that PCO did not impinge upon or undermine functions and powers of judiciary, see *Tajamal Hussain Malik v Federal Govt of Pak* PLD 1981 Lahore 462. As the Chief Justice of Lahore High Court, he led a full bench upholding the dissolution of the Benazir Bhutto government in 1990, see *Khawaja Tariq Rahim case.*

[262]See for detail H Khan (1997), Fruits of Judicial politics: Mr Justice (R) Muhammad Rafiq Tarar, *supra* note 111, 127. It also appeared in daily *The News*, 21 December 1997.

[263]P Musharraf (2006), *In the Line of Fire: A Memoir* (Free Press, New York, 2006) 83.

[264]H Khan (1998), Government and Judiciary 1994 to 1997: the Crisis of State, *supra* note 111, 151.

[265]Huntingdon, Preface, Baxter, *supra* note 202 vii.

[266]*The State v Zia-ur-Rehman* PLD 1973 SC 49, 70. Where it was held that court is not above the constitution nor it can strike down any provisions of the constitution.

elected parliament.[267] The slogan to defend the parliament came up in the Nawaz and Sajjad controversy. Some members of the Pakistan Muslim League (PML) thought that parliament was not protected enough against other organs of the state in the constitutional set-up.[268] Addressing the South Asian Association for Regional Cooperation in Law (SAARCLAW) Conference, Prime Minister Nawaz stated that the "the line of demarcation between interpretation and transformation should not be overlooked" by the judiciary when interpreting the constitution.[269] The argument against this was that the magnitude of damage to the judiciary was greater at the hand of politicians than at the hand of military dictators,[270] and hence, the judiciary was to keep a tight reign over the executive and should not give any leniency or indulge to its functionaries.[271] The powers of the judiciary were not supra-legislative powers, but were corrective in nature.[272]

The judiciary under Sajjad exhibited features of state institutions like the military in Pakistan, such as little accountability, strong ambitions, no internal democracy and an elite class orientation. But why was it superior to the other institutions? The impression that "the judges generally led secluded lives"[273] was no longer valid. Supreme Court Chief Justice Sajjad met with Prime Ministers Benazir Bhutto and later Nawaz Sharif, as well as president and Chief Of Army Staff General Jehangir Karamat several times.[274] These meetings were about future legislation.[275]

This was not driven, and it must be stated, by Sajjad's personal ambitions, but by the power that the judiciary had acquired during the era of the globalization period, when the state was going through a transitionary phase. The judiciary became strong enough to challenge the private interests of the military.[276] The judiciary had

---

[267]SKA Khursheed, Whether Parliament is Supreme? *PLJ* (1998) Magazine Section 45, 47; But the writer at the same time stressed his dissatisfaction with the legislature and not the judiciary. Even for delays in the courts, according to the writer, the legislature was responsible as it did not amend the procedural laws, see also SMKA Khursheed, Existing Laws Requiring Amendments *PLD* (1993) Journal 69.

[268]Shah, *supra* note 49, 496.

[269]As cited by Shah, *supra* note 49, 742, Appendix 8.19.

[270]A Chaudhry, Role of the Bar in Administration of Justice *PLJ* (1998) Magazine Section 187, 189; The writer was a member of the Punjab Bar Council at that time.

[271]Justice (Ret) KMA Samdani, Rule of Law *PLD* (1999) Journal 91, 92.

[272]MA Mirza JSC, Judicial System of Pakistan *PLD* (1998) Journal 125, 135.

[273]H Khan (1997), Judicial appointments in the perspective of Independence of Judiciary, *supra* note 111, 112. A paper read at the 6th SAARC LAW Conference at Karachi, 3–5 October 1997; also published in *PLJ* (1997) Magazine Section 177.

[274]Shah, *supra* note 49, 335, 428.

[275]Mian, supra note 61, 218, 273.

[276]An example is the *Wahab-ul-Khairi*case. In a PIL case, he challenged the private interests of the military. The petition was dismissed on technical grounds [Re: Supreme Court of Pakistan case No. CP 1593/98]. Without checking the title of the land 33866 acres of land owned were allotted to Brig (rtd) Muhammad Bashir in 1993. A landless peasant brought a case against in Lahore High Court and the court gave a decision in favour of Karim in spite of the fact that the district govt favoured Brig Bashir. In appeal, the SC upheld the ownership of Karim on land in 2003 and

moved from a position of non-interference in election matters, to monitoring the elections, to checking the educational degrees of the members of the assembly.[277] Before 1994, the Supreme Court had a very consistent view, not to engage in election matters, as there was a special mechanism for this in the constitution as established in the *Javed Hashmi* case in 1989.[278] However, the Supreme Court in the *Mustafa Jatoi* case reversed this view in 1994.[279] Similarly, in the *Muhammad Muqeem* case,[280] the Supreme Court decided to disqualify a loan defaulter from a political post to eradicate corruption from the political culture. The dissenting judge was of the opinion that the loan should be recovered through banking procedures for it had nothing to do with elections.

Around that period a known jurist, Syed Muhammad Kalim Ahmad Khurshid, responded to the judgment in the *Abdul Rahim* case. In that judgment, the court explicitly declared that courts in Pakistan undisputedly have the powers to strike down law. It is also clearly stated that rigorously prescribed parliamentary sovereignty has a very limited scope. Rather, in Pakistan, the constitution is supreme and it is judiciary that is supreme in Pakistan as opposed to Parliament.[281] According to Kalim, the understanding of the judiciary so far had been that the provisions of the Constitution could not be struck down. He gave the examples of the *Zia-ur-Rehman* case,[282] *Fauji Foundation* case,[283] *United Sugar Mills* case[284] and finally *Mehr*

(Footnote 276 continued)

quoted from John Steinbeck's *The Grapes of Wrath* and cautioned against accumulation of property in few hands [Civil Appeal No. 30 of 1999, dated 24 September 2003]. Detail given by Ayesha Siddiqa, see Siddiqa, *supra* note 20, 204, 118, 159.

[277]Later in cases by Chief Justice SC Iftikhar in 2008.

[278]*Election Commission of Pakistan through its Secretary v Javed Hashmi and others* PLD 1989 SC 396.

[279]*Ghulam Mustafa Jatoi v Additional District and Session Judge/Returning Officer, NA 158 and others* 1994 SCMR 1299. Ghulam Mustafa Jatoi (former caretaker minister) and Asif Zardari (husband of Benazir Bhutto and later president of Pakistan) were contesting elections. Jatoi was disqualified without notice being a defaulter in the list of Banking Council of Pakistan. SHC upheld the order in the light of Javed Hashmi case. But SC headed by Nasim Chief Justice SC reversed the order and let Jatoi contest the elections.

[280]*Muhammad Muqeem Khoso v President of Pakistan* PLD 1994 SC 412; A member of the National Assembly and a defaulter of ADBP loan was disqualified for 7 years by the election commission on a reference sent by the president. He went in appeal and SC upheld the order with a majority of 2 to 1 under PPO 17 of 1977.

[281]*Abdul Rahim and 2 others v Mesrrs UBL Pakistan* PLD 1997 Karachi 62, 86.

[282]PLD 1973 SC 49 ("it is not the function of the judiciary to legislate or to question the wisdom of the Legislature in making the particular laws").

[283]Fauji Foundation and another v Shamim-ur-Rehman PLD 1983 SC 457 [judiciary should not strike down a legislation on the ground of mala fide. This may lead to a conflict between judicial power and political power.

[284]Federation of Pakistan v United Sugar Mills Ltd Karachi PLD 1977 SC 397; Fourth Amendment by Bhutto reducing judicial powers of HCs, SC made it clear that laws should be interpreted in such a manner that it should be saved and not destroyed.

Zulfiqar Ali Babu case.[285] The doctrine of basic structure, for Kalim, denies the right to the sovereign people. It stopped their elected representatives from implementing policies demanded by them. Furthermore, if there are no limits on the parliament, the court should not invent them. The parliament is the guardian of the rights and liberties of the people. He went to the extent to say that "Any threat to the Parliament to refrain from Legislation may fall within the ambit of Article 6 of the Constitution of Islamic Republic of Pakistan, 1973", which is treason. Ajmal Mian's position refused to dilate upon the sensitive political question using the tradition of judicial restraint. It was his belief that a judge should speak through his judgments.[286] This retreat of the judiciary after Sajjad was temporary. Ajmal gave a clear message that the right of courts to interpret a provision of the statute is a 'very potent legal weapon', as he used it in *Judges*' case as well as in *Shahid Nabi* case.[287] Added to this were rise of PIL in the mid-1990s and above all the new role of the judiciary in 'Good Governance' began at the end of the decade. To complete the analysis, it is necessary to understand the nature of PIL at that time.

4.6 The Mid-1990s: Crucial Years for Public Interest Litigation

Rights can be Suspended, not Courts: This period was marked with judicial activism and respect earned through PIL, enhanced by the attacks from the legislature. Individual rights could be suspended but not the courts, according to *Farooq Ahmed Laghari v Federation of Pakistan*. While deciding this case, the courts articulated their own domain, accepted the suspension of fundamental rights to deal with emergency, but denied the second proclamation to stop the courts. Furthermore, it stated that the judiciary itself was not accountable and "no writ can be issued by a High Court of the Supreme Court against itself or against each other or its judges" when exercising their constitutional jurisdiction.[288] In another very important case, the court strongly defended its right to PIL in 1996.[289] The court did not allow any legislation to take away its jurisdiction.

Limits to Public Interest Litigation and Political Questions: At the same time, the limits of PIL as an alternative stream of justice were becoming evident, including its use as a political tool. Khosa pointed out that judges should not try to

[285]Mehr Zulfiqar Ali Babu v Govt of Punjab PLD 1977 SC 11 [as per Ajmal Mian and Saiduzzaman JJ, court is not at liberty to inquire into the mala fide on the part of the legislature].

[286]Addressing to the annual dinner of Sindh High Court Bar Association Karachi *PLD* (1998) Journal Section 123.

[287]*Ibid*; see Nabi Malik v Chief Election Commissioner PLD 1997 SC 32.

[288]Mian, *supra* note 61, 108.

[289]*Shahida Zahir Abbasi v President of Pakistan*, PLD 1996 SC 632. The court defended its jurisdiction to hear the appeal against its decision of Field General Court Martial of the accused of a military coup.

be wiser than the law while trying to do justice, and that judgments should not be used to restrict the rights of others.[290] PIL was also criticized as a key reason behind the backlog of cases. Courts refused PIL cases that were considered frivolous and not genuine PIL cases, declaring them a 'packing of the courts'.[291] In some cases, the courts did not trust bona fide petitioners and the courts checked the misuse of PIL for personal benefit.[292] M.D. Tahir filed many cases and was unmindful of criticism of frivolous action.[293] At the same time, genuine cases of PIL were refused, like the case of Zainab Noor and the lawyers against VIP culture (an unnecessary given protocol to important persons).[294]

Menski ultimately found there was a decline of PIL in Pakistan because of 'distractions of the big politics'.[295] *Al-Jehad Trust v Federation of Pakistan* was a case he cites as, like in India, PIL was used in struggles over the division of power between the judiciary and the executive. In other cases, the judiciary sought to fill in gaps in legislation that were inconveniencing citizens.[296] Another objection was the misuse of PIL by middle-class entrepreneurs for their personal gains.[297] Menski proposed a balance between public interest activism and private interest.[298] In his view, the judiciary could play a role in monitoring standards.[299] Yet, Menski argued there was a false dichotomy between 'normal' litigation and PIL.[300] Supreme Court Chief Justice Ajmal found that because of PIL, public utility services did improve to

[290] *Yusuf Haji Ismail v. Husain Mumtaz* PLD 1989 Karachi 299.

[291] Comments of Ahmad Saeed Awan J in *Tariq Saeed v Director, Anti-Corruption Establishment* MLD 1864. The point to remember here is that Ahmad Saeed Awan J was one of those political appointees by Benazir Bhutto who were removed by CJ Sajjad. It should be considered that the period showed the height of use and abuse of judicial activism.

[292] *Hamid Majid v Discipline Committee* 1991 SCMR 2317 & *Farrough Ahmed Siddiqui v Province of Sindh* PLD 1996 Karachi 267.

[293] Human Rights Commission of Pakistan- HRCP (1997) 71.

[294] Human Rights Commission of Pakistan -HRCP 1998 Report.

[295] W Menski (1997), Public Interest Litigation: A strategy for the future. The Fourth Cornelius Memorial Lecture, *supra* note 151, 130.

[296] *Ameer Bano v SE Highways* PLD 1996 Lahore 592; Residents of Bhawalpur complained that construction of the highway was slow and as a result the sewage system is disturbed. Muhammed Aqil Mirza J Lahore High Court resolved the issue 'through consensus' using PIL. He ordered the lifting of the bans on jobs by the government so that the municipal corporation can recruit more employees to complete the construction.

[297] H Khan (1998), Role of Bar in the Administration of Justice, in, *supra* note 111 170. Essay was also published in *PLJ* (1998) Magazine Section 148; This was a paper read in the seminar held by the Punjab Bar Council.

[298] W Menski (1997), Public Interest Litigation: A strategy for the future. The Fourth Cornelius Memorial Lecture, *supra* note 151, 107.

[299] AR Alam, The Law of Public Interest Litigation in Pakistan *supra* note 151, 63.

[300] We Menski (1997), Public Interest Litigation: A strategy for the future. The Fourth Cornelius Memorial Lecture, *supra* note 151, 131.

some extent. But according to him, the judges did not use this facility sufficiently. The concept of the Quetta Declaration was valuable but remained only on paper.[301] By the end of the 1990s, PIL in Pakistan was of some use by cutting the excesses of free market capitalism, through consumer protection, and market-oriented environment protectionism. A detailed analysis is in the last empirical chapter about 2000s. The consolidation of PIL was also evident in the lawyers' movement, which swept through the country in the 2007 onwards. PIL and its principles had become an integral part of the constitution in spite of criticism and misuse.[302] Ultimately, I view PIL as a legal development that evolved with political developments in Pakistan but which became co-opted within the good governance paradigm.

4.7 'Good Governance': A Class Explanation of Musharraf's Coup (October, 1999)

The liberal project became disenchanted with the democratic experience. Nawaz Sharif's success in the 1997 election was one step forward, yet it occurred in the context of a decade-long tradition of non-issue and non-policy politics or 'de-ideologized' politics.[303] For Rasul Bakhsh Rais, the transition to democracy was not working due to the feudal political 'culture'. The underdeveloped civil society was not in a position to enhance this democratic polity.[304] Devoid of structural issues, and class formations, 'institutionalist' studies were analyzing the voting behaviour in elections to solve the question of who is voting for whom and why?[305] One such study, by Andrew R. Wilder, examined the self-interested rational voter who sought patronage in order to reject the claim that social factors like traditional 'feudal' relationships and ties of family, clan or tribe determine voting behaviour.[306]

---

[301]Mian, *supra* note 61, 145.

[302]AR Alam, The Law of Public Interest Litigation in Pakistan, *supra* note 151, 62.

[303]Waseem, *supra* note 68, 14.

[304]Though his opinion is democracy will solve its own problems, see RB Rais, Benazir's Return to Power, 1992–94, Kennedy, *supra* note 45, 14.

[305]The findings of Andrew R Wilder (1999) are that the common perception is wrong that social factors like traditional 'feudal' relationships and ties of family, clan or tribe determine voting behaviour. Rather, political determinacy like party, party leadership identification in urban areas and patronage orientation in rural areas are important in voting behaviour, see Wilder, *supra* note 34, 3.

[306]Wilder made the basis of rise of Pakistan Muslim League-N and decline of Pakistan People's Party in urban areas of central Punjab, along with increasing prosperity, a factor behind Nawaz Sharif's reliance on patronage in 1988 onward in central Punjab. For him this was also the reason of decline of organized labour and hence decline of Pakistan People's Party as part of the poor in 1988–90, see Wilder, *supra* note 34.

In terms of class formations, the tug of war between the two fractions of the reigning class saw both sides using the state apparatus of bureaucracy and judiciary against each other. The decade of 1985–95 led to the politicization of the bureaucracy, particularly the District Management Group and Police Group with large-scale postings.[307] According to Saeed Shafqat and Saeed Wahlah, every regime, whether civil and military, tried to curtail the powers and authority of the Civil Services of Pakistan, and break its 'institutional will and capacity'.[308] Apart from this, we can translate this change in Civil Services as class formations affecting the state formations. Every regime tried to re-mould the frame of the bureaucracy and judiciary. Nawaz suspended 87 civil servants in 1997 and formed a task force for civil reforms.[309] Close to the end of the 1990s, all the class forces agreed to break the back of civil bureaucracy, including the hegemonic metropolitan bourgeoisie and emerging petty bourgeois 'liberal' project. The World Bank worried about the high transaction costs of doing business in Pakistan.[310] Until 1998, the World Bank clearly stood against over-centralized organizational structure and seriously eroded internal accountability, as well as the politicization of civil-service decision-making in Pakistan.[311] Reformist economic managers of the World Bank were struggling hard to restrain and block the pursuit of populist policies by the political leaders.[312]

The dilemma for the reigning class was that the political leadership was given the task of the state's strategic imperatives and the economic needs of its populace, and they did not have the authority or resources to meet these needs.[313] Democratic regimes were vulnerable to both, an overthrowing by a military-backed president and to voters' expectations. They reached short-term 'politically optimal solutions'

[307]S Shafqat & S Wahlah, Experimenting with Democratic Governance: The Impact of the 2001 Local Government Ordinance on Pakistan's Bureaucracy, in, Charles H Kennedy & Cynthia A Botteron (eds) *Pakistan: 2005* (Oxford University Press, Karachi, 2005) 198, 208.

[308]*Ibid* 203.

[309]S Shafqat, Pakistani Bureaucracy: Crisis of Governance and Prospects of Reform 38:4 *The Pak Dev Rev* (1999) Part II 995.

[310]The Word Bank (2001), Bari et al., (2002); World Bank SME Policy Note, World Bank Islamabad, 2001; Bari, F. Cheema A., and Haque E., Regulatory Impediments, Market Imperfections and Firm Growth: Analyzing the Constraints to SME Growth in Pakistan, A Study Conducted for the Asian Development Bank (ADB) 2002. As cited by BA Khan & F Bari, Pakistan: Economic Challenges for a New Millennium, in, Craig Baxter (ed) *Pakistan on the Brink: Politics, Economics and Society* (Oxford University Press, Karachi, 2004) 131.

[311]The World Bank, Pakistan: A Framework for Civil Service Reforms in Pakistan, Report No. 18386-PAK (15 December 1998).

[312]I Hussain, Pakistan and IMF, International Expert Workshop organized by the German Foundation for Development (DSE), Berlin (1–2 July 2002) 2, as cited by Kennedy, *supra* note 307, 51, 78.

[313]A Jalal, Pakistan's Tangle: The Politics of Conflicting Security and Economic Interests 34: 1 *Government and Opposition* (1999) as cited by *ibid.*

to stay in power.[314] Aid programs, like the Rural Works Program, the Integrated Rural Development Program, the People's Works Program, and the *Tamir-e-Watan Program,* were established to bypass bureaucracy and so that the elite could direct patronage towards the members of the national and provincial assemblies.[315]

Proponents of the liberal project were not happy with this situation. They vigorously attacked development planning, as the policy-makers were asking local Members of National and Provincial assemblies—MNAs and MPAs—where schools should be located. Funds were given as a prestige and to please MNAs and MPAs.[316] Their conclusion was that "if the state can't deliver, it should leave the poor alone",[317] or that NGOs should lead development.[318] Insofar as there was a critique of Structural Adjustment Programs,[319] the liberal project recognized the need for breaking the nexus of politicians and the bureaucracy with land reforms and decentralization. However, land reform was a 'structural issue', and the quick solution was decentralization and 'good governance', which the metropolitan bourgeoisie (through International Financial Institutions) had already developed as a response to critiques of Structural Adjustment Programs. Suffice it to say, this milieu was ready for a regime change to one that prioritized the principles of 'good governance' instead of democracy, and consequently welcomed the 'liberal' coup of General Musharraf.

References

A Mian, CJSC (Ret, As he then was), *A Judge Speaks Out: An autobiography* (Oxford University Press, Karachi, 2004).

A Siddiqa, *Military Inc.: Inside Pakistan's Military Economy* (Oxford University Press, Karachi, 2007).

AR Wilder, *The Pakistani Voter: Electoral Politics and Voting Behaviour in Punjab* (Oxford University Press, Karachi, 1999).

B Bhutto, *Daughter of the East: An Autobiography,* 2nd edn (Simon & Schuster, London, 1988 & 2007).

C Baxter (ed), *Pakistan on the Brink: Politics, Economics and Society* (Oxford University Press, Karachi, 2004).

---

314 M Grindle & J Thomas, *Public Choice and Policy Change, The Political Economy of Reform in Developing Countries* (John Hopkins University Press, Baltimore, 1991) 62.

315 M Waseem, Local Power Structures and the Relevance of Rural Development Strategies: A Case Study of Pakistan 17:3 *Community Dev J* (1992) 1, 3, 228.

316 TA Siddiqui, *Towards Good Governance*, (Oxford University Press, Karachi, 2001).

317 *Ibid* 165; This confrontation between state and NGOs became high in flood relief of 2009.

318 See a full formation of such a case in SR Khan & S Aftab, Structural Adjustment, Labor and the Poor *in Pakistan*, Research Report Series# 8, Islamabad (1995), see also J Bennett (1998), Development Alternatives: NGO-Government Partnership in Pakistan, Working Paper Series#3, Islamabad (1998).

319 T Banuri, SR Khan & M Mahmood. *Just Development: Beyond Adjustment with Human Face* (Oxford University Press, Karachi, 1997).

C Lasch, *The True and Only Heaven: Progress and its Critics* (W. W. Norton & Company, New York, 1991).
CE Black (ed) *Comparative Modernization: A Reader* (Free Press, New York, 1976).
CH Kennedy & CA Botteron (eds), *Pakistan: 2005* (Oxford University Press, Karachi, 2005).
CH Kennedy & RB Rais (eds) *Pakistan: 1995* (Vanguard, Lahore, 1995).
D Kux, *The United States and Pakistan 1947-2000: Disenchanted allies* (John Hopkins University Press, Baltimore, 2001).
DC Engerman, N Gilman, MH Haefele & ME Latham (eds), *Staging Growth: Modernization, Development, and the Global Cold War* (University of Massachusetts Press, Amherst, 2003).
DI Narejo (ed), B Bhutto, *Wither Pakistan: Dictatorship or Democracy* (Al-Hamd Publications, Lahore, 2007).
DM Trubek & A Santos (eds), *The New Law and Economic Development: A Critical Appraisal* (Cambridge University Press, Cambridge, 2006).
H Khan (ed), *The Judicial Organ: Speeches and Articles* (Freedom Forum for Human Rights and Development, Lahore, 1999).
H Khan, *Constitutional and Political History of Pakistan,* 2nd edn (Oxford University Press, Karachi, 2009).
I Husain, *Pakistan: The Economy of an Elitist State* (Oxford University Press, Karachi, 1999).
JM Dawood. *The Role of Superior Judiciary in the Politics of Pakistan* (Royal Book Company, Karachi, 1994).
JS Addleton, *Undermining the Centre: The Gulf Migration and Pakistan.* (Oxford University Press, Karachi, 1992).
L Panitch, The New Imperial State, 2 *New Left Rev* (March/April 2000).
LW Pye, Political Science and the Crisis of Authoritarianism: The Vindication of Modernization Theory, 84:1 *Am Polit Sci Rev* (1990).
M Grindle & J Thomas, *Public Choice and Policy Change, The Political Economy of Reform in Developing Countries* (John Hopkins University Press, Baltimore, 1991).
M Hussain & A Hussain, *Pakistan: Problems of Governance* (Vanguard, Lahore, 1993).
M Khan, Patron-client Networks and the Economic Effects of Corruption in Asia, 10 *EJDR* (1998).
M Waseem, Local Power Structures and the Relevance of Rural Development Strategies: A Case Study of Pakistan, 17:3 *Community Dev J* (1992).
NH Shah, CJSC (Ret, as he then was), *Memoirs and Reflections* (Alhamra Printing, Islamabad, 2002).
O Siddique & Z Hayat, Unholy Laws & Holy Speech: Blasphemy Laws in Pakistan - Controversial Origins, Design Defects and Free Speech Implications, 17 *Minn. J International L* (2008).
O Tornquist, *What is Wrong with Marxism: On Capitalists and State in India and Indonesia* (Manohar, New Delhi, 1989).
P Musharraf (2006), *In the Line of Fire: A Memoir* (Free Press, New York, 2006).
PR Newberg, *Judging the State: Courts and Constitutional Politics in Pakistan* (Cambridge University Press, New Delhi, 1995).
R Braibanti, *Chief Justice Cornelius of Pakistan: An Analysis with Letters and Speeches* (Oxford University Press, Karachi, 1999).
Rahnema & V Bawtree (eds), *The Post-Development Reade*r (Zed Books, London, 1977).
SA Shah, CJSC (Ret, as he then was), *Law Courts in a Glass House: An Autobiography* (Oxford University Press, Karachi, 2001).
SA Zaidi, *Pakistan's Social and Economic Development: The Domestic, Regional and Global Context* (Rupa Co., New Delhi, 2004).
Shahid-ur-Rehman, *Pakistan: Sovereignty Lost* (Mr Books, Islamabad, 2006).
SJ Burki, *A Revisionist History of Pakistan* (Vanguard, Lahore, 1998).
SP Huntington, Political Development and Political Decay, 17 *World Politics* (1965).
SP Huntington, *Political Order in Changing Societies* (Yale University Press, New Haven, 1968).

T Banuri, *Democratic Decentralization and the Judiciary* (SDPI, Research Report, Islamabad, 1992).

T Banuri, SR Khan & M Mahmood, *Just Development: Beyond Adjustment with Human Face* (Oxford University Press, Karachi, 1997).

TA Khan, *The Post-Colonial State in The Era of Capitalist Globalization: Historical, Political, and Theoretical Approaches to State Formation* (Routledge, New York, 2012).

TA Siddiqui, *Towards Good Governance* (Oxford University Press, Karachi, 2001).

V Chibber, *Locked in Place: State-Building and Late Industrialization in India* (Princeton University Press, Princeton, 2003).

W Menski, AR Alam & MK Raza (eds), *Public Interest Litigation in Pakistan* (Platinum Publishing Ltd./Pakistan Law House, London/Karachi, 2000).

Chapter 5
Good Governance by Judiciary—The 2000s

After the painful struggles against four democratic regimes in 10 years, the judiciary was more than ready to welcome the coup of General Musharraf. This time, the judiciary had its own agenda, as prescribed by the good governance paradigm. To implement it, it was necessary to restore the 'juridico-bureaucratic' structure. I argue that the main legal tool it used was Public Interest Litigation. The judiciary justified its actions by pointing to the supremacy of the constitution.

The strength, role and morale of the judiciary as the custodian of a new phase of global modernity under the rubric of rule of law projects and good governance is evident from the papers presented at the International Jurists Conference Islamabad in 2006.[1] The juridico-bureaucratic structure had become so strong that the Opposition (the Pakistan People's Party and Pakistan Muslim League-Nawaz) insisted that the judiciary's powers must be put in check before democracy can be restored. The bar associations were upset with the judiciary–military bureaucracy alliance and, at its height, published a blunt white paper in 2003.[2] The Opposition could, however, only act when a deal was signed internationally between the PPP and the western powers as well as when the Charter of Democracy was signed between the two main opposition parties (Pakistan People's Party and Pakistan Muslim League-Nawaz).

---

[1]International Judicial Conference, Islamabad, Pakistan (August 11-14, 2016) available at <http://www.supremecourt.gov.pk/ijc/ijc.htm>, last visited on 20 May 2016.

[2]Pakistan Bar Council, White Paper against Judiciary, available at <http://pakistanbarcouncil.org/wp-content/uploads/2012/07/White-Paper_Complete_.pdf>, last visited on 01 November 2012.

M. Azeem, *Law, State and Inequality in Pakistan*, International Law and the Global South, DOI 10.1007/978-981-10-3845-7_5

This class formation caused cracks in the juridico-bureaucratic structure, which gave rise to the lawyers' movement of 2007. After the success of the lawyers' movement, in 2008, the judiciary was ready to go one step further, and argued for 'constitutional governance' and 'constitutional democracy' rather than parliamentary democracy. This concluded with the attempt to establish a 'judicial dictatorship'.

5.1 Institutional Rearrangement: Installing the Governance Structure

By the end of the 1990s, people were disenchanted with neoliberal policies. International Financial Institutions bestowed massive responsibilities on the shoulders of the corrupt elite. The projects of rule of law came in response. The main architect of the 'rule of law' in the World Bank is considered to be Ibrahim Shihata, who was the senior vice president of the Bank from 1983 to 1998. He emphasized governance, 'good order', and a system of rules and institutions as a prerequisite for the development of developing countries. This was accompanied by Kofi Annan's famous declaration in 1997, to make good governance "the single most important factor in eradicating poverty and promoting development",[3] and hence, all the development agencies, namely the U.S. Agency for International Development, the Inter-American Development Bank[4] and the World Bank, became committed to this. The World Bank developed the Global Governance Indicators, reflecting institution building, in transitional economies as explained in the first chapter of this book. The 2000s were thus the decade of putting the state back in the analyses of International Financial Institutions, but this time in the name of good governance.

[3]Annual Report of the Secretary General on the Work of the Organization, UN Doc A/53/1 (1998) [114] as cited by R Birner, Improving Governance to Eradicate Poverty and Hunger, available at <http://www.ifpri.org/sites/default/files/publications/oc63ch42.pdf>; S Pahuja, *Decolonizing International Law: Development, Economic Growth, and the Politics of Universality* (Cambridge University Press, Cambridge, 2013) 194 where she has a detailed analysis of Shihata's rule of law writings at the bank.

[4]US Agency for International Development, At the Freedom's Frontiers: A Democracy and Governance Strategic Framework (December 2005) 5, available at <http://drg.usaidallnet.gov/dgpubs/document_details.php?document_key=8>. According to this, "USAID and the State Department define democracy and governance programmes as 'technical assistance' which goes to 'democracy programmes' to promote the rule of law and human rights", etc. Inter-American Development Bank, Strategy for Promoting Citizen Participation in Bank Activities (19 May 2004) available at <http://www.iadb.org/en/publications/publication-detail,7101.html?dctype=All&dclanguage=en&id=16746%20>.

The Good Governance model did not push the developmental state, which had made the 'Asian Miracle' in the early 1990s.[5] Instead, it was for the legal order that could make the market economy possible.[6]

The 'development policies' now proposed were to fight against corruption through legal reforms in the civil service, as well as criminal law, administrative law and judicial reforms. Terminology and rhetoric used by officials and intellectuals included meritocracy in the bureaucracy, guaranteeing transparency in public administration, ensuring the monitoring of government procurement processes, reducing red tape, curbing arbitrariness and discretion in administrative and judicial decisions. The judiciary was to hold public officials or politicians responsible for their acts of interfering with market processes and private investment. Hence, the World Bank began giving 'technical assistance loans' for judicial reforms. The first loan was granted to Venezuela in 1992. Now, these loans range from $2.5 million (in U.S. dollars) to Yemen to $58 million to Russia. According to one estimate, the World Bank was supporting 330 'rule of law' projects dealing with judicial reforms in 100 countries in early 2000s. Per the World Bank's Annual Report of 2003–2004, it spent $3.8 billion on loans for judicial reforms since 1993.[7] All of the above processes began in the early 1990s, with the transition from the push for a non-interventionist state under deregulation, decentralization and privatization to a state set up to promote the formal market under good governance at the end of the 1990s. These 'waves' of externally funded law reform in the transition economies of Eastern Europe and Asia were strongly influenced by 'new institutional economics' for their theoretical framework.[8] According to this school of thought, good institutions can make an economy efficient, and benefit the individual as well as society (of course, with the implied assumption of a perfect market, competition and information). Furthermore, the thinking went that existing institutions could be reformed under a much wider and looser theory of social change. 'Pragmatic' or

---

[5]The East Asian 'miracle' told a slightly different story. This development was the result of an activist 'developmental state' that aggressively promoted economic development and financial stability. M Woo-Cummings (ed) *The Developmental State*, (Cornell University Press, Ithaca, 1999). Amsden (1989) and Wade (1990) proved that success was due to the effective role of the state as initiator and coordinator in the process of development. See AH Amsden, *Asia's Next Giant*: *South Korea and late Industrialization* (Oxford University Press, New York, 1989); R Wade, *Governing the Market*: *Economic Theory and the Role of Government in East Asian Industrialization* (Princeton University Press, Princeton, 1990). Fukunari Kimura (2004) claimed that South East Asian development was due to the usage of dual track approach, that is, import substitution and export led growth. F Kimura, New Development Strategies under Globalizations: Foreign Direct Investment and International Commercial Policy in Southeast Asia, in, A Kohsaka (ed) *Development Strategies*: *Beyond the Washington Consensus* (Palgrave Macmillan Ltd, England, 2004) 115, 123.

[6]RA Posner, *Economic Analysis of Law*, 4th edn (Little, Brown and Company, Boston, 1992).

[7]A Santos, The World Bank's Uses of the "Rule of Law" Promise in Economic Development, in, Trubek & Santos (ed) *The New Law and Economic Development: A Critical Appraisal*, (Cambridge University Press, Cambridge, 2006) 253.

[8]See Chap. 1 for a detailed discussion of this.

purpose-built, economic, political and particularly legal institutions are the focus of institutional economists. The official presentation on this front can be found in the World Bank document, *Comprehensive Development Framework.*[9] Apart from the legal and development critique of this inclusion of the 'social' in preposition of the World Bank[10] or this proper place of law in it,[11] this book is to evaluate the centrality of law for political development. In this perspective, we can see the relationship between the metropolitan bourgeoisie and the Musharraf regime, and why it did not vocally object to this overthrow of the democratic regime of Nawaz. Furthermore, we can see how the rising petit bourgeoisie (or the 'civil society') joined hands with good governance and its emphasis on legalism and constitutionalism (or what I refer to as the 'liberal legal project'). That is how 'rule of law' became more important than democracy in Pakistan for the metropolitan bourgeoisie and 'civil society'. Below, I detail this state formation and its class formation under good governance in the 2000s.

5.2 State Formation in the Era of Good Governance

General Pervez Musharraf served as the tenth president of Pakistan from 2001 to 2008. He had been brought to power through a military coup in 1999. His governing policies were a clear move from Structural Adjustment Programs to the good governance paradigm as "structural reforms cannot be successfully implemented if

[9]James D Wolfensohn, President of the World Bank Group, started in 1995 with debt issue but after one year found 'cancer of corruption' as the main issue. 'The Challenge of Inclusion'of "the weakest and the most vulnerable from the margins of society" became the issue in 1997. This developed as CDF in 1999. JDWolfensohn, Joint Annual Discussion (September 28–30, 1999) 2, available at <http://www.imf.org/external/am/1999/speeches/pr02e.pdf>.

[10]K Rittich, The Future of Law and Development: Second-Generation Reforms and the Incorporation of the Social, Trubek *supra note 7*, 203; SE Merry, Measuring the World: Indicators, Human Rights, and Global Governance, in, D Partridge, M Welker & R Hardin (eds) *Corporate Lives: New Perspectives on the Social Life of the Corporate Form* (Wenner-Gren Symposium Series, 2011) 52:3 *Current Anthropology*, S83-S95.

[11]John K M Ohnesorge (2008) rebutted the law and development approach of development agencies and its critics like Trubek (2006) as their experience was based on Anglo-American and Brazilian experience. He used the South East Asian 'miracle era' as a case study to give evidence for proper role of law in development. He drew on the work of Alice H Amsden and Dani Rodrik to illustrate how the economic development used law instead of the formalist logic of law as found in law and development scholarship. My problem with his approach is it still does not illuminate the relationship of state and class relations. For example, in South Korea and Taiwan, the U.S. as a hegemonic class successfully promoted land reforms which were vital to political and economic development. This did not happen in Pakistan where the U.S. kept the reigning class as a feudal class. Lag or lead of economic or political development in relation of law and development does not take us far if the nature of contradiction are not analyzed within which both processes travel. See JKM Ohnesorge, Developing Development Theory: Law and Development Orthodoxies and the North East Asian Experience, 28:2*U. Pa. J. Int'L Econ. L.* (2008) 219.

quality of economic governance remains poor".[12] This 'governance' compliance was bolstered post-9/11 by the U.S. connection and its involvement, both politically and economically.[13] The American threat, for an alliance in the U.S. war against terror, for Musharraf, was a threat of de-modernization, that is, to be sent back to the stone ages. Income inequality was not an issue and could be fixed by the right policies. He did not blame the International Monetary Fund for governance issues in Pakistan. In 2004, he appointed Shaukat Aziz, a Citibank employee with a humble 'middle class' background, as Prime Minister; Dr. Ishrat Hussain, who came from the World Bank, as the Governor of the State Bank of Pakistan; and a local industrialist Razzak Dawood as the Commerce minister.[14]

For General Musharraf, the prior democratic regimes were "autocratic, usually plutocratic and lately kleptocratic", with parties centred on the shifting coalitions of clans and tribal leaders which led to poor governance when they come to power. Political parties were "no more than family cults, a dynastic icon at their head", such as Benazir Bhutto.[15] He wanted a 'sustainable democracy', democracy that should be tailored according to the needs of a nation. He also had a populist side, "I am no socialist, yet I share these ideals".[16]

Musharraf passed a Local Government Ordinance in 2000, which he called a silent revolution. Later, the Pakistan Muslim League-Quaid-e-Azam was formed with the help of the National Accountability Bureau (NAB) and Intelligence Services of Pakistan. General Musharraf established NAB, declaring its mandate to as being to control corruption and improving major economic issues.[17] The U.N. reported that Rs.100 billion was lost to corruption in Pakistan each year and Transparency International ranked Pakistan twelfth in 1999 on the Corruption Perception Index.[18] The U.S., U.K. and Swiss governments showed their willingness to help NAB fight against corruption.[19] NAB's rapid and ruthless pace horrified the business community and Finance minister, Shaukat Aziz, had to assure the business community they would not be harassed by the Bureau.[20] Shortly after, the Bureau sent a message of confidence to the business community for out-of-court settlements.[21] General Khalid Maqbool, Chairman of the Bureau, promised to pursue business-friendly policies to avoid any negative impact on the trade and

---

[12]P Musharraf, *In the Line of Fire: A Memoir* (Free Press, New York, 2006) 182.

[13]AS Akhtar, *Overdeveloping State: The Politics of Common Sense in Pakistan, 1971-2007*, SOAS, University of London, PhD Thesis (2008) 126.

[14]P Musharraf, *In the Line of Fire: A Memoir* (Free Press, New York, 2006) 201, 185, 145.

[15]*Ibid* 164.

[16]*Ibid* 155.

[17]*The Nation*, (27 October 1999) 5.

[18]*The Nation*, (27 October 1999).

[19]As prosecutor General of NAB declared. *The Nation*, (30 December 1999) 12.

[20]Addressing the All Pakistan Cloth Exporters Association in Faisalabad, *The Nation*, (12 March 2000) 18.

[21]*The Nation*, (01 January 2000) 1.

investment climate.[22] By pacifying and terrifying different fractions of the landed and capitalist elite through corruption cases, all the actors of the historical bloc (including the metropolitan bourgeoisie, landed and capitalist elite) came back in anew 'institutional arrangement' with the old structure intact. This time, 'civil society' also shared a place in this class formation under the banner of 'rule of law' and 'good governance'. Where was the judiciary in this?

5.3 Judicial Decisions Under Dictatorship: Restoring the Juridico-Bureaucratic Structure

General Musharraf followed the same steps in relation to the judiciary as previous military regimes, but there was a difference. The difference was that the judiciary had its own agenda this time. The new role of the judiciary came as a part of conditionality for aid for political and economic development. The Asian Development Bank, in December 2001, financed a $350 million loan for judicial reform in Pakistan. This Project, numbered 38612, was titled *Islamic Republic of Pakistan: Support to Governance Reforms in Pakistan* (*Financed by the Government of the United Kingdom*) for "Improving governance and preventing corruption". It was launched in Pakistan as the 'Access to Justice Program'. The judiciary was now a 'coequal partner' of three organs of the state, rather the two organs of the state, as there was no legislature for the next two years.

Let us look at the self-awareness of the judiciary of its new role. After the episode of Chief Justice Sajjad, the new Chief Justice Ajmal (who served from Dec 23, 1997 to June 30, 1999) knew the limits of judicial activism. Being the main initiator of the separation of powers decision in 1989, and being the main writer in the decision of the *Judge's case* in 1998, he was well aware of the emerging power of the judiciary also. He maintained the discourse set during the regime and connected it with the new priorities of the hegemonic class, under a push for good governance. He wanted a 'system of governance' according to the constitution promulgated by the third U.S. president Thomas Jefferson.[23] A very important component of the emerging 'good governance' paradigm was dispensation of justice, as a part of legal reforms. Ajmal Mian CJSC stressed the need for justice "timely, expeditiously and economically" as an important part of the *administration of justice* in a civilized society [my emphasize].[24]

---

[22]*The News*, (21 February 2001) 10.

[23]A Mian, CJSC, Speech at a Seminar on Rule of Law, *PLD* (1999) Journal Section 128, 129 - He started using words 'democratic governance' and 'constitutional rule'; A Mian, Addressing SHC Bar Association, *PLD* (1999) Journal Section 130, 131; Rule of law started getting connected with the newly popular word "governance" in judiciary, A Mian, Address of CJSC at the Annual Dinner of LHC Bar Association Rawalpindi Bench on 11-2-199, *PLD* (1999) Journal Section 33.

[24]A Mian, CJSC, Addressing the Annual Dinner of Karachi Bar Association on 14/11/1998, *PLD* (1999) Journal Section 1, 2.

After Ajmal, the next Supreme Court Chief Justice Saiduzzaman Siddiqui (July 01, 1999 to Jan 26, 2000) felt a stress on adopting "civilized means and methods of governance" which was essential for economic development. For this, there were expectations on the judiciary to play a role.[25] By the end of 1999, he used the word "good governance".[26] Was using this discourse of 'good governance' by Chief Justices a coincidence when the IFIs had just began this paradigm, and Musharraf also found 'good governance' as the 'pre-requisite' to achieve the objectives of his regime?[27] Meanwhile, Chief Justice Siddiqui was now able to claim that the struggle for an independent judiciary had been realized and it was now free and independent.[28] Probably, pointing to the demoralizing effects due to the 'judicial adventures' of the Chief Justice Sajjad court, Siddiqui reiterated the retreating position of the *Zia-ur-Rehman* case of the 1970s regarding the supremacy of the legislature, and that the judiciary had no superiority over the other two organs of state.[29] Though the judiciary can check the constitutional limits of the Legislature, yet this function should "be performed with great circumspection". He pointed out that the struggle for the independence of the judiciary and its separation from the executive was a running theme in every 'constitutional governance' debate and declared that it was achieved in Pakistan. He made clear how the appointments of judges, even in all tiers of judiciary, were in the hands of the judge's, in accordance with the *judges' case*.[30] Furthermore, the "judiciary plays a crucial role in improving governance and strengthening the political economic and social institutions in the country".[31] I want to make two points very clear before moving to the role of the judiciary during Musharraf's regime; one, that the judiciary was confident vis-à-vis the dictatorial regime of Musharraf; secondly, that it was aware of the new role for 'good governance' which had just emerged.

Following his coup, General Musharraf enacted the Provisional Constitutional Order to govern the country in accordance with the constitution.[32] The military takeover was challenged in the Supreme Court in a number of writs. In January of

---

[25]S Siddiqui, CJSC, Speech of CJSC at the Certificate Distribution Ceremony at Federal Judicial Academy (1-8-1999), *PLD* (1999) Journal Section 136, 138.

[26]S Siddiqui, CJSC, Addressing All Pakistan Women Lawyers' Convention at Lahore on 27 November, 1999.

[27]Mushrraf's first speech after the military coup in 1999, available at <http://fas.org/news/pakistan/1999/991017-mushraf_speech.htm>, last visited on May 14, 2016.

[28]JS Siddiqui, CJSC, (as he then was), *PLD* (1999) Journal Section 97, 100. JS Siddiqui, Judiciary in Pakistan: An Overview, *PLD* (2000) Journal Section 52, 59; a speech delivered at National Defense College, Islamabad to the Senior Cadre Officers of the Armed Forces of Pakistan and Friendly Countries in Asia, Africa, Europe and North America. A speech delivered on a Seminar on Law Reforms dated 3-7-1999.

[29]S Siddiqui, JSC, Speech at the Seminar titled Law, Justice and Welfare State, *PLD* (1999) Journal Section 97, 99.

[30]*Ibid* 100.

[31]*Ibid* 101.

[32]*Provisional Constitutional Order (PCO)*, PLD 1999 Central Statutes 446.

2000, General Musharraf promulgated the Oath of Office (Judge's) Order, which required the judges to take a fresh Oath.[33] The Supreme Court Chief Justice refused to take Oath[34] and one Supreme Court judge from Punjab and four Supreme Court judges from Sindh followed suit. None of the Judges of High Courts refused to take Oath.[35] The remaining team of judges, led by Irshad Hasan Khan as Chief Justice, took the Oath. Following this, a bench of 12 judges of the Supreme Court upheld the military takeover in the *Zafar Ali Shah* case.[36] The coup was validated on the basis of the doctrine of necessity and the principle of *Salus Populi Suprema Lex* as embodied in the *Begum Nusrat Bhutto* case. Nawaz Sharif was sentenced in a hijacking case on 6 April 2000.[37]

After gaining the stamp of approval from the judiciary, General Musharraf promulgated an order in 2001, titled the President's Succession Order, declaring the office of the president vacant and therefore it was under his mandate to take on the presidents' functions until a successor was found.[38] General Musharraf then announced a referendum to be held on 8 April 8 2002, for him to be elected as president.[39] The referendum was challenged in the Supreme Court, which declared the petition premature and left the consequences of the referendum on the incoming parliament.[40]

The *Zafar Ali Shah* case gave General Musharraf powers to amend the constitution and he initiated constitutional amendment packages for 'sustainable democracy' and 'institutional strengthening'. He revived the controversial Article 58(2)(b) which had been removed in the 13th Amendment by the elected parliament of Nawaz Sharif. He formed a National Security Council, putting the chiefs of armed forces together with civilian government officials to give a constitutional

[33]*Oath of Office (Judges) Order*, 2000, PLD 2000 Central Statutes 38.

[34]In January 2000, Musharraf discussed a new Oath with Supreme Court Chief Justice Saiduzzaman Siddiqui, and Siddiqui refused. On 26 January 2000, 89 out of 103 judges took oath under the Provisional Constitutional Order and these were six Supreme Court judges and the rest were HCs judges. Senior most Irshad Hasan Khan became Chief Justice of the Supreme Court. See ZK Maluka, Reconstructing the Constitution for a COAS President: Pakistan, 1999 to 2002, in, C Baxter (ed) *Pakistan on the Brink: Politics, Economics and Society* (Oxford University Press, Karachi, 2004) 53, 59.

[35]H Khan, *Constitutional and Political History of Pakistan*, 2nd edn (Oxford University Press, Karachi, 2009) 480.

[36]*Zafar Ali Shah v General Pervez General Musharraf*, PLD 2000 SC 869. In the *Nusrat Bhutto case*, the petition was declared not maintainable. Whereas in the *Zafar Ali Shah* case judges declared the petition maintainable but made "lengthy declarations far from reality". See Maluka, *supra* note 34, 53, 61.

[37]*The Guardian*, (07 April 2000) available at <http://www.theguardian.com/world/2000/apr/07/ pakistan. lukeharding>.

[38]*President's Succession Order*, 2001, PLD 2001 Central Statutes 392.

[39]*Referendum Order*, 2002 (Chief Executive Order 12 of 2002); PLD 2002 Central Statutes 218.

[40]*Hussain Ahmad v General Pervez Musharraf*, PLD 2002 SC 853.

cover to military hegemony.[41] The amendments were challenged in the Supreme Court, which held that parliament, not the court, was the appropriate forum to consider these amendments.[42]

In 2001, the Supreme Court Chief Justice Irshad Hasan Khan was in a position to claim that after the 1999 coup, the judiciary continued its work and retained its independence by exercising judicial review, maintaining rule of law and securing fundamental rights. He argued that the separation of powers between the judiciary and the executive was achieved and the judiciary is independent in Pakistan. He claimed that the judiciary enjoyed administrative, financial as well as decisional independence.[43] After retirement, he was appointed as Chief Election Commission, and helped to rig the 2002 elections.[44]

In the 2002 elections, an undergraduate degree was a prerequisite to be a candidate.[45] Musharraf's Conduct of General Elections Order 2002 was challenged before the Supreme Court in June 2002. After three days of hearing, the Supreme Court dismissed the petition in July 2002 and concluded that an educational qualification did not violate the principles of Pakistan's Constitution or democracy.[46] The petition also involved issues such as gender, class, faith, religion, language, race, education, etc. but the Supreme Court rejected those. The court found that the 'right' to run for a public office to be a statutory right, not a fundamental right. In countering the charge of supporting an 'elitist democracy' by this educational qualification clause, the court argued that the business of the state system requires competence. The institutional argument of the court was based not on the character of the officials but on 'political culture', which it defined on the basis of David Sill's article in International Encyclopedia of the Social Science. This, for Cynthia A. Bottern, was very behavioural and led to the argument of education increasing good governance as "the hallmark and soul of democracy". The writer empirically made clear that this educational requirement made an impact in temporarily daunting its opponents.[47] We can recall that the judiciary once again

---

[41] *Legal Framework Order*, 2002 (Chief Executive's Order 24 of 2002), PLD 2002 Central Statutes (Supplement) 1604.

[42] *Watan Party v Chief Executive*, PLD 2003 SC 74.

[43] IH Khan, CJSC (as he then was), Judicial System, Administration, and Training in Pakistan, *PLD* (2001) Journal Section 103, 111, National Judges College, Beijing, Peoples Republic of China (05 September 2001).

[44] Pakistan Bar Council, White Paper against Judiciary, available at <http://pakistanbarcouncil.org/wp-content/uploads/2012/07/White-Paper_Complete_.pdf>, last visited on 01 November 2012.

[45] *Local Government Ordinance*, 2001, and *Conduct of General Elections Order*, 2002, made Matriculation a condition. See *Conduct of General Elections Order*, 2002, and *Chief Executive's Order 7* of 2002, PLD 2002 Central Statutes 193.

[46] *Pakistan Muslim League (Q) v Chief Executive of Pakistan*, PLD 2002 SC 994, 1011.

[47] In Sindh, out of 204 Union Councils the membership of 36 union council and 66 Nazims were elected uncontested, indicating feudal/tribal power in the rural areas at 216. See CA Botteron, Validating Educational Qualification as a Prerequisite to Hold Elective Office: The Supreme Court and the Pakistan Muslim League (Q) Decision, in, CH Kennedy & CA Botteron (eds) *Pakistan: 2005* (Oxford University Press, Karachi, 2005) 158, 179.

stood with controlled democracy, exclusion and marginalization in the name of education.

Sheikh Riaz, the Supreme Court Chief Justice from February 2002 to January 2004, gave judgments in favour of General Musharraf, including appointments of judges he favoured to the Supreme Court,[48] upholding the referendum of April 2002,[49] and the Legal Framework Order.[50] The court defended its decision of taking the Oath, declaring that it had three options; either refuse to take the oath, thereby causing court closure, leading chaos/anarchy and denial of justice to the ordinary citizens of Pakistan. Or the courts could have completely surrendered to the regime and refused all petitions against the same. The last was to accept the situation and save the institution, save the fabric and save the guarantee of human rights, this being the option the courts opted for this. General Musharraf tried to keep him as Chief Justice, despite him having crossed the age of retirement, by amending the Legal Framework Order in October 2004. Lawyers protested, and the retirement age provision was restored under the 17th amendment to the constitution and the Supreme Court Chief Justice had to retire. Sheikh Riaz Ahmad CJSC was exceedingly corrupt and the military regime kept him just to serve the regime.[51] The new Chief Justice, Nazim Husain Siddiqui, who served from 31 December 2003 to 29 June 2005, also supported the military regime. His most important verdict was in favour of the 17th Amendment, through which General Musharraf could retain two offices, namely the President of Pakistan and the Chief of the Army Staff.[52] Supreme Court Chief Justice Nazim also tried to revive the amendment regarding delaying the retirement age by three years,[53] but he was unsuccessful.

General Musharraf then created a party, the Pakistan Muslim League-Quaid-e-Azam, by pulling politicians away from present popular parties. Most, if not all, politicians faced corruption cases, and were vulnerable to NAB and the Intelligence Services of Pakistan. Next, he promulgated the Conduct of General Elections Order on 27 February 27 2002.[54] Under this law, elections were held on 10 October 2002, followed by allegations of rigging and state interference. His party won the elections. Rational theory followers like Andrew R. Wilder, who

[48]*Supreme Court Bar Association v Federation of Pakistan*, PLD 2002 SC 939.

[49]*Hussian Ahmad v Pervez General Musharraf*, PLD 2002 SC 853. While reviewing *Provisional Constitutional Order No.* 1 of 1999 read with *Oath of the Office Order no 1* of 2000, the judiciary commented on its Provisional Constitutional Order position in *Qazi Hussain Ahmad v Pervez General Musharraf*, PLD 2002 SC 813.

[50]*Watan Part v Chief Executive*, PLD 2003 SC 74.

[51]Khan, *supra* note 35, 566.

[52]*Pakistan Lawyers Forum v Federation of Pakistan*, PLD 2005 SC 719.

[53]Khan, *supra* note 35, 566.

[54]*Conduct of General Elections Order*, 2002, *Chief Executive's Order 7* of 2002, PLD 2002 Central Statutes 193.

analyzed the 1997 elections, were stuck with legitimizing the status quo in the 2002 elections because there were open pre-poll manipulations, bribes and coercion. The reason behind Musharraf's success was an "inability of the politicians to rise above their narrow interests".[55]

An alliance of religious parties (Muthida Majlis-e-Aamal-MMA) was formed and it drafted the 17th Amendment of which the Legal Framework Order was a part. The opposition of the MMA, while bargaining for the Legal Framework Order on the 17th Amendment, also gained concessions, including a reduction in the age of Supreme Court judges from 68 to 65 (because the older judges were putting stamps on those decisions regarding Musharraf), removal of the National Security Council and the elimination of Chief of the Army Staff (COAS)—concessions that remained in place until 2004. Musharraf undid all these 'institutional arrangements' by bringing the National Command Authority in place of the National Security Council, and creating the President to Hold Another Office Act, which was passed on October 2004.[56] On 27 December 2003, the 17th Amendment was passed by the National Assembly, followed by its passing in the Senate on 30 December 2003, but without Article 152A (National Security Council).

The 17th Amendment 2003, Legal Framework Order 2002, and President to Another Office Act, 2004 were challenged in the Supreme Court and a five-member bench, headed by Chief Justice Nazim Hussain Siddique, heard all the petitions together. The petitions were all dismissed by a consolidated judgment on 13 April 2005.[57] The court stated that the "remedy lay in the political and not in the judicial process". The appeal in such cases was to be made to the people, not the courts. In the 2005 local elections, even the Punjab judiciary was involved in the rigging. The Chief Justice of Lahore High Court was an active participant.[58] Justice Iftikhar Muhammad Chaudhary had already signed the judgments favouring a takeover by the military, an unconstitutional referendum, the Legal Framework Order and a statute know as President to hold Another Office Act 2004.

It is usually stated that the judiciary was under duress and vulnerable to undertake the dictates for the rulers. As we have seen, it had always been a part of the state structure. The same was true during Musharraf's regime. The judiciary was very much central to 'good governance' for Musharraf, as it allowed him to keep the main opposition away from politics and in exile.

---

[55]AR Wilder, Elections 2002: Legitimizing the Status Quo, in, C Baxter (ed) *supra* note 34, 101, 125.

[56]CH Kennedy, Political Issues in 2004, in, CH Kennedy & CA Botteron (eds) *Pakistan: 2005* (Oxford University Press, Karachi, 2005) 1. This essay was first published as CH Kennedy, Pakistan 2005: Running Very Fast to Stay in the Same Place, 24:1 *Asian Surv.* (2005).

[57]*Pakistan Lawyer's Forum v Federation of Pakistan*, PLD 2005 SC 719.

[58]*Ibid* 503, 504 fn 32.

5.4 Class Formations Under 'Good Governance'

5.4.1 An Undermined Legislature

The usual reason given for why the judiciary opposed the legislature was the claim that it did not legislate. Justice Khoosa concluded that, in the 1990s, legislators spent their time passing motions about breaches of their privileges. The 'logical conclusion' was that under these circumstances, the judiciary in Pakistan had to arrest the repugnancy of parliamentary laws. Therefore, he noted the "judiciary is enjoying a sway over both the Legislature and the Executive".[59] It was also claimed that the legislators in Pakistan did not know the rules for drafting legislation, or the relevant jurisprudence, and judges are to apply these laws with responsibility.[60] The reason for PIL, for Justice Nasir Aslam Zahid, itself rested on the understanding or inability/failure of the legislature and executive to bring about social and economic justice to the poor people.[61] Furthermore, if the elected governments were equally inept, then the remedy could not be regular and fair elections. Citizens cannot find a forum to challenge their elected representatives, as they are only accountable at polls. In conclusion, PIL provides such a forum.[62] The other possibility is the separation of powers as a check on the legislature and executive,[63] and this also enhances the responsibility on the judiciary. Furthermore, since there is widespread illiteracy, people can only get any accountability through the judiciary.[64] In addition, the Supreme Court "shall have to fill-in the empty shows of the opposition" and to provide a dialogue.[65] It was clear that it was thought that every function of the legislature needed to be done by the judiciary.

---

[59]ASK Khoosa, ASC, Legislature, Executive, and Judiciary: Conflict and Cohesion, *PLD* (1994) Journal Section 64, 71, 67.

[60]JS Malik, Supreme Court: A Fountain of Justice, *PLJ* (1999) Magazine Section 146, 149, 151; see also NA Zahid, JSC (retd as he then was), The Role of Judiciary Protecting the Rights of the People- Judicial Activism, International Jurists Conference, Islamabad, Pakistan (2006). Pervez Hasan has the same view about environment litigation. See DP Hassan, Shehla Zia v. WAPDA: Ten Years Later, *PLD* (2005) Journal Section 48, 54, presidential address at the First Annual Seminar of Pakistan Environmental Law Association held at Dr. Pervez Hassan Environmental Law Center, University of the Punjab (New Campus) Lahore on 14 March 2004 for the Lifetime Achievement Award conferred by PELA on Mr Justice Saleem Akhtar (R).

[61]NA Zahid, JSC (retd as he then was), The Role of Judiciary in Protecting the Rights of the People- Judicial Activism, International Jurists Conference, Islamabad, Pakistan (2006).

[62]"Superior courts contributing to the process of democracy through PIL". An example of the judiciary as a legislature is, for example, of PEPA-*Pakistan Environmental Protection Act*, 1997, and *Bonded Labour System (Abolition) Act*, 1992 (Darshan Masih Case). See AR Alam, Public Interest Litigation and the Role of Judiciary, International Jurists Conference, Islamabad, Pakistan (2006) 6.

[63]K Azfar, The Role of Judiciary in Good Governance, International Jurists Conference, Islamabad, Pakistan (2006).

[64]S Ahmad, CJSHC, Good Governance and the Role of Judiciary, International Jurists Conference, Islamabad, Pakistan (2006).

[65]SA Zafar, The Role of Supreme Court in Contemporary Age, International Jurists Conference, Islamabad, Pakistan (2006).

5.4.2 Struggle Against the Judiciary's Encroachment on the Legislative Powers

The judiciary's main demand in 2000 was to bring in Service Tribunals, Custom Courts, Income Tax Tribunals, Banking Tribunals and even Revenue Courts under the administrative control of either High Courts or the Supreme Court as they are the forums which adjudicate most matters. They should gradually and progressively be separated from the executive, it was argued.[66] This demand began to face a backlash. In the *Sirtaj Bibi* case,[67] the writer Irshad Ahmad gave a critique of the prior *Anwar Ali* decision and found that the judiciary was encroaching upon the powers of the executive.[68]

The judiciary had exclusive rights to appoint the judges at this point. Earlier, the executive appointed the judges after consulting with the Supreme Court Chief Justice, who requested favours. Now, the judges were appointing judges, except that the Chief Justice was in office 'for the pleasure of the president' and the president can appoint anyone through the Supreme Court Chief Justice. This did not make much difference, but the principle inspired the protest against the new 'exclusive' right of the judiciary in the appointment of judges. Shahida Jamil, while criticizing this 'Indian novelty' of the appointment of judges, reminded the judiciary that it had totally shifted the power of the appointment of judges to the judiciary in complete disregard to the *trias politica* percept. Due to this, an imbalance had been created.[69] The discontent of the two main parties in opposition —the Pakistan Muslim League (PML-N) and the Pakistan People's Party—was evident in the Charter of Democracy of 2006.[70] What about the lawyers?

---

[66]MP Awan, Separation of Judiciary: Bit by Bit, *PLD* (2001) Journal Section 99, 102.

[67]*Government of Sindh and others v Mst. Sirtaj Bibi and another*, PLD 2001 Karachi 442. This case was about the *Land Acquisition Act* 1984 where the Sindh Government acquired land and took a possession of it but challenged the compensation evaluated by the collector. Later the govt. withdrew from the acquisition. District judge did not reduce the amount of compensation and the matter went into the High Court which ordered to de-notify all the notification regarding acquisition proceedings. There is no such provision in *Land Acquisition Act* 1984 such that the court can do this.

[68]I Ahmad, Former Federal Secretary, Separation of Powers, *PLD* (2002) Journal Section 237.

[69]S Jamil, The Independence of Judiciary, International Jurists Conference, Islamabad, Pakistan (2006) 10, 12.

[70]They recommended an independent commission which would consist of 50% from the ruling coalition and 50% from the opposition. This charter was signed between the leaders of the PPP headed by BB and that of PML-N headed by Nawaz Sharif in London on 14 May 2006. Paras 3 and 4 of Section A (Constitutional Amendments) were concerned with appointment of judiciary and the role of judiciary in constitutional manners. For the appointment of judges, a commission was proposed consisting of judiciary and Bar Councils representatives and provincial and central law officers. This commission would forward three names for each vacancy to Prime Minister who will move one name for each vacancy to a Joint Parliamentary Committee consisting of fifty members of opposition and the ruling party. There were also provisions in the Charter for the abolition of Anti-terrorism and Accountability courts (3(d)). To bring about democracy within the

The bar had already put forth the idea of a Judicial Commission comprising the bar, the bench and people involved in the appointment and removal of the judiciary.[71] This proposal was blatantly in favour of the bench and bar minimizing the role of legislature. The proposal of the potential legislature, (including the Pakistan People's Party and Pakistan Muslim League, PML-N), an agreement signed as the Charter of Democracy, was critiqued by the bar, as it was obvious that the Charter conferred "a disproportionate high degree of discretion in the Prime Minister and the Joint Parliamentary Committee".[72]

5.4.3 Supremacy of the Constitution as Supremacy of the Judiciary

Ultimately, the judiciary established its supremacy by invoking the supremacy of the constitution. In the 1970s, the judiciary had an explicit stance that it was not above the constitution and could not strike down any provisions of the constitution, even if a particular provision ousted the jurisprudence of the Court.[73] Until 1988, Pakistani courts were reluctant to assume the functions of the legislature and always interpreted under well-settled canons of the construction.[74]

From the mid-1990s, the new constitutional construction was done through three areas: constitutional litigation, alternate rulings that have social consequences, and through rulings regarding how to balance opposing societal interests or values.[75]

(Footnote 70 continued)

judiciary itself Chief Justice was bound to exercise its powers with two senior most judges (3(d)). An important aspect of this Charter was the proposal of a Federal Constitutional Court to resolve constitutional and let the Supreme Court and High Courts hear regular civil and criminal cases.

[71]Pakistan Bar Council, White Paper on the Role of Judiciary (June 2003) 43. The members of the bench included Chief Justice (chairman), two senior most judges of the Supreme Court, Chief Justices of the High Courts. Members of the bar in this composition are Vice Chairman of Pakistan Bar Council, the President of SCBA, four presidents of HCBAs at the principle seats of HCs. Members from the legislature were one member from the ruling party, one nominated by the leader of opposition, one member of senate from each province.

[72]Khan, *supra* note 35, 567.

[73]*State v Zia-ur-Rahman*, PLD 1973 SC 49, is a particular case in this regard which is already discussed in Chap. 4.

[74]SM Haider (1988) claimed this on the basis of observation of Justice S. M Murshed Chief Justice East Pakistan High Court in *Abdus Sattar v Arag Ltd. and others*, PLD 1964 Dacca 773. See SM Haider, American Constitution and Assimilation of Modern Legal Norms in Pakistan, *PLD* (1988) Journal Section 121.

[75]AG Chaudhry, Half- Hundred Canons of Constitutional Construction, *PLJ* (1994) Journal Section 74, 75.

This opened up many possible methods of political governance.[76] The constitution and amendments in themselves undermined the legislature. Apart from 58(2)(b), the Shariat Bill of 1985 and the 1986 Constitution Bill (9th Amendment) created structures above the legislature. The former created a non-legislative body to oversee Islamization programmes, whereas the latter made the Federal Shariat Court as a kind of supreme government body.[77] The Objective Resolution[78] put a supernatural authority over the elective representatives. The Federal Shariat Court acquired the role of a supra-legislature body and, by declaring any law unconstitutional, it undermined legislature.[79]

Sajjad Ali asserted the supremacy of the constitution to be a 'positive contribution' and that it was the right of the judiciary to interpret the constitution, even to the extent of finding solutions to the legal and political crisis as a practical mechanism for the 'governance' of a developed and a developing country.[80] Similarly, his immediate successor or parallel Chief Justice Ajmal Mian[81] also believed in a whole system of governance in accordance with the letter and spirit of the constitution. He considered the rule of law as *sine qua non* for good governance, and the economic progress of a country,[82] as laying the basis for the full concept of constitutional governance in the future. This 'constitutional arrangement' was not to be changed for a democratic regime,[83] but only when asked by a military

---

[76]Journey of progressive approach from Munir to Haleem goes through from the comments of Munir Chief Justice Federal Court in *Jibendra Kishore v East Pakistan*, PLD 1957 SC 942, to Cornelius, Chief Justice Supreme Court, in *Abdul Aala Mounddodi v Govt of West Pakistan*, PLD 1964 SC 673, to Chief Justice Haleem in *Benazir Bhuttoo v Federation of Pakistan*, PLD 1988 SC 416, to *Benazir Bhutto v. Federation of Pakistan*, PLD 1989 SC 66. Later, in 1993, Nasim made a clear statement in favour of progressive approach in *Muhammad Nawaz Sharif v Federation of Pakistan*, PLJ 1993 SC 473.

[77]Chaudhary M. Altaf Hussain (1986) Ninth Amendment and Shariat Bills - Some Aspects, *Dawn*, (21 October, 1986) as cited by Newberg. See PR Newberg, *Judging the State: Courts and Constitutional Politics in Pakistan* (Cambridge University Press, New Delhi, 1995) 196.

[78]It became the part of the Constitution in Article 2A as amended by Zia.

[79]Before 1979, HCs declared some laws as being against Holy Quran and Sunnah. Appeals were heard against this in Shariat Appellate Bench of the Supreme Court comprised of Ulema. The FSC bypassed the Supreme Court and heard appeals against the trials of *Huddood* cases. It infringed the independence and sovereignty of the parliament as it could review the law as being Islamic or not. But Nasim Hasan Shah, Supreme Court Chief Justice while reflecting on the future of judiciary in Pakistan clearly stated that Federal Shariat Court, Appellate Shariat Bench in the Supreme Court are not parallel judicial systems and they are integrated because of the supervision of Supreme Court over them. See NH Shah, Administration of Justice *PLD* (1994) Journal Section 123, an address to the course participants of the National Defense College, Rawalpindi on 31 October 1993.

[80]SA Shah, CJSC (as he then was), Process of Constitution-making in Pakistan and the Role of Judiciary, *PLD* (1995) Journal Section 123, 128.

[81]Keeping in view the controversy during Nawaz regime in 1997 mentioned in Chap. 5.

[82]A Mian, CJSC (as he then was), Seminar on the Rule of Law, *PLD* (1999) Journal Section 128. This was a speech delivered on 3 June 1999.

[83]*Mahmood Khan Achakzai v Federation of Pakistan*, PLD 1997 SC 426.

ruler.[84] Furthermore, it is argued that the power of judicial review is given to the judiciary by the constitution, which was enacted by the people of Pakistan through their elected representatives and hence is a 'democratic power'.[85]Due to the role of the judiciary in national life, it was said that it had become "a national forum for achieving consensus[86]". If the judiciary is to run democracy, what is the role of mainstream legal parties?

5.4.4 Opposition: Correcting the Judiciary Before Democracy

In this situation, it was meaningless for the opposition to speak about democracy without reducing the powers of the judiciary. Here, it is important to understand Benazir Bhutto's approach to 'political governance'. Benazir Bhutto needed support and aid from democracies[87] like the U.S. and U.K. For her, General Musharraf's decision to stand with America after 9/11[88] was the right one, and Professor Huntington correctly pointed out the clash of civilizations, as, in her words, "Al-Qaeda will try to provoke the clashes of civilization".[89] This was not inevitable[90] and could be prevented, she argued, but only if the U.S. relied on her, as she claimed the Pakistan People's Party was the only civilian and political structure with popular support to form government outside the intelligence agencies and the military.[91]

Benazir Bhutto did not forget that she was speaking in the era of 'good governance'. Her views came to overlap with the trends in global modernization. The reliance on American concepts was inevitable as even the U.K. was relying heavily on this paradigm.[92] She stressed the importance of rights and 'governance' to

---

[84]As done by the judiciary in LFO case, *Pakistan Lawyers Forum v Federation of Pakistan*, PLD 2005 SC 719. The case against the LFO was heard by a five—member bench headed by Justice Nazim Hussain Siddiqui, Supreme Court Chief Justice, and dismissed on 13 April 2005.

[85]JF Karim, JSC (retd as he then was), Judicial Review on Administrative Actions, 6th International Jurists Conference, Islamabad, Pakistan (2006).

[86]SA Zafar, The Role of Supreme Court in Contemporary Age, 6th International Jurists Conference, Islamabad, Pakistan (2006).

[87]Commencement address at Harvard University on 8 June1989.

[88]B Bhutto (2004), Concentrating power in One Institution has Negative Consequences, in, SS Bokhari (ed) *Benazir Bhutto (*2006*): Speeches and Statements* (Musawat Publications, Islamabad, 2006) 83, 87. This was an address at Woodrow Wilson Center, Washington DC on 9 February 2004.

[89]B Bhutto (2005), Democracies Do Not Make War against Other Democracies, *Bhutto ibid*, 139, 140. This was an address to the Writers, Intellectuals in Florida, U.S. on 8 March 2005.

[90]B Bhutto (2007), in, DI Narejo (ed) *Whither Pakistan*: *Dictatorship or Democracy?* (Al-Hamd Publications, Lahore, 2007) 58.

[91]*Ibid* 243.

[92]Haider, *supra* note 72, 129.

undermine terrorism and the need to empower citizens and build a society "on the edifice of the majesty of law". Rights were the core value of her 'governance'. She stated that debt relief should be tied to good governance. For her, rule of law came before democracy, as a country needs the rule of law more than democratic elections.[93] The move should be from a civil society to a democratic society, as this was the pattern around the world and the case in Europe and America.[94] She quoted George Bush, saying "men and women in every culture need liberty like they need food and water and air".[95] She argued that poverty defamed the image of India and Pakistan[96] and 'good policy' was the key solution. For Benazir Bhutto, leadership was the courage to take actions that are necessary in the long run but *not popular* [my emphasize].[97] She claimed leaders should not follow opinion surveys for decisions, but like the American President Franklin Delano Roosevelt, to know where the people stand and then educate and lead them.

She was not in a hurry for democracy and wanted it to evolve, claiming that for this to happen, there needed to first be an independent and impartial judiciary. Democracy cannot function if a handful of judges follow their own political agenda and distrust political leaders, she argued. Benazir Bhutto summed up the last half a century in Pakistan as a "century of law, politics and a politicized judiciary" and complained that, as a Prime Minister, she was twice denied the right to appoint judges. During the Nawaz Sharif regime (1997–99), "we are crushed under a mountain of litigation", she said, as that regime believed in incapacitating the leader of the opposition through judicial abuse. Some examples of legal abuse that she gave were that four hours before the judgment, there was a government order that froze her funds. No contempt petition against the regime was heard. Also, judges who worked for the Prime Minister's family business tried Benazir Bhutto. One judge's son was working with the lead parliamentarian of the ruling party. Another judge worked as the Deputy Attorney General when Benazir Bhutto was behind bars for nearly six months, and his father sentenced Benazir Bhutto's father. Benazir Bhutto fired him but his brother was elected as a parliamentarian from the Prime Minister's home constituency. He wrote the order to convict Benazir Bhutto before the trial was over. The nephew of a General who hanged her father, Z.A. Bhutto, was appointed unanimously by the Supreme Court to try her husband, Asif Ali Zardari.

---

[93]Bhutto, *supra* note 88, 47, 50. This was an address at the Conference to Commemorate Women's Week in South Africa, Johannesburg on 07 August 2001.

[94]Bhutto, *supra* note 88, 63. This was speech on Civil Society and Women's Participation in Political Process, Rome, Italy on 18 July 2003.

[95]*Ibid.*

[96]Bhutto, *supra* note 88, 81. This was an address at a meeting of professional Women San Jose-USA on 18 November 1 2003.

[97]B Bhutto (1999), I am Determined not to let Down Those who Believe in a Democratic, Modern, Moderate, Muslim State, in, SS Bokhari (ed) *Benazir Bhutto (2006): Speeches and Statements* (Musawat Publications, Islamabad, 2006) 17. This was an address at SDPI Seminar, Islamabad on 5 March 1999.

According to her, women-hating, bigoted judges with gender, political and theocratic biases were lined up against her and her family. The same judge who tried Zardari refused help when a woman was killed in an honour killing. Another judge trying Benazir Bhutto was so biased against women that the Human Rights Commission of Pakistan-HRCP complained against him. He believed that women had no right to work.[98] While some judges had taken loans from state banks and were under pressure. Benazir Bhutto was so scared of the courts that she refused to return back to Pakistan and fight for democracy, believing that all her time would be wasted in courts.[99]

For the solution, she asked the international community to step forward and assist in the process of instituting the rule of law in Pakistan. She wrote to the UN Rapporteur on Judges and the Judiciary, the former British Attorney General Sir John Morris and two American Chief Justices, outlining the judicial abuse she was suffering. Morris and the two American judges found her conviction flawed. She complained that if the West condemned judicial political victimization in Burma, then why not in Pakistan?[100] She suggested that Pakistan needed 'judicial accountability', and proposed changing the contempt law to allow free public scrutiny of judgments when delivered. She requested the UN Rapporteur on Judges and Judiciary fund NGOs to investigate wrongful prosecution and trials. "Unless judges and Generals are accountable along with Prime Ministers and Parliamentarians, power can and will be abused", she explained. Referring to the Pakistani Human Rights groups, she put forward a proposal for a separate constitutional court to deal with constitutional issues. She also suggested changing the law of conflict of interest, since judges who had a conflict of interest with Benazir Bhutto and her party were insisting on sitting on the benches. Furthermore, the parliament was an independent organ of the government and there should be a parliamentary investigation in case of impropriety, she said, adding that opposition leaders should be equally represented in this investigation.[101]

5.4.5 The Liberal Legal Project

Those who championed the liberal project were disenchanted with the democratic regimes of the 1990s. By the 1999 coup, they came to the conclusion that decentralization was the solution, and part of good governance. That is why the NGO

[98]Bhutto, *supra* note 88, 25, 26, 33. This was an address at the Commonwealth Ethnic Bar Associations on 30 October 2000.

[99]B Bhutto (2007), BBC Interview, in, DI Narejo (ed) *Whither Pakistan: Dictatorship or Democracy?* (Al-Hamd Publications, Lahore, 2007) 189.

[100]*Ibid*, 181.

[101]*Ibid*, 101.

elite[102] was part of Musharraf's coup with Omar Ashgar (a Marxist turned social democrat) as a Minister in Musharraf's new set up. The dilemma for liberals was how to correct the 'overdeveloped state',[103] as well as how to correct democracy because the feudals continued to be in power. Decentralization, as a part of 'good governance', seemed a point of compromise between the 'neoliberal metropolitan bourgeoisie', and the rising 'liberal' petit bourgeoisie (the liberal layer of 'civil society'). The former wanted to get rid of 'state capture', which was a nexus of politicians and civil bureaucracy.[104] The latter wanted a share in the new developmental paradigm and the inclusion of 'social' in good governance.[105] Practically, they wanted to get rid of the feudals through land reforms to correct democracy, but who could do it?[106] The only option was to at least get rid of the 'centralized state'.

Shahrukh Rafi Khan gave a cost-benefit analysis of decentralization and local government to the National Reconstruction Bureau to convince them that the project was viable.[107] He offered the example of the Banuri's project[108] and argued that the governance issue was a 'power issue'. For him, the district administration and courts served the large landlords. Therefore, even if the land is distributed, there would be police and court abuse, and that the courts would not let land reforms happen. The only solution to him was decentralization of financial and

[102]I am using this term in a very loose sense of the term 'project'. I mean foreign funded NGO related liberal research and rights projects as a whole. SDPI and its writers are just one example, but there are many others. NGOs are dominated by upper class liberals in Pakistan. Their projects shifted with the changing priorities and politics of the IFIs. Omar Asghar was running a well-established NGO named 'Sanghi'.

[103]The concept developed for postcolonial state by Hamza Alavi and discussed in Chap. 1 of this book.

[104]When the paradigm could not bear fruit in 2000s, its own architects blamed 'state capture' (a form of elite corruption) in countries with developing and transitional economies. For instance, promoters of the World Bank project, Kaufmann and Kraay, have argued that 'state capture' by the elite is the "illicit influence of the elite in shaping the laws, policies and regulations of the state". This results in a negative effect of per capita income on governance in developing and transitional economies because the fruits of the growth go to benefit a certain elite. The phenomenon is observed by the writers in transitional economies of the former socialist bloc. They recall 'historical' evidence of the influence of 'robber barons' in the United States at the turn of the 20th century and crony capitalism in the Philippines under Marcos. This is indicative of 'misgovernance' by the writers. See D Kaufmann and A Kraay, Growth without Governance, Policy Research Working Paper No. 2928 (2002) 30.

[105]Rittich, *supra* note 7.

[106]SR Khan, A Qadir, AS Akhtar, A Saleem & F Sadiq, The Case for Land and Agrarian Reforms in Pakistan, Policy Brief Series #12, SDPI, Islamabad, Pakistan (2001) 1.

[107]SR Khan, Costing the National Reconstruction Bureau's Local Government Plan (2000), Policy Research Series#1, SDPI, Islamabad, Pakistan (2000).

[108]T Banuri, Ahmad, & Afzal, Democratic Decentralization in Nature, Power, People: Citizen's Report on Sustainable Development, SDPI, Islamabad, Pakistan (1995).

administrative authority.[109] Women's rights-based NGOs welcomed the reserved seats for women in his local government plan.[110]

This argument of good governance through decentralization was made on the basis of the liberal and connected liberal legal project of the Sustainable Development Policy Institute-SDPI collective, this was also built on SDPI's 1992 work.[111] This suggested that the formal legal system in Pakistan is workable and the only problem is governance, case management, delay reduction, automation, the court information system, human resources and infrastructure.[112] The 'liberal legal project' also clearly placed its position in line with recommendations of the S.A. Rahman Commission (1958), the Hamood-ur-Rahman Commission (1967–70), the Law Committee (1978), as well as the Commission on Reform of Civil Law (1993).[113] It opposed the Jirga system (North Western Frontier Province-NWFP) and the Panchyat system (in Punjab) because, according to the writers, both were losing their effectiveness due to extraneous influences.[114] Tariq Banuri, while suggesting these organizational reforms, pointed out that he avoided the topic of a parallel judicial system (because the judiciary was reacting to it) and hence gave the opinion of overhauling the existing mainstream system, particularly at the lower level. He recommended four 'Is', namely; incentives, institutions (internal and external accountability institutions), infrastructure for 'efficiency' and infrastructure (judicial courts buildings equipment).[115]

The liberal project thus weakened the state apparatus without furthering democracy. In this effort, the stake of the metropolitan bourgeoisie was not neglected, but was integrated along with the role of NGOs as 'civil society' to steer good governance. These changes reflected a deep frustration with the liberal

---

[109] SR Khan, Devolution of Power to the Grassroots Level, Policy Paper Series#25, SDPI, Islamabad (2000).

[110] SG Khatak, Women and Local Government, Working paper Series#24, SDPI, Islamabad (1996).

[111] M Yasin & T Banuri (eds) *The Dispensation of Justice in Pakistan* (Oxford University Press and Islamabad: SDPI, Karachi, 2004). Tariq Banuri included his essay of 1992 as a first essay in this book at 3-43. Dr. Faqir wrote a piece about PIL in the same book at 58-72.

[112] M Yasin & S Shah, System of Justice, in, M Yasin & T Banuri (eds) *The Dispensation of Justice in Pakistan* (Oxford University Press and Islamabad: SDPI, Karachi, 2004) 93, 111.

[113] Mohammad Yasin had contempt for lawyers and found that dropouts joined the legal profession. He himself had been a brigadier. He found the legal profession overcrowded. See Yasin, Administration of Justice in Pakistan, *ibid* 75, 87; see also Yasin, Attempts at Reforms, *ibid*, 151, 152.

[114] The essay was concluded in 1993 but since then, according to the writer, the situation changed. HCs and the Supreme Court tried to bring Frontier Crime Regulation, etc. under their regular court system. It backfired and a movement of Sharia and Qazi courts started which ended operation in Swat in 2000 s. See SS Ali & K Arif, Traditional/Alternative Dispute Resolution Mechanism in Pakistan,, *ibid,* 115, 133.

[115] Banuri, Improving the Provision of Justice in Pakistan, *ibid*, 169.

project, whose proponents were deeply confused as to what was going on.[116] The clichés that Pakistan is not an agricultural country, as well as, Pakistan is a rural country were defeated.[117] There was a 'statistically' proven middle class, but analysts of 'liberal' legal and political project questioned why the liberal institutional arrangements/rearrangements were not working. Why was there no socially responsible modern and democratic middle class?[118]

While analyzing Musharraf after 1999, after seven pages, Akbar Zaidi ran out of room for further comments. He presented Musharraf's politics as the politics of opportunism and argued that he was a person who "merely stated the obvious".[119] The main anxiety of the liberal project was that 'Good Governance' assistance in critical policy areas (administrative and political reforms) led to the disproportional policy influence of foreign donors. Musharraf used this discontent[120] to strengthen himself, whereas it could have been used to bring much needed changes in the state's 'behaviour' and even 'identity' as a member of twenty-first century international society.[121] The military was not providing sufficient finances for social development.[122]

For the liberal legal project, the main objective of international donors for improvement of the government was to make the country more 'market-friendly'. This objective was to be meant through supervision of the civil society though it was absent from practice.[123] The project was not cost effective as an enormous amount was being spent on consultation and similar activities. Even if they were cost effective, laws are not necessary for improving justice for the poor, rather they are a burden, under the good governance approach. There is no word of participatory democracy in their project. There is no mention of obligations of a just state.[124] They insisted that the Access to Justice Program should bind the state with the UN Conventions on Social, Economic and Political Rights and ILO Declaration

---

[116]SA Zaidi, Continuity Rather than Change: Elections 2002, in, *Continuity and Change: Socio-Political and Institutional Dynamics in Pakistan* (City Press, Karachi, 2003) 175.

[117]S Akbar Zaidi, *Issues in Pakistan's Economy*, 5th edn (Oxford University Press, Karachi, 2009). S. Akbar Zaidi claimed in his introduction that agriculture was now capitalist and the 'feudal lord' is now a capitalist farmer. There were only pockets of 'feudal' tendencies. His claim is based on Reza Ali's work. See Reza Ali, Underestimating Urbanization, *ibid* 127.

[118]Zaidi pointed out the rise of *arthi*, transporter as the new middle classes in rural areas as well as the division of landholdings as a reason of demise of feudal power. See SA Zaidi, *Pakistan's Social and Economic Development: The Domestic, Regional and Global Context* (Rupa Co, New Delhi, 2004) 11.

[119]Zaidi, The Politics of Opportunism, *supra* note 116, 85.

[120]A Shah, Aiding Authoritarianism? Donors, Dollars and Dictators, in, CH Kennedy & CA Botteron (eds) *Pakistan: 2005* (Oxford University Press, Karachi, 2005) 51.

[121]DT Hagerty, The United States-Pakistan Entente: Third Times' a Charm?, Baxter, *supra* note 34, 1, 2.

[122]AS Agha, The Political Economy of National Security, Zaidi, *supra* note 116, 101, 113.

[123]A Ercelawn & M Nauman, Market-Based Justice: The Asian Development Bank and Legal Reforms, Zaidi, *supra* note 116, 151.

[124]*Ibid.*

of Principles. This way, the state will become pro-poor. This critique emphasized the inability of Access to Justice Program-AJP in not considering the state as a part of the problem of injustice and how judiciary itself is the part of the state.[125]

While the liberal legal project was coopted with Musharraf in good governance, is it not an irony that the 'quasi-liberal' project (Cornelius tradition) was on the forefront of fighting against the military–judiciary alliance. Lawyers from the exiled Nawaz and Hamid Khan professional groups were against the pretentious 'liberal project' under Musharraf. The Provisional Constitutional Order-PCO courts did not decide a single case against the military regime, but rather supported it in cases, such as imposition of emergency, the referendum, appointment of junior judges, graduation bar for contesting elections, etc. All this frustrated the Cornelius tendency to the level that Hamid Khan took back the Junior Judges Elevation case, submitting the statement that "since the judiciary is no more independent, we do not want to proceed with the case".[126] This group was responsible for the lawyers' movement, which was later joined by Pakistan People's Party and the frustrated the liberal project.

5.5 Judiciary as Custodian of Global Modernity Under 'Good Governance': Steering the Juridico-Bureaucratic Structure (2000–2006)

A simple electronic search on the main Pakistan law site of the words 'good governance' nicely illustrates how the judiciary adopted the World Bank's good governance paradigm. The phrase 'good governance' appears in one case in 1996, and once again in 1998. As soon as Musharraf announced 'good governance' for the country and the Asian Development Bank efforts to loans for good governance in Pakistan started, the use of this word increases, to five cases in 2000, and five, six, eight and nine in 2002, 2003, 2004 and 2005, respectively. This was a period of close alliance between the judiciary with Musharraf. In the disputed years of 2006, 2007 and 2008, the number of cases including the phrase of good governance is three, three and two, respectively. When again in 2009, 2010 and 2011, the judiciary turned up as the sole custodian of good governance in Pakistan, the phrase was referred to five, eight and sixteen times, respectively. The details of these cases can further illustrate the nature of the role of the judiciary in adopting the good governance discourse.

Whereas Musharraf was getting legitimacy around good governance, the courts were also harping on the chorus of "democracy, good governance [and] economic stability" and also ensuring that the judiciary is independent as a prerequisite of it.[127] The judiciary agreed with the corruption campaign against the politicians for the sake

[125] *Ibid* 156.

[126] Maluka, *supra* note 34, 53, 75.

[127] *Zafar Ali Shah v Pervez Musharraf*, 2000 SCMR 1137.

of good governance.[128] When Musharraf began his decentralization plan to limit the powers of the bureaucracy, the judiciary claimed it stood with good governance as an idiom for "upright, honest and strong bureaucracy".[129] Cases were launched that reflected on local governance and decentralization as package of good governance.[130] We can see "settled principles of good governance" in judicial decisions.[131] Good governance adopted the form of a 'doctrine' for equality of justice, welfare of the people and to reduce income and earning inequality by the judiciary.[132]

Over time, the judiciary's domain of 'good governance' expanded and started encompassing issues such as the norms of transparency,[133] health education,[134] allocation of welfare funds and schemes.[135] The judiciary also opined as to the future likelihood of good governance.[136] For Supreme Court Chief Justice Nazim Hussain Siddiqui, "good governance is a key to progress, development and ultimate prosperity".[137] Furthermore, for him, the "rule of law is the most important thing".[138] For Supreme Court Chief Justice Iftikhar, "institutions are the units of the system of governance", which indicate the strength or weakness of any polity.[139] Rule of law as an 'essential component' of good governance[140] became "the rule of good governance", until 2008.[141]

After Musharraf, it seems that the judiciary alone was the initiator and custodian of good governance. It actively intervened in different state departments in regards

---

[128]PLD 2000 SC 869.

[129]*Shamas-ul-Bahadar v Nasir Ahmed*, PLD 2002 SC 68. See also *The Province of Punjab v IbrarYounasButt*, PSC 2003 SC 1357.

[130]*Muhammad Ramzan and 3 others v Govt of Pak.*, 2004 YLR 1856; *Clifton Centre Association (CCA) Clifton, Karachi v City District Government*, PLD 2003 KHC-Sindh 477.

[131]*Zaka Ullah Bajwa v Chief Secretaryi Govt. of the Punjab, Lahore*, 2005 SCMR 13.

[132]*Ikram Bari and 524 others v National Bank of Pakistan*, 2005 SCMR 100.

[133]*Sheri-CBE and others v Lahore Development Authority*, 2006 SCMR 1202. See also *Govt. of NWFP v Muhammad Tufail Khan*, PLD 2004 SC 313; *Iqbal Akbar v Province of Sindh*, 2002 MLD 1835.

[134]*University of the Health Science Lahore v Sh. Nasir Subhani*, PLD 2006 SC 243 (against grace marks given to a student).

[135]PLD 2007 Lahore 61.

[136]In the Matter of: Reference No.2 of 2005 by the President of Pakistan, PLD 2005 SC 873.

[137]NH Siddiqui, CJSC, Speech: the 24th Certificates Awarding Ceremony for the Additional Districts & Session Judges/Participants of the 24th Training Course at the Federal Judicial Academy, Islamabad, *PLD* (2004) Journal Section 65, 66.

[138]NH Siddiqui, CJSC, Address by Mr. Justice Nazim Hussain Siddiqui, Supreme Court Chief Justice on the Commencement of Judicial Year, 2004-2005, *PLD* (2004) Journal Section 111.

[139]IM Chaudhry, Address at the Opening Ceremony of Judicial Year 2006-2007, *PLJ* (2006) Journal Section 353.

[140]*Syed Yaqoob Shah v XEN, PESCO (WAPDA), Peshawar*, PLD 2002 SC 667.

[141]*Mumtaz Sultana v State Bank of Pakistan*, PLC 2008 KHC-Sindh.

to transfers, appointment, promotion and benefits.[142] As the judiciary emerged from the struggle to uphold the rule of law through the lawyers' movement it strongly asserted its rule of law stance to steer the good governance of the country.[143] The judiciary stood for overarching good governance, even in 2008, when the elected government was in power. The range of the judiciary's good governance interference expanded not only in number, but also in scope. For example, the judiciary took a stand against discretionary powers "without application of mind"[144] by the bureaucracy, and it also intervened in issues relating to institution building,[145] how institutions operated,[146] hiring and firing in institutions,[147] completion of government-contracted projects, policy matters,[148] delegated legislation,[149] tort law,[150] police,[151] law and order and security,[152] confidence of investors,[153] and not

[142]*Safdar Ali Shahito v Province of Sindh through Chief Sec. Sindh*, PLC 2011 KHC-Sindh 956; *Atta Ullah Khan Malik v Fed of Govt. of Pak. Through President of Pak.*, PLD 2010 Lahore 605; *Lal Khan v Employee Old Age Benefit Institution through Chairman*, PLC 2010 KHC-Sindh 1377 (against posting); *Muhammad Furqan v Speaker of National Assembly*, PLC 2010 Islamabad 1013; *Tahira Qureshi v Azad Govt. of the State of Jammu and Kashmir through Chief Sec.*, PLC 2010 HC-Court-Azad Kashmir 209; *Sameena Parveen v Govt. of Punjab through Secretary Education, Civil Secretariat, Lahore*, 2009 SCMR 1 (extending benefits in one decision to all); see also *Tara Chand v Karachi Water and Sewerage Board, Karachi*, PSC 2005 SC 368; see also *Muhammad Abbas v Govt. of Punjab and others*, PSC2005 Lahore 671; *Haji Muhammad Ismail Memon, advocate v Haji Muhammad Ismail Memon, advocate*, PLD 2007 SC 35 (incident of death of an old retired civil servant and his wife was brought in the notice of Supreme Court directly); *Binyamin Masih v Govt of Punjab through Secretary Education*, 2005 SCMR 1032 (lack of efficiency).

[143]*Tariq Azizuddin v Fed. Of Pak.*, 2011 S.C 1130; see also *Mst. Iffat Nazir v Govt. of Punjab through Secretary of Population Welfare Department*, PLC 2011SC1124; see also 2010 SCMR 1301.

[144]*Majeeb Ahmad v Province of Sindh through Chief Sec. of Sindh*, 2011 PLC 1193.

[145]*Imran Hussain v WAPDA*, 2011 PLC 116; *Imran Hussain v WAPDA through chairman WAPDA*, PLD 2010 Lahore 546.

[146]*Muhammad Aslam v Vice-Chairman*, 2010 PLC 266.

[147]Job contracts like the no reason clause (without assigning any reason), *Samina Kanwal v Director Forestry Research Institute Faisalabad, Punjab*, 2011 PLC 1553.

[148]Unreasoned orders, *Ashfaq Hussain v Govt of Punjab*, 2011 PLC 799.

[149]*Khalid Mahmood v NWFP through Chief Sec Peshawar*, PLD 2011 Pesh 120; see also *Messrs Gul Cooking Oil and Vegetable Ghee (Pvt.) Ltd. Through Chief Executive v Pakistan through Chairman Revenue Division, CBR, Islamabad*, PLD 2007 Pesh 39 (legislative powers of the president in the tribal areas cannot be delegated to provincial assembly).

[150]*Islamic Republic of Pakistan v Abdul Wahid*, 2011 SCMR 1836.

[151]PLD 2011 SC 277; *Suo Muto* Case No. 24 of 2010; and HR Case No. 57701-P, 57719-G, 57754-P, 58152-P, 59060-P, 54187-P and 58118-K of 2010.

[152]*Watan Party v Federation of Pakistan*, PLD 2011 SC 997.

[153]*Engro Fertilizer Ltd. v Islamic Republic of Pakistan and Federation of Pakistan*, PLD 2012 Karachi 50. In this case, the plaintiff spent US $1 billion and the government was not giving gas. See also *Pakaposhi Flour Mills Jaglote through Manzoor Mir v Provincial Govt. through Chief Sec. Gilgit-Baltistan* (right of freedom of trade and business).

to mention fundamental rights.[154] For the judiciary, good governance was the demand of the day.[155]

The interesting aspect of all these cases is that governance is promoted quite apart from planning with its sequencing and pacing in political and economic development, but good for all times. Good governance is uncritically accepted and disconnected with social and economic issues, as well as the overall state and society. Other options to advance political and economic development are absent from the judiciary's concerns.

The rule of law was *sine qua non* for good governance and economic progress of a country,[156] and there is no need to emphasize that the same trajectory too course in the U.S. Just a cursory glance at the books in Pakistan's Federal Judicial Academy reveals that most texts focus either on the U.S. legal system or Islamic law. As a member of the World Trade Organization, each and every sphere of law in Pakistan were amended, repealed and/or enacted in these years.[157] These laws affected local industry and agriculture significantly, but there is no legal analysis of them. Instead, there is only rhetoric emphasizing these laws were necessary for market economy under the World Trade Organization legal regime and World Bank Good Governance.

The height of this thrust of the internationalization of laws can be seen in the resolutions taken up at the International Jurists conference held in Pakistan in 2006. It was emphasized there that developing countries should follow the international commitments of Intellectual Property-IP laws as they are in the interest of the nation.[158] Similarly, there was significant stress on adopting the Rules of Arbitration of the International Chambers of Commerce to get foreign

---

[154] *Muhammad Yasin v Federation of Pakistan*, PLD 2012 SC 132.

[155] *Amir Farooq v Govt of Pakistan through Ministry of Housing and Works*, 2012 PLC (CS) 153; also *Watan Party v Federation of Pakistan*, PLD 2012 SC 292.

[156] A Mian, CJSC (as he then was), Speech Delivered at a Seminar on Rule of Law dated 3-6-1999, *PLD* (1999) Journal Section 128.

[157] There was a range of laws which paved the path for the introduction of a market economy in Pakistan: *Anti-Dumping Duties Ordinance*, 2000, *Countervailing Duties Ordinance*, 2001, *Safeguard Measures Ordinance*, 2002, are a direct result of WTO regime. The laws not alluding to GATT and WTO are: *Intellectual Property Organization of Pakistan Ordinance*, 2005; *Public Procurement Regulatory Authority Ordinance*, (2002); *Industrial Relations Ordinance*, 2002; *Board of Investment Ordinance*, 2000; *Privatization Commission Ordinance*, 2000; *Trade Marks Ordinance*, 2000; *Patents Ordinance*, 2000; *Registered Designs Ordinance*, 2000; *Registered Lay-Out Designs of Integrated Circuits Ordinance*, 2000; *Securities & Exchange Commission of Pakistan Act*, 1997 There were amendments also made in the *Customs Act*, 1969 lowering import tariffs.

[158] 6th International Jurists Conference on IP Laws and Globalization, Islamabad, Pakistan (2006); see also K Mansoor, Intellectual Property Law and Globalization, 6th International Jurists Conference, Islamabad, Pakistan (2006); see also HI Khan, Intellectual Property Law and Globalization, 6th International Jurists Conference, Islamabad, Pakistan (2006).

investment.[159] Alternative Dispute Resolution (ADR) was the main component of the judicial reforms and the assurance was given that the "necessary legal framework for Alternative Dispute Resolution-ADR in Pakistan is laid down".[160] Until 2006, jurists were clear that ADR was a necessary evolution from commercial litigation, without being tied to any juristic philosophy.[161] International environmental standards, even market-led ones, such as the International Standard Organization—ISO certification, were seen as positive, as was child labour certification, which refused goods from Pakistan produced by child labour.[162] An international human rights discourse was adopted, accepted and acknowledged by national courts very quickly.[163] Given the largely unregulated market economy, consumer protection and related legislation was requested from the state.[164]

Laws, the rule of law, and the role of the judiciary, according to the judiciary in Pakistan, were seen as a 'qualified human good' as opposed to E.P. Thompson's, 'unqualified human good'.[165] Yet, it has to be observed that foreign funds poured in from the Asian Development Bank to allow these developments and a Federal Judicial Academy to oversee judicial reforms was established.[166] There was so

---

[159]N Sarwar, New ICC Arbitration Rules to Enter into Force on First January, *PLJ* (1998) Magazine Section 32.

[160]NH Siddiqui, CJSC, Access to Justice and Alternate Dispute Resolution, *PLJ* (2004) Magazine Section 378. In this seminar, the advantages and disadvantages of ADR were considered on 02 May 2004; see also IM Chaudhry, Speech, *PLJ* (2004) Magazine Section 378; TH Jilani, JLHC, The Maladies of Delayed Justice and Growth of A.D.R., *PLJ* (2004) Magazine Section 404; see also SSR Rizvi, *PLJ* (2004) Magazine Section 423, the writer was Advocate General Punjab.

[161]In the 6th International Jurists Conference 2006, the jurists found it a matter of urgency that "the *Recognition and Enforcement (Arbitration Agreements and Foreign Arbitral Awards) Ordinance*, 2005 be made an Act of Parliament", "the Washington (ICSID) Convention 1965 be incorporated into Pakistan law", and "the *Arbitration Act*, 1940 be replaced by a law, embodying contemporary norms, which implements the UNCITRAL Model Law on International Commercial Arbitration, 198. See also TH Jilani, Delayed Justice and the Role of ADR, 6th International Jurists Conference, Islamabad, Pakistan (2006).

[162]DP Hassan, The Role of Judiciary and Judicial Commissions on Sustainable Development in Pakistan, 6th International Jurists Conference, Islamabad, Pakistan (2006).

[163]SS Ali, Applying Islamic Criminal Justice in Parallel Systems: Exploring Gender- Sensitive Judicial Responses to Hudood Laws in Pakistan, 6th International Jurists Conference, Islamabad, Pakistan (2006).

[164]DAS Humayan, Consumer v Corporate Sector: Judicature's Role in Balancing the Equation, 6th International Jurists Conference, Islamabad, Pakistan (2006). The writer is a founding director of Consumer Rights Commission of Pakistan (CRCP).

[165]EP Thompson, *Whigs and Hunters*: *The Origins of Black Act* (Penguin Books Ltd, Harmondsworth, 1975) 266.

[166]The federal judicial academy was established in 1988 with the help of Asia Foundation. This idea was first given by Judge Clifford Wallace of a US Circuit Court of Appeals and the Senior Advisor to the Asia Foundation on Legal Education and Judicial Administration to then Supreme Court Chief Justice Muhammad Haleem. See M Haleem, Speech delivered on the Inauguration Ceremony of Federal Judicial Academy, *PLJ* (1988) Magazine Section 143. See also S Akhtar, JSC, In-Service Training for Civil Judges and Judicial Magistrates, *PLD* (2006) Journal

much money for judicial reforms, that either funds were underutilized,[167] or they were forced onto Pakistan, and were then denied by then Minister of Law, Justice and Human Rights, Shahida Jamil.[168] Is it not interesting that the judiciary was asking for financial independence from the executive, but that judicial reforms were a project of financial dependence on International Financial Institutions. One commentator criticized the judicial reforms loans on the grounds that a loan cannot be used to start a programme, only to maintain a programme.[169] A study by Osama Siddique published in 2013 analyzed in detail the law reforms of 2000s as an alien concept of justice but one that attracted disparate champions like the Supreme Court Chief Justice, U.S. aid and the Taliban. I want to add liberals to this group of admirers. The speedy justice in the above pursuits, for Siddique, showed a "remarkable obliviousness to the historical, institutional and sociological factors that alienate Pakistanis from their formal legal system".[170]

A further point worth remembering is that during the 2000s, while the demand of de-linking with U.S. was popular due to drone attacks,[171] the connection of the rule of law and legal projects is always presented as apolitical. There is no footnote even, except when raised by the Supreme Court Chief Justice, in the form of a "global, systematic, military, diplomatic and financial strategy" to deal with terrorism.[172] Gradually, concepts from the "good governance paradigm" entered judgments of the superior courts, as explained above.

(Footnote 166 continued)

Section 19; see also CH Nawaz, Federal Judicial Academy Training of Trainers Workshop Program- August 2002, *PLJ* (2004) Magazine Section 158.

[167]$350 million (Rs. 20 billion) were given by Asian Development Bank, but in 2005, Douglas Porter, the Senior Governance Specialist from President Mission of the ADB had to inform the government that the funds were underutilized. Punjab still has Rs. 337 million out of Rs. 671 million, Sindh got Rs. 277 million but could only utilize Rs. 41 million, NWFP could only Rs. 91 million out of Rs. 226 million and Baluchistan got Rs. 124 million but spent only Rs. 61 million. See W Ahmad, Judicial and Legal Reforms in Pakistan, *PLJ* (2005) Magazine Section 361. For a detailed analysis see also L Armytage, Pakistan's Law and Justice Sector Reforms Experience- Some Lessons, *PLJ* (2004) Journal Section 100.

[168]S Jamil, The Independence of Judiciary, 6th International Jurists Conference, Islamabad, Pakistan (2006) 1, 15. The writer is a Bar at Law and had been the Former Minister of Law, Justice & Human Rights during the Musharraf's regime.

[169]RH Rahi, Access to Justice Program and the Prevailing Judicial System, *PLD* (2006) Journal Section 84, 85.

[170]O Siddique, *Pakistan's Experience with Formal Law: An Alien Justice* (Cambridge University Press, Cambridge, 2013).

[171]Since 9/11, anti-American sentiments grew with 74% of Pakistanis viewing America as an enemy. See *The Global Post* (28 June 2012).

[172]IM Chaudhry, CJSC (as he then was), Terrorism and the Criminal Justice System, International Jurists Conference, Islamabad, Pakistan (2006).

5.5.1 Public Interest Litigation Until 2006: A Comfortable Substitute for Democracy

It was inevitable that the Public Interest Litigation tool in the arsenal was also altered to suit global needs. The future of the world was impossible unless Human Rights were guaranteed and recognized at the national, regional and international levels.[173] Public Interest Litigation represented a new era of judicial culture where courts gave substantive justice and acted as a "catalyst for socio-economic change".[174] Judicial activism and empowerment transformed Public Interest Litigation into a 'silent revolution'[175] or a social engineering project.[176]

The legislature was the continuous target of Public Interest Litigation supporters, and an easy target, as the legislature was manned by feudal forces.[177] The judiciary was to provide social justice.[178] The job of 'salvaging democracy' was on the shoulders of the judiciary.[179] Public Interest Litigation represented the "democratization of access to justice".[180] For Ahmad Rafay Alam, Public Interest Litigation was nurturing a 'stable democracy'.[181] It was seen as a democratic tool as most petitions were against the state which meant that the litigation was a forum for a debate. The denial of writ petitions on technical grounds meant denial of the democratic forum provided by Public Interest Litigation. Furthermore, the increase in Public Interest Litigation cases was seen as an indication that citizens needed an outlet. "In our burgeoning democratic environment, elections alone may be too little and too far apart", Alam explained. His genuine worry was that Public Interest Litigation and the judiciary should not be the only democratic forum, so he suggested a Public Interest Litigation filter that could be a 'democratic alternative'[182]

---

[173] MN Abbasi, JSC, Human Rights in Pakistan: Concepts and History of Human Rights, *PLD* (2004) Journal Section 90.

[174] S Ahmad, CJSHC, Good Governance and the Role of the Judiciary, 6th International Jurists Conference, Islamabad, Pakistan (2006).

[175] S Minallah, Judiciary as a Catalyst for Social Change, 6th International Jurists Conference, Islamabad, Pakistan (2006). The writer was a Research Anthropologist and executive Director of Enthno-Media and Development.

[176] EA Khan, Role of Judiciary in Good Governance, International Jurists Conference, Islamabad, Pakistan (2006).

[177] JJ Iqbal, The Role of Judiciary as a Catalyst of Social Change, 6th International Jurists Conference, Islamabad, Pakistan (2006).

[178] NA Zahid, JSC, The Role of the Judiciary in Protecting the Rights of the People- Judicial Activism, International Jurists Conference, Islamabad, Pakistan (2006).

[179] SMA Shah, CJSC, Salvaging Democracy - Judiciary our Last Hope: Going Beyond Public Interest Litigation, 6th International Jurists Conference, Islamabad, Pakistan (2006) 1.

[180] *Ibid*6.

[181] AR Alam, ASC, Public Interest Litigation and the Role of the Judiciary, 6th International Jurists Conference, Islamabad, Pakistan (2006) 13.

[182] The petitioner for PIL had to prove that he or she had attempted to work with democratic institution to get his or her rights.

much like the constitution provides a filter of 'alternative remedy' in writ jurisdiction. "In any event, it would be against the nature of the Public Interest Litigation jurisdiction to strictly enforce such protocols", he argued.[183]

Wasim Sajjad, Chairman of the Senate, expressed his concerns and suggested that the role of the court could be suggestive as far as social changes are concerned.[184] Supreme Court Justice, Nasir Aslam Zahid, while appreciating Public Interest Litigation warned that the judiciary should not take over the functions of the legislature or the executive.[185] Hamid Khan came forward in its favour and argued there was a need for a very strong judiciary to face down the government.[186]

The above connection took its shape under Supreme Court Chief Justice Iftikhar. He took very popular steps against the land mafia to provide the public with basic needs, such as parks.[187] Iftikhar first followed General Musharraf and decided cases in his favour, but later he used Public Interest Litigation to fix prices against pharmaceuticals and oil and gas companies. According to the claim of the Supreme Court Chief Justice himself, Public Interest Litigation provided speedy and inexpensive access to justice for the common man.[188] A further exhibition of such a 'pro-people' approach was the banning of wasteful expenditures on marriage functions, because it led to frustration, anger and hostility among the poor.[189] So not the wealth, but its exhibition was the main issue in this thinking.

5.5.2 *2006: The Judiciary's Own Consciousness of Its Linear Development and Weaknesses in Leading Global Modernity*

On the other hand, around 2006, the judiciary was also aware of its weaknesses. It felt that it was now at the 'Final Frontier'.[190] Khoosa identified the developments in the judiciary in its historical trajectory. The first stage was the *cognitive stage*, where

---

[183]AR Alam, ASC, Public Interest Litigation and the Role of the Judiciary, 6th International Jurists Conference, Islamabad, Pakistan (2006) 10.

[184]W Sajjad, The Role of the Judiciary as a Catalyst of Social Change, 6th International Jurists Conference, Islamabad, Pakistan (2006). The writer is Bar-at –Law, Honorary Fellow, Wadham College, Oxford and Leader of the House in the Senate of Pakistan.

[185]Zahid, *supra* note 178.

[186]H Khan, Role of an Independent Judiciary in Countries of South Asia, Particularly Pakistan, 6th International Jurists Conference, Islamabad, Pakistan (2006) 1.

[187]Commonly called as the *Mini golf case*. There was an attempt to convert a piece of land reserved as a park by CDA into a golf park for rich people. The court found it as an attempt to shut out deprived sections from the facility who are not in a position to afford luxury of joining the golf club. See Iqbal Haider, PLD 2006.

[188]Address on 5 May 2007 in Multan during the lawyers' movement. See MA Malik, *The Pakistan Lawyers' Movement: An Unfinished Agenda* (Pakistan Law House, Karachi, 2008) 120.

[189]*Ch Muhammad Siddique v. Government of Pakistan*, PLD 2005 SC 1.

[190]ASK Khoosa, JLHC, Independent Judiciary: The Final Frontier, *PLD* (2007) Journal Section 1.

the need was to identify the constitutional hindrances. From this, the *Judges' case* arose accordingly.[191] The second stage came when the judiciary consolidated its gain, thus the *consolidation stage*. The third stage was the *Public Interest Litigation stage*, that is, the judiciary focused on how to deliver this gain to the public. For him, the *final frontier* was the stage in which to protect the judiciary from threats within the judiciary itself, including personalities, peer pressure and the concentration of power in the hands of the judicial heads.[192] Ijaz Ahmad, Justice of the Supreme Court, also spoke of removing personal prejudices, which cannot be controlled by regulations or laws. External independence meant freedom from the control of the executive.[193] These were not calls for judicial restraint,[194] and could only be translated as a call for the judiciary to act in an insular manner, like the military and bureaucracy. That is why, when the lawyers movement was criticized about the Chief Justice's judicial activism, this criticism was not understood by the lawyers.[195]

5.6 Lawyers' Movement: From Supremacy of the Constitution to Supremacy of the 'Rule of Law'

The judiciary's image after the coup needed uplifting. The relationship of the bar and the bench as two wheels of the chariot of justice were out of alignment.[196] The superior judiciary was violating the fundamental rights by supporting unconstitutional forces. As a result, the legal fraternity was helpless. The position of the judiciary can be described in the words of an Italian proverb, "[w]e condemn death penalty to tiny thieves and pass rewards to robbers and bandits". The judiciary was standing against democracy.[197] The potential legislature (including the PPP and PML-N, which had its leadership in exile) was annoyed with the decisions in cases

[191]ASK Khoosa, *PLD* (1994) Journal Section 101. According to Asif Saeed Khan Khoosa, he gave copies to the judges. Based on this, he claimed the credit of decision of *Al-jahad Trust case*, PLD 1996 SC 324.

[192]Khoosa, *supra* note 190, 6.

[193]I Ahmad, JSC, Independence of Judiciary, 6th International Jurists Conference, Islamabad, Pakistan (2006).

[194]Only one voice was a cry in the desert around the period of judicial activism of Justice Iftikhar, Supreme Court Chief Justice. That was that of Malik Qamar Afzal, ASC (2006). He wrote the first coherent, though incomplete dialogue against monologue of strong judiciary. See MQ Afzal (2006), ASC, Judicial Review: A Study of Judicial Activism vis-à-vis Judicial Restraint, *PLD* (2006) Journal Section 67.

[195]Munir A Malik (2008) replied to this criticism. See Malik, *supra* note 188, 12.

[196]MM Qayyum, President SCBA, Welcome Address dated 21 January 2006 by the Supreme Court Bar Association's Dinner in the Honour of Mr. Justice Iftikhar Muhammad Chaudhry, Chief Justice of Pakistan, *PLD* (2006) Journal Section 12.

[197]AA Kurd, Role of Bar in Protection of Human Rights, *PLJ* (2006) Magazine Section 342, 343. This essay was read by the writer in front of Iftikhar Chief Justice and other judges of the superior courts as Vice-Chairman, Pakistan Bar Council.

like *Javed Hashmi, Yousaf Raza Gilani* and then *Shahbaz Sharif*. The Supreme Court Bar Association-SCBA tried to bridge the gap between the judiciary and politicians and emphasized that the country's former leadership was in exile and should be called back and cases against them should be heard. The situation lasted till 2005.

Supreme Court Chief Justice Iftikhar, who was known for lacking the polish of leading Pakistani lawyers and graduated from the Ivy League university of Cambridge, according to the New York Times,[198] started taking *Sou Moto* actions on issues involving human rights violations and public importance. He challenged land allotments to influential people in Gwadar, as well as the *Murree Scheme case* regarding degradation of the environment, and the *Steel Mill* case.[199] Supreme Court Chief Justice Iftikhar also objected to the fact that 500 people had disappeared under the suspicion of terrorism by intelligence agencies, and as a result 100 were quickly released.[200] In the beginning of his judicial year, Iftikhar Supreme Court Chief Justice clearly stated that he'll continue judicial activism.[201] The height of this activism came in *Steel Mill* case, where the Supreme Court stopped the privatization of Steel Mill Karachi, which was unacceptable for General Musharraf. He called Chief Justice Iftikhar and demanded his resign. The Chief Justice refused and Musharraf filed a reference against him in the Supreme Judicial Council. On 18 April 2007, the Supreme Court Chief Justice filed a petition before the Supreme Court, challenging General Musharraf's reference against him. A full bench of thirteen members of Supreme Court accepted the petition on 20 July 2007.[202] This happened due to the pressure of events that occurred between 6 March and July 2007 through the highly popular Lawyer's Movement. Protests by lawyers, the media, with the wide inclusion of the general public against General Musharraf made the petition's acceptance possible. Presidential elections were due and there was a controversy whether General Musharraf could hold two offices (president as well as Chief of Army Staff). In a number of petitions, the vires of dual office law was challenged.[203] A nine-member bench, headed by Justice Bhagwan Das, heard the petition and by a majority of six to three declared these petitions unmaintainable.

---

[198] Jane Perlez, *New York Times* (09 April 2008).

[199] *Watten Party through its President v Federation of Pakistan*, Constitution Petition No 9 of 2006 & Civil Petition Nos 345 & 394 of 2006, decision dated 23 June 2006, available at <http://www.supremecourt.gov.pk/web/user_files/File/CJD_Pakistan_Steel_Mills_Case.pdf>.

[200] Perlez, *supra* note 198.

[201] IM Chaudhry, Address at the Opening Ceremony of Judicial Year 2006-2007, *PLJ* (2006) Journal Section 353.

[202] *Mr. Justice Iftikhar Muhammad Chaudhary v The President of Pakistan*, PLD 2007 SC 578.

[203] *President to Hold Office Act*, 2004.

5.6.1 Emergency Against Judicial Activism and Public Interest Litigation

General Musharraf was re-elected as president on 6 October 2007, but there was a petition pending against the nomination papers of General Musharraf, which was fixed for hearing on 5 November. General Musharraf panicked and imposed emergency on 3 November 2007 and the constitution was held in abeyance.[204] Seven judges of Supreme Court, headed by Chief Justice Iftikhar, overturned the Provisional Constitutional Order-PCO and restrained the Chief of Army Staff and Corps commanders, and other military officers from acting under that degree. A bench of seven judges, headed by the new Chief Justice Abdul Hameed Dogar, overruled the order against Provisional Constitutional Order-PCO. It was declared as void, quorum non judice and without lawful authority.[205] In the *Tikka Muhammad Iqbal* case of 2007 and the Provisional Constitutional Order case of the *Watan Party*, the Zafrullah Khan court strongly criticized the judicial activism of brother judges and justified the Provisional Constitutional Order.[206] The order criticized Public Interest Litigation in cases like fixing prices of fruits and vegetables and stoppage of various projects like New Murree City, Islamabad Chalets, Lahore Canal Road and others. It was an emergency action against judicial activism and Public Interest Litigation, and was not against the legislature.

Under the Provisional Constitutional Order, fundamental rights were suspended; the Oath of Office (Judges) Order of 2007 was promulgated according to which those judges not taking oath would cease to hold office.[207] Of the Supreme Court judges, seventy two per cent did not take oath. In the Sindh High Court, more than 70% refused. It was a revolt by the judiciary and followed by a terrible attack on lawyers. The Proclamation of Emergency by General Musharraf on 3 November was against the judiciary disturbing law and an order in itself, interfering with government policy, affecting economic growth, ordering the release of terrorists and hence outstepping the limits of judicial authority. General Musharraf claimed the judiciary was eroding the trichotomy of power[208] and disturbing his so-called "third phase of transition to full democracy".[209] Two points are important here. Before this, the charge sheet had always been against the legislature. Secondly, General Musharraf requested the U.S., E.U. and Commonwealth countries to give Pakistan time to advance democratically as it was trying to reach their level. He gave ten

---

[204] *Proclamation of Emergency Act*, 2008, Federal Statutes 108; and *Provisional Constitutional Order 1* of 2007, PLD 2008 Federal Statutes 110.

[205] N Iqbal, *Dawn* (Nov 7, 2007).

[206] *Dawn* (Nov 24, 2007). See *Tikka Iqbal Muhammad Khan v General Pervez General Musharraf*, PLD 2008 SC 6.

[207] *Oath of Office (Judges) Order*, 2007, PLD 2008 Federal Statutes 112.

[208] Complete order in *The Dawn* (4 November 2007).

[209] First phase was Martial Law (1999-2001), second was quasi-democratic regime (2002-07), 2007 was expected to be full democracy.

examples of U.S. president Abraham Lincoln breaking laws and usurping rights to save the constitution.[210] This confirms that in this era of good governance, the judiciary was sharing the seat of power of the hegemonic metropolitan bourgeoisie. Meanwhile, the affective legislature, in terms of the leadership of the two main parties of the reigning classes, was in exile. Finally, on 28 November 28 2007, General Musharraf handed over the command of the army to General Ashfaq Parvez Kayani and took the oath as a civilian president. Emergency Law and the Provisional Constitutional Order were challenged in the Supreme Court, decided by Provisional Constitutional Order judges and headed by Abdul Hameed Dogar on 23 November 2007, who declared the emergency proclamation void.[211]

5.6.2 *Rule of Law or Politics: Class Formation and the Lawyers' Movement*

The struggle around the lawyers' movement as seen in its slogans and aspirations was a struggle for the rule of law.[212] It was fought between the military, the bench and the bar (between the khaki military coat and the black-lawyers coat) but it succeeded because of the support of the two main political parties. The lawyers' movement paved the way for the political leadership to assert the supremacy of civilian institutions.[213] Here, however, civilian supremacy is defined not as the supremacy of the legislature or people, but as the supremacy of the rule of law and the constitution.[214] Judges and lawyers were ready to negate Keith B. Callard's claim that "no one is willing to die for the preservation of the constitution in Pakistan".[215] It was also translated into a fight to restore civilian supremacy as there was civil-military imbalance in the country,[216,217] and that is what allowed the mainstream parties to join the movement, which, I argue, explains the 'success' of the movement.

The academic literature also relied on institutional explanations, focusing on the supremacy of one institute over the other, or vice versa. Joel A. Mintz compared the

---

210 I Haque, *Dawn* (4 November 2007).

211 *Tikka Iqbal Muhammad Khan v General Pervez General Musharraf*, PLD 2008 SC 6.

212 Asma Jehangir (2008) in Foreword of the book of Munir A. Malik. See Malik, *supra* note 188, iv.

213 Malik, *supra* note 188, xii.

214 Address of the Chief Justice Iftikhar at Aiwan-e-Adal at 6.00 am dawn 16 July 2007 as cited by Munir A Malik. See Malik, *supra* note 188, 122.

215 Counter claim made by IM Chaudhry, CJSC, On the Occasion of Orientation/Consultation Workshop on Access to Justice Development Fund, *PLJ* (2007) Journal Section, 342, 345.

216 Remarks of Dr Pervez Hassam, Roundtable in Justice, Accountability and International Experience, Islamabad, Pakistan (2-3 May 2007). See DP Hassan, Establishing an effective Rule of Law in Pakistan - The Way Forward, *PLJ* (2007) Journal Section 118.

217 AS Akhtar, *Overdeveloping State: The Politics of Common Sense in Pakistan, 1971-2007*, SOAS, University of London, PhD Thesis (2008) 236.

bravery of Supreme Court Chief Justice Iftikhar with the U.S. founding fathers to overcome tyranny and establish a regime of 'laws and not men'.[218] Tariq Hasan called the Supreme Court Chief Justice a 'judicial activist' on the basis of Public Interest Litigation. This was devoid of any political analysis about Public Interest Litigation.[219] Tayyaba Ahmad also tried to connect judicial activism to the Public Interest Litigation of Chief Justice Iftikhar, who she saw as understanding the "ebb and flow of judicial independence in Pakistan". She analyzed the importance of this development to Pakistan's internal affairs and its role as an actor in the war on terror.[220] Similarly, Shoaib A. Ghias found the reason for the Chief Justice's rise and conflict with Musharraf to be Public Interest Litigation and his opposition to economic liberalization, for instance, through challenging the Steel Mill privatization. He used the framework of judicial power and the legal complex in an authoritarian context, which comes from the old dichotomy of dictatorship versus democracy.[221] Not to mention, Naveed Ahmad praised Iftikhar and declared the Lawyers' Movement as laying down "a foundation stone for the reinstatement of rule of law culture in the country".[222] Let me advance a class formation and structural analysis of this 'event'.

The PML-N and the PPP, who represented landed classes and indigenous bourgeoisie, were effectively removed from sharing power during Musharraf's regime.[223] Most of the lawyers were connected with these two main parties, and both the parties became united on the issue. Furthermore, religious forces were annoyed after the Lal Masjid operation and General Musharraf's support of the U.S. in its war against terror. In the North Western Frontier Province-NWFP, Latif Afridi, the newly elected president of the bar, was from Awami National Party-ANP, was close to the leadership and was successfully bringing out workers. Qazi Muhammad Anwar of the PPP was a member of the Punjab Bar Council. Jamiat Ulmae-e-Islam-Fazlul Rehman, JUI-F and Jamat-e-Islami, JI lawyers were active in North Western Frontier Province-NWFP, where the main parties were in opposition to the government.[224] There is no need to mention the support of PML-N, whose government was removed by Musharraf's coup and Tehrik-i-Insaf, who were against

[218]Nova Southern University gave an honorary Doctor of Laws degree to Chief Justice Supreme Court Iftikhar. He compared his bravery with U.S. founding fathers to overcome tyranny and establish a regime of "laws and not men". See JA Mintz, Introductory Note: A Perspective on Pakistan's Chief Justice, Judicial Independence, and the Rule of Law, 15:*1 ILSA J Int'l & Comp. L.* (2008-2009) 1, 2.

[219]T Hasan, The Need of Judicial Activism and Chief Justice Supreme Court Iftikhar Chaudhry as a "Judicial Activist" on the basis of PIL, 15:1 *ILSA J Int'l & Comp. L.* (2008-2009) 9.

[220]TA Qureshi, State of Emergency: General Pervez Musharraf's Executive Assault on Judicial Independence in Pakistan, 35 *N. C. J. Int'l L. & Com. Reg.* (2009–2010) 485, 489.

[221]SA Ghias, Miscarriage of Chief Justice: Judicial Power and the Legal Complex in Pakistan under Musharraf, 35:4 *Law Soc. Inq.* (2010) 985, 987.

[222]N Ahmad, The Rule of Law - A Substratum of Justice, 8:2 *JCLLE* (2012) 11, 1.

[223]Akhtar, *supra* note 13, 236.

[224]Malik, *supra* note 188, 88.

Musharraf for his war against terror. For a while in the lawyer's movement, then, the support of politicians was needed; jurists abandoned their monopoly on 'wisdom' and accepted the political leadership to safely navigate the ship of the state.[225] At the same time, the lawyer's movement was told that only independent judges could provide them any kind redress from Waderas (Feudalism), Seths (capitalists) or police bureaucrats,[226] which actually pointed to the composition of the legislation.

To sum up, the lawyers' movement was political, if not opportunist, to the core, as opposed to being 'neutral'. The reigning class (the PPP and the PML-N), and the 'liberal' and 'quasi-liberal' projects (led by the MMA and PTI) and even extremist parties joined hands. The metropolitan bourgeoisie slowly played its hegemonic role to help this transition.

5.6.3 Lawyers' Movement: A Political Movement for a 'Non-Political' Judiciary?

Contempt towards the legislature, both by the military and judiciary, had always been accompanied by contempt for politics. The lawyers' movement was a 'political struggle to the core' but claimed to not be about electoral politics.[227] It claimed it should not be understood as partisan politics.[228] The Bar Associations claimed to be a professional group with diverse political opinions and it was argued their unity meant that no political party was backing any of them. The lawyers' movement insisted that the issues of the removal of the Chief Justice and opposition to the military were connected; later, the lawyers' movement made Musharraf leave and they continued agitating against the elected government. Chief Justice Munir stated that the lawyer's movement did not invite political parties but parties joined for their own agendas.[229]

The judiciary wanted every institution of the state to be held accountable except it. The Supreme Judicial Council was a 'dormant body' as it had not investigated any case against a judge of superior courts for his misconduct for the last 20 years or so.[230]

---

[225]Malik, *supra* note 188, xiii.

[226]Malik, *supra* note 188, 76.

[227]A detailed answer of the allegations of politicization of judiciary was given by Munir A Malik in Not Motivated by Politics, *Dawn* (11 May 2007).

[228]Also speaking in Chakwal on June 16, 2007 and on May 26, 2007. The seminar was held by the Supreme Court building with the Chief Justice as keynote speaker on the principles of Separation of Power. Lawyers there raised slogans against General Musharraf. See Malik, *supra* note 188, 114, 109.

[229]Malik, *supra* note 188, 103; see also DP Hassan, Environmental Protection, Rule of Law and the Judicial Crisis in Pakistan, *PLJ* (2007) Magazine Section 278, 280. See also the Remarks made at the International Congress on Environmental Law, Rio de Janeiro, Brazil (22-24 May 2007).

[230]A Mian, CJSC, *A Judge Speaks Out: An Autobiography* (Oxford University Press, Karachi, 2004) 348.

Chief Justice Iftikhar could have been brought before the Council, but wasn't due to the resistance of the lawyers movement.[231]

It was stated that there should be caution about the accountability of the judges, so the Chief Justice should be suspended, not removed and there should be an acting Chief Justice. If judges under inquiry are objecting to certain judges, new judges should be found. So the impeachment of the Chief Justice was legally allowed. The Supreme Judicial Council was a legal forum, and suspension was the normal course of action. If the charges were under political motives, political offences could be separated from legal ones.[232]

In this scenario, the image projected of the maligned Chief Justice was that of the custodian of the constitution and his office was "most strong, protected, non-accountable and untouchable" as per the constitution.[233] He was entitled to more security protocol than the president of Pakistan, and hence, could use government helicopters and airplanes, as these were public property.[234] Chief Justice Iftikhar was told to hold dual office after restoration, firstly, that of the Chief Justice of Supreme Court of Pakistan and secondly, Chief Justice of Peoples of Pakistan.[235] The height of this romance of judges was that judges were said to be pro-people.[236] The irony of the lawyers' movement was this: while the judges were expected to support the people, in effect, the people's courts were established before a people's democracy.

Finally, it should be noted that on March 28, 2007, the Chief Justice did not follow the speech written by Barrister Gohar Ali Khan and Munir A. Malik while addressing the Rawalpindi High Court. Rather, he had his own prepared written speech titled, 'Access to Justice' after the name of the judicial reform project of the Asian Development Bank in Pakistan. It was about the separation of power to ensure the rule of law and good governance.[237] Munir's approach was also full of good governance concepts.[238] The nature of this 'external' support for the lawyers' movement speaks to its acceptance within the governance project.[239]

---

[231]Arguments of Sharif-ud-din Pirzada. See MA Malik, *The Pakistan Lawyers' Movement: An Unfinished Agenda* (Pakistan Law House, Karachi, 2008) 189.

[232]See for a detailed analysis, M Saboohi, Article 209 of Pakistan Constitution: Dilemma or Possible Explanation?, *PLJ* (2007) Journal Section 413, 440. This essay was written to address the different legal positions and discusses impeachment of judges around the world and offers, particularly, a detailed comparison of U.S. and U.K. It found that in Pakistan impeachment takes place by the peers themselves [417]. Accountability of judges is left to Pakistani rulers and it lacks public confidence [421]. Only the president can initiate impeachment [424].

[233]RNH Khan, former JLHC, Supreme Judicial Council, *PLJ* (2007) Magazine Section 134.

[234]*Ibid* 138.

[235]Malik, *supra* note 188, 197.

[236]Malik, *supra* note 188, xi.

[237]This can be assessed even from the summary found in Malik, *supra* note 188, 81.

[238]Even the title of the chapter seems like a package of good governance. See Malik, *supra* note 188, xi.

[239]This is not to make an accusation of 'foreign hands' in the lawyer's movement but to focus attention on the nature of the discourse promoted in the support. See particularly the support of

5.7 After the Lawyers' Movement: Reclaiming Parliamentary Sovereignty

After the restoration of democracy, the relationship of democratic, civilian and legislative leaders with the restoration of judges was a reluctant one. On December 2007, Benazir Bhutto made clear that she was with the 'independent judiciary', but 'not the judges'. Her position to not support the involvement of the judiciary in politics, like in Bangladesh, is also telling.[240] General Musharraf lifted emergency on 16 December 2007 and 14 Supreme Court and Federal Shariat Court judges took the oath on 16 December 2007.

Zardari entered into an agreement with the PML-N, called the Murree Declaration, on 3 November 2007. This was a move to restore the judiciary, including Chief Justice Iftikhar, within 30 days of the formation of government. Elections were held on 8 January 8 2008, a month after Benazir Bhutto's assassination, the PPP won the elections thereafter under the chairmanship of Zardari.

The federal government was formed on 31 March 31 2008, but Zardari was now reluctant to restore the judges. He was interested in seeing the criminal charges against him removed and to get rid of the condition of graduation for his election in the national assembly. The Provisional Constitutional Order court did this on 21 April 2008, it paved the path for Zardari to become president after the resignation of General Musharraf on 7 August 2008. Zardari reneged from the promise of the restoration of judiciary. Pakistan Bar Council-PBC and the other Bar Councils decided to boycott the Provisional Constitutional Order judges, continuing for a period of two months.

Particularly in the Lahore High Court Bar Association-LHCBA, the lawyers were clearly divided amongst the 'professionals' (rejectionist parties like Imran Khan's Tehrik-e-Insaf, Jamaat-e-Islami-JI, etc.) and the 'Khoosa' group (or the Pakistan People's Party).[241]

Zardari offered a constitutional package, which was rejected by the PML-N.[242] The amendments of this package, related to the judiciary, were considered as violative of the judiciary's independence. The concerning amendments were related to the appointment of Chief Justices and judges of superior courts and their removal, as well as the amendments that curtailed the *sou motu* jurisdiction of the Supreme Court.[243] Talks among the PPP and PML-N in Dubai did not succeed and

(Footnote 239 continued)

Human Rights Watch mentioned in Munir's book. See MA Malik, *The Pakistan Lawyers' Movement: An Unfinished Agenda* (Pakistan Law House, Karachi, 2008) 136. Similarly, Harvard Law School's award of a Medal of Freedom to Chief Justice Chaudhry. The Canadian Bar Association president participated in a march of Ontario lawyers. The Quebec Bar and Law Society of Upper Canada were also concerned. See Malik, *supra* note 188, 251.

[240]*The Pakistan Observer* (14 December 2007).

[241]Editorial, *Daily Times* (24 February 2008).

[242]*Pakistan Observer* (12 April 2008).

[243]Malik, *supra* note 188, 272.

Zardari made it clear that the mandate was given to the PPP for *Roti, Kapra aur Makan* (food, clothes and houses), and not to restore the judges. He called the Murree Declaration a political statement and made clear that he had been in jail for eight years, a victim of the judiciary. He said the Supreme Court reverted back a case against him to the accountability court, though he had already served the sentence. He even denied the fact that the change that took place in the country was due to the historic 'no' of the deposed Supreme Court Chief Justice and the subsequent lawyers' movement, which resulted in lawyers having their legs broken. He even noted that international powers were behind the return of democracy in Pakistan. He reminded the public that Benazir Bhutto was not in favour of restoring the judiciary.[244]

Finally, the situation was such that the opposition was stuck with the law and constitution (or the restoration of judiciary) and the government with law and order (in terms of fighting terrorism). The PPP wanted 'slow' and 'constitutional' changes to remove the constitutional engineering by General Musharraf, whereas 'quick change' or 'radicalism' meant the restoration of the judiciary and was necessary.[245] Finally, the guarantors moved and brokered another deal[246] under the hegemonic bloc. Supreme Court Chief Justice Iftikhar met with Asif Zardari and with retired Justice Tariq Mahmood, who was the Supreme Court Bar Association former president and leader of the lawyers' movement. Supreme Court Chief Justice Iftikhar also met a six-member delegation of the U.S. congress led by Tiernerry, head of the National Affairs of the sub-committee of the House Oversight and Government Reform Committee.[247]

5.7.1 *From Parliamentary Democracy to Constitutional Democracy*

Until 1998, the concept of Constitutional Governance through judicial review was not considered to be 'super legislative', or above the Constitution, and was instead considered to be "corrective in nature with anxiety to protect the constitution".[248] Later, the judiciary was considered the 'custodian' of the constitution and a 'watchdog' over the other organs of the state. It became a 'safety valve' or the 'balance wheel' of the constitution.[249] This role was required, especially when the judiciary felt

[244] *The News* (29 April 2008); *The Pakistan Observer* (29 April 2008); *Dawn* (29 April 2008).

[245] Politics of Change through Amendments, Editorial, *The Dawn* (21 May 2008).

[246] D Perino, White House Press Secretary, report Anwar Iqbal, *Dawn* (5 March 2008).

[247] N Iqbal, *Dawn* (27 March 2008).

[248] MA Mirza, JSC, Judicial System of Pakistan, *PLD* (1998) Journal Section 125, 135; see also S Akhtar, Justice of the Supreme Court, In-Service Training for Civil Judges and Judicial Magistrates, *PLD* (2006) Journal Section 19, 20.

[249] Ibid.

marginalized after military coups when there was no constitution.[250] Thus, in a way, the supremacy of the constitution meant the judiciary's own supremacy.

After the lawyers' movement, the judiciary was clear that it was not bowing down before parliamentary democracy. For Barkat Ali Khan, parliamentary democracy was not enough because the written constitution itself was limited and the parliament in Pakistan deviated from this principle and ignored its basis of fundamental rights and the rule of law. That is why we need constitutional democracy and constitutional governance, whereby the majority is restrained within the framework of the constitution and hence there is legal restraint. Constitutional democracy and constitutional governance make the government 'responsible', Khan argued. Does this mean that a constitutional government is a responsible government rather than a representative government? The writer went further, and made clear that Pakistan followed the principle of British parliamentary democracy but does not accept English doctrine of absolute supremacy of the legislature. So it is a system of constitutional supremacy, not parliamentary supremacy.[251]

We should recall that during the period of early modernization (the 1950s to the 1970s), it was argued that a controlled type of democracy, like a strong presidential system, was needed. Afterward, in 1980s under Zia, the constitution (with the judiciary as its custodian) was to envisage democracy, understood as "not a system of self-government but a system of control and limitations of the government".[252] Has Pakistan entered an era of judicial dictatorship (2008 and onward) in the name of good governance? Let me close the book on the role the judiciary has played in democracy in Pakistan on these remarks. Below is the conclusion regarding the judiciary's second claim, that it had protected human rights.

5.8 'Loud' Rights in a 'Shallow Democracy': A Structural Analysis

> I picked up my daughters one by one from their cots to the courtyard of the house and slaughtered them. I had learnt over time that I would never be able to generate enough resources to give honourable lives to my daughters.[253]

Of course, the event referred to in the quote is disturbing, but I am concerned with its interpretation. The statement that, "I had learnt over time that I would never be able to generate enough resources" shows that poverty is deeply structural. There is

---

[250]DJ Iqbal, former JLHC, The Independence of Judiciary, 6th International Jurists Conference, Islamabad, Pakistan (2006) 1.

[251]Barkat Ali Khan (2008) at 632-633; see also DF Hussain, *PLJ* (2008) Magazine Section 627. The author was Secretary of the Law and Justice Commission of Pakistan.

[252]Comments of Supreme Court Chief Justice Haleem, PLD 1988 SC 416, 515-16.

[253]Confession of a father surrendering before the police, as quoted by RMH Patel, ASC, Family Laws and Judicial Perceptions, 6th International Jurists Conference, Islamabad, Pakistan (2006).

a helplessness that settles in after decades. What role can 'hope' play, the buzzword courts used to justify Public Interest Litigation? The man is questioning his "ability" to "generate enough resources" and charity in the form of legal aid and court directions are not his issue. He points out the relation of "enough resources" and "honourable lives" and not a mere 'right to life', as is romanticized by the judiciary in the *Shehla Zia case*.

In Pakistan, Public Interest Litigation began with the court intervening in political matters like the *Benazir Bhutto* case and the *Khar* case of 1988. It started with these 'high profile' political cases and, after a few gestures of being for the 'public', became a tool in the hands of the privileged legal players. New business opportunities in Public Interest Litigation have led new lawyers to become interested in it, and it became the focus of the middle class in the 1990s.[254] After more than a decade, it intervened in issues in *non-class* terms around women, widows, orphans, children, condemned prisoners and other deserving persons as 'weaker segments of the society'.[255] My question is, is it possible to approach class issues through Public Interest Litigation?

5.8.1 Bonded Labour

Starting from the *Darshan Masih* case, the issue of bonded labour is unresolved, even in neighbouring India.[256] Menski's post-structural defense of Public Interest Litigation is that while South Asian middle-class activists and their Western supporters had never seriously put themselves in the feet of a bonded labourer in 'South Asian conditions of life', that should not be an excuse. At least the courts stood with the disadvantaged and argued that more resources should be directed to them.[257] However, this does not explain the actual place of law in social change.

---

[254]The situation was not different in India. See V Gauri, Public Interest Litigation in India: Overreaching or Underachieving?, available at <http://elibrary.worldbank.org/doi/book/10.1596/1813-9450-5109>, last visited Feb 22, 2014; see also S Muralidhar, India: Public Interest Litigation Survey 1997-1998 33-34 (Annual Survey of Indian Law, 1997-98) 525<http://www.ielrc.org/india/litigation.php>, last visited on 22 February 2014.

[255]IM Chaudhry, CJSC, Keynote Address, the Inaugural Session of National Judicial Conference (16-18 April, 2010) 9, available at <http://ljcp.gov.pk/Menu%20Items/NJC-2010/PDFs/PRESS%20COPY%20OF%20INAUGURAL%20ADDRESS%20OF%20HCJ%2016.04.2010.pdf>, last visited 02 December.

[256]Bonded labour was abolished in India in 1973 by Article 11 of the Constitution, by the *Bonded Labour System Abolition Act*, 1992, and the *Bonded Labour System (Abolition) Rules* of 1995. See W Menski, Public Interest Litigation: A strategy for the future. The Fourth Cornelius Memorial Lecture, in, W Menski, AR Alam & MK Raza (eds) *Public Interest Litigation in Pakistan* (Platinum Publishing Limited, London, 2000; and Pakistan Law House, Karachi, 2000) 106, 121.

[257]W Menski, Introductory Overview of Public Interest Litigation in Pakistan; Past Future, in, W Menski, AR Alam & MK Raza (eds) *Public Interest Litigation in Pakistan* (Platinum Publishing Limited, London, 2000; and Pakistan Law House, Karachi, 2000) 1.

In Pakistan, activists and social movements adopted Public Interest Litigation from the very beginning in the *Darshan Masih case*.[258] To end the issue of bonded labour, they adopted extensive legal means, but they also joined hands with the Pakistan Mazdoor Kissan Party (or the Pakistan Workers and Peasants Party) to fight the issue from a political base.[259] In the 1990s, these movements started relying on foreign funds to establish schools for the children of the bonded labourers and to fight legal battles. Slowly, the leadership of these NGOs left the class struggle political debate and the class itself (the class position of the bonded labourer). The focus became for them to help the poor and their rights only. This departure by political and apolitical NGOs was complete when the Pakistan Workers and Peasants Party decided to step back from the bonded labour NGO movement, which was fully indulged in accepting foreign fund assistance. After sometime, foreign funds dried up for bonded labour activities, as the priorities of donor agencies changed to women rights, the environment and consumer protection for emerging markets by the end of the 1990s. Foreign funds moved directly to decentralization under good governance in 2000s. The lack of funds in bonded labour projects resulted in infighting between groups of NGOs, further reducing the interest of the middle class and petty bourgeois NGOs in the issue, as these classes were more interested in 'good governance' decentralization. Courts, as a part of state formation, responded accordingly.

According to Ghulam Fatima, General Secretary of the Bonded Labour Liberation Front-BLLF, there was relief given in the *Darshan Masih* case, but this was just a decision. Later, the *Bonded Labour Act* was passed, but the Supreme Court still could not abolish bonded labour inspite of this legislation. According to her, the Supreme Court was busy in big political cases and could not be bothered with 4.5 million brick kiln workers.[260] On 12 September 2012, the Bonded Labour Liberation Front asked the Supreme Court why there was not a focus on the violation of judgments passed by the court. Her stance was that the activists could hardly compel the courts to give decisions, but then the courts overlooked their own decisions. That is why a slogan used by the group was '*tum fayslay bhi khaw*

[258]Indian courts followed the legislation in bonded labour, whereas in Pakistan, the judiciary followed the Indian judiciary. It gave the decision of *Darshan Masih*, after which the Pakistani legislature responded. India passed *Bonded Labour System (Abolition) Act*, 1976 and prominent cases followed were *People's Union for Democratic Rights v Union of India*, AIR 1982 SC 146, *Bandhua Mukti Morcha v Union of India*, AIR 1984 SC 802, *Balram v State of MP*, AIR 1990 SC 44.

[259]Interview with Abdullah Komoka, Secretary General, *Pakistan Mazdoor Kissan Party* (Pakistan Workers and Peasants Party-PMKP) dated 02 December 2013.

[260]These figures are according to BLLF. It does not include other small informal sector industry and agriculture labour where bonded labour is rampant. Fatima defined that every labourer who is 'bound' and gets less than Rs. 5000 per month (approx. $50) is a bonded labourer. Contractors only took young men. The bonded labourer was given Rs. 2500 ($25) and 40 kgs of wheat per month. He and his family are expected to work round the clock for the landowner. They are used to settle enmities and are even used to commit thefts and other illegal activities for the landowner. Interview with Ghulam Fatima, General Secretary Bonded Labour Liberation Front, BLLF, dated 20 December 2012.

gayay; tum qawaneen ura gayay' which means 'You have eaten away the decisions; you have thrown away the laws.[261] Fatima stated that '*contempt of court*' was a common complaint in elite politics, but her issue was *contempt for workers* by the judiciary. For example, judges frequently claimed that bonded labourers were fraudulent, they argued that bonded labourers who took advances of Rs.50,000 ($500) were 'habitual' debtors, rather than question why the brick owners indebted the labourers for life with these petty loans. Once, a judge said, "Oh, there are bonded labourers in the court. They ran away with my Rs. 45,000".[262] What a judge, what a court! Fatima's view was clear—bonded labour cannot be abolished as long as the feudal system remains, all the feudal lords themselves being brick kiln owners and sitting in the assemblies. District Nizams (local governments heads) themselves were invigilating the implementation of law and were torturing the bonded labourers. 33% of women in the legislative bodies were not from movements but from the same elite political families, though they often had no political background. Until and unless there is to be representation of the working class in the assembly, there will be no change.[263]

5.8.2 *Gender and Public Interest Litigation*

The most highlighted contribution of the judiciary was its protection of the right to property for women.[264] The constitution of Pakistan gives ample opportunities for women's rights,[265] but they are not enforced.[266] The judiciary, being part of the social formation, also carried the prejudices of a male-dominant society. Supreme Court Chief Justice Ajmal Mian admitted that the position of women in Pakistan was not good, as in U.S. and Canada, but added that it is not as bleak as is often presented in the Western media, as Pakistan has women with roles in various walks

[261] *Ibid.*

[262] *Ibid.*

[263] *Ibid.*

[264] In the *Ghulam Ali* case, PLD 1990 SC 1, the court clearly stood for female's (daughter's) rights in inheritance even if the legislature was lagging. Even in the *Kalsoom Bibi* case, 2005 SCMR 135, the court took notice of deprivation of females from property in the form of gift and relaxed the rule of the burden of proof on the respondent beneficiary. See also the *Muhammad Ashraf* case, 1989 SCMR 1390.

[265] The Constitution of Pakistan has three sets of provisions related to rights. First, background provisions (2A, 3, and 4) which are preamble of the Constitution. Second, the provisions relating to fundamental rights (Article 8, 9, 14, 23, 24, 25, etc.) third set of provisions are Principles of Policy (Article 33, 35, 37 (a), 37e, etc.).

[266] MF Naseem, Constitutional Guarantees for the Rights of Women and their Implementation, *PLJ* (1998) Journal Section 31, 35. The writer is LLB (Hons) (Wales), LLM (London), PhD (London) of Lincoln's Inn Barrister-at-Law.

of life.[267] Subordinate and superior judiciaries are also involved in decisions with a gender bias and they could not surpass their various prejudices.[268] According to Retired Justice of the Lahore High Court, Nasira Javed Iqbal, "judges are ready to believe the worst about women" and are supporting male aggressors by sending women back to their homes from where they ran away from forced marriages and also lowering the threshold of provocation (which is a defense in a murder case) in honour killings and in punishing the rapists.[269] The criminal justice system has utterly failed in protecting women against honour killings, domestic violence, Karo Kari, forced marriages, rape and family feuds.[270] Even courts allowing marriage according to women's wishes reduce sentences if the contending parties or the family kills such women.[271] Farzana Bibi had to protest, "It is highly unfortunate that the so-called custodians of the constitutional rights of the citizens are violating the constitution by upholding and reinforcing archaic tribal value systems, chauvinism, fanaticism and political expediency".[272] The liberation of women always comes with a proviso among the most enlightened jurists. While talking about how male-dominated thinking is suppressing women, in the very next sentence, a jurist can jump to a proviso, such as this "does not mean that there should be a license to obscenity or that women should be let completely loose and encouraged to become paranoid about their rights, independence and feminism".[273]

The problem exists at every level of the judicial structure. Female judges are not given proper courtrooms, residential facilities, medical facilities or promotions by the male-dominated judiciary. Retired Justice of Lahore High Court, Fukhrunisa

---

[267]He gave the reference of *Business Recorder* (03 January 03 1999) in his book. This judicial education program on gender issues was held by the Asia- Pacific Advisory Forum on Judicial Education on Equality Issues in Lahore on 2 January 1999. Madam Justice L' Heureux-Dube of Canada was present. See Mian, *supra* note 230. He dedicated one page out of his 383 pages autobiography about this topic. Justice Sajjad Ali Shah's 834 pages long repetitive auto-biography did not include the word gender (though it does mention the Ghouri missile), women or women's rights (though World Bank) or female/feminism. Same is the case with Anwar-ul- Haq's collection of speeches.

[268]NJ Iqbal, JLHC (retd as she then was), Judiciary and Gender Bias, International Jurists conference, Islamabad (2006). The counter claim is that the superior judiciary is always vigilant but the subordinate judiciary has also played an effective role in the protection of human rights. See MN Abbasi, JSC, Human Rights in Pakistan: Concepts and History of Human Rights, *PLD* (2004) Journal Section 90, 105.

[269]The punishment for a rapist is the death sentence but it has not been granted till date. See *ibid.*

[270]Unfortunately, the pioneer of PIL, Afzal Zullah, Chief Justice Supreme Court (1 January 1990 to 18 April 1993) was in favour of the reduction of sentences on the question of family honour, *ibid.*

[271]Mohammad Riaz and Mohammad Feroze were given life imprisonment for killing their sister marrying after her own heart. LHC found it worth 18 months only, and, released them. The court held, "in our society nobody forgives a person who marries his sister or daughter without the consent of parents or near relatives". *Ibid.*

[272]*Ibid.*

[273]MF Naseem, Constitutional Guarantees for the Rights of Women and their Implementation, *PLJ* (1998) Journal Section 31, 35.

Khokhar claimed that there are only 6% women in the subordinate judiciary and no female judge in the Supreme Court.[274] The judiciary often accused the legislature of not legislating. What about the fact that amendments in Section 3 of the *Family Court Act* of 1994 made mandatory the presence of at least two judges in family court in each district, which has not been implemented by the judiciary? In 1994 (while Benazir Bhutto was Prime Minister), five female judges were appointed but none of them were allowed to work as Chief Justices of High Courts, though two of them could easily be considered for Lahore High Court and Peshawar High Court of North Western Province-NWFP. Both were superseded and were allowed to retire without elevation to the Supreme Court. Supreme Court Chief Justice Sajjad (as he then was in 1995 when Benazir appointed female judges) was even respectful of the idea and insisted that they should fulfill the 'constitutional requirements'. He refused the appointment of a 'lady judge' from judicial service to be appointed as a judge. Benazir Bhutto insisted, but according to Sajjad, she was not sufficiently senior.[275]

At the same time, judges used plural legal frameworks to remove the rigours of the laws adopted in the name of Islam.[276] The judiciary did not touch the Hudood Laws, but no one was executed and the courts did not convict anyone. Doctors refused to do amputations.[277] According to Samar Minallah, the judiciary played a proactive role in abolishing the customs of Swana, Vanni or Sang Chatti,[278] which are 'culturally sanctioned forms of violence' and an abuse of fundamental rights by *Panchayts* or *jirgas*, who claim the customs are "an indigenous means of alternate dispute resolution mechanisms".[279] The judiciary in Pakistan strongly stood against the Jirga presenting itself as a 'modernist' force. Through an amendment, Section 310-A, in the Pakistan Penal Code-PPC, the *Swana* custom was criminalized in 2004. On December 16, 2005, the Chief Justice declared *Jirgas* to be a negation of the concept of 'civilization', but this viewpoint did not go uncontested. Justice Javed Iqbal, while discussing delays in the judicial system, appreciated the

---

[274]F Khokhar, JLHC (retd as she then was), Judiciary and Gender Bias, 6th International Jurists Conference, Islamabad, Pakistan (2006).

[275]SA Shah, CJSC (retd as he then was), *Law Courts in a Glass House*: *An Autobiography* (Oxford University Press, Karachi, 2001) 229.

[276]SS Ali, Applying Islamic Criminal Justice in Plural Legal System: Exploring Gender- Sensitive Judicial Responses to Hudood Laws in Pakistan, 6th International Jurists Conference, Islamabad, Pakistan (2006) 1, 11. The writer was Professor of Law, University of Warwick and Professor at the University of Oslo, Norway. Formerly, Professor of Law, University of Peshawar, Pakistan; Provincial Minister for Health, Population and Women's Development, Government of the NWFP, Pakistan; and Chair of the National Commission on the Status of Women, Pakistan.

[277]Interview with senior lawyer, Abid Hassan Minto, dated 2 December 2012.

[278]*Swana*, *Vanni*or, *Sang*, *Chatti* are the customs women/girl are given in dispute settlement of usually murder cases to keep traditional peace. The proceedings are conducted by *jirga* or traditional *panchayats*.

[279]S Minallah, Judiciary as a Catalyst for Social Change, 6th International Jurists Conference, Islamabad, Pakistan (2006). The researcher is an anthropologist and Executive Director, Ethno Media and Development.

fewer delays in the courts under the Baluchistan system, giving the informal *Sardari* system as the reason for the lower case load. He favoured the system's mediation to create a "win–win" situation in litigation as opposed to the zero-sum outcome of adjudication system.[280] The feudal chiefs, or *sardars,* themselves sitting in legislation could not legislate against them.[281] Even Benazir Bhutto appreciated the *Jirga* and conducted it by herself.[282]

Let us then turn to the potential for women's emancipation in Public Interest Litigation. Suffice it to say that, in Pakistan, 80% of rapes are never reported and only the most resilient and resourceful go for to file a First Information Report-FIR.[283] Secondly, the following factors reduce the relief further:

Gender bias in judiciary itself

What percentage reaches the higher judiciary?

What percentage of cases the court takes notice of

What percentage it can implement the decisions

To what extent legal relief is relief when social, economic and political relief are not available,

Even in those cases which were reported and persuaded on behalf of weak and very poor,[284] the actual motivators have been NGOs for the last two decades. The media also claims credit as in *Mukhtaran Mai case.*[285] So, one is compelled to conclude that activism and political struggle are the saviours, not the judiciary.

Even when these activist groups go for relief to these judges, it is a minor part of their own work. Women's rights activists had to fight against the judges and their conservative approach. The judiciary does not only refuse today's NGOs when they go for broader political aims, they can also suffer the reduction of their funding. Let us recall Alavi's analysis in the very early days of the women's movement in Pakistan.[286] He condemned the Left view of the women's rights movement as

---

[280] J Iqbal, The Role of Judiciary as a Catalyst of Social Change, 6th International Jurists Conference, Islamabad, Pakistan (2006) 1, 15.

[281] In 2006, a parliamentarian and a District Nazim (administrator) were involved in handing over five girls to the rival party. Supreme Court here took a *suo motu* notice. Sindh High Court Sukhar bench explicitly declared holding a Jirga as illegal and unconstitutional and banned them. Inspite of this, feudal members of the Sindh government enacted the *Sindh Amicable Settlement of Disputes Ordinance (SASDO)*, 2004. In 2002 in the *Aba Khel Vanni* case in Mianwali, the Nawab of Kalabagh himself handed over 8 girls to resolve a very old dispute.

[282] See B Bhutto, *Daughter of the East*: *An Autobiography,* 2nd edn (Simon & Schuster, London, 2007).

[283] Khokhar, *supra* note 273.

[284] Like the famous *Mukhtran Mai* case.

[285] N Sethi, Role of Media in Dispensation of Justice, 6th International Jurists Conference, Islamabad, Pakistan (2006). He was the Editor-in-Chief, *Daily Times* and the *Friday Times*, Pakistan.

[286] He tried to analytically understand the roots of the women rights movement in Pakistan (as seen in the work of the Women's Action Forum, Democratic Women's Association, Sindhiani Tehrik, and Women's Front).

bourgeois elitist,[287] and he gave a class analysis of the movement and its different layers. The agricultural Green Revolution relieved peasant women from outdoor work but increased repression on them within the household. He commented on how women's income in middle-class families presaged a restructuration of family life and redefinition of moral values. "The whole problem arises from the crisis of middle class and lower middle household economy", he argued. For him, respect and dignity are middle-class concepts.[288] Working class women were less involved in women's rights movement. He felt the need to find ways to go beyond the "confines of the salaried urban middle class and lower middle class women and to work for mobilizing women for the wider sections of society".[289] To bring the story to the present, opting only for law-centred and legal struggles also says a lot about the women's movement in Pakistan. Excessive legal struggles do not show the strength of the movement, but the weakness of class struggle and their thin mass base.

5.8.3 Public Interest Litigation and the Environment

The biggest claim for success by Public Interest Litigation is in the area of environment. Dr. Pervez Hasan, a pioneer in this area,[290] evaluated the *Shehla Zia case*.[291] For him, Pakistan has among the most advanced environmental laws[292]

---

[287]B Ali, Elitist View of Women's Struggle in Pakistan, *EPWEcon. Polit. Wkly* (14 May 1988), cited by Alavi as an example. See H Aalvi, Pakistan: Women in a Changing Society, *EPW Econ. Polit. Wkly* (1988) 1328.

[288]H Alavi, Pakistan: Women in a Changing Society, *Econ. Polit. Wkly* (1988) 1328.

[289]*Ibid* 1330.

[290]See, generally, P Hasan and A Azfar, Securing Environmental Rights through Public Interest Litigation in South Asia, 22:3 *VELJ* (2004) 216. See also P Hasan, Judiciary Leads the Way, 15:1 *The Environmental Forum* (1998) 48. An earlier recognition of the evolving role of the Pakistan judiciary is noted in P Hassan, From Lyon the Otsu: Laws on Conservation and Wise Use of Wetlands, in, *Towards Wise Use of Wetlands* (Asian Wetlands Symposium, 1992) 22.

[291]DP Hasan, *Shehla Zia v. WAPDA*: Ten Years Later, *PLD* (2005) Journal Section 48; a presidential address at the First Annual Seminar of Pakistan Environmental Law Association held at the Dr. Pervez Hasan Environmental Law center, University of the Punjab (New Campus) Lahore on 14 March 2004 for the Life time Achievement Award conferred by PELA on Mr. Justice (R) Saleem Akhtar.

[292]The *Pakistan Environmental Protection Ordinance*, 1983, establishment of Pakistan Environmental Protection Council chaired by the President of Pakistan. The 1983 Ordinance followed the experience of developed countries and set up a Federal Pakistan Environmental Protection Agency as well as Provincial Environmental Protection Agencies (EPAs) in the four provinces. The National Conservation Strategy was adopted in 1992 followed by Provincial Conservation Strategies. Later the *Pakistan Environmental Protection Act, 1997* was promulgated. National Environmental Quality Standards (NEQS) were developed to guide industrial and other. The National Environmental Action Plan (NEAP) announced by the Government of Pakistan in 2001.

but nothing has happened on this front due to "a wide gap between legislative goals, declared national policies and their implementation".[293] This gap between policy and implementation is highlighted in the good governance discourse, and the problem is reduced to a 'governance' issue. The *Shehla Zia* case exemplifies the policy and implementation gap.

Shehla Zia's life was endangered by the electromagnetic effects of a high voltage transmission line designed to go through a posh area of Islamabad; thus, the court ordered an end to the construction. While Shehla was not interested in pursuing the case, however, money was spent by NGOs, as well as the Pervez Hasan, who represented both local and international corporations that pollute the environment, and was appointed as *amicus curie*.[294] As opposed to this, the actual lives of millions are endangered when slum dwellers are moved from state land under the high voltage wires.

From the Environment Commission in the *Shehla Zia case*[295] to the *salt mines* case[296] to the *Mahmood Booti* case,[297] the elite interest of environment cases is repetitive. But the problematic part in the analyses of these elite environment commissions is the 'public–private' model, which results in 'built to operate and transfer' investment of the private sector. This is not more that the market endeavouring to control its own excesses.

5.8.4 Conclusion

I argue on the basis of previous analysis that the notion of rights as a relief for the subordinate classes has a very limited emancipatory value when the subordinate classes have no power. Subordinate classes can invoke the legal political institutions of the state but this route is usually unproductive. It results in huge costs to both parties, including lengthy delays. Lawyers engaged are parasitic middlemen (and women), and workers have found formal legal codes cumbersome and

---

[293]DP Hasan, The Role of Judiciary and Judicial Commissions on Sustainable Development in Pakistan, 6th International Jurists Conference, Islamabad, Pakistan (2006) 48. The writer was an Advocate of the Supreme Court of Pakistan and High Courts of Pakistan, Senior Partner, Hasan & Hasan (Advocates), Lahore President, Pakistan Environmental Law Association. B.A (Punjab), L. L.B (Punjab), L.L.M (Yale), S.J.D. (Harvard).

[294]Interview with Imran Akram, barrister and solicitor, Law Society of Upper Canada, Punjab Bar Council, and Adjunct Professor at the University Law College, Punjab University, dated 10 November 2013.

[295]In the *Shehla Zia* case, NESPAK (a semi government construction enterprise) was made the commission to look at the plan of the grid station of WAPDA (a state sector power producing and distributing agency).

[296]*General Secretary, West Pakistan Salt Mines Labour Union (CBA) Khewra, Jhelum v Director, Industries and Mineral Development, Punjab Lahore*, 1997 SCMR 2061.

[297]*City District Government v Muhammad Yousaf*, I.C.A No. 798/2002 filed before the Lahore High Court. Here, in this case, the petitioner challenged the use of a site for dumping solid wastes.

illegible.[298] The 'addiction to litigation' cannot be a substitute for mass mobilization. *Roti, Kapra aur Makaan* (meaning Food, Clothing and Shelter)—a quote from the Pakistan People's Party founding manifesto—was the old programme (1970s), geared towards substantive needs. The current rhetoric is one of legalism and rights and, it remains hollow.[299] In the 'good governance' framework, the rule of law is posited as fundamental to a wide range of societal and developmental goals, including expanding and deepening the reach of democratic institutions, empowering the working classes and granting rights. Locally, the judiciary's claim about its role of political development and governance rests on two connected claims. The judiciary could not defend democracy in the face of military coups but could by protecting fundamental rights. Throughout my book, I engaged with both claims in an interconnected manner in relation to political development (or governance). My analysis suggests that the judiciary has been crucial in the reproduction of state and political inequality in Pakistan. The rights discourse of the judiciary has been a poor substitute for this democratic deficit.

References

A Kohsaka (ed), *Development Strategies: Beyond the Washington Consensus* (Palgrave Macmillan Ltd., England, 2004).

A Mian, CJSC (as he then was), *A Judge Speaks Out: An Autobiography* (Oxford University Press, Karachi, 2004).

AH Amsden, *Asia's Next Giant: South Korea and Late Industrialization* (Oxford University Press, New York, 1989).

C Baxter (ed) *Pakistan on the Brink: Politics, Economics and Society* (Oxford University Press, Karachi, 2004).

CH Kennedy & CA Botteron (eds), *Pakistan: 2005* (Oxford University Press, Karachi, 2005).

DI Narejo (ed), B Bhutto, *Whither Pakistan: Dictatorship or Democracy?* (Al-Hamd Publications, Lahore, 2007).

DM Trubek & A Santos (ed), *Introduction: The Third Movement in Law and Development Theory and the Emergence of a New Critical Practice* (Cambridge University Press, Cambridge, 2006).

EP Thompson, *Whigs and Hunters: The Origins of Black Act* (Penguin Books Ltd., Harmondsworth, 1975).

H Khan, *Constitutional and Political History of Pakistan,* 2nd edn (Oxford University Press, Karachi, 2009).

JKM Ohnesorge, Developing Development Theory: Law and Development Orthodoxies and the North East Asian Experience, 28:2 *U. Pa. J. Int'L Econ. L.* (2008).

M Woo-Cummings (ed), *The Developmental State* (Cornell University Press, Ithaca, 1999).

M Yasin & T Banuri (eds), *The Dispensation of Justice in Pakistan* (Oxford University Press and Islamabad: SDPI, Karachi, 2004).

MA Malik, *The Pakistan Lawyers' Movement: An Unfinished Agenda* (Pakistan Law House, Karachi, 2008).

[298]During the work in Okara and Charsada around peasant struggles, lawyers admit playing such a role. See Akhtar, *supra* note 13, 208.

[299]DM Hasan, cited by Akhtar, *supra* note 13, 219.

N Ahmad, The Rule of Law - A Substratum of Justice, 8:2 *JCLLE* (2012).
O Siddique, *Pakistan's Experience with Formal Law: An Alien Justice* (Cambridge University Press, Cambridge, 2013).
P Hasan and A Azfar, Securing Environmental Rights through Public Interest Litigation in South Asia, 22:3 *VELJ* (2004).
P Musharraf, *In the Line of Fire: A Memoir* (Free Press, New York, 2006).
Partridge, M Welker & R Hardin (eds) *Corporate Lives: New Perspectives on the Social Life of the Corporate Form* (Wenner-Gren Symposium Series, 2011).
R Wade, *Governing the Market: Economic Theory and the Role of Government in East Asian Industrialization* (Princeton University Press, Princeton, 1990).
RA Posner, *Economic Analysis of Law,* 4th edn (Little, Brown and Company, Boston, 1992).
S Pahuja, *Decolonizing International Law: Development, Economic Growth, and the Politics of Universality* (Cambridge University Press, Cambridge, 2013).
SA Ghias Miscarriage of Chief Justice: Judicial Power and the Legal Complex in Pakistan under Musharraf, 35:4 *Law Soc. Inq.* (2010).
SA Shah, CJSC (as he then was), *Law Courts in a Glass House: An Autobiography* (Oxford University Press, Karachi, 2001).
SA Zaidi, *Issues in Pakistan's Economy,* 5th edn (Oxford University Press, Karachi, 2009).
SA Zaidi, *Pakistan's Social and Economic Development: The Domestic, Regional and Global Context* (Rupa Co., New Delhi, 2004).
SS Bokhari (ed) *Benazir Bhutto (2006): Speeches and Statements* (Musawat Publications, Islamabad, 2006).
TA Qureshi, State of Emergency: General Pervez Musharraf's Executive Assault on Judicial Independence in Pakistan, 35 *N. C. J. Int'l L. & Com. Reg.* (2009–2010).
W Menski, AR Alam & MK Raza (eds) *Public Interest Litigation in Pakistan* (Platinum Publishing Ltd., London, 2000; and Pakistan Law House, Karachi, 2000).

Chapter 6
Some Theoretical Implications

6.1 A Departure from a 'Liberal' Analysis About Pakistan

This book has sought to empirically substantiate the theoretical claim that the judiciary had been a crucial link in the reproduction of the state and political inequality in Pakistan. Even a strong judiciary is not a substitute for a truly representative legislature and the dominant rights discourse cannot replace the demand for a deeper and broader democracy. This conclusion challenges the dominant liberal and Islamic approaches to state and judiciary of Pakistan which play within dichotomies of democracy versus dictatorship and liberalism versus Islam. The supposedly neutral managerial solution of 'good governance' is only the latest instance of the liberal approach, and it forms the common sense of the elite whose constant concern is the deviation from 'ideals' of state and society as found elsewhere.

Drawing on Gramsci's idea of classes and hegemony, the book has argued that a large majority of the population was excluded and marginalized during periods of both democracy and dictatorship, while the ruling classes jointly established hegemonic control over the society. It has aimed to show how a hybrid of a U.S. type liberal legal and constitutional arrangement and a local Islamic law in Pakistan together glossed over the structural exploitation, marginalization and exclusion in society and came to further undermine a weak legislature. Contrary to dominant critical perspectives, the book has argued that it was not the civil-military bureaucracy which alone shaped the hegemonic terrain, but the judiciary has been the architect of the prevailing political design and discourse. I have identified therefore a juridico-bureaucratic structure in the post-colonial state of Pakistan.

The popular discourse around the judiciary is that it is considered as under attack by the dictators and corrupt politicians in the legislature and deserving support, protection and autonomy. Or, it elicits complaints that it has not risen to the occasion to save democracy. The book has aimed to show how judiciary was not only a crucial part of postcolonial state structure but was the main architect of

M. Azeem, *Law, State and Inequality in Pakistan*, International Law and the Global South, DOI 10.1007/978-981-10-3845-7_6

constitutional and legal arrangements during modernization of 1950s–60s. Apologetic arguments for when the judiciary supported dictatorial regime goes along the lines of though it could not save democracy, yet it saved itself and protected fundamental rights of the people. This claim is largely derived from the decisions of the Chief Justice Cornelius 'collective', and is uncritically accepted in legal circles in Pakistan and abroad. The book has sought to closely analyze and deconstruct this assumed connection of rights with democracy to argue that, judges first wanted a controlled democracy and then were in favour of rights to address any democratic deficit. A mix of a liberal US type presidential system and Islam was used to restrict popular participation and a strong judiciary was instituted to protect rights.

Drawing insight from a detailed legal history of Pakistan, therefore, this book contributes to the 'law and development' literature an analysis of the changing role of law and the judiciary, from the period of collapsing modernization to the current stage of globalized capitalism. Most law and development scholarship cannot adequately explain why law has become central in current phase of New Institutionalism. The modernization theorist Ralph Braibanti, in the tradition of Samuel Huntington, discusses the possibility of law to stop popular participation in Pakistan, promoting 'institutionalism' (particularly legal institutions) as a response to failed modernization and the consequence of increasing political resistance and participation. Braibanti accuses participatory, popular and agitational politics for the declining role of law, but also illustrates how Pakistani courts used law to pacify the demand for popular participation (the details are in Chap. 2).

The book explains the techniques of the rise of the judiciary in 1990s and 2000s. The rights discourse in the form of Public Interest Litigation came in the wake of the demise of working class politics and in the presence of a meager welfare state. In this period, an alliance of International Financial Institutions with a rising middle class (petit bourgeoisie) served as check on corrupt political elite and stubborn bureaucracy. Foreign funded NGOs with a very thin mass base crowded courts, and romanticized the rule of law, human rights, PIL and the devolution plan. The state (legislature and civil bureaucracy) weakened ideologically in that process and the judiciary rose in this gap. Its height took the form of the Lawyers' and Judges' Movement. All this was the development a new complex hegemony. Sadly missing was an organized working class and a thrust towards deeper and broader democracy and substantive economic equality. They were now 'legal subjects' with formal rights entitlements, and more to come in abundance, if there were only 'rule of law'. Yet this book suggests to legal theorists to go around and beyond law to address political and social issues, given the hitherto self-serving role of the judiciary.

I will briefly now touch on the theoretical implications of this study for international legal scholarship in the area of law and development. To more fully 'engage' with this literature is beyond the scope of this book.

6.2 Theoretical Implications for Law and Development, Looking at the Work of Douglas North, Brian Tamanaha, David Trubek

Most mainstream critics have pointed out imprecision in Good Governance indicators (WGIs) making comparison between contexts difficult. It has also been noted that the indicators have a bias towards the views of the business elite. Yet most donor agencies follow these indicators and there is no alternative basis for political and social development. The lesson of this book should be that rather than continuously arranging, rearranging or building another institution to oversight the existing ones, the paradigm of change should take into account structural obstacles like unequal distribution of land wealth and centre-periphery dependency relations as a starting point. So far the only focus of governance interventions is on the constitutive side of governance, whereas structural aspects demand a turn to the distributive side of the governance interventions.

6.2.1 Douglas North

The neglect of distributive aspect of governance goes to the core issue of problematic understanding of the state and politics in WGIs and New Institutionalism as seen in the work of Nobel Prize winning economist, Douglas North. He emphasizes out the importance of institutional structures for the performance of economic system as were neglected by the economic historians.[1] He particularly emphasized the importance of rules of the game (institutions) for property rights enforced by the state and these, for him, are essential for economic growth. These may be formal (constitution, statutes, by laws, etc.) or informal (culture, religion).[2] Here state acts as a third party, developing an impersonal body of law and enforcement and lowers the cost of transactions.[3] Connected and relevant to this for our study in this book is North's clear statement about Third World countries that they have poorly defined and/or ineffective property rights and lack formal structure (and enforcement). This, for North, results in high transaction costs and underpins efficient markets.[4]

Apart from a critique which can be levelled against North for its theoretical positions in new and old economics, new institutionalism and transactional cost economics,[5] a few relevant critical points from the point of view of study in this

[1]DC North, *Structure and Change in Economic History* (Norton, New York, 1981) ix.

[2]*Ibid* 7.

[3]*Ibid* 37.

[4]DC North, *Institutions, Institutional Change and Economic Performance* (Cambridge University Press, Cambridge, 1990) 67.

[5]See for broad introduction of this field, PG Klein, New Institutional Economics, in, Boudewijn Bouckaert and Gerrit De Geest (eds) *Encyclopedia of Law and Economics* (Edward Elgar, 1999).

book are as follows. In Chap. 1 it was discussed that there is no separation of state from civil society and there is no separation of political from the economic in Pakistan like other postcolonial countries. State itself is composed of big land-holding classes and business elite connecting it with international capital through centre-periphery dependency relations. This metropolitan bourgeoisie acting as a hegemonic class historically used juridico-bureaucratic structure as a seat of power. Defining property rights through state (and laws related to trade, tariff, foreign investment, etc.) means strengthening biased dependency relations and unequal distribution of land and wealth. Taking property rights as a prerequisite for economic growth may be problematic as they may themselves be a hindrance on the path of political and economic development. This disconnection of institutions (legal, property law) and state from politics is very particular to Douglas North. In his basic model of studying Europe in 1973, he ignores the effects of crusades, technological innovations and accumulation of capital.[6] For him, efficient economic organization is the prerequisite of growth to whom individual respond. He ignores the inequality of strategic actors in new rules of the game. That is, who will benefit from the change of rules is missing in his formation. Furthermore, he expects individual to obey the rules of the game on utilitarian principles.

The problematic nature of this understanding of state, which lay behind governance interventions of financial institutions, became evident in transitional economies as soon as the local ruling elite started misappropriating state controlled assets during deregulation and privatization of early 1990s. Where the paradigm could not bear fruit, its own architects blamed 'state capture' (a form of elite corruption) in countries with developing and transitional economies. For instance, promoters of the World Bank project, Kaufmann and Kraay, have argued that 'state capture' by the elite is the "illicit influence of the elite in shaping the laws, policies and regulations of the state". This results in a negative effect of per capita income on governance in developing and transitional economies because the fruits of the growth go to benefit a certain elite. The phenomenon is observed by the writers in transitional economies of the former socialist bloc. They recall 'historical' evidence of the influence of 'robber barons' in the United States at the turn of the twentieth century and crony capitalism in the Philippines under Marcos. This is indicative of 'mis-governance' by the writers.[7] State in this 'state capture' understanding seems neutral, autonomous, outside the classes and hence the state has been 'captured' by some corrupt elite.

Now governance interventions began to give a central role to the judiciary to fix this corrupt elite and the stubborn bureaucrats, adding in another problematic prescription in the legal remedies for developing countries. This book rather argues for a class-based understanding of the state rather than a perception of an

[6]AJ Field, New Economic History and Law and Economics, in, Boudewijn Bouckaert and Gerrit De Geest (eds) *Encyclopedia of Law and Economics* (Edward Elgar, 1999) 728, 738.

[7]D Kaufmann & A Kraay, Growth without Governance, Policy Research Working Paper No 2928 (2002) 30.

unfortunate 'capture' of a neutral set of institutions. This study presented state formation as political practice ('hegemony' as nuanced concept of this phenomenon in Gramscian tradition). Through a detailed historical and empirical study of postcolonial judiciary in Pakistan it argued for its role in the reproduction of state and political inequality, indicating the limits of the reliance on judiciary to fix problems of governance in developing countries.

6.2.2 Brian Tamanaha

The lack of a critical understanding of law and state theory can be seen in the writings of Brian Z. Tamanaha, who is the most popular 'internal critic' of World Bank's rule of law projects. Tamanaha's work is the best illustration of the divides within the liberal legal project itself and possible remedies within its institutional framework. Tamanaha (1997) proposed a 'pragmatic-realist approach' as opposed to the corrosive onslaught of postmodernism based on anti-foundationalism. According to him when he walks in the streets, nothing seems changed and realism creeps around. He advocated a realistic approach to socio-legal studies based on philosophical pragmatism as epistemological foundations promoted by Legal Realists. He contested critical socio-legal theory which, according to him, is harmful to "epistemologically unsound, potentially harmful to socio-legal enterprise". A realistic approach will respond to all the problems that dog the field.[8]

Subsequently disillusioned with the instrumentalism within legal realism he sought 'values', or law as an asset of ideals, and law as the common good. Tamanaha criticizes the instrumental approach to law in the Rule of Law project of the World Bank, tracing its historical trajectory through the Legal Realists, 'the social' in law, pragmatism and cause litigation. He reveals how instrumentalism has a class orientation.[9] He regrets the deprivation of two ideals in US legal system, law as an asset of ideals and law as the common good for public welfare, over the last 200 years.[10] He draws on E. P. Thompson who rejected the Marxist notion of law as an instrument in the hands of the dominating elite.[11] Thompson believed that

[8]BZ Tamanaha *Realistic Socio-Legal Theory: Pragmatism and Social Theory of Laws* (Oxford University Press, Clarendon, 1997) xii.

[9]Tamanaha very clearly describes how the business interests influence legislators and administrators. According to him, financial interests take three basic forms: individual corporations, associations (corporate trade groups as well as trade unions), and institutes. He then tells about "K-Street projects", names of groups, Pharmaceutical industry, patterns of domination, two-way movement of the lobbying industry (202), how offices give benefit to industry (example of PHRMA, it's a very good example of relation between state, business and NGOs); see *Ibid* 195, 196, 198, 199, 200, 202, 204.

[10]BZ Tamanaha, *Law as a Means to an End: Threat to the Rule of Law* (Cambridge University Press, Cambridge, 2006) 215.

[11]*Ibid* 247.

even though the law did not live up to its idealized characterizations, to give up the traditional non-instrumental views of law as rhetoric would be an error and Tamanaha concurs.[12] He challenges "anyone who doubts Thompson's conclusion about the benefits offered by the rule of law" for they "must merely examine the situation in those countries around the world where it is lacking—at blighted societies in which power has its way with scant restraint, and the powerless have little protection[13]".

Tamanaha's move from a 'pragmatic-realist approach' to quest for 'non-instrumental' view of law required filling gaps in theories of law. He tried to bring harmony between formalism and realism. His justification was that the legal formalists lawyers and judges found law as autonomous, comprehensive, logically ordered and determinate. This shows judges can judge by pure mechanical deduction. On the other hand in 1920s and 1930s, Roscoe Pound and Benjamin Cardozo gave a legal realist view where law was filled with gaps and contradictions, indeterminate, with exceptions to all legal rules, principles, precedents and hence judges decide according to their personal preferences and construct desired outcomes. For Tamanaha, there was no division between formalism and realism and he joined 'values' as formal with judging according to politics.[14] But the independent role of politics affects judges, courts and the art of judging is absent from Tamanaha. His writings lack a nuanced understanding of state theory, the place of judiciary within the state and the state's relation to social whole. Furthermore, Tamanaha's lack of any substantive position within liberal thinking, that is, instrumentalism of pragmatism-realism to formalism (moral ground for law) to finally somewhere in between, makes his critique of critical thinking, like on CLS and legal pluralism, highly incoherent.[15] E.P. Thompson's position about rule of law as an 'unqualified good' turns to a 'qualified human good' in Tamanaha. This ignores the complexity of Marxist analysis of law and debates within tradition (we have discussed the problematics of Thompson's position in Chap. 1).

An application of Tamanaha's 'moralist' and 'pragmatic-realist' approach to rule of law projects in developing countries is more illustrative. He 'bridged the gaps' (though gulfs in developing countries) between scholars and practitioners of the World Bank with an approach which is 'pragmatic one[16]'. Here legal pluralism[17] is

---

[12] *Ibid* 247.

[13] *Ibid* 247.

[14] BZ Tamanaha, *Beyond the Formalist-Realist Divide: The Role of Politics in Judging* (Princeton University Press, Princeton, 2010).

[15] BZ Tamanaha, The Rule of Law and Legal Pluralism in Development, in, BZ Tamanaha, Caroline Sage & Michael Woolcock (eds) *Legal pluralism and development: scholars and practitioners in dialogue* (Cambridge University Press, New York, 2012).

[16] It is because scholars are thinking about the situation from a distance whereas practitioners are carrying projects within constraints. *Ibid*; Preface, xv.

[17] Legal pluralism defined, the existence of multiple legal systems within the given community or sociological space. See Merry, S Engle, 1988, Legal Pluralism, Law & Society 22 (55): pp 869-96, see also Benda-Beckmann, F Von, Who's Afraid of Legal Pluralism? 47: 37 *J Legal Plur* (2002) 82.

advocated being 'realist[18]' and to be 'pragmatist' it is based on the 'disappointing progress' of building rule of law in societies with poorly functioning legal systems. This position of Tamanaha, therefore, is quite close to that of Douglas North. Tamanaha is aware of pluralism as a colonization project and warned that these local tribunals must not be overly 'idealized' even if they are *of* the community, because it does not make them *for* the community. There can be clashes between two local systems or two religions. He further added that the legal pluralism as a colonization project was to create harmony. For him, colonization was the first wave of legal pluralism and the second is going now.[19] Tamanaha is descriptive at the formal level of clash between 'local' and formal legal reforms. Our study on Pakistan shows how local (Islam, culture) and formal (liberal), though contradictory, reinforce the exclusion at the political level and exploitation at the structural level. The theoretical 'hybrid' of 'realism' and 'formalism' of Tamanaha derived from 'U.S. centric' context is not only a description of the confusion of the context itself but is also a poor fit for developing countries.

6.2.3 David Trubek

Moving on to the heart of law and development scholarship, David Trubek and his collective published two books in the last decade connecting legal changes with economic development under neoliberalism, calling them 'experiments'[20]. These books also do not provide a rigorous and proper critique of the new institutionalism behind the current phase of law and development, unlike Trubek's critical rigour of the 1970s against Critical Legal Studies and Law & Society.[21] While the first wave of law and development in 1970s was in crisis, Trubek tried to develop the 'sociology of law' as a response and its height is his 1974 article, "Scholars in Self-estrangement", co-written with Marc Galanter.[22] The crux of Trubek's works is pointing out the importance of 'scientific method' used by Weber to study the

[18]Tamanaha, *supra* note 36.

[19]Tamanaha, *supra* note 39.

[20]DM Trubek & A Santos (eds) *Law and Development Theory and the Emergence of a New Critical Practice* (Cambridge University Press, Cambridge, 2006); see DM Trubek et al, *Law and the New Developmental State: The Brazilian Experience in Latin American Context* (Cambridge University Press, Cambridge, 2014).

[21]See for example, DM Trubek, Where the Action Is: Critical Legal Studies and Empiricism, *Stan L Rev* (1984) *6*; see DM Trubek & M Galanter, Scholars in Self- Estrangement: Some Reflections on the Crisis of Law and Development Studies in the United States, *Wis L Rev* (1974) 1062; see also DM Trubek, Towards a Social Theory of Law: An Essay on the Study of Law and Development, 82:1 *The Yale LJ* (1972); see also DM Trubek, Max Weber on Law and the Rise of Capitalism, *Wis L Rev* (1972) 720-753.

[22]*Ibid.*

relation of capitalist development and law. Trubek found that the economy and polity merged together to some extent in the developmental state in developing countries, as opposed to western capitalist societies. Trubek concluded that Weber cannot be applied to developing countries. But how should the postcolonial state, and the 'developmental state' of postcolonies in this case, be understood? Disavowing any theoretical position currently, Trubek has not been in a position to answer this.

While Trubek was busy in developing a theory of sociology of law, the deductive school of thought in new institutional economics brought back the usefulness of institutions as the 'Ideal Type' in the vein of Max Weber.[23] Trubek merely saw all of the interest in law in new institutionalism as "economists interested in development discover[ing] law". For Trubek this was different than in the 1950s and 1960s when legal institutions were available as needed. Now "all of a sudden development economists began to focus on law"[24]. For him this focus on law as an institution was to facilitate market transactions and to constrain undesirable state intervention. This statement is not only descriptive but is in line with the theoretical premises of new institutionalism.

While new institutionalism was taking the shape of 'Good Governance', Trubek engaged with its pragmatic-realist layer in the name of 'New Governance'. These for him were mechanisms designed to increase flexibility, improve participation, foster experimentation and deliberation, and accommodate complex multilevel systems using examples drawn from the European Union and the United States.[25] These are alternative approaches to governance are opposed to traditional, top down, command and control governance,[26] and involve use of soft law along with hard law.[27] Here law is problem-solving through networks, experimentation, standards and deliberations, that is, multilevel networks which are 'law-like processes' developed and based on the empirical study of three cases: EU's Water Framework Directive, the Tuna-Dolphin case and the WTO Council and Committee system.[28] These transnational arenas, institutions and processes create 'opportunity structures' and suggest transnational solutions as a supplement to national

---

[23]As claimed by K Ford, The Veblenian Roots of Institutional Political Economy, Working Paper No. 2011-07, Department of Economics Working Paper Series, University of Utah (2011) 13.

[24]Trubek (2014), *supra* note 20, 10.

[25]DM Trubek & LG Trubek, New Governance and Legal Regulation: Complementarity, Rivalry or Transformation, 13 *Colum J Eur L* (2007) 542.

[26]JS Mosher & DM Trubek, Alternative Approaches to Governance in the EU: EU Social Policy and the European Employment Strategy, 41:1 *J Common Mark Stud* (2003) 63.

[27]DM Trubek & LG Trubek, Hard and Soft Law in the Construction of Social Europe: The Role of the Open Method of Co-ordination, 11:3 *Eur LJ* (2005) 343; see also DM Trubek, P Cottrell & M Nance, 'Soft Law', 'Hard Law' and EU integration, in, Scott & de Burca (eds) *New Governance and Constitutionalism* (Hart, 2005) 65; New Governance approaches in EU use 'soft law' at the place of or along with 'hard law' which was the product of treatise, regulations, and the Community Method. This essay is just about soft law in New Governance approaches.

[28]DM Trubek & MP Cottrell, Law as Problem Solving: Standards, Networks, Experimentation, and Deliberations in Global Space, 21 *Transnat'l L & Contemp Probs* (2012) 359.

systems.[29] In a nutshell, new institutional experiments are a process where IFIs are changing and are more permissive to developing countries.[30] So for Trubek, we should not out rightly oppose[31] or accept IFIs but rather engage with the processes.

At the same time, quite in line with the failures of neoliberalism at the end of 1990s, Trubek's collective was able to reach 'New Critical Practice'. This critique involves challenging commonly held assumptions about the neutrality of private law, unrestricted market fundamentalism, gaps between rhetoric and reality, problematic efficiency doctrines and false universalism. Most important of this new critical practice was a reminder of the forgotten issues of distribution and hegemony of the economic order in third moment of law and development.[32] But how Trubek's proposed 'New Governance' could realize distribution is unclear, nor is it clear how the hegemony of the economic order would permit such distribution. Finally, I believe the 'new critical practice' has found refuge in the 'New Developmental State' as an exemplar of pragmatism.

The 'New Developmental State'[33] in Trubek's analysis is the legacy of twenty-first century complexity where three forces shape local law, namely IFIs, local policy makers and international law. In this situation only governments, academics, judges and leaders of the bar and some 'elite' law schools in places like Brazil, China and India have taken up the challenge of building a body of knowledge about law and development appropriate for our times.[34] This new developmental state recognized the elements of the new political economy of development, namely imperfect markets, market failure, strategic trade theory, networks, technological capacity, innovation, etc. and domestically developed a kind of private-public partnership approach.[35] There is no general theory of law that might allow for institutions capable of managing the complex needs of the new developmental state, but rather such management requires 'new governance', democratic experimentalism and hybridity.

Trubek misses the theoretical underpinnings of the legal state in this third wave of law and development under new institutionalism. The countries of the Global

---

[29]DM Trubek, J Mosher & JS Rothste, Transnationalism in the Regulation of Labour Relations: International Regimes and Transnational Advocacy Networks, *Law Soc Inq* (2000) 1187.

[30]Trubek based his study on the BRICS. See DM Trubek, Reversal of Fortune? International Economic Governance, Alternative Development Strategies, and the Rise of the BRICS, European University Institute Florence, Italy (June 2012) 2.

[31]That is of Faundez 2011 that International economic law and policy (IELP) of IFIs is against developing countries as claimed by Trubek. See *ibid.*

[32]Trubek, Introduction: The Third Movement in Law and Development Theory and the Emergence of a New Critical Practice, *supra* note 11.

[33]DM Trubek, DR Coutinho, & MG Schapiro, Toward a New Law and Development: New State Activism in Brazil and the Challenge for Legal Institutions, 4 *WB L Leg Rev* (2013) 281.

[34]DM Trubek, Law and Development in the Twenty-first Century Forthcoming, McAlinn & Pejovic (eds) *Law and Development in Asia* (Routledge 2011) 3.

[35]DM Trubek, Developmental States and the Legal Order: Towards a New Political Economy of Development and Law, Conference on Social Science in the Age of Globalization National Institute for Advanced Study on Social Science, Fudan University, Shanghai (December 2008).

South and the people of these countries are tied into extensive new legal and institutional arrangements, such as the WTO and other global legal regimes. As global actors, Southern countries are disadvantaged in these systems as the institutional arrangements that are promoted are a restraining factor for any independent and alternate path of political and economic development. In that sense, too much law is antithetical to development for the marginalized. Above all, legalism can be a distraction from the needed political and economic development (devoid of development defined broad or narrowly) for these global marginalized countries and the marginalized peoples therein. Trubek missed this point 40 years ago while evaluating first wave of law and development and this left him uncritical or mildly critical of second and third wave of law and development in 1990s and 2000s. I suggest any new wave of law and development should concretely engage with development of the marginalized of the global subaltern countries. This means reviewing the legal global regimes promoted in the 1990s–2000s as well as local legal amendments, repeals and legislature under this global thrust. This way, my position is different than uncritical or mildly critical embrace of legal arrangements under new institutionalism by Trubek.

6.3 Post-Development, TWAIL and Critical Legal Studies

More importantly, this is also different from one sided polemics of post-development strand of international law which reduces problem to discourse, 'intentions' and authority and understands 'development' only negatively. In this regard, the edited works of collectives of Sally Engle Marry, Jean Comaroff and Tim Linsey are important. Comaroff et al. rightly points out the centrality of law and emerging fetishism, but cannot identify causal relations of law with changes in political and economic instances.[36] Sally Engle Merry and her collective's works are dominantly within the Foucauldian framework, and show linkages between power and knowledge[37] behind governance indicators and indicators as technologies of knowledge production and global governance.[38] What this book adds to this approach is how a 'local' legal framework (Islam) accepts and accommodates the liberal thrust at a discursive level. Both together reflect the nature of changes in the practice of hegemony for the exclusion of the dominated classes. Based on this, I have found no reason to accept Tim Lindsey's divide of the formal law as

[36]L Comaroff & JL Comaroff, *Law and Order in the Postcolony* (University of Chicago Press, Chicago, 2006).

[37]SE Merry, KE Davis & B Kingsbury, *The Quite Power of Indicators* (Cambridge University Press, Cambridge, Merry et al. 2015).

[38]KE Davis, A Fisher & B Kingsbury, *Governance by Indicators: Global Power through Quantification and Rankings* (Oxford University Press, Oxford, 2012).

imperialist and informal/indigenous custom/law as defensive in the name of legal pluralism.[39]

Similarly, Third World Approaches to International Law (TWAIL) was the timely response to a uni-polar world emerged after the Cold War and the new legal regimes unleashed after the WTO was signed in 1995.[40] TWAIL critically investigates the hegemony of the few dominant nations over a majority of the global 'South' or 'Third World', and the Westphalian assumptions of universality, positivism and Eurocentricity in international legal theory and its practice.[41] TWAIL itself is aware of its inability to effectively critique neoliberal international law or project alternative vision of international law. Apart from TWAIL's own identification of its limits of 'resources' and 'problems' for research by scholars from the South[42] the research in this book can have implications for a few very basic constituent elements of TWAIL's theory.

TWAIL lumped together all the First World and used the terms 'empire' and 'imperialism' problematically.[43] Imperialism in TWAIL is 'de-territorialized and de-centred' and is very particular to the concept of 'empire as found in the work of Michael Hardt and Antonio Negri. TWAIL considers the remaining world as 'Third World'. All contradictions are collapsed to lying between these two worlds. Consequently, it ignores the relationships and contradictions within and among capitalist countries as well as among the least developed (e.g. Sub Saharan Africa) and the more developed countries (e.g. BRICS).

This book shows imperialist centre-periphery dependency relations are not located outside but has been internal to the state and society of Pakistan in the form of a hegemonic class of which the military is also a part. Therefore, legally backed but despotic regime changes in Pakistan were not debated at WTO forums. Legal amendments, repeals, enactments, which are blunted at the implementation stage

[39]T Lindsey (ed), *Law Reform in Developing and Transitional States* (Routledge, London & New York, 2007).

[40]For the introduction of TWAIL, see BS Chimni, Third World Approaches to International Law: A Manifesto, 8 Int'l Comm L Rev (2008) 3; see also A Anghie, What is TWAIL?: Comment, 94 Proceedings of the American Society of International Law (2000) 39.

[41]For the critique of Westphalian assumptions, see C Cutler, Critical Reflections on the Westphalian assumptions of International Law and organization: a crisis of legitimacy, 27:2 Rev Int'l Stud (2001) 133; and see A Anghie, Finding the Peripheries: Sovereignty and Colonialism in Nineteenth-Century International Law, 40:1 Harvard Int'l LJ (1999) 1 for the critique of imperialism and positivism in International law; for hegemony in International law, see N Krisch (2005), International Law in Times of Hegemony: Unequal Power and the Shaping of International Legal Order, 16:3 Eur J Int'l L, 369.

[42]Chimni, supra note 40, 3.

[43]TWAIL scholars interchangeably use the concepts of 'imperialism' and 'empire' without subtle difference. See for the critique of the concept of 'empire' and difference of these terms AA Boron, *Empire and Imperialism: A critical reading of Michael Hardt and Antonio Negri* (Zed Books, London, 2005). The writer criticized the problematic concept of de-territorialized and de-centred character of imperialism in 'empire.' See also M Hardt and A Negri, *Empire* (Harvard University Press, Cambridge, 2002).

are supposed to be corrected by the judiciary through 'good governance' interventions. Latin American countries, only due to rising working class politics, resisted international law regimes in a way never possible in Pakistan, but also as not anticipated by TWAIL.

Critical Legal Studies (CLS) as a legal tradition carries forward modern leftist thought (Marxist and neo-Marxist),[44] critical social theory and poststructuralist deconstruction.[45] While criticizing mainstream liberal legal thought in the U.S., CLS itself has received extensive critique.[46] CLS exposed the contradictions of the liberal legal project and in that sense seemed doctrinal and not empirical. Based on this, Trubek pointed out that the mission of the CLS is to change the consciousness by a counter-hegemony.[47] CLS took this as an end in itself, placing itself therefore within liberal legalism. This book in contrast traced contradictions of the liberal legal project as contradictions of hegemony resulting from the persistent inequality at structural level. The 'consciousness' of judges, lawyers and public was not either 'liberal' or 'Islamic' but were both at the same time. The same judges, lawyers and public were for 'rule of law' during the Lawyers' Movement and showered rose petals on Mumtaz Qadri, the murderer of Governor Punjab when the Governor supported a poor Christian woman wrongfully accused of blasphemy.[48]

CLS's limits was not uncontested and was challenged by the subalterns. The key here is political practice and structural location of the subaltern in the system, giving rise for instance to Critical Race Theory (CRT) as well as feminist critical theories. In simplest terms CRT wanted legal practice and civil rights discourse for the marginalized Black community whereas CLS was interested in 'critique'. CRT borrowed methods of CLS for the critique of liberal legal project but kept its political commitments with the civil rights movement and scholarship. At a deeper level this reflected a tension between 'radical emancipation' and 'radical critique'[49]. At a theoretical level it was a move within the critical tradition from 'modernist' to 'postmodernist' and then back to 'modernist' thought,[50] as also occurred in feminist critical theories.[51] The question of how to use law and legal institutions for political

---

[44]Dealing with ideology, hegemony and consciousness in the tradition of Karl Korsch, George Lukacs, Gramsci, and Althusser. Other names given to this trend in Marxism are Western Marxism, Hegelian Marxism or Critical Marxism.

[45]D Brosnan, *Serious but Not Critical*, 60 *S Cal L Rev* (1986) 259.

[46]OM Fiss, *The Death of the Law*, 72 Cornell L Rev (1986-87), 1.

[47]Trubek, *supra* note 21.

[48]See <http://www.pakistanchristianpost.com/detail.php?hnewsid=5170>; <http://www.dawn.com/news/1242637>, last visited 14 December 2015.

[49]AP Harris 1994, Forward: The Jurisprudence of Reconstruction, 82: 4 *Cal Law Rev*.

[50]*Ibid*; for a clash between modernists and postmodernist thinking in critical tradition see R Kennedy, Racial Critique of Legal Academia, *Harv L Rev* (1989); for this tension in feminist critical tradition, see D Patterson, Postmodernism/Feminism/Law 77 *Cornell L Rev* (1992) 254; see also D Faber and S Sherry, Telling Stories out of School: An Essay of Legal Narratives (1993).

[51]DL Rhode, Feminist Critical theories, *Stanford L Rev* (1990).

and economic struggles has haunted the critical tradition. What is the take of research in this book which is also in the critical legal tradition?

6.4 Social Change Beyond Law: Final Reflections

The main contribution of this book is seeking to keep central the structural hindrances to social and political development in postcolonial societies like Pakistan. Tackling this is beyond the limits and capacity of the judiciary given its own location in the class-state. Having thus offered a 'critique', should we then abandon law?

Wendy Brown describes the contradictory nature of rights,[52] and the legalistic turn in Left circles. Furthermore, she argued against the irrelevance of critique of legalism.[53] Its rebuttal and the South Asian version of cause litigation debate is Public Interest Litigation (PIL), chiefly articulated by scholar Upendra Baxi. He is not nihilistic and accepts the universality of human rights. He distinguishes between the politics *of* human rights and politics *for* human rights. The former is the use of human rights languages by IFIs for legitimacy for governance and domination which is constantly reproducing human right-lessness and suffering. The politics *for* human rights is human rights activism 'militant particularism' of the local against global.[54] Baxi insists that the real birth place of rights is the farm and factory, which for him is 'realism'[55]. That is, "people's praxes of resistance and struggle"[56].

Missing in Baxi's work is an analysis of what links people's politics *for* human rights and NGOs and donor agencies' politics *of* human rights. The reason is possibly Baxi's theoretical eclecticism[57] which is at the mercy of the 'ebb and flow' of the movement. While Baxi points to the 'farm' and 'factory' as the places where the rights are produced he cannot tell us why courts are needed to get these rights (or for that matter, why 'family' is not such a site). He does not leave any space

[52]W Brown, State of Inquiry: Power and Freedom in Late Modernity (Princeton University Press, Princeton, 1995).

[53]W Brown & J Halley, *Left Legalism/Left Critique* (Duke University Press, Durham, 2002); Essays in the book examine the tension between state-centred left legalism and left theoretical critiques of the state, the law, and identity on the other.

[54]U Baxi, The Future of Human Rights, 2nd edn (Oxford University Press, New Delhi) xiv-xv.

[55]*Ibid* 80.

[56]*Ibid* 94; He notes different responses to the potential of human rights as 1- wariness by taking it as imperialist manoeuvers, 2- dialogism, taking HR as a dialogue between perpetrators and violated, 3-evangelism in taking HR as a new kind of religion, 4- romanticism, HR at the UN and its conferences, 5- free choice taking global capital opposed to universal HRs of human beings, 6- bureaucratization taking HR as inter-governmental efforts.

[57]OC Okfor, Marxian Embraces and De-couplings in Upendra Baxi's Human Rights Scholarship: A Case Study, in, Susan Marks (ed) International Law on the Left; Re-examining Marxist Legacies (Cambridge University Press, Cambridge, 2008).

beyond the legal state and judiciary to address the problematic nature of Indian democracy and secularism, as pointed out by critics like Arundhati Roy.[58]

In response I would comment that, firstly, legal practice and its use for political ends cannot be left unquestioned when strategic actors in a legal arrangement are highly unequal. Courts may be the choice of professional lawyers, NGOs and even state and politicians. But labour and peasantry may first need organizing at 'farm' and 'factory' level. This may need politics as a class. Courts cannot organize them nor can give them a political voice. Without this even the political gains through courts cannot be materialized as seen subsequent to *Masih* bonded labour liberation case in Pakistan.

Secondly, the automatic critique of economic reductionism and the instrumentality of law is problematic where both the sharpness of economic and political inequality and the instrumental uses of law are in actual effect. Exposing instrumentality is a prerequisite for claiming 'relative autonomy' or 'impartiality' from the law or state. The analysis should not end here but be extended to trace and show how law gives legitimacy to inequality to reproduce hegemony. In this situation of inequality, extensive legalism and going to courts is to channel social conflicts into legal rituals, symbols, judges and case law. It is getting moral consensus from Jinnah or Gandhi for existing institutions of property, contract and themselves as extension of human rights. The preoccupation of 'rights-consciousness' reassures people that rights resides in the state and can be achieved through the state, allowing the state and courts to define the terms of the struggle. It creates alienation.[59] Without success in political struggle as a pre-requisite, legal struggle is 'constitutionalizing', 'institutionalizing', and 'legalizing', inequality and is 'structuration' through institutional practices.[60] The primacy of politics over legal struggles does not mean abandoning legal struggles but it means placing people first and not the state, and suggests a power oriented approach and not rights oriented approach, and a clear understanding of the structural location of the marginalized.

Marx and Engels attached the legal struggle with the most backward sections of the socialist movement that articulate their revolutionary demands in legal terms.[61] Whether the rule of law is an 'unqualified human good' or not, there seems no obligation for marginalized and subalterns to submit and limit themselves to courts for their political actions. From revolutionary epoch to peaceful moments, they can decide differently. Once it is clear that they are dominated, it is essential to demystify grand laws, robed judges, to reveal limits of law and bring to light social,

---

[58]A Roy, Democracy: Who is She when She's at Home?, Outlook (6 May 2002).

[59]P Gabel & P Harris, Building Power and Breaking Images: Critical Legal Theory and Practice of Law, 11 *NYU Rev L & Soc Change* (1982-3).

[60]For Giddens structuration is a conscious historical process when capable human agents interact with wider social system and structures. See A Gidden, *Central Problems in Social Theory: Action, Structure, and Contradiction in Social Analysis* (University of California Press, Berkley, 1979) 29.

[61]P Beirne, Piers & R Quiney, in, P Beirne & R Quiney (eds), Marxism and Law (John Willy & Sons, New York, 1982) 6.

political and economic basis of legal system. This cannot be achieved through going to courts for political solutions but extending the analysis of courts to politics.

To sum up, the nature of exploitation and marginalization in a legal arrangement determine the features of a legal system. For any legal analysis, therefore, there is a need to know the form of rule and class essence of a particular state, the concrete historical conditions and the conditions and power balance of class struggle. Once this is known, only then can one can know the role of legal struggle, and where it is a futile exercise. Critique and analysis comes first and foremost. This is particularly true in highly unequal class divided societies. We are not critical enough if, in our analyses, what exists is equal to what can exist.

References

A Anghie, Finding the Peripheries: Sovereignty and Colonialism in Nineteenth-Century International Law, 40:1 *Harv Int'l LJ* (1999).

A Anghie, What is TWAIL?: Comment, 94 *Proceedings of the American Society of International* Law (2000).

AA Boron, *Empire and Imperialism: A Critical Reading of Michael Hardt and Antonio Negri* (Zed Books, London, 2005).

AP Harris, Forward: The Jurisprudence of Reconstruction, 82:4 *Cal Law Rev* (1994).

B Bouckaert and GD Geest (eds) *Encyclopaedia of Law and Economics* (Edward Elgar, 1999).

BN Krisch, International Law in Times of Hegemony: Unequal Power and the Shaping of International Legal Order, 16:3 *Eur J Int'l L* (2005).

BS Chimni, Third World Approaches to International Law: A Manifesto, 8 *Int'l Comm L Rev* (2008).

BZ Tamanaha, *Beyond the Formalist-Realist Divide: The Role of Politics in Judging* (Princeton University Press, Princeton, 2010).

BZ Tamanaha, C Sage & M Woolcock (eds), *Legal Pluralism and development: Scholars and Practitioners in Dialogue* (Cambridge University Press, New York, 2012).

BZ Tamanaha, *Law as a Means to an End: Threat to the Rule of Law* (Cambridge University Press, Cambridge, 2006).

BZ Tamanaha, *Realistic Socio-Legal Theory: Pragmatism and Social Theory of Laws* (Oxford University Press, Clarendon, 1997).

C Cutler, Critical Reflections on the Westphalian Assumptions of International Law and Organization: A Crisis of Legitimacy, 27:2 *Rev Int'l Stud* (2001).

D Brosnan, *Serious But Not Critical*, 60 *S Cal L Rev* (1986).

D Faber and S Sherry, Telling Stories out of School: An Essay of Legal Narratives, 45:4 *Stanford Law Rev.* (1993).

D Patterson, Postmodernism/Feminism/Law 77 *Cornell L Rev* (1992).

DC North, *Institutions, Institutional Change and Economic Performance* (Cambridge University Press, Cambridge, 1990).

DC North, *Structure and Change in Economic History* (Norton, New York, 1981).

DL Rhode, Feminist Critical Theories, *Stanford L Rev.* (1990).

DM Trubek & LG Trubek, Hard and Soft Law in the Construction of Social Europe: The Role of the Open Method of Co-ordination, 11:3 *Eur LJ* (2005).

DM Trubek & LG Trubek, New Governance and Legal Regulation: Complementarity, Rivalry or Transformation, 13 *Colum J Eur L* (2007).

DM Trubek & M Galanter, Scholars in Self- Estrangement: Some Reflections on the Crisis of Law and Development Studies in the United States, *Wis L Rev* (1974).

DM Trubek & MP Cottrell, Law as Problem Solving: Standards, Networks, Experimentation, and Deliberations in Global Space, 21 *Transnat'l L & Contemp Probs* (2012).
DM Trubek, DR Coutinho, & MG Schapiro, Toward a New Law and Development: New State Activism in Brazil and the Challenge for Legal Institutions, 4 *WB L Leg Rev* (2013).
DM Trubek, J Mosher & JS Rothste, Transnationalism in the Regulation of Labour Relations: International Regimes and Transnational Advocacy Networks, *Law Soc Inq* (2000).
DM Trubek, Law and Development in the Twenty-first Century Forthcoming, McAlinn & Pejovic (eds) *Law and Development in Asia* (Routledge, 2011).
DM Trubek, Max Weber on Law and the Rise of Capitalism, *Wis L Rev* (1972).
DM Trubek, Towards a Social Theory of Law: An Essay on the Study of Law and Development, 82:1 *The Yale LJ* (1972).
DM Trubek, Where the Action Is: Critical Legal Studies and Empiricism, *Stan L Rev* (1984).
FB Beckmann, Who's Afraid of Legal Pluralism?, 47:37 *J Legal Plur* (2002).
JS Mosher & DM Trubek, Alternative Approaches to Governance in the EU: EU Social Policy and the European Employment Strategy, 41:1 *J Common Mark Stud* (2003).
KE Davis, A Fisher & B Kingsbury, *Governance by Indicators: Global Power through Quantification and Rankings* (Oxford University Press, Oxford, 2012).
L Comaroff & JL Comaroff, *Law and Order in the Postcolony* (University of Chicago Press, Chicago, 2006).
M Hardt and A Negri, *Empire* (Harvard University Press, Cambridge, 2002).
OM Fiss, *The Death of the Law*, 72 *Cornel L Rev* (1986–87).
R Kennedy, Racial Critique of Legal Academia, *Harv L Rev* (1989).
Scott & D Burca (eds) *New Government Constitutionalism* (Hart, 2005).
SE Merry, KE Davis & B Kingsbury, *The Quite Power of Indicators* (Cambridge University Press, Cambridge, 2015).
SE Merry, Legal Pluralism, Law & Society, 22:5 *Law Soc. Rev.* (1988).
T Lindsey (ed), *Law Reform in Developing and Transitional States* (Routledge, London & New York, 2007).
U Baxi, The Future of Human Rights, 2[nd]edn (Oxford University Press, New Delhi).
W Brown & J Halley, *Left Legalism/Left Critique (*Duke University Press, Durham, 2002).
W Brown, *State of Inquiry: Power and Freedom in Late Modernity* (Princeton University Press, Princeton, 1995).

FSC
www.fsc.org
MIX
Papier | Fördert
gute Waldnutzung
FSC® C083411

Kolibri 360 GmbH
Ferdinand-Jühlke-Straße 7
99095 Erfurt, Deutschland
produktsicherheit@kolibri360.de